THE GRETSCH DRUM BOOK

by Rob Cook
with John Sheridan

© 2013 by Rob Cook

ISBN Assignments
978-1-888408-20-1   paperback
978-1-888408-21-8   hardcover
978-1-888408-22-5   ebook format
978-1-888408-23-2   Mobipocket format

Library of Congress Control Number: 2013905667

Rebeats Publications
608 N State St, Alma, Michigan 48801
www.Rebeats.com

Printed in the United States of America
All rights for publication and distribution are reserved. No part of this book may be reproduced in any form or by any electronic of mechanical means including information storage and retrieval systems without publisher's written consent.

ACKNOWLEDGMENTS

ROB COOK would like to thank:
John Aldridge (my brother from another mother to whom I owe more than can be expressed), Philip Anderson, Florence Asciolla, Gary Asher, Sam Bacco, Edward Ball, Roy Burns, Jon Cohan, Mark Cooper, Paul Cooper, Derek Crawford, the late Bill Crowden, Mike Curotto, Jeffrey Davenport, Robert Delich, Bill Detamore, Deric Dickens, Brian Drugan, Karl Dustman, Gretchen Elsner-Sommer, Gary Folchi, Dave Ford, Hannah Ford, Gary Forkum, Rick Gier, Dave Gordon, Kim Graham, Luther Gray, Fred W. Gretsch, Dinah Gretsch, Michael Hacala, Bill Hagner, Ryan Hajj, Bill Hartrick, Emi Keffer, Paul Librizzi, Joe Luoma, Dave Mattacks, Steve Maxwell, Lloyd McCausland, Winnie Mensink, Monmouth Music, Joe Montineri, Ferit Odman, John Palmer, Joe Partridge, Jim Pettit, Professional Drum Shop of Hollywood (Stan & Jerry Keyawa), Revival Drum Shop (Keary Ortiz & Jose Medeles), Lee & Dorcas Ruff, Brian Scheidecker, Rob Scott, Nick Seiwert, Colin Schofield, John and Andrea Sheridan, Lena Thomas, Will Tillman, Nick Trocchia, Rick VanHorn, Andy Weis and the late Robert Zildjian.

There is simply no substitute for years of experience studying the products of a particular drum company. My biggest debts of gratitude are owed to John Sheridan, Lee Ruff, and their wives Andrea and Dorcas. The generosity they showed as they opened their homes, archives, and parts bins to me was remarkable. I don't mean to rank the contributors, but a close third has to be Fred W. Gretsch; another gracious host who has been not only generous with permission to use images and information from his archives but very uplifting with his encouragement.

JOHN SHERIDAN would like to thank:
John Aldridge, Florence Asciolla, Sam Bacco, Edward Ball, Roy Burns, Mark Carter, Paul Cooper, Dawn Colwell, Terry Dennis, Deric Dickens, Micky Dolenz, Charlie Donnelley (the father of vintage drums), Dan Duffy, Karl Dustman, Jimmie Fadden, George Folchi Sr. (my other father), Gary & George Folchi Jr., Ernie Gadzos, Susan Gallagher, Bob Gatzen, Rick Gier, Dinah & Fred W. Gretsch, Bill Hagner, Bill Hartrick, Gene Haugh, Billy Jeansonne, John Keenoy, Emi Keffer, Fritzi & "Duke" Kramer (who I miss), Tom Lanahan, Dave Mattacks, Steve Maxwell, Joe Mazza, Roger Morin, Billy Murphy, Angela Neese, Phil Nestor, John Palmer, Joe Partridge, Louis Porsi, Brian Scheidecker, Nick Seiwert, Colin Schofield, Lena Thomas, Will Tillman, and Nick Trocchia.

Special thanks to Rob Cook for getting the ball rolling and seeing this project through to its fruition. Of course, I must thank my wife Andrea, not only for her support throughout, but also for her computer savvy and organizational skills that kept me going. Last, but certainly not least, I thank Fred W. Gretsch for all of his personal help, steadfast encouragement, and for keeping the great Gretsch legacy alive and well.

Special thanks to the folks at KMC Music who took time from
doing today's Gretsch drum business to contribute to this project.
Special assistance was received from
John Palmer, Paul Cooper, Kim Graham, and Nick Seiwert

Table of Contents

foreward by Lee Ruff
foreward by Fred W. Gretsch
foreward by John Sheridan
preface
Where Gretsch Was and Is; a timeline chart illustrating Gretsch facilities 1883-2013
Family tree

Chapter 1   1883-1967 1
     Gretchen Elsner-Sommer (Gretsch family history essay)
     Richard Gretsch
     The Men Behind The Drums
         Richard Dickson, Duke Kramer, Phil Grant, Bill Hagner

Chapter 2   The Baldwin Era 1967-1984 23
     Baldwin overview 1967-1982, Charlie Roy, Karl Dustman

Chapter 3   Fred W. and Dinah Gretsch 39
     Fred W. Gretsch interview, Fred W. and Dinah Gretsch

Chapter 4   Endorsers 53

Chapter 5   Dating Guide 82
     Badges & Serial Numbers 83
     Catalogs 96
     Colors 105
     Outfits (& Electronic Drums) 117
     Snare Drums 157
     Lugs 191
     Hoops 198
     Shells 201
     Strainers 212
     Mufflers/Tone Controls 219
     Cymbal Stands 222
     Hihat Stands 228
     Pedals 230
     Tom Holders 223
     Tom Legs 239
     Spurs 242
     Snare stands 244
     Gretsch & cymbals 246

Appendices
I	Promotional Items	253
II	Ridgeland, SC production	255
III	Drums & Wood	256
IV	Ferit Odman, Andy Florio	258
V	Andy Florio	259
VI	Brooklyn Series cocktail kits	260
VII	Hannah Ford	261

Index 264

Resource Page 268

Foreword by Lee Ruff

My name is Lee Ruff. I have been playing and collecting Gretsch round badge drums and related items exclusively for 53 years. I toured as a full time jazz drummer for 10 of those years. I have been a full time drum instructor and part time player for the remaining 43 years. At a young age, it occurred to me that my jazz drumming heroes were all playing Gretsch. I got my first Gretsch Progressive Jazz drum set in 1960. It was quite obvious that my little Gretsch set sounded completely different than the drums made by the other major drum companies. Being the curious tinkering type, I completely dismantled that first set of drums, examined them carefully, and then reassembled them. My Gretsch drums were made in a very unique way when compared to the drums that my many musician friends owned. The sound was much more blending and sweet for jazz. They sounded fat and round to my ear. They never seemed abrasive or thin to me. Those 60s Progressive Jazz drums were exactly what worked for my taste. Since those early days, I continued purchasing more Gretsch round badge drums as I could afford them. I always kept my existing sets, constantly adding to my stable. In a period of 25 years or so, I had amassed quite a collection. Every year I always dismantled "all" of my drums for cleaning and lubrication. I had a habit of keeping notes on little changes that I observed through the years. I began thinning out my collection about 10 years ago. Every time a set or a snare would leave, I felt like I was losing a family member. I now have a somewhat reasonable, manageable collection. During the last 20 years, I have also restored Gretsch drums that had suffered significant abuse or damage. In the early 90s I attended my first drum show. I was startled to see so many Gretsch round badge parts and single drums being sold. It soon became apparent to me, that a lot of "dealers" were separating original factory matched sets. Even more disturbing, some of those people were actually tearing the drums apart and selling the individual parts. Over the years that followed, I watched this practice exacerbate. As computers became household items, this practice continued to increase. Unfortunately, since the onset of online auctions, the practice of selling vintage drums one piece at a time has become very, very common.

Finding Gretsch round badge drums today that have not been "messed with" has become very difficult. Unfortunately, many true Gretsch enthusiasts have unknowingly spent serious money on drums and sets that have been put together with mixtures of parts from different eras. On the internet and at drum shows, I have seen tons of drums, that have been grossly misrepresented as all-original or factory-matched. In reality, they were put together with mismatched parts. In recent years, I have felt a compulsion to share some very defined knowledge, which is based exclusively on my 53 years of careful viewing, cleaning, playing, and owning many original Gretsch round badge drums. When I was given the opportunity to share this information in this publication, I jumped at the chance. I sincerely hope this information will help provide a comprehensive guideline for both present and future generations of Gretsch enthusiasts of the round badge era (especially 1955 thru 1969). The information and photos are tangible proof of my impressions. When no tangible examples were available, I have done my best to rely on my recollections. I'm certain there is some information that is overlapping, as many little transitions occurred. Also, after studying these drums for all these years, it is evident that many variations and inconsistencies took place. My advice is to utilize "all reliable, documented" sources available when evaluating the age and authenticity of vintage Gretsch drums. It is complicated. I continue to learn more as the years pass. There will always be questions asked, where the only honest answer is, "I don't know".

Heretofore, there has been tons of erroneous, inaccurate, and/or incomplete information published. Unfortunately, there has been information in print based on pure conjecture. There has been information that simply generalizes too much to do much good. Lastly, there has been information taken from brochures, letters, catalogs, interviews, etc. Though very significant, these sources can leave many, many gaps and doubts, when applied to the drums themselves. I personally have no interest in controversy. My sole motivation for providing this precise information is to "add to the toolbox" of the Gretsch investor. All "credible" sources available, "used in concert", can help the enthusiast acquire a "feel" for the evolution of Gretsch drums. I believe that with the information in this book, when studied with an open mind, one can easily evaluate the originality and approximate ages of vintage Gretsch drums. As in the collecting of antique furniture, vintage automobiles, vintage guitars, etc., the original "survivor" pieces tend to command the most value. When viewing restored items (including drums), the accuracy, "consistency," and degree of restoration should be strongly considered when determining value. It's a "buyer beware" world out there. Good luck in your searches for vintage Gretsch drums, and above all, have fun.

Many thanks to Rob Cook for his knowledge and ongoing promotion of vintage drums. His tireless efforts in authoring this and other publications, coupled with his patience, tenacity, and organizational skills are commendable. I am truly honored to be one of the many dedicated contributors to this effort. I have known John Sheridan for over 20 years. I applaud his ongoing interest, dedication, research, and promotion of the Gretsch Company.

Foreword by Fred W. Gretsch

When Rob Cook approached me about his writing a book about the history of Gretsch drums, I was thrilled. Rob's reputation as a writer and researcher–as well as the promoter of America's oldest and largest vintage and custom drum show–has established him as a key figure in the field of drum history. Now, with the able assistance of John Sheridan, Rob has produced a work to be proud of. I know I am, and I want to start this foreword by thanking Rob and John sincerely for their tireless efforts.

Of course, when Rob and I began our discussions about the book, I warned him that in writing the history of Gretsch drums and the Gretsch Company, he was also going to have to include the history of the Gretsch Family. As I write this, in May of 2013, we're celebrating our 130th year in the music business. I'm proud to represent the fourth generation of Gretsch drum-makers, in an unbroken line that leads back through my father, William "Bill" Gretsch, and my uncle, Fred Gretsch Jr., to my grandfather, Fred Gretsch Sr.—who helped to establish the Gretsch reputation for innovation with the introduction of the first ply drumshells in 1920. From Grandpa Fred the family line extends back to my great-grandfather, Friederich Gretsch, who founded the business in 1883. No other drum company can claim a similar lineage. And I want to say here and now that we plan to keep the business in the family for at least another hundred years.

In the early years of the business the Gretsch Company was more of a multi-line distributor than a manufacturer—a fact that Rob Cook details extensively in his text. You'll learn about Gretsch's involvement in cymbal history (which dates back to the 1890s), and about a wide and fascinating array of other products and brands. Rob is nothing if not thorough.

But it's likely that most readers will come to this book because of their love for Gretsch drums. And I'm enormously proud to be able to say that the history of Gretsch drums is inseparably linked to the history of music in America…and beyond. Just consider this: In 1933 New York City was becoming the music capital of the world. Radio broadcasts from New York were the source of entertainment to the nation. Live theaters lined Broadway. And a new and spectacular venue called the Radio City Music Hall was opening. Meanwhile, Gretsch was already celebrating its 50th anniversary!

Four years later Gretsch began a collaboration with the famous percussionist of the Radio City Music Hall orchestra, Billy Gladstone. In addition to being a great player, Billy was also a recognized inventor, and his partnership with Gretsch initiated a tradition of artist-driven innovation that has continued ever since.

In the 1930s and '40s, the drummers who were performing in the nightclubs of Harlem made regular pilgrimages across the East River to visit the Gretsch factory at 60 Broadway in Brooklyn. Big-band stars like Chick Webb, "Papa" Jo Jones, Dave Tough, and Louie Bellson contributed their ideas and suggestions—not least of which was Louie's first double-bass kit in 1946. The parade of Gretsch artists continued into the be-bop era of the 1950s with greats like Kenny "Klook" Clarke, Max Roach, Art Blakey, and Elvin Jones—all of whom took part in the now-legendary "Gretsch Nights At Birdland." As jazz continued to progress into ever-more-diverse territory, stylistic specialists like Shelley Manne, Chico Hamilton, and Mel Lewis established their own unique niches. And in the 1960s the entire drumming world was floored by a young phenom named Tony Williams.

Of course, jazz wasn't the only music that was going on in the 1960s. That was also when rock 'n' roll exploded onto the scene…and Gretsch drums helped to fuel that explosion. That parade was led by the legendary Charlie Watts, drummer for the Rolling Stones—then and now. Charlie just celebrated fifty years of performing with "the world's greatest rock band," and I'm proud to say that all of those performances have been on Gretsch. My wife Dinah and I had the chance to visit with Charlie several times in recent months, and each of those visits was a personal pleasure for us.

When—like jazz before it—rock diversified in the 1970s, Gretsch became the life-long choice of one of "progressive rock's" seminal figures: Genesis drummer Phil Collins. What drummer could miss the look and sound of Phil's distinctive single-headed Gretsch toms?

The regard for Gretsch drums exhibited by superstars like Chick Webb, Tony Williams, Charlie Watts, and Phil Collins has continued to the present day, as evidenced by a roster of Gretsch drummers that includes Taylor Hawkins (Foo Fighters), Stanton Moore (Galactic), Mark Schulman (Pink), Keith Carlock (Steely Dan), Stephen Ferrone (studio and touring great), and Cindy Blackman-Santana (jazz and rock powerhouse). So has our regard for the input that we receive from those stars, which continues to drive Gretsch's innovation.

On a personal note, I mentioned that I'm a fourth-generation member of the family business. My grandfather brought me into the business in the 1950s, and I'm still in it today, some forty-eight years later. But I'm certainly not alone. I'm pleased to be joined by my wife, Dinah, whose business skills and warm, outgoing personality have made her an integral part of the Gretsch operation—and my indispensable partner—for thirty-four years. Dinah's own accomplishments within our industry are impressive. These include the establishment of the Mrs. G's Music Foundation—a charitable entity that supports music education in rural schools—as well as a host of other philanthropic efforts.

But the generational lineage doesn't stop there. For more than nineteen years Dinah and I have been ably supported at Gretsch Company headquarters by daughter Lena Thomas, who is a skilled administrator and operations manager. Between Lena, Dinah, and me, that's just over 100 combined years of "sweat equity" in the family business. And I'm pleased to report that the sixth Gretsch generation includes sixteen-plus grandchildren, many of whom are pursuing educational tracks that will help them continue the family legacy for years to come. (Who knows…Rob may have to start work on Volume II soon!)

In the meantime you have this volume to read and enjoy.

Fred W. Gretsch

Foreword by John Sheridan

Born 1955 in the Jamaica section of Queens, NYC, my first interest in drums came as a small boy watching a jazz drummer on television. Not yet aware of technique, I became spellbound at his ability to play tap-dance rhythms on a cymbal and rolls that made his snare drum sound like a buzz saw! And the contraption itself: a glistening barrage of drums and cymbals. What is each one for and how does it all go together? It was all so intriguing!

Though clearly fascinated by drums, the obsession didn't take hold until I saw a live drummer at my sister's wedding. I spent most of that 4-hour reception transfixed while he played with the band. That was it; I was hooked! Up to this point, I had been a promising young art student, but suddenly that didn't matter. Music became my new art, and I would best express myself through playing drums.

I sent for every drum catalog available, including Gretsch, which arrived from the neighboring borough of Brooklyn. My family was from Brooklyn, so I felt a kindred spirit in Gretsch. Of course, it would be some time before I could afford my first Gretsch drums, but when they arrived, it was an eye-opener, as well as an ear-opener. It was also a "feel"-opener, due to Gretsch's unique response. Unlike my previous kit, Gretsch drums inspired me to play differently ... on another level, if you will.

This inspiration led me to learn as much about Gretsch drums as possible. (I was also playing Gretsch guitars and just as eager to know about them as well.) Along the way, I gained much knowledge from longtime key Gretsch personnel, such as "Duke" Kramer, Bill Hagner, and Dan Duffy. Likewise, I became friends with such Gretsch cognoscenti as Charlie Donnelley, Jay Scott, and Lee Ruff, among others. I also accumulated a vast archive of vintage Gretsch company literature, including catalogs, price lists and ads; yet remained mindful to carefully temper such information with hands-on/peer experience. In my research, I discovered much about Gretsch instruments overall. The common thread, of course, is their unique sound and feel; they are inextricable from one another. It comes from the brilliant recipe that Gretsch has carefully refined over generations, continuing to please players and listeners alike… as well as collectors.

I have gigged and recorded extensively for more than 40 years. I began collecting/dealing in vintage drums in 1992, and have been offering new Gretsch drums, parts and gretschgear.com swag since 2005. From 1996 to 2002, I worked at Precision Drum Company where, among other duties, I helped restore many old Gretsch drums. Since 2007, I've managed Monmouth Music, an authorized Gretsch dealer. These varied experiences, along with the aforementioned key people, have helped provide me with a strong knowledge of Gretsch, as well as a unique perspective regarding Gretsch drums and Gretsch guitars. This has not only enabled me to write many insightful articles for vintage-themed drum and guitar magazines, but to also consult for many Gretsch enthusiasts, including Fred W. Gretsch.

I've known Rob Cook for 13 years and have spent a good part of that time working with him on this book. There have been many people who have helped us along the way; I know I speak for both Rob and myself when I say thank you for all your contributions and I sincerely hope that everyone enjoys this book as much as we've enjoyed bringing it to you.

John Sheridan
June 2013

John at Lincoln Center with unusual 12x22

Preface
Rob Cook

The mission statement that has guided the assembly of the information in this book: The Gretsch Drum Book provides a business history of the Gretsch Drum Company and documents the instruments they have produced for the purpose of assisting Gretsch owners and potential owners in determining authenticity.

One might assume that the most important resource to the author of a book such as this would be the business records of the 130 year-old company. The correspondence, memos, depositions, manufacturing & sales records have unfortunately pretty much all been discarded. Though the firm has been in business continuously for 13 decades there is no single set of archives that has been accumulating for that entire time frame. Fred W. Gretsch has over the last 30+ years built a fairly substantial archival museum that has been very helpful in piecing the story together, but much more has been needed. As evidenced by the long list of people I am indebted to (Acknowledgements), this kind of project is a joint effort. With this project more than any other I have relied on the expertise and advice of others. The list includes music industry associates past and present, collectors, fans, Ebay sellers, former employees and their families. I am especially indebted to the Gretsch family and many Gretsch drum experts who have examined thousands of Gretsch drums. The experts have not always agreed, and sometimes are quite passionate and adamant about their disagreements. I regret that this book may upset, even anger some of them but there was simply no way to avoid a bit of that.

Rick Gier is the only person I've heard of who has made some well-reasoned estimates regarding production numbers. His serial number studies indicate that about 116,000 Round Badge drums were produced with labels and serial numbers between 1962 and 1969. These are the years and the drums that really have inspired the heart of this book's research. The drums of this era (and of course the preceding two decades) are identified with the American jazz idiom. The American jazz giants used Gretsch to produce rhythms that started a world-wide ripple effect of influence. My friend Dave Mattacks (Fairport Convention, Paul McCartney, Elton John, George Harrison, Jimmy Page, etc.) is a great example. Dave explained to me that he saw Harold Jones with the Basie band in Glasgow, Scotland, in the mid-1960s. He loved the band, loved Jones' playing, and had never heard a kit sound so good, especially the bass drum. Dave went to his local music store and ordered his first Gretsch set the following day.

Are Gretsch drums for everybody? Probably not. I've spoken to drummers who claim Gretsch drums cannot be tuned properly. Dave Mattacks: *"I don't agree with some players who find difficulty getting a sound out of them– especially the snare drums. It may not be easy... one has to work at it, but the rewards are definitely there! The thing about Gretsch drums is that players are drawn to them because they have a lot of character and identity. There truly is a "Gretsch sound" like it or not. (Character is something arguably missing in contemporary sets– Yamaha aside, and I do mean that!) I'm particularly keen on the rocket lug-era drums. I have several snare drums from that era & find that with some careful attention to detail (assembly and tuning), the playability & sound is excellent."*

The Gretsch sound did not happen by accident. It was the result of a group effort by a unique alignment of artists, craftsmen, and businessmen. That's the story I've tried to tell in these pages. I'm sure there are a few errors; feel free to call them to my attention and I'll try to correct them in future editions. For now, well, here it is!

Rob Cook
Alma, Michigan

Where Gretsch Was And Is

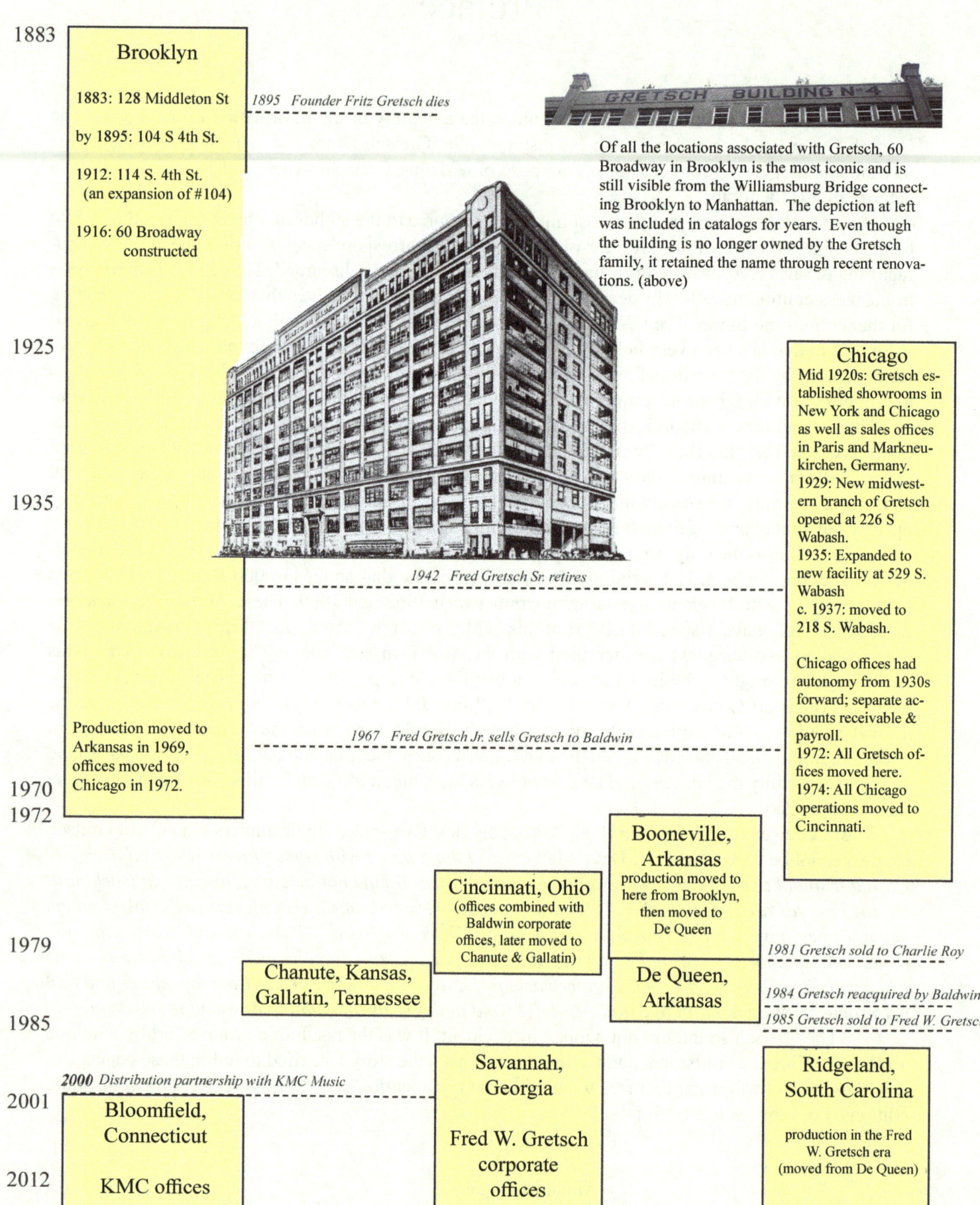

1883

Brooklyn

1883: 128 Middleton St

by 1895: 104 S 4th St.

1912: 114 S. 4th St. (an expansion of #104)

1916: 60 Broadway constructed

1895 Founder Fritz Gretsch dies

Of all the locations associated with Gretsch, 60 Broadway in Brooklyn is the most iconic and is still visible from the Williamsburg Bridge connecting Brooklyn to Manhattan. The depiction at left was included in catalogs for years. Even though the building is no longer owned by the Gretsch family, it retained the name through recent renovations. (above)

1925

Chicago

Mid 1920s: Gretsch established showrooms in New York and Chicago as well as sales offices in Paris and Markneukirchen, Germany.

1929: New midwestern branch of Gretsch opened at 226 S Wabash.

1935: Expanded to new facility at 529 S. Wabash

c. 1937: moved to 218 S. Wabash.

Chicago offices had autonomy from 1930s forward; separate accounts receivable & payroll.

1972: All Gretsch offices moved here.

1974: All Chicago operations moved to Cincinnati.

1935

1942 Fred Gretsch Sr. retires

Production moved to Arkansas in 1969, offices moved to Chicago in 1972.

1967 Fred Gretsch Jr. sells Gretsch to Baldwin

1970
1972

Booneville, Arkansas
production moved to here from Brooklyn, then moved to De Queen

Cincinnati, Ohio
(offices combined with Baldwin corporate offices, later moved to Chanute & Gallatin)

1979

Chanute, Kansas, Gallatin, Tennessee

De Queen, Arkansas

1981 Gretsch sold to Charlie Roy

1984 Gretsch reacquired by Baldwin

1985

1985 Gretsch sold to Fred W. Gretsch

2000 Distribution partnership with KMC Music

2001

Bloomfield, Connecticut

KMC offices

Savannah, Georgia

Fred W. Gretsch corporate offices

Ridgeland, South Carolina

production in the Fred W. Gretsch era (moved from De Queen)

2012

GRETSCH (Business) Family Tree

Anna Maria von Gerichten   M   William Gretsch
1854

When they married, William had two sons; they then had 9 together. William's Anna Maria's two younger brothers moved to California and eventually all of her children did as well. Her oldest son was Karl Friedrich Wilhelm "Fritz." Fritz, arrived in American in 1873. The brothers and sister of Fritz were: Anna Maria, Philippina Paulina, Augusta Catharina, Ludwig Carl Franz, Anna Maria Philippine, Carl Peter, Phillip Wilhelm, Jacob, plus half-brothers August and William.

Fritz Gretsch   M   Rosa Behman Schnapauff
1879

Fritz & Rosa had seven children. Fritz began his business in 1883, died of cholera April 28 1895. Rosa incorporated in 1903 with sons Fred and Walter. (Walter & Fred would part ways in 1924.)
Children of Fritz & Rosa:
Fred Gretsch,
Walter Gretsch, Louie Gretsch,
Elsa Gretsch, Helene Gretsch,
Hertha Gretsch, and Herbert Gretsch

Fritz
1856-1895

Fred Gretsch
(1880-1952)
M
Charlotte Sommer
1904

Children: William Gretsch, Fred Gretsch Jr., Harold Gretsch (died in infancy), Richard Gretsch

William
1906-1948

Fred Jr.
1905-1979

Richard
1908-2010

William Gretsch
M
Maxine (Sylvia) Elsner
1942

1942 was a big year for William; his father retired, he became president of the family business, and he married. His tenure at the head of the family firm would last only 6 years as he died young in 1948.
Children: Charlotte, Katherine "Katie", Fred William, Gretchen Gertrude "Gee Gee"

Fred Jr. joined the family business upon graduation from Cornell in 1926. He became president when his brother William died in 1948. He sold the business out of the family in 1967.

Richard worked at Gretsch as a youngster, but after getting an engineering degree from the University of Michigan pursued a career in business.

Fred William Gretsch   M   Dinah

Fred W Gretsch (son of William, nephew of Fred. Jr.) was working in the family business when he learned that his uncle Fred was selling it to Baldwin. He wanted to buy the business himself, but did not have the money. He was finally able to buy the company and make it a Gretsch family business again in 1985.

Fred William Gretsch with his uncle Fred Jr and grandfather Fred

Chapter 1   1883-1967

Family history, by Gretchen Elsner-Sommer
For more photos and essays, please visit the site Gretchen has been maintaining since 1986,
http://lookingoppositely.com]

Let me introduce myself. I was born Gretchen Gertrude Gretsch on January 15, 1948 in Chicago, Illinois. At the time, my father Bill Gretsch was president of the Fred Gretsch Manufacturing Company. My mother Maxine Elsner, Sylvia, as my father always called her, was from Joplin, Missouri and a graduate of Northwestern University. She was the first Gretsch woman I have discovered who graduated from college. Following Bill Gretsch's example, both of his brothers would also marry college graduates.

To celebrate my birth, my parents held a large christening party at the Dania House on Kedzie Avenue in Chicago not far from where we lived on Palmer Square. The invitations were disguised to look like a letter from the Internal Revenue Service calling each invitee to a meeting…it was a very clever joke.

The "christening" was really a business party, attended by about a hundred music dealers, store owners, musicians and other Chicago music people. Afterwards, a booklet of photos from the event was put together and distributed to all the attendees. The cover of the booklet refers to my parents as the "Bill and Sylvia Gretsch Production Company" and each of their children as new models….Charlotte, March 1944, Katie, April 1945, Fritz (Fred W.), July 1946, and me, "Gee Gee", January 1948.

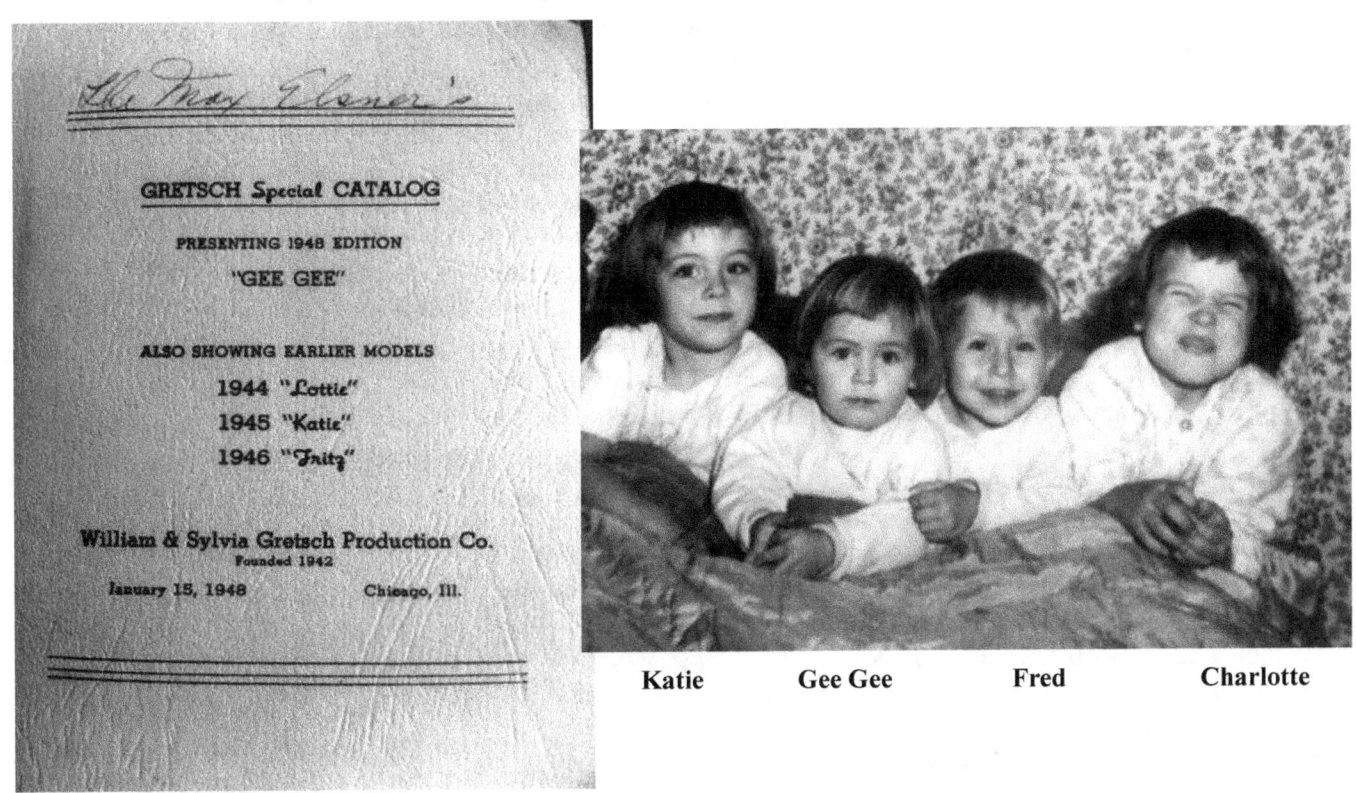

Katie   **Gee Gee**   **Fred**   **Charlotte**

That was my father, he was a real jokester and he loved the music business, mixing it constantly with family and fun. Unfortunately, my father died just 8 months later. I, of course, have no memory of him, but his absence left me with a strong interest in what is no longer visible.

For years, I have been interested in the women of the Gretsch family: women I never met, women whose names were so infrequently mentioned. I've worked hard to imagine just who these women were, the mothers, the daughters, the sisters and the aunts of all the Fred Gretschs who I always heard so much about. I wondered, too, about my father, Bill Gretsch, whose name was so rarely mentioned. As I grew older, I began researching facts, seeking out family stories and writing things down.

The following essays are born from disappearance, absence, imagination and investigation.

Gretchen Elsner-Sommer, nee Gretsch

I

In 1854, when my great, great grandmother Anna Maria Von Gerichten married William Gretsch in Mannheim in what would later become Germany, she had no idea that her two step-sons, William age 9 and August age 7 and all of her nine "yet to be born children" would follow in her younger brothers' footsteps and travel to America to seek their fortunes. The young bride probably imagined that her children would follow the path of her new husband and enter the world of business. Business indeed was the choice of all of sons– none of her children stayed in Europe.

The letters which Anna Maria's brothers sent her from the gold fields of California as they set up their business must have ignited the imagination of her growing family. As her brothers moved from "clerk" and "merchant" to owners of a General Store, a distillery and later a hotel, their progress was watched by the families they left behind. Letters from her husband's brother Jacob Gretsch, who had settled in Brooklyn, New York, would have only served to broaden her children's familiarity with the landscape of opportunities America offered.

So, almost twenty years later, when Anna Maria's oldest son, my great grandfather Fritz Gretsch, arrived in Brooklyn, he was not coming to a land completely foreign to him. Fritz, the founder of what would become the Fred Gretsch Manufacturing Company, arrived in America on his 17th birthday in 1873, just eighteen months after the death of his mother. For all of her children, Anna Maria's death provided a point of departure from their homeland. Although her two step sons came to America before her death, it was in the 15 years after her death that each of her eight children would make their way to America.

Fritz and his siblings had uncles and aunts on both coasts of the American continent and many American-born cousins: Gretsch cousins on their father's side and Von Gerichten cousins on their mother's. From the store on Markplatz in Mannheim which Wilhelm Gretsch operated to the successful California business endeavors which their von Gerichten uncles initiated, the world of business was well-known to these Gretsch children from Mannheim. Coming to America, they had paths to follow and connections to make.

Saving family letters was not a Gretsch trait; there are no family letters from this period and very few from subsequent generations. However, family letters and daily newspapers were certainly helpful in familiarizing Fritz and his siblings with the business and cultural landscape which awaited them in America. Two older half brothers, August Gretsch, who had served in the American Civil War, and William Gretsch, the oldest of the Mannheim children, had come to Brooklyn in 1868 and played a part in helping their younger siblings get situated. There was also a large female family presence here in America to welcome Fritz and his siblings. In 1872, the year before Fritz left Mannheim for America, his cousin Pauline Gretsch arrived in Brooklyn. The home of their uncle, Jacob Gretsch in Brooklyn would serve as a gathering point for all the Gretsch cousins from Germany as they arrived through the 1870s and 1880s from Mannheim. Pauline had come no doubt to help out in her uncle's household. When Paulina arrived, Jacob's second wife Anna was ill and their young daughter, Wilhelmina needed watching after. Jacob's older daughter, Emilie was beginning her teaching career so Pauline, it seems, would be a great help to Anna. Unfortunately, little is known about Pauline and her time in America. We do know

Dora, Bertha, Emilie, and Wilhelmini Gretsch
Brooklyn, New York circa 1890

that she was the daughter of Carl Gretsch, a younger brother of Jacob and William. And we know that she was the first Gretsch woman of her generation to come to America. Pauline was no doubt an inspiration and a catalyst to all her girl cousins who would soon follow her. In the late 1870s, after the death of Jacob's second wife, his remarriage and the birth of three more children, Fritz's three sisters came to America following Pauline's, and of course their brothers' lead.

Despite the lack of existing family letters, it can be assumed that Fritz's older half brother William came to work with his step-mother's brothers in California. From passport papers and city directories we know that William worked in San Francisco with Conrad von Gerichten in his distillery business. Later, William set up his own wine business in Manhattan. This east coast business was just getting underway when his younger brother Fritz arrived from Mannheim in 1873. By 1875, "William Gretsch wines" can be found in the city directories. It is interesting to note that in the same year in which William Gretsch opened his wine store in Manhattan, his father Wilhelm Gretsch died in Mannheim. Soon afterwards, the family store which had operated for fifteen years on Markplatz, the center of Mannheim, was closed.

Perhaps what brought Fritz across the Atlantic was the assumption that he would work with William in his new business. It is a common immigrant experience that one family member settles in a land, sets up a business and other relatives come to work in that same business. William, after all, had come to America and joined in the business of his California uncles. Fritz, however, never took to that family business. (But his younger brother Louie who followed Fritz to America did work for William.) Although there is no record of Fritz's earliest years in America, it is clear that although family played a big part in Fritz's getting settled and making his own way in America, he branched off to begin his own business. On his arrival in Brooklyn, Fritz was welcomed in 1873 by his father's brother Jacob who had come to America in the early 1850s. He was also welcomed by his American born cousins, Emilie (Mil) Gretsch born in Brooklyn in 1854, and her half sister, Wilhelmina (Min) born in 1864. Pauline Gretsch, the cousin from Germany was also living with Jacob's family. Emilie was already teaching schools in the Brooklyn Public School system and would continue to teach there for 42 years, retiring in 1912. In 1916, Emilie, the oldest of Jacob's children wrote a chapter on the Gretsch family in Schlegel's German-American Families in the United States. This book was published in New York in 1916 by the American Historical Society. Here, Emilie chronicles the early rise of the Gretsch music business but interestingly leaves out any trace of the aforementioned wine business and the California von Gerichten connections.

When Fritz arrived in Brooklyn in 1873, there was already quite a comfortable home situation awaiting him. For almost 20 years, Jacob Gretsch had made his residence in Brooklyn. In the intervening years, Jacob was widowed and remarried and now had two daughters, so the young Fritz found himself surrounded by the comforts of a family home. Jacob's oldest daughter Emilie, along with her sister Wilhelmina, never married and the sisters lived together in a house they jointly purchased in the early 1890s. After Fritz's death, Aunt Min and Aunt Mil were very close to Fritz's children. They filled, I imagine, a grandmotherly role.

In 1875, just two years after Fritz's arrival in America, his father died in Mannheim. Now, all of Fritz's remaining siblings--Louis, Katie, Pauline, Philippine, Jacob, Philip and Carl made their way to Brooklyn. Little is known about Fritz's oldest sister, Anna Maria. It is assumed that she too came around this time; we do know that by the late 1890's she was a widow, living in New York with her only child, Wilhelmina. We do know for certain that the three younger Gretsch girls, Katie, Paulina, and Philippine, all came to New York in the late 1870s. Katie went on to California and lived for a while near her mother's brother's family in San Diego. There she married and had a daughter, Helma von Hellerman. Unlike her siblings, Katie later returned to Germany. She lived for years in Dresden near some of her Von Gerichten cousins. These cousins were born in California but chose to return to Germany with their German born-parents.

After the death of Jacob's second wife and his remarriage, Pauline and Philippine, sisters of Fritz, came from Germany to live with their uncle and to help raise Jacob's growing family, William born in 1877, Dora born in 1878 and Ralph born in 1879. Another brother of Fritz, Philip, stayed for awhile in Brooklyn but then went to San Francisco where he worked for a time with his uncles.

By 1884, the Gretsch family of Manheim had completed its migration to America. Fritz stayed close to his siblings as they settled in America as can be seen by his signature as witness at his sister Pauline's wedding in 1878.

In 1879, amidst all of this family activity, Fritz married Rosa Behman Schnapauff, an American born woman of German descent. Rosa's parents had died in the cholera epidemic in New York in the 1850s and she was adopted as a baby by a childless couple, Caroline and Adolph Schnapauff. Together, Fritz and Rosa would have seven children. Today only two small pictures of Rosa survive and none of her letters or papers have been saved. The stories told by her grandchildren have kept her memory alive. Ted Clauss, the son of Rosa's oldest daughter Elsa, remembers that he was his grandmother's favorite grandchild. Marion Gretsch Wells, daughter of Rosa's third son Louis enlarges Rosa's story by remembering that when Rosa died each of her children felt that he or she was she favorite child. These memories of her grandchildren have keep alive Rosa's genius for seeing each of her children's worth and supporting each of their individual talents. Her young husband Fritz, as he struggled to start a new business in a foreign country in a foreign language was no doubt an early recipient of Rosa's keen insights and unfailing support.

As a testament to Fritz's enterprising spirit, three different documents from this period– his wedding certificate (1879), the US Census (1880) and the birth certificate of his first son (1880)– each give Fritz a different occupation. Fritz is listed as a "colorizer" in his marriage certificate, as a wholesale grocer in the birth record of his first child, and finally, in the census, as a bookkeeper in a music store. This was probably the beginning of his work with Albert Houdlett and Company. Rosa's father was also listed as a "colorizer" in the 1880 census, so perhaps this is how Rosa and Fritz first met.

The 1880 Census shows the newlyweds living in the same building as Rosa's parents. This building would be torn down in the years to come to sustain the footing of the Williamsburg Bridge. In 1883, after the birth of his second son and soon after the completion of the Brooklyn Bridge, Fritz began his own business.

More children quickly followed as the family grew right alongside Fritz's musical instrument business: first, three sons: Fred (1880), Walter (1882), Louie (1883); then Elsa (1885), Helene (Oct 1887), Hertha (November, 1887); and finally Herbert (November 1891).

In February, 1890, Fritz and Rosa purchased a house on Hart Street, a neighborhood of new two story, single family homes. The builder of the homes and his family lived just a few blocks down from the Gretsch family. In this same period, Fritz continued to buy property around his business on Middleton Avenue. In 1893, when he saw that there were plans in the works for a bridge to connect Manhattan to Williamsburg, he began buying property on South Fourth Street, near the proposed footing of that bridge. This area held many memories for Fritz and Rosa. The building of the bridge demolished the apartment home where Rosa and Fritz had lived as newlyweds, the same building where their first son was born. The area reached not only into their past but also into their unknowable future. The footing of the bridge on the Brooklyn side, the same site of their newlywed apartment, was also just a stone throw away from the site of several buildings that would soon house the growing Gretsch business first on South Fourth street and then in years to come on Broadway itself.

Pictures from this time show the family at Sea Cliff, Long Island enjoying a day at what was at that time a favorite spot for family fun. Steamships made daily round trips from New York to Sea Cliff. Other ships up the Hudson River made the Catskill mountains another place where Jacob Gretsch's children and Fritz's children would vacation together.

The mid-1890s was a time of growth for the business and a time of imagining a bright future. In the spring of 1895, a very dynamic Fritz planned his first trip back to his homeland. He was now a determined American businessman. Most likely, he no longer called himself Fritz.

William, Fritz's older step brother, having left his American wine and liquor business in the hands of Fritz's younger brother Louis, was now living in Heidelberg and would meet Fritz in Hamburg. Together, they would travel to Mannheim to visit relatives. Perhaps, plans were even made for Fritz to travel to Markneukirchen. There, Fritz could make arrangements to distribute in America the fine handmade instruments for which Markneukirchen was famous. Dresden, where Fritz's sister Katie, now lived with many of their von Gerichten cousins, was not too far from Markneukirchen. Perhaps, a visit there was also planned.

The day before he left, Fritz signed a will witnessed by his neighbors. The closeness of the date to his departure and the nearness of the witnesses to his family home, suggest a hurried action. It was a last minute thought to write that will, a thought that was quickly executed.

Perhaps in the midst of all the plans for the journey, the cholera scare that had instigated the quarantine of many ships in New York harbor just three years earlier was recalled. The "Furest Bismark" was one of those ships quarantined in 1892 and the "Furest Bismark" was the ship on which Fritz sailed to Hamburg on April 11,

1895. In his will, Fritz left everything to his wife, Rosa. He obviously trusted her above all others.

Records show that Fritz died on April 28 in Hamburg from cholera. Like his mother, Anna Maria, he died at a fairly young age leaving behind him a large young family. It was the end of a dream and the beginning of a new era in the family.

II
Rosa, Fred Sr. and Walter

The family story, I've always been told, explains that after Fritz's sudden death, everyone encouraged his wife to sell the business. Rosa, however, was intent on carrying on her husband's work. Her answer to their discouraging suggestions was "I will put Fred in long pants and have him run the business before I will sell it." That was exactly what she did….. after an appropriate amount of time.

It's hard to believe that no family history has been passed down about this important period immediately after Fritz's death. Brooklyn property papers show that one of Rosa's first moves after her husband's death was to buy up several of the mortgages that her husband had purchased. This gave her, among other things, full ownership of the family home on Hart Street. Rosa was taking control. Because of the fear of cholera, it was not until November, 1895 that Fritz's body was finally returned to the United States. Then Rosa made another firm statement confirming her determination to keep her husband's legacy and her children's future in the public view. Rosa purchased for her husband and her family a burial plot in the prestigious Green-Wood Cemetery. This was a break of tradition for the burial of Gretsch family members. This purchase set Rosa and Fritz apart from the earlier Gretsch family members and assigned her family, in their final resting place, a space of more dignity and stateliness.

Caroline Schnaupauff, Rosa's mother and the children's grandmother, lived with the family until her death in 1897. At that time, Rosa took in a boarder. Perhaps this idea came from Fritz's youngest sister, Philippine Gretsch Morgner. "Tante Bena" as the Rosa's children affectionately remembered her was already taking in boarders in her Manhattan home. Later in 1902, Rosa followed in Philippina's footsteps again when Rosa sold the family home on Hart Street and moved with her children to Bath Beach. This section of Brooklyn was near Coney Island and a recently built transit line led directly to the heart of Brooklyn. The area was quickly developing. Philippine ran a boarding house there and Rosa moved her family into a nearby home. Philippine was by this time a widow like Rosa and raising her only child, Johanna.

The boarder who Rosa chose in 1897 was Jacob Hyman, a retired Jewish businessman who would have an immense impact on the family. Jacob Hyman had no immediate family of his own. He had, however, a great deal of business experience in the Brooklyn/New York area, many friends in banking, and a tremendous love of children. Rosa could not have made a better choice for her family. Jacob Hyman lived with the family off and on until his death in 1915. There is no doubt that he helped Rosa and her young sons as they transitioned through the world of business in Brooklyn. Jacob Hyman loved the outdoors, he loved matinees and he loved children. Newspaper articles report that he enjoyed taking the young Gretsch children on fishing trips on the many ponds and tributaries around Brooklyn. He also frequently took them to the matinee which he attended daily. Articles from the Music Trade Magazine in the early 1900's show that Walter Gretsch, Rosa's second son, also loved to fish and that he often mixed his fishing trips with his business trips. The young Walter would have learned this love of fishing from Jacob Hyman.

When Jacob Hyman died in 1915, he left his fortune to the Gretsch girls. Half was left to Hertha, the youngest daughter, and a quarter to Elsa and a quarter to Helene. His will set in motion a well published court case in Manhattan as the will was contested by his distant cousins. Articles about the case appeared in newspapers around the country. The appeals were finally overturned and a small fortune was left to the Gretsch girls, just as Jacob Hyman had intended. Nothing was left to the Gretsch boys. Probably Jacob, having helped steer the boys through the world of business and banking in Brooklyn, felt that they were well taken care of. Hertha, the youngest of the Gretsch girls had as a child contracted Scarlet Fever. She was left with a weak heart and her future did not look promising. Jacob Hyman's will changed that. Newspaper articles from the time, speculate that Jacob Hyman left Hertha the money because as a young girl, Herha sat so quietly in the fishing boat. A front page story in the Washington Post from January 28, 1915 reports "She Sat Still, Got Fortune."

Jacob Hyman's will was settled on May 6, 1915. On May 7th, the Lusitania was sunk. The tensions in

Europe and the beginnings of the First World War are probably what delayed Hertha's travels. It wasn't until 1918 when Hertha was in her late twenties that she left Brooklyn to travel to Washington State to visit her cousin Johanna. From there no doubt, she went on to visit her von Gerichten cousins in San Diego and San Francisco. She was making the first steps in her trip around the world that would last 3 years.

Rosa did not realize when her third and youngest daughter left Brooklyn that Hertha was planning on traveling around the world. Perhaps Hertha had not even admitted to herself what she was plans were. We have no record of her travels. According to Ted Clauss, Rosa's grandson, Rosa just kept getting letters from farther and farther away. Ted, who was the son of Rosa's oldest daughter Elsa, also remembers his mother receiving these far-away letters from Hertha. That the letters arrived always having postage due infuriated his mother, Hertha's older sister. Elsa had to stop what she was doing and search for money to pay the postman. On the other hand, the flutter which these letters caused in the household and their foreign stamps and markings always fired up the young Ted Clauss' imagination. It is this precise flutter which remained in Ted's memory, and caused him to pass down one of the only family memories of Hertha's amazing around the world adventure. Hertha's travels didn't stop when she returned home in 1922. She was soon off again for another long period of traveling abroad. The memory of these travels are only recorded in passport application papers.

Helene, Rosa's second daughter, studied in Boston and New York for an acting career under the name of Helene Hope. She graduated from The American Academy of Dramatic Arts in 1910. She was on the road touring with a theater company in Ohio in 1915 when the papers reached her about Jacob Hyman's bequest. Rumor has it that she married John P. Welsh secretly before the war so as not to interrupt her theatrical career while her husband was at war. No record of her marriage has yet been found. Jack Welsh and Helene had no children and separated soon after Rosa's death in 1934.

On June 2, 1903, Rosa and Fred and Walter incorporated the Fred Gretsch Manufacturing Company. The prominence of Rosa's position in the papers is important. Her name always appears first. Fred was now 23 years old, Walter had just turned 21. Two of Rosa's sons were now of legal age, their place in the company could not be questioned. It was time for Rosa to leave her sons in charge, now that they actually were "in long pants."

Soon afterwards, in January of 1904, Fred married Charlotte Sommer. Charlotte was the only daughter of a family of six children. Her brothers so adored her that several of them named their daughters in her honor. Charlotte's father William Sommer owned a small grocery and butcher store in Manhattan. Charlotte's mother Theresa Leicht came from a family of furniture makers who owned several properties in mid-Manhattan.

Charlotte and Fred's small wedding took place in the bride's family home on West 54th Street in Manhattan; an Evangelical Lutheran pastor officiated. However, by the time their first child was born 18 months later, the Catholic Church was a very definite part of Charlotte's life. All of her children were raised Catholic and would throughout their lives remain devoted to their Catholic faith.

In 1905, with the birth of Fred and Charlotte's son, Fred Gretsch Jr., the legacy of Fritz was crystallized. In December of 1906, a second son, my father William, was born. The family called him "Willie Walter" then to distinguish him from William Charles Gretsch a grandson of Jacob Gretsch and a cousin of the same age as the new born. The following summer, my father, just an infant, contracted polio. One can only imagine the fear which enveloped the young family as their infant son suffered with this devastating disease. Polio left my father with a crippled leg and he would always walk with a limp. Polio however didn't affect his "outsized" personality, and he is remembered as being the liveliest and the most fun loving of the three Gretsch brothers. In 1908, another son, Richard, was born.

In 1907 Rosa, having safely guided the business into the hands of Fred and Walter, was ready to concentrate on another aspect of her life. In that year, Rosa married David Kling. Rosa's grandson Ted Clauss reported that David Kling was a very handsome man, a debonair man but definitely not a business man.

For a short time, Rosa's third son Louie joined his older brothers in their father's business. Louie, however, did not take to the music business and soon left to pursue a career in banking. It was at this time (circa 1907) that he brought a friend from the bank home for dinner. "Choose one!" Louis said to Joe Clauss as he pointed to his three sisters, Elsa, Helene and Hertha, who were seated at the dinner table. Joseph Clauss chose Elsa. In the years to come, Louis turned to developing real estate in Brooklyn and was quite successful.

Back at the Fred Gretsch Mfg. Company, Fred and Walter worked together to enlarge the business in many areas. They both traveled to Markneukirchen and set up deals with small musical instrument makers there and in other German, Italian and French cities. But the uneasiness of their relationship can be viewed through the lens of their breakup in 1924. At that time Walter and William Brenner, who also worked for Fred Gretsch Manufacturing Co. formed "Gretsch and Brenner", which also distributed musical instruments.

Mention must also be made of Fred Gretsch Sr.'s interest in Banking. Both Fred and Walter became close to Nathan Jonas, a Brooklyn banker, at the time of the building of the Gretsch building #4 in 1915. Jonas's wife Jennie and Charlotte also became good friends. Nathan Jonas was also the founder of the Brooklyn Jewish Hospital to which Fred and Charlotte also donated. It is likely that the beginnings of this important relationship were encouraged by Jacob Hyman, the boarder Rosa had brought into the family, who also was involved with the Brooklyn Jewish Hospital.

Perhaps it was by way of the encouragement of Nathan Jonas that Fred Sr. was elected a member of the Board of the Lincoln Saving Bank in 1918. Fred Sr. liked the work and began working on the Finance Committee in 1925. He was elected to Vice President in 1930 and President in 1940. In 1950, he was elevated to Chairman of the Board of Trustees. In August of 1953, Charlotte and Fred's oldest son Fred Jr., following in his father's footsteps, was elected Vice President of the Lincoln Savings Bank.

In the summer of 1924, at the same time as the formation of "Gretsch and Brenner," Fred and Charlotte Gretsch took their oldest son Fred to Europe. The next summer they took their second son Bill and the following summer, their youngest son Richard. Richard's diary survives and tells of visiting the Gretsch office in Paris, traveling to Markneukirchen, Erfurt, …and other German musical cities. If the diaries of the older boys had survived they would no doubt tell of similar travels. In the years immediately after the split between Walter and Fred Sr., Fred Sr. was certainly grooming his boys for the Fred Gretsch Mfg. Company.

Charlotte once told her youngest son, Richard, that as soon as she started packing her trunks for the long ocean voyage, she could feel the rolling of the ship and began to feel sea sick. Charlotte's address book from this time, which was given to her by her friend Jenny Jonas, lists friends, family and shops in France, Switzerland and Germany whom she would have visited on these trips.

In the Spring of 1928, Fred Sr. returned to Europe with his oldest son, Fred Jr. who had graduated from Cornell University in 1926 and was now working in the business. Charlotte was at first going to accompany them. However, near the day of departure, she was not feeling well did not go along on this trip. Her illness did not seem serious and it was assumed that she would meet up with her husband and son later. Her condition worsened, however, and her husband was sent a wire that he should return immediately. Charlotte died in a Hospital before her husband and son returned. She was 47 years old. Forty-five years later, her youngest son Richard told me this story with tears in his eyes. It was a tremendous shock to the whole family.

Just six years later in December of 1934, Rosa died after suffering from a long illness. Soon after, Rosa's daughter, Helene, separated from her husband and moved in with her widowed brother Fred and his three grown sons. Helene waited until the death of her mother before she left her husband, Jack. Her address on legal papers of that time proclaims these changes in her life. From a distance of more than three quarters of a century, it appears that Helene's timing, her entrances and exits, was well intact although her stage career was well behind her.

The following year, Hertha, whose childhood bout with Scarlet Fever left her with a rheumatic heart, also passed away. Her niece Gertrude Gretsch, who was thirteen years old at the time, always remembered her aunt Hertha as a very romantic person: tall, beautiful, elegantly adorned in large hats and surrounded by rumors of the romance she had had in India with a prince. When Hertha's final illness began, Gertrude, a young teenager unfamiliar with medical terms, understood that her aunt was dying of "Romantic" Fever. Gertrude, Walter Gretsch's only child, would introduce her own brush with romance and adventure into the Gretsch family with her marriage to John Jacob Astor in September, 1944. Astor's father had gone down in the Titanic in 1912. His mother, pregnant with John at the time, had waited in a life boat to be rescued. Gertrude's marriage was not a happy one for long. It ended in a prolonged court case which was reported in many papers. Like her romantic Aunt Hertha in 1915, Gertrude Gretsch Astor made headlines with a much reported court case in the early 1950's.

In this long period from Rosa's incorporation of the Gretsch business in 1903 until her death in 1934, great changes occurred not only in the business but also in the family. The seven Gretsch children, who were all considered infants in the eyes of the law when their father died in 1895, had grown to adulthood. Rosa's oldest daughter Elsa and all her sons had children of their own while the youngest girls, Helene and Hertha, had carved for themselves quite unique adventures. The business left by Fritz in its young years had matured into a very successful and still growing enterprise. It had survived the split between the two oldest sons as Fred kept the original business, the "Fred Gretsch Manufacturing Company" and Walter opened "Gretsch and Brenner."

Fred Sr., with his three sons growing in their knowledge and experience of their father's world, had come a long way in successfully steering the Fred Gretsch Manufacturing Company into the next generation. The youngest son Richard chose to pursue a career in engineering but the older boys Fred and Bill, by the time of Rosa's death were firmly established in the Gretsch business.

In 1944, just a few years after Walter Gretsch's death, Walter's only child, Gertrude, asked her Uncle Fred Gretsch to give her away in her wedding to John Jacob Astor. The family rift which might have been caused by the splitting up of the business in 1924 was effectively closed by this generous gesture and thankfully never worked its way into the next generation.

III
Fred Jr., Bill

Standing at a hundred years' distance from this early 20th century photograph, I finally see the women who stood close by and just out of frame as the photographer set to work that day. Informed by a history I was never taught and having recently become a grandmother myself, I finally sense the influence in this photograph of my grandmother and her mother. Their presence, standing unrecorded outside the limits of the lens, is as certain to me as the image of my father and his brother, little boys at play in a child sized grocery store, which this photograph portrayed and passed on to future generations.

Above the boys' heads, at the top of the toy market is a sign which reads:
GRETSCH BROS. MARKET
-BRANCH STORE-
SOMMER BROS. 910 6th Ave City

Bill (left) and Fred Jr. (behind counter)

Sometime in my teenage years when I first saw this image, I was intrigued to see my family name "Gretsch" coupled with "Sommer" the name of my father's cousins whom I barely knew. I remember asking questions. The answers were as vague to me then as the image I had of my grandmother Charlotte Sommer Gretsch who died long before I was born.

This clear photograph of the "Gretsch Bros.", my father and my uncle, playing in the "Branch Store" of the real life market of their grandfather "Sommer Bros. 910 6th Ave." in the "City" of Manhattan, is mesmerizing in its detail. The toy-sized grocery store is set up indoors, in what was at the time the family home of the "Gretsch Bros." on President Street in the Crown Heights section of Brooklyn. Highly polished and fluted woodwork reaches up along one edge of the image, past the faux brick chimney of the playhouse and out of frame. Just below the woodwork, a small section of the rich parquet wood floors on which the playhouse rests is visible and suggests that this little market enjoys a very certain comfort in its Brooklyn surroundings.

This elegant setting is mirrored in the polite interaction of the two exquisitely groomed and uniformed little grocers. Freddy, the oldest boy has thick dark hair much like his mother's. My father, Willie Walter, is blond with fine hair as straight as my own. The boys are outfitted in matching tailored, heavy cotton, pin stripped tunic shirts and knee button pants. Long white aprons, emblematic of the grocers they pretend to be, complete their costumes.

Just as clearly as I see the elegant woodwork stretching out of frame, I visualize my grandmother standing silent and also graceful at a close distance from the scene. While Charlotte watched the photographer arrange and rearrange the cumbersome lights around her two oldest children, she was also listening carefully for the sounds of her youngest waking from his nap. No doubt, the outfits of her sons reminded her of other boys who in her own childhood were similarly dressed. First, her older brothers, Philip and Louis and then her younger ones Charles, John and Leo, all worked through the years of their childhood at their father's market on 6th Ave. Charlotte, the only sister, was surely in charge of mending and maintaining her brothers' "grocery boy" uniforms. It was not difficult for her now to recreate these costumes brand new for her own little boys.

Perhaps, Charlotte's mother, Theresa, sat close by watching the photographer work on that winter day of 1910. The boys' grandmother must have wondered at the casualness and ease of modern photography. For Theresa, just the possibility of having pictures taken in one's home would have seemed a modern miracle compared to the days when her own children were young. Theresa's memories of this family market stretched further back in time than those of her daughter. Theresa remembered easily the small family owned "eating house" or restaurant on 8th Ave. and later the butcher shop which preceded the finally successful "Sommer Bros. Market" of her husband William and his brother Louis.

Remembering the struggles of these earlier businesses and watching her young grandsons playing in the stylish rooms of this modern Brooklyn town house, Theresa may have been reminded of long ago rooms not so well fashioned which encircled the play of her own children on 9th Ave. in Manhattan just on the outskirts of Hell's Kitchen. Surrounded by her only daughter's children and the wonders of modern life, Theresa may have also recalled her daughters born before Charlotte, daughters who did not survive their infancy. One, Theresa's

Fred Jr. (left) and Bill with their display at the Music Trades Convention in Chicago, July 15, 1946

first child, Susan Regina, was named after both of her grandmothers, Susanna Mayer Leicht and Regina Winklein Sommer. The other, Theresa, was named in honor of her mother. These sisters who Charlotte never knew were daughters that Theresa would never forget.

There is no Christmas tree in this photo. However, the winter dress of the boys and my own memory of other German Christmas scenes with children playing happily beneath a tree, leads me to imagine that this child sized grocery store had recently been a Christmas gift. Such a special present might easily have been designed with the boys in mind and then assembled by one of the many skilled craftsman employed at their father's

The drum portion of the trade show display from the previous page.

musical instrument factory on South Fifth Street in what was then called the Eastern District of Brooklyn. As children, these "Gretsch Bros." would play at being grocers but the real work of their adult lives would be in their father's music business.

In the years surrounding the taking of this picture, the boys' father Fred and his brother Walter were busy with plans for erecting an even larger factory on Broadway not far from their first joint building venture on South Fifth Street. Both of these modern structures were completed very soon after the opening of the Williamsburg Bridge in the same neighborhood.

In the first decade of the twentieth century, this new bridge quickly brought business opportunities from Manhattan to this once distant part of Brooklyn. Both new factories built by the boys' father and uncle were signs of the success of this once small family business and both buildings proudly bore the name "Gretsch" high above their many stories. The sign which hung above the toy market, however, clearly points to the importance of another family business across the East River in Manhattan.

At the same time that the Gretsch history was being written larger everyday, it was Charlotte who supervised her children's play and it was most probably Charlotte who saw the importance of connecting her children with the family history which she remembered on the other side of the Williamsburg Bridge.

Encircled in my childhood by a proud Gretsch legacy in which my grandmother Charlotte's voice is silent, it is not hard to imagine that her life was surrounded by a long series of unrecorded efforts and responsibilities. Following backwards on a path of influence which stretches into the modern life of mothers and grandmothers, it is quite possible to see that it was my grandmother who supervised the building of the tiny market in this photograph…she who composed the wording of the sign which hung above the market, connecting her sons to their history in Manhattan…she who had the sign painted…she who arranged the photographer's visit.

After the photograph was taken, it was Charlotte who ordered duplicate copies of this formal record of the existence of the Sommer Bros. grocery store, the only record which would be passed on to future generations. For without this long ago photograph, I would have never asked the questions which have lead to my discovery of the forgotten family history in Manhattan. It was Charlotte who placed the photograph prominently in the center hallway of the family home on President's Street, thus preserving a small piece of family history long after the Christmas presents of 1909 were forgotten.

In the years after Rosa's death, her oldest son Fred Sr. gave more and more control of the music business over to his oldest son as Fred Sr. pursued more fully his interest in banking.

My father who was now called "Bill" Gretsch was sent to Chicago in the early 1930's to work in the Gretsch office which was getting started there. Bill's outsized business style was not a good fit with the tradition minded, Gretsch business offices of Brooklyn. In the 1930s, Chicago was a hot bed of new music, new musicians and new ideas. My father, an outgoing, fun loving, adventurous business man, was in his element.

In the fall of 1937, he met my mother Maxine Elsner whom he always called "Sylvia." Everyone who met my mother through my father called her Sylvia. Everyone who met my mother before that point called her "Maxine." Her parents, of course, always called her Maxine. I don't think they were pleased with her unofficial name change, especially since she was named after her father whose name was Max. My mother liked it though. In January, 1938, just months after my parents first met, my mother signed a telegram sent to my father: "Sylvia." My mother obviously liked her name change. From her birthplace city of Joplin, Missouri, my mother came to Northwestern University to study the new field of "Radio." In her college application, she wrote that she had been preparing for a career on the radio since she was ten. Since the early 1930s when Northwestern offered its first courses in radio, the University was known for preparing their students for opportunities in this quickly developing field.

Bill and Sylvia had a long and often stormy courtship. He was a fun loving bachelor and she was a career minded woman. In late November, 1942, while she was working as editor of a west coast magazine, and while Bill was working for Gretsch in New York, Bill called Sylvia on the phone. Days later she described their conversation in a letter to her aunt, "we argued for half an hour and then decided to get married." They met halfway between New York and California in a small Missouri town called "California" and were married in mid-December. Sylvia converted to the Catholic faith and raised all their children in this religion.

Maxine (Sylvia) Elsner Gretsch

Earlier in 1942, Bill was named by his father, who was retiring, president of the Fred Gretsch Manufacturing Company. Bill's brother, Fred, who had been running the company, volunteered for the Navy in December, 1941 soon after Pearl Harbor and was enrolled in Officer Candidate School. Because of the lingering effects of his childhood polio, Bill was, much to his disappointment, unable to join the fight. His younger brother Richard joined the military. Bill would run the company throughout the war and shortly beyond. [Ed. note: Bill moved from Chicago back to New York when he became president and guided Gretsch through it's "scaled down production" war years. Metal was in short supply and Bill's ingenuity was tested as he made drum fittings out of wood and plastic. Bill was involved in the war effort serving as a member of the War Production Board, and worked with the Red Cross to supply instruments to thousands of soldiers.]

I found it interesting that Bill chose to marry at this time. His marriage echoes his own father's marriage in 1904. Perhaps my father felt that now that he was president of the company, he was in a position to marry. His father, after all, had proposed marriage to his mother soon after the business was incorporated in 1903. Both Gretsch men, father and son, so different in so many ways, had postponed their marriages until their business lives were well in hand.

For the following six years, through the second world war and through the recovery, Bill ran the Gretsch Company …. until his death in 1948. This is where I end the story….here in 1948, the year I was born, the last of Maxine's "Sylvia's" four children: Charlotte, Katherine, Fred William and me.

Looking back over these pages at the lives of Anna Maria, Emilie, Pauline, "Tante Bena", Rosa and Charlotte, I find myself looking oppositely from the family business which over the years has flourished and thrived. Instead, I find myself concentrating on the peripheries of its success…. on the women in the family whose stories are unwritten, whose pictures and letters are missing…..women who were well loved and forgotten.

Gretchen Elsner-Sommer 2012

Though Fred Gretsch bore three "heirs apparent," in the end this would be the generation that sold the family musical instrument business. Richard worked at the family business as a youngster, but followed an entirely different career path since it appeared to him that his father and two brothers were firmly entrenched. William would die young, however, and Fred Jr. would sell the business out of the family.

Richard Gretsch   1908-2010
The following is from Gretsch House Telegram Volume 10 #1, 2004

The youngest of three brothers, Richard Francis Gretsch was born in 1908 and grew up with his brothers Bill and Fred in the family home in Forest Hills, New York.

Dick remembers trips to Europe (by ship) with his father to their offices in Paris and Germany. The trips could last up to a month, and the brothers took turns traveling with their father. The boys also enjoyed train trips to Chicago. When not working, the boys took turns caddying for their father who paid them $1 plus a 25-cent tip. Golf was a prominent pastime in the Gretsch household and continued to be so throughout Dick's life. Dick's father Fred shared his love of gold with his close friend Nathan Jonas, founder of Manufacturer's Trust Company. Together in 1921, they decided to create a match between the winner of the American Open Golf Championship and the British Open Golf Championship, creating the first unofficial championship of the world. The two men contributed $2,000 each to bring the match to the Sound View Country Club in Great Neck, New York. The 36-hole match was held on Labor Day and was won by Jim Barnes, the American Champion. The winner received $1,250 in cash and a trophy and the loser received $500 cash. This purse was said to be, up to that point, the largest ever posted for a golf match of this nature in the U.S.

Dick and his brothers worked at the Gretsch factory at 60 Broadway in New York on Saturday mornings packaging phonograph needles and filling orders. He remembers climbing into the truck for weekend trips to Cold Spring Harbor on Long Island to pick up drum heads from the tannery and to the docks of New York to collect imported product. He is careful to point out that all these business adventures as a young man were done on weekends, NOT on school days.

All three of the Gretsch brothers took piano lessons. Their Grandmother, Rosa Kling (their father's mother), was a talented pianist believed in the importance of studying music. (None of them, however, could play the instruments the family sold.)

Dick and his brothers all attended school in Forest Hills, up to the 6th grade which was as high as they would go. After that they then walked "a couple of miles" to and from school in Richmond Hill, the neighboring school district, regardless of the weather– "rain, snow, sleet or hail."

Dick's older brother Fred had attended Cornell and there was a plan for Dick to enroll there as well. He completed his high school studies in February, and was set to start at Cornell in September. In the meantime, he visited a friend attending the University of Michigan and decided to enroll there instead. Tuition at the time was $98 for state residents, $125 for out-of-state residents. Dick shipped his laundry home each week where it was washed, folded, and shipped back to him. He was allocated $100 per month for expenses and was required to provide a written account for everything spent or he would not receive the next month's expense money. Any surplus was to be applied to the next month's expenses.

The Gretsch brothers were quite mischievous in nature and tended to befriend like-minded classmates. The many tales of their college years could make any parent turn pale and any law officer cringe. There were endless practical jokes played, most of which one could not get away with today. They communicated primarily by telegram, and quite often those telegrams ended up being delivered by police officers. It was common for the boys to fictitiously sign their telegrams with notorious criminal names or to mention that the solution to a crime currently in the papers awaited police at the recipients location. One of Dick's college buddies was driving to Florida after graduation and didn't want to drive through traffic so he sent a telegram to the police departments in all the towns along his route that the then-famous Charles Lindberg would be passing through on a certain date and time and he would appreciate the utmost privacy on his passage through their town. In most towns a police escort awaited him and the school children lined the streets waving flags of celebration.

Dick at University of Michigan

Dick returned to New York after receiving his Engineering degree from Michigan. There he worked for the Brooklyn Edison company while studying law at St. John's at night. He eventually moved to Hollywood, California where he worked for Kleigl Lights, the first totally silent movie studio lighting system. (The earlier carbon-arc lights were noisy.) While there, his brother Bill asked Dick to get product placements for Gretsch instruments in the movies. In one telegram sent December 28, 1933, Bill says, "Contact all main studios. We are planning 1936 sales campaign. Will give studio that will feature our instruments in major picture free publicity in 10,000 retail windows through the United States. Must have advance on picture with plenty of still shots showing our instruments."

When Dick returned to New York from California, he learned that he could travel West all the way around the world for less than it would cost him to travel directly East to New York. Being a very clever fellow, that is exactly what he did and the entire trip cost some ridiculous sum like $136!

Upon his return to New York, Dick took a position managing utility properties for the Manufacturer's Trust Company. In 1942, during World War II, Dick was called up to serve in the Army War Show. The show was meant to inform the public on how war effort funds were being spent. Lieutenant Richard F. Gretsch, electrical engineer, utilized his Hollywood lighting experience to work alongside the director of Radio City Music Hall and the head of the Yale School of Drama to create "an elaborate lighting system necessary for the desired dramatic effects." They brought the Army War Show to eighteen cities, to stadiums without any electrical wiring. It was Dick's job to manage a team of men to wire the stadiums for each show. The show consisted of a "cross section of the Army," featuring a tank, anti-tank, and several service units.

Dick's life from that point forward remained focused on the Electric Utility business, while his brothers Bill and Fred ran the family business. Dick stayed involved in the Gretsch business as a member of the board and in the management of Gretsch buildings and properties.

In 1944 Dick married Barbara Jean Ininger, also a Lieutenant in the Army, who he met in the Pentagon. Together they relocated to Wisconsin to work at a utility there until he made a final move to Connecticut. (Dick's father did not like to visit him in Wisconsin because he could not pronounce the name of the town, Oconomowoc, and had difficulty telling the train conductor where he wanted to get off.) Dick and Jean raised eight children after which Jean attended medical school and opened a private medical practice at the age of 53.

An update: Richard "Dick" Gretsch Sr. At The Century Mark

The following is from an article written by Rick Van Horn at about the time Richard celebrated his 100th birthday.

As he looks forward to celebrating his one hundredth birthday on June 14, Richard "Dick" Gretsch Sr. has a lot to look back on. He's led a fascinating life full of noteworthy milestones. But misty-eyed reminiscing isn't really Dick's style. He's too busy.

A long-time Connecticut resident, Dick currently makes his home at the Glen Crest retirement center in Danbury. He lives independently in his own apartment, the walls of which are covered with framed photos, newspaper articles, and certificates that document his personal and professional accomplishments. A small patio is brightened by several flowering plants and a bird feeder that attracts jays and robins.

The apartment might seem the quintessential home for the quiet retiree—were it not for the room that serves as Dick's office. There, a printer busily spits out emails from friends and business associates. A desk is piled high with correspondence, stock market reports, and the latest copy of The Wall Street Journal. A savvy player in the market, Dick's diverse portfolio includes shares of Coca-Cola purchased at $1 per share and now worth $58.

Dick Gretsch has been actively involved in the business of business for all of his adult life. And he sees no reason why turning a hundred years old should change that. Accordingly, he spends every weekday morning at yet another desk. This one is in the Danbury headquarters of the Housatonic Industrial Development Corporation, where Dick is chairman of the board of directors.

Dick works daily in his office at the Housatonic Industrial Development Corp. in Danbury.

Dick is also a fixture within the Danbury social scene. An avid golfer for most of his life, he lunches every day but Monday at the Ridgewood Country Club, where he's been a member for almost sixty years. (Mondays find him at Jim Barbary's restaurant.) The club holds Dick in such high regard that they've commemorated his hundredth birthday by installing "The Dick Gretsch Birthday Birdhouse" just outside the window adjacent to his favorite dining table.

Dick is still active with Housatonic Industrial Development on a daily basis. He approves loans, signs checks, and offers input into additions to the board of directors. He's also a voracious reader, perusing the Hartford Business Journal, the Fairfield County Business Journal, the New England Business Journal, the New England Real Estate Journal, and, of course, the Wall Street Journal. He also corresponds with fellow alums from the University Of Michigan.

Returning to Dick's apartment, a quick look at the memorabilia on the wall reveals a Developer Of The Year award from the state of Connecticut, a letter of congratulations on the occasion of his ninety-ninth birthday from President Bush, and a proclamation from Connecticut Governor Jody Ralle officially designating June 14, 2008 as Richard Gretsch Sr. Day. It's characteristic of Dick's independent

Dick holds a framed proclamation from Gov. Jody Ralle, officially designating June 14, 2008 as Richard Gretsch Sr. Day in the state of Connecticut.

nature, however, that the first two items he points out are a photo of the 1935 University Of Michigan track team that he managed, and a certificate celebrating his 1940-41 handball championship at the New York Downtown Athletic Club.

Stepping into his home office, Dick opens a drawer in his desk, displaying hundreds of carefully sorted state quarters and presidential dollar coins, which he avidly collects. Then he pulls out an impressive-looking badge that reads, "Richard Gretsch, special deputy sheriff, Fairfield County, Connecticut." "Back in the mid-'80s," says Dick, "I used to play golf three times a week with the mayor of Danbury and the head of the state police. Being friendly with those guys got me this badge. "So behave yourself," he adds with a laugh.

[Ed. note: ***Richard passed on May 22, 2010 at age 101.***]

THE MEN BEHIND THE DRUMS

None of the Gretsch family members were drummers nor drum builders, but they were smart enough businessmen to know that it would take drummers to design and market drums and skilled craftsmen to build them.. From the 1920s forward, Gretsch employed people capable of positioning Gretsch drums as world class professional instruments. Among the longest-tenured employees was Bill Hagner who worked with Gretsch from 1941 until 1985. In a 2012 interview with Rick VanHorn (provided by Fred W. Gretsch), Hagner mentioned some other Gretsch personnel:

Phil Nash: He was a vice president. He was fairly old even when I first joined the company—in his late-eighties or early-nineties.

Emerson Strong: He was a type of corporate secretary. There were three offices in the Brooklyn building, outside the factory. Strong's was first, then Phil Nash's, and then Fred Gretsch Jr.'s.

Harold Woods: He was the factory manager when I got there. But he couldn't get along with Bill Gretsch when Bill was running things, so Bill let him go. When Fred Gretsch Jr. took over again after Bill died, Fred hired Harold back. We worked together, of course. Harold used to go on a cruise every year between Christmas and New Year's, because he knew that I was taking inventory and the whole shop was closed. One year, on the Monday of his return, he came into the office, walked over to the window, shook hands with me—and had a heart attack and died.

Charlie Fromm: Charlie was a long-time employee of Gretsch. He was fairly old when I got there in '41. I think you could best describe him as a factory foreman. If I wanted to learn something, he was very good at explaining.

John DeRosa: I made Johnny my finishing department foreman. His picture is in Chet Falzerano's book.

Vincent D'Domenico: Vincent was the foreman of the wood shop. He was a good man for Gretsch at the beginning…like a whole wood shop unto himself. But later, when I took over as factory manager, Vincent couldn't keep up with the trends going forward. Production just got too fast for him. So I made him a tool-and-die maker.

Jerry Parito: He was Vincent's assistant.

Mike and Bill Zotta: They were the drumshell builders when I started in 1941.

Sid Lakin: Sid was my chucker. He worked making drumshells as I described elsewhere.

December 29, 1945, photo of the Gretsch "Executive Staff" at an event at Carnegie Hall. (L-R) Fred Gretsch Jr., Duke Kramer, Phil Grant, Richard Dickson, William Walter Gretsch

Al Garofolo: He worked with Dick Dickson in drum assembly.

Jimmy Webster: Jimmy was the major figure in representing Gretsch guitars to the market. He was also very involved in the actual design, with constant suggestions and requests: "Put mufflers in the guitars… change the tailpiece…change the bridge…change this, change that." He wanted new features to market every year. One day I asked him, "Jimmy, where do you get all these ideas from?" He told me, "From my neighbor. He's an engineer." (Laughs.)

Carmine Capolo: Carmine worked as a tuner on the guitar assembly line. He'd put the strings on, then tune and adjust every guitar before it went out.

Tony Carello: He was the man who glued tops and backs on guitars.

Dan Duffy: As we expanded I had to get a guitar player in to test the guitars. Dan was our guitar player.

Carl Diaz: He was a woodworker.

Margaret McCarthy: She was a clerk out in the office.

RICHARD DICKSON (1889-1955)
A skilled British drum maker immigrates to the USA and begins a career with Gretsch

Richard Dickson was born in 1889 in Westminster, London, England. His career path was established quite early; when he was 22 the 1911 census listed him as a drum maker. He later explained to an interviewer that his interest in drums began at age 13 and as a young man he served as an apprentice to the Hawkes & Son Drum Company, founded in 1865. An area of specialization for Hawkes was military drums with cast sterling silver shells. This also became the specialization for young Dickson as a journeyman; his military induction papers listed his civilian occupation as a military drum maker.

Richard married on Christmas Day 1915, practically on the eve of his departure to the military. His bride Florence was 21.

Richard enlisted in the British army in January of 1916 at the age of 25. His enlistment with the London Regiment (Kings Royal Rifle Corps) was listed as a "short service engagement," which meant his service would terminate at the end of World War I. He was a slight man at the time of his enlistment, at 5'6", 124 lbs. His first foreign deployment was to Salonica (now called Thessalonica.) The Greek government had requested British assistance to protect the Serbs, though

by the time it arrived, the Serbs had been defeated. From there, Dickson traveled to Egypt as part of an occupational force. Egypt had at the onset of WWI been part of the Ottoman empire; by the time Dickson arrived it was a British Protectorate. His final foreign posting was as part of the final British Expeditionary Force to France in 1918. His discharge came in 1920. For his service, Rifleman Richard Dickson was awarded the British War Medal and the Victory Medal.

Richard's skill set was demonstrated with the significant military drums he manufactured. He made sterling silver drums for the Grenadier Guards, the most senior regiment of the British infantry. An even more prestigious assignment came from the Duke of Windsor (Edward VIII, earlier known as the Prince of Wales), who personally requested his services in making the Duke's ceremonial drums.

Richard had what was considered a very good job working for Hawkes and was content with his life. He was reluctant to move to the United States in 1925, but gave in to the urging of his mother-in-law who had moved to America in 1916. His young family (a

**Staff photo, Hawkes & Son of London.
Richard Dickson is seated, center**

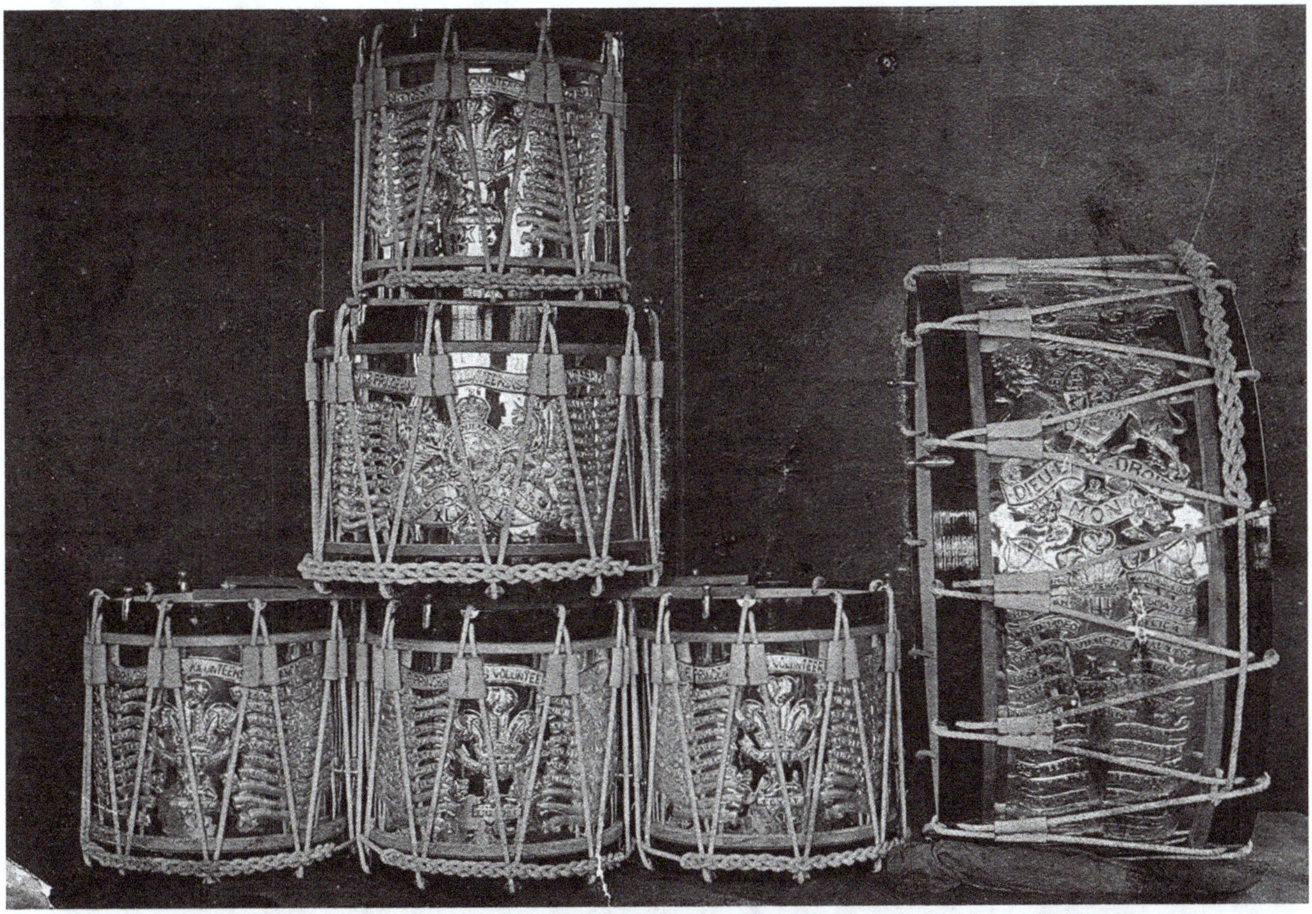

Ceremonial drums made by Richard Dickson for the Edward VIII, Duke of Windsor, known earlier as the Prince of Wales

son had been born less than a year after his military discharge) made the move, arriving in New York on Richard's birthday, May 28, 1925.

It is unclear whether Richard Dickson was recruited to work for Gretsch making drums in New York while he was still in England, but it is quite possible. In a 1939 interview, he said, "I came over to New York for the Gretsch Manufacturing Company..." Regardless of whether his skill set was actively recruited, clearly they were valuable to Gretsch and it is a safe assumption that he supervised Gretsch drum construction for most of his 30-year tenure at Gretsch.

Richard Dickson spent the rest of his career in the employ of Gretsch. He retired in 1954, passed away in 1955.

Richard's daughter Rosemary worked for Gretsch in 1950 and 1951 at the age of 17-18.

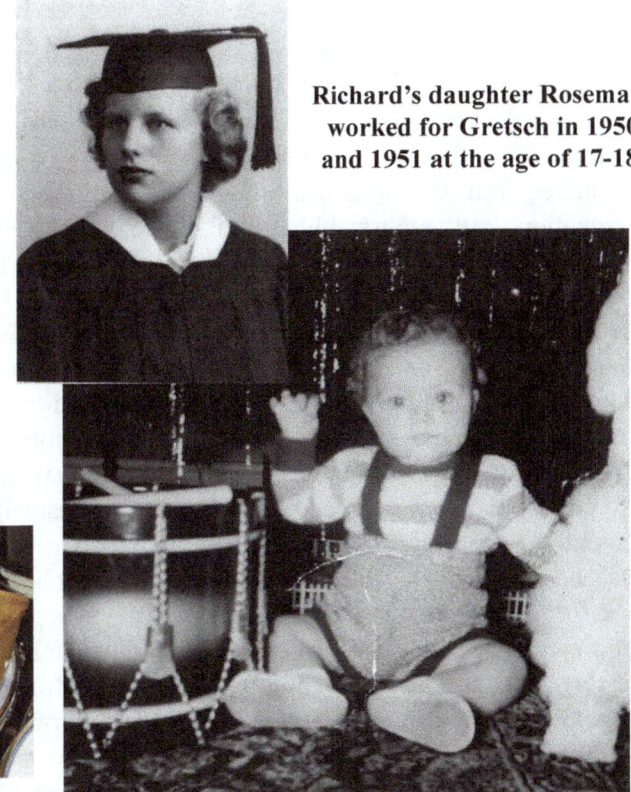

Makeup case that Richard Dickson made for a relative from a 15" Gretsch shell

Richard's son Donald with the drum Richard made for him as a Christmas present

17

Richard Dickson, Jo Jones, Phil Grant

PHIL GRANT (1914-2002)

Phil Grant came from a musical family. For many years his mother and father both taught in the Music Department of Pennsylvania State College. Phil Grant graduated from the same institution with a degree in Educational music. After graduation, Phil taught public school music. He played professionally in several popular dance bands. Before the war, Grant was the snare drum, tympani, and xylophone specialist with the Goldman Band and the Pittsburgh Symphony.

Grant served as a communications officer in the South Pacific during World War II, retiring from the Navy after the war with the rank of Lieutenant. The Carnegie Hall program for the event he organized there on December 29, 1945, introduced Grant as the new head of the Educational Department of The Fred Gretsch Mfg. Co. and mentioned that this event was his first civilian activity.

Grant was the public face of Gretsch as a salesman, inventor, innovator, and general company liason for over twenty years. He was bitterly disappointed by the sale of Gretsch to Baldwin and did not feel that he received proper compensation for his years of service. While employees who were released by Baldwin at the time of the sale in 1967 received severance packages, Grant did not because he stayed on as a Gretsch employee. When he retired in 1972, his pay stopped. Fred Gretsch Jr. also felt that this was unfair to Grant, and presented Grant with $5,000.00 worth of Baldwin stock. Grant sold the stock and used the money to finance the purchase of a general store in Middletown Springs, Vermont.

Phil Grant with the Goldman Band in Central Park, New York City

DUKE KRAMER (1916-2005)

Duke Kramer was 19 and playing sax in local Chicago clubs when he met Bill Gretsch in 1935. (Bill Gretsch was at the time managing the company's Chicago Distribution office.) Gretsch hired Kramer, paying him $11 weekly to polish horns.

Over the years, Duke Kramer became a Gretsch institution. His official duties covered pretty much everything at one time or another: purchasing agent, salesman, bookkeeper, general manager, plant manager, inventor, mentor, and advisor to four of the five Gretsch presidents.

Working with Chet Atkins and Jimmie Webster, Kramer forever changed the look and sound of guitars. In similar fashion, he worked at getting Gretsch drums into the hands of the best musicians in jazz and popular music.

Duke was one of a handful of employees who survived the Baldwin acquisition in 1967 and he ran the Cincinnati office of the Gretsch division until his retirement in 1980. When Baldwin was in bankruptcy in the early 1980s, Duke was brought in to run the Gretsch business and was key in arranging the sale back to the Gretsch family. (Fred W. Gretsch worked under Duke for a couple years in the late 1960s as a salesman, and it was Duke who made the call to Fred W. in 1984 asking if he wanted to buy it back.)

Duke continued to work with the new family-owned Gretsch and played a critical role in bringing Gretsch guitars back into production. Fifty years after he was hired by Fred's father, Bill Gretsch, Duke Kramer was again on the road talking to musicians and instrument dealers assuring them that the "Great Gretsch Sound" would soon return.

Duke Kramer

with the Jazz Kings in Chicago circa 1934 (center)

BILL HAGNER

Bill Hagner was a part of Gretsch history for more than forty years. Starting as a clerk just out of high school, Bill eventually became the plant manager at the storied Gretsch factory at 60 Broadway in Brooklyn, New York. There he oversaw production of drums, guitars, banjos and other items. On April 12, 2012, not long before his eighty-seventh birthday, he shared some of those recollections with Rick VanHorn. Parts of that interview, courtesy of Fred W. Gretsch:

"I started on November 28, 1941, just about a week before the attack on Pearl Harbor. I'd just finished high school and I was going to New York University at night. I saw an ad in the paper that Gretsch was looking for clerks in the factory. Women generally took those jobs, but they tended to quit in order to have babies. The job was right in the middle of the factory in a little office. I'd take the elevated train to Brooklyn each day from my home in Queens."

"One day very soon after I came to work for Gretsch, vice president Phil Nash said to me, 'I want to tell you something right from the start. Someday this is going to be a big company. So I advise you, if you have any interest in a career, learn everything you can about what you're doing, and stay with it.'"

Bill recognized good advice when he heard it, and he acted on it. "There were about thirty workers in the factory," he says, "and they were paid on piece work. It was part of my job to record how many pieces each worker had made each day, for payroll purposes. When I came to an operation that I wasn't familiar with I'd come have that worker show me how it was done. That's how I learned most of the factory operations. While I was paying people for the jobs they did, I was learning what those jobs were all about."

"Fred Gretsch Sr. would walk around the factory at 3:30 every Monday," says Bill. "One time he stopped me and said, 'I have something here I'd like to show you.' Out of his pocket he took a piece of shaped metal, saying, 'You see this piece of metal? It's chrome plated. I took it off a can opener. Someday you're going to need a handle just like this to throw off your snare strainer.' That's the foresight this man had. He was very nice."

In 1942 Fred Gretsch Sr. turned the supervision of the Gretsch factory over to his son, Fred Gretsch Jr. But Fred Jr. joined the Navy shortly after America entered World War II, and factory supervision then passed to his brother, Bill Gretsch (father of Fred W. Gretsch).

"Bill Gretsch was a good man," says Bill Hagner. "I

Bill Hagner, 2012

always felt that he trusted me. We were good friends. He was a nice man. I enjoyed working with him. Unfortunately he passed away in 1948, which is when Fred Jr. came back and took over the company."

The Gretsch factory wasn't particularly large in the pre-war years. Like many other small manufacturers, it was departmentalized by the type of operation, not by the item being produced. Woodworking operations for all instruments were done in the wood shop. In the back of the factory was where drum shells would be glued. "We didn't have panel work in those days," says Bill Hagner. "Every drum had to be cut to size, glued, and put in a big chuck and pounded into shape. We also had two double-spindle lathes. If we needed one for woodworking we used it; if we needed it for another operation, we used it for that. We made drums, tambourines, and even wastepaper baskets." Wastepaper baskets?

"Hell, yes," Bill replies with a laugh. "When things were bad in the early 1940s we'd take a 9x13 shell, paint it differently, slap a bottom onto it, and sell it as a wastepaper basket. We had to do something to keep going back then."

Gretsch And The War Effort

When America entered World War II, Gretsch, like many other manufacturers, was pressed into service to support the war effort. "We got a contract with the government to make the wooden components for gas masks," Bill recalls. "We did that at night after the regular day-shift work was done. Most of the workers would go home at five o'clock. But I'd keep about ten people, and we'd work until one o'clock in the morning. And let's just say that sometimes we'd have a good time when there was an air-raid drill, because we had to put out all the lights in the building."

But the fun didn't last too long for Bill. On the 19th of January, 1943, he was drafted into the Army Air Force. His service lasted through the end of the war, after which time he returned to work at Gretsch.

"After the war was over," he says, "all heck broke loose. Everybody wanted something…more and more and more. So we had to keep expanding the factory." Among the "somethings" that people wanted was banjos. And Gretsch was a key figure in the manufacture of these instruments. "I never had time to learn how to play a banjo," says Bill Hagner, "but I liked making them. We used to dress them up to look really nice. The best one we made was the Symphony Banjo. Everything was gold-plated, and it had diamonds all around the headpiece and tailpiece.

Management came to me in the mid-1950s when Arthur Godfrey was a huge star and said, 'We have to give Arthur Godfrey a banjo. It'll boost sales.' So we made a Symphony Banjo for him…a beautiful thing. But Godfrey came on TV with his ukulele, so everybody wanted ukuleles and we converted a lot of space to making ukuleles. "A little later, when I was in New York, I went to the studio where they did the Godfrey show and I asked one of his assistants, 'What did he ever do with the banjo?' He told me, 'He's got it home in a closet.' (Laughs.) But we did sell a lot of ukuleles."

The late 1940s and 1950s also saw an increase in the demand for drumsets. Popular music was evolving from the sound of big bands to small-group jazz, and Gretsch drums became a favorite of the leading drummers in that emerging style. The look of these drumsets was also evolving…which posed a production challenge for Bill Hagner. He had to select the color and style of material to cover Gretsch drums. "Fortunately for me," says Bill, "I made friends with our supplier of pearl drum covering material. He'd meet me at the beginning of the year with samples of all the new colors they were going to come out with. And he'd say, 'Which ones do you want in order to beat everybody to them?' It was a great connection for us.

"Several years later," Bill continues, "I had an interesting experience with drum coverings. When it was time to choose the colors for that year, I picked three. And I asked everybody in the factory to tell me which ones they liked. The one they liked least was the one I picked. That was Champagne Sparkle, and it became the best seller we ever had!"

Additional Outside Help

Bill adds that Gretsch did business with several outside suppliers and services. In addition to Jasper Wood Products—which was started in 1925 by the Gramelbacher family—there was Walberg & Auge, who manufactured stands, tom holders, and other hardware. "We made our own tom holders at the beginning," says Bill. "They were brass castings, and they were okay. But Walberg & Auge created a lot of innovative hardware designs, like the famous 'Rail Consolette' tom holder, and we started using those parts. The only things that fell under my responsibility were floor tom legs and bass drum spurs. I'd make those 'cause they were fairly easy to lathe."

Another outside provider was Advanced Pressure Casting. The New Jersey-based company did die-casting for Gretsch from the 1920s on. "Early Gretsch drums used single-flanged brass hoops with claw hooks," says Bill. "But later we developed the die-cast hoops that Gretsch drums are famous for. Advanced made those hoops and other cast parts. "Every die-cast part had to be polished on buffing wheels," Bill continues. "It took about six operations to do a hoop or a set of lugs. My plating department couldn't keep up… they had to do copper plating, then nickel plating, and finally chrome plating on hundreds of parts, including parts for guitars and banjos as well as for drums. When we needed help, we went to Norwood Plating in Brooklyn."

Gretsch Artists

In his many years at Gretsch, Bill Hagner interacted with many top guitar and drum endorsers. Preeminent among these was guitar great Chet Atkins, with whom Bill says he spent a lot of time. "Chet would call me at the beginning of a year," Bill recalls. "He'd say, 'Bill, let's work on this year's new model.' So I'd go to meet with him in Nashville. I spent a whole week with him in his office once. He was a gentleman's gentleman…a true professional. He'd take me out to a different place for lunch every day, and everyone knew him.

Bill Hagner interacted with the legendary Billy Gladstone, who made a name as an inventor and drum craftsman as well as a talented performer. Says Bill, "Billy Gladstone was a drummers' drummer, with a lot of class. We became very good friends in the late 1940s and early '50s. Back then, Radio City Music Hall would show movies with live stage shows in between showings. Billy was the snare drummer in the pit, and his wife was the third girl from the left in the Rockettes. Every time they'd run a new movie at Radio City, she'd leave a ticket for me to see the show. Then I'd meet them afterwards and we'd go up to their place on Sixth Avenue. Billy was so nice to talk to. He told me how he had run away from Europe to escape the war. We'd talk until two or three in the morning.

"After I'd known Billy for a while, his wife became ill and died. Billy took it hard. At one point rehearsals were under way to take the Broadway show *The Sound Of Music* on the road. A friend called Billy and suggested that he see about taking the drum chair in that show, to keep himself busy. When Billy went to the rehearsals and introduced himself to the guy in charge, that guy said, 'Oh yeah. Well...you want to go over there and play something on the drums for me?' There were people dancing and singing and doing other things all around Billy, but when he started to play a drum roll, everyone just stopped to listen. That's how good a drummer he was."

"Everything had to be perfect with him. He came to me and showed me exactly what he wanted on his shell. All Billy wanted us to do was supply him with raw shells. And those shells had to be perfectly round, with edges that were absolutely true. He didn't want holes drilled in them or anything. He did all that himself, because again, everything had to be perfect. There couldn't be staggered lugs, or lugs that were the slightest bit out of alignment. Everything had to be right down the middle. The slightest irregularity would kill the sound for him...and he had a perfect ear."

Bill Hagner also worked with some of the great Gretsch drumset artists. One was a very young Louie Bellson, who was making a name for himself with bandleader Tommy Dorsey. Bill recalls, "Louie came to me and said, 'I want to get more drums on my kit. I want two bass drums, one big tom in the middle, and couple of small ones around the top of the kit. Oh... and the most important thing: I'll be at the Paramount Theater. When they put the lights out, I want my set to glow!' "Well I had to do something first about that glow business, because I didn't know anything about it. Eventually I found some white phosphorescent material that could be sprayed onto the drums. We had three spray booths at the time. One would be spraying drums while the other two were spraying guitars. They brought Louie's set in, sprayed it with that white stuff, and then left to let it dry overnight. When we came in the next morning what we saw was unbelievable. The stuff had floated all over the room. It covered the walls...the ceilings...everywhere—including six or eight racks of guitars. We had to do them all over again."

"Phil Grant was the guy that all the artists dealt with," Bill continues, "and that every drummer out there wanted to get to know. At one time Phil brought fifty drummers up to the factory. (Laughs.) They killed me for hours with questions. Over the years, as more and more Gretsch drummers got to know me, it became sort of a headache for me. 'Hey Bill, I have a problem' or 'I need this part' or 'Can you fix my drum for me?' I used to get that from drummers all the time."

When Fred Gretsch Jr. sold the Gretsch Company to Baldwin—who promptly moved manufacturing operations from Brooklyn to Booneville, Arkansas, Bill Hagner was kept on as plant manager to supervise the relocation and to oversee ongoing operations over the next few years. Bill was later transferred to Baldwin's sales department in Cincinnati, where he stayed until 1976 when he was offered an opportunity to purchase the Gretsch drum factory from Baldwin. (see page 26.) With financing help from Fred Gretsch Jr., he made the purchase, thereby establishing the Hagner Musical Instrument Company in Arkansas. Though initially successful, the operation was not able to meet contractual production demands, and ownership of the factory reverted to Baldwin.

"After Fred W. Gretsch bought the company back from Baldwin," says Bill Hagner, "He remembered me. He asked me if I'd go down to DeQueen, Arkansas, where Baldwin had moved the manufacturing equipment, and arrange to have it shipped to his building in Ridgeland, South Carolina. I went down and loaded trailers, pickup trucks, and everything else I could find to get that move made."

After helping Fred W. Gretsch with the move, Bill and his wife moved back to New York. There Bill pursued a successful career in real estate, working with government reverse mortgage programs. He retired in 2002.

THE BALDWIN ERA 1967-1984

The popularity of rock music in the 1960s made for explosive sales growth for instrument manufacturers. This attracted the attention of many conglomerates who were in acquisition mode.

CBS (Columbia Broadcasting Systems) purchased a number of instrument manufacturers in the 1960s and 1970s: Electro-Music (Leslie), Fender, Rogers, Steinway, Gulbransen, Gemeinhardt, Rodgers, and Lyon & Healy.

Norlin (formerly known as the Ecuadorian Corporation, a holding company for various businesses in Ecuador) purchased Chicago Musical Instrument Company in 1969 which instantly made Norlin the largest manufacturer of Instruments in the USA. Their brands included Gibson, Lowery, Story & Clark, Moog, and others. Norlin was then the victim of a hostile takeover by the brokerage and private investment bank Rooney Pace Group (RPG) in 1984. (RPG founders Patrick Rooney & Randolph Pace played fast and loose with financial laws. Pace, who later became CEO of Norlin, was charged with securities laws violations in 1981, and Rooney was convicted of income tax fraud in 1983 and sentenced to jail.)

CCM (Crowell, Collier, McMillan), the publishing conglomerate, between 1967 and 1970 acquired Slingerland, C.G. Conn Ltd., Ostwald Uniforms, the C.E. Ward Company, and G. Schirmer. (Antitrust action was threatened because of their acquisitions.)

To many familiar with the music industry, the name "Baldwin" does not really sound like a conglomerate. Founded in 1862, the company legacy for it's first century was that of a piano company. How did a piano company manage to survive a century of changes in popular music culture, major wars, and economic calamities? In addition to making excellent products and utilizing creative financing such as large scale consignment plans, there was diversification. One of the first significant acquisitions was the purchase of the Hamilton Organ Company in 1889, resulting in the name change from Baldwin Piano Company to Baldwin Piano and Organ Company.

In an attempt to cash in on the rock music boom, Baldwin made an unsuccessful attempt to acquire the Fender company. When that failed, they acquired the well-known English guitar maker Burns. Baldwin imported Burns parts from England and shipped them to Booneville, Arkansas, where they already had a banjo factory. The Burns guitars were assembled from the imported parts in Booneville.

At the time of the 1967 sale to Baldwin, Gretsch drums were being manufactured in Brooklyn, with offices in Brooklyn and Chicago. Fred Gretsch Junior, who consummated the sale, had held the position of President of Gretsch at the time of the sale, and became a director of Baldwin when the sale was finalized. At the time of the sale, guitar sales, in retrospect, had already peaked. The largest number of production staff ever employed in Brooklyn, about 150, was during 1966 and 1967. The sale price was rumored to be $4 million.

Morley Thompson, who became president of Baldwin in 1970, seems in retrospect to have had a near mania for acquisitions. Throughout the 1970s and into the early 1980s, Thompson oversaw the acquisition of dozens of financial services firms. Among Thompson's missteps was the purchase of Mortgage Guaranty Insurance Corp., a residential mortgage insurer. To come up with the $1.2 billion for that purchase, Baldwin took out almost $600 million in short term loans from eight banks. When the mortgage insurer's profits slid by 20%, it became very difficult for Thompson to service the debt, particularly the $440 million that came due in March of 1983. By May, Thompson had taken a "leave of absence," never to return. Insurance regulators seized control of six of the company's insurance companies which pretty much froze most of the company's assets. The board began to plan for bankruptcy reorganization. By the time Baldwin-United (the name was changed when Baldwin merged with the investment company United Corp. in 1977) filed a reorganization plan in August of 1985, $1.4 billion in assets had already been liquidated in an attempt to settle some of the claims. The Gretsch drum company was among those liquidated assets. The bankruptcy was major news; it was the largest corporate bankruptcy in the United States to date. Baldwin-United's liabilities at the time of the bankruptcy totalled $9 billion, which represented more than the *combined* liabilities of the four largest bankruptcies before it.

Who bought the Gretsch drum company from Baldwin during the bankruptcy reorganization? It remained a division of Baldwin Piano & Organ Company which was purchased from Baldwin-United by Baldwin Piano & Organ CEO Richard Harrison in partnership with the company's president Harold Smith. It cost them $65 million, which was over 90% financed by Security Pacific Business Credit and General Electric Credit Corporation. This transaction took place in June of 1984. (The Gibson guitar company would acquire Baldwin Piano and Organ from General Electric Credit in 2001 after another bankruptcy.)

Before continuing from June 1984, let's back up and look at what happened to the Gretsch Drum Company from 1967 to 1984.

Gretsch workers were members of the United Electrical Radio and Machine Workers Union (UE), and were organized in 1966. There were repeated strikes in New York which disrupted production and there were even incidents of product sabotage. The factory superintendant at the time, Bill Hagner, once loaded up a caravan of trucks and cars with enough parts to build 100 drum kits, then drove out of the city with 15 non-striking foremen. They traveled to a supplier in Massachusetts (Walberg & Auge) to assemble the drums. The strikes continued, so Baldwin finally moved Gretsch production out of New York, to their existing facility in Booneville, Arkansas in 1969. The move was made in the summertime, which made it possible to recruit vacationing high schoolers to help unload the flatbed trailers arriving from New York.

A condition of the 1967 sale of Gretsch to Baldwin was that Baldwin would retain Phil Grant and Duke Kramer on five-year employment contracts. When production was moved to Booneville, Grant was transferred there, a move he was not happy about.

It was as if Gretsch had come apart at the seams, losing their identity in the process. For years, Phil Grant had worked closely with New York's jazz drummers, responding to their needs with Gretsch product developments. Now he was detached from that support system and expected to produce drums in an environment that he resented. By the end of his 5-year employment contract in 1972, Grant was eager to leave the company. He was bitter that he was not offered any kind of severance, something that also bothered Fred Gretsch Jr. who gave Grant $5,000 worth of Baldwin stock. Grant sold the stock and used the money to open a general store in Vermont. At about the same time (1972), the New York offices were closed and administration was moved to the Chicago offices. Those offices were closed within another year or two, and combined with Baldwin's operations in Cincinnati.

Jerry Perito. He is a cousin of Vinnie Didominico who appears in catalogs from the 1930s. Both worked in Brooklyn until the move in 1969. Jerry was one of the few who did transfer to Arkansas in the employ of Baldwin, as did Bill Hagner.

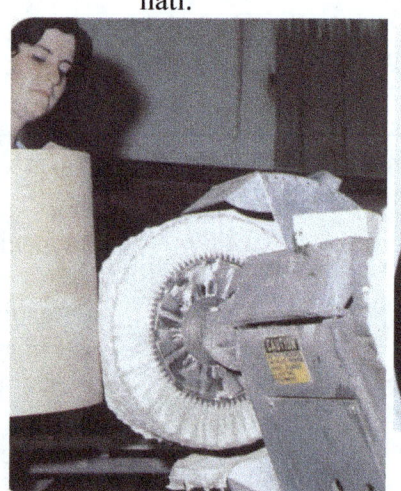

Booneville, Arkansas production photos

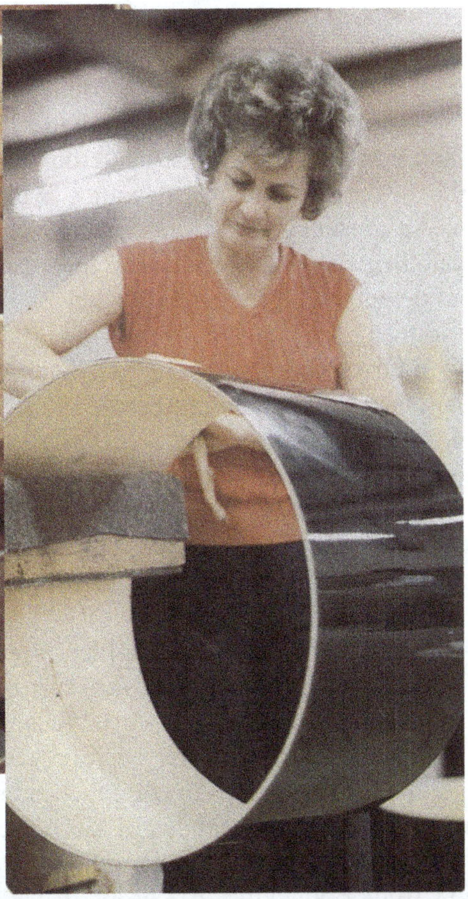

Booneville, Arkansas production photos

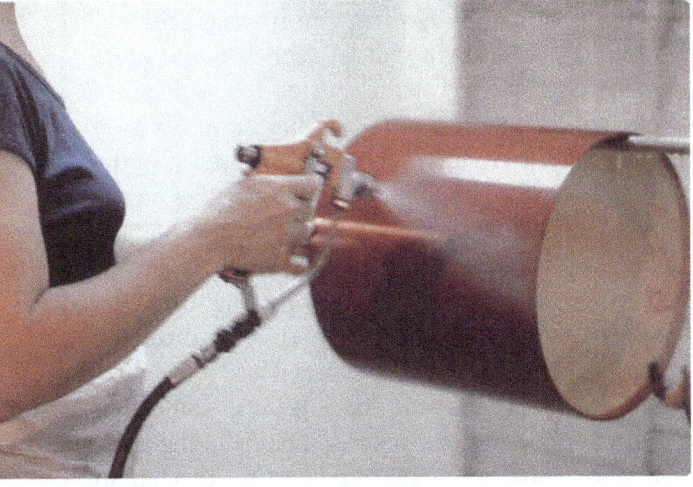

New York plant superintendant Bill Hagner had moved the manufacturing from Brooklyn to Booneville, but few of the foremen could be convinced to relocate to Arkansas. Hagner himself was transferred after a year-and-a-half in Booneville; after getting the operation up and running and training the staff, he was reassigned to Baldwin's corporate offices in Cincinnati. Hagner felt at the time that this was a mistake, and was later quoted as saying that a Baldwin VP apologized to him years later, admitting that Hagner should have been left to operate the Booneville operation the same way he'd run the Brooklyn shop.

The Booneville facility was set up in a converted two-story barn, a huge change from the Brooklyn environment. Local labor was recruited from the farming workforce and had to be trained to operate the drum manufacturing equipment. In January 1973, the barn burned down. After analyzing the damage and retooling costs, Baldwin decided to give up on American guitar and drum production altogether. They considered moving production of Gretsch drums and guitars to Japan and Mexico and some of the surviving Booneville manufacturing equipment was auctioned off. It was the employees who convinced Baldwin to keep production in Booneville. Bill Hagner managed to persuade them that moving production out of the country would destroy the Gretsch name, and he offered to supervise the rebuilding of the factory and it's production personally. He formed a company called Hagner Musical Instruments and took personal responsibility for instrument production, with an exclusive sales agreement with Gretsch. (Gretsch was the only customer of Hagner Musical Instrument Company, and ownership of the Gretsch name on the instruments produced remained the property of Baldwin.) Hagner moved from Cincinnati back to Arkansas to rebuild the manufacturing facility in April of 1973. On December 15th the factory was again largely destroyed by fire. It destroyed inventory and machinery, but this time the recovery was speedy. Control of the Booneville operation reverted to Baldwin (from Hagner Musical Instrument Company) in 1978 when Hagner was having difficulty keeping up with demand.

In spite of Gretsch's lackluster returns, Baldwin continued to invest in the musical instrument industry. They acquired Kustom, based in Chanute, Kansas, in 1979. The company was renamed Kustom/Gretsch, and the drum offices (not manufacturing) were moved from Cincinnati to Chanute. In 1981, the decision was made to stop guitar production and move drum production from Booneville, Arkansas, to De Queen, Arkansas, to consolidate it with other Baldwin operations such as the manufacturing of Sho-Bud steel guitars. Plant manager Ben Johnson (hired in 1978) was pleased with the workforce in De Queen, expressing pride in their ability to work skillfully with wood. Why was guitar production halted? They simply were not selling. Gibson and Fender were selling plenty of solid-body electric guitars, but sales of hollow-body electric models like Gretsch made were very slow. According to one report, Gretsch still had enough inventory on hand in 1982 to last two years.

Certainly by this point it was becoming obvious to Baldwin that Gretsch was not quite the cash cow they had expected when they acquired it. They had detached the drum division from the environment that had nurtured it in the jazz idiom and done nothing to capitalize on the rock and roll boom. Duke Kramer later blamed that on Phil Grant, saying that Grant had considered rock a fad and that all advertising, catalogs, artist relations, and anything else drum-related was under Grant's direct supervision.

In fairness to Grant, he was somewhat hamstrung by Baldwin when it came to the artist relations program, which all but came to a halt in the 1970s. Baldwin had some very high-profile artist relationships with their expensive pianos, but did not see the value in drum and guitar endorsements that were petty in comparison. They even wanted Duke Kramer to drop Chet Atkins, the number one Gretsch guitar endorser. Sticks and heads were reluctantly supplied to top drum endorsers, but precious little advertising featured the endorsers and eventually most artists drifted away from their Gretsch affiliations. Kramer later said that the only guy who hung on was Tony Williams.

In 1982 Baldwin sold Kustom/Gretsch to Charlie Roy, who was managing both divisions for them from Chanute, Kansas, at the time. (Charlie had been managing Kustom at their Chanute headquarters at the time Baldwin acquired Kustom.) Terms of the sales contract are not public knowledge, but Roy became president and primary stockholder of the new Kustom-Gretsch company. Roy indicated that he planned to again produce guitars in the near future and a number of prototypes were produced over the next few years, but production never geared up again. Roy moved his offices from Chanute, Kansas, to Gallatin, Tennessee, to be near Nashville, a major music hub. Roy could see that the Gretsch drum division was not keeping pace with the competition, and brought in Karl Dustman.

Karl Dustman Joins Gretsch

Kustom Gretsch issued a press release on June 2, 1983 announcing the appointment of Karl Dustman as Percussion Marketing Manager for Gretsch. In the release, Kustom Gretsch president Charlie Roy called attention to Dustman's 11-year tenure with Ludwig where he held a number of marketing and educational positions.

Karl's comments on joining Gretsch:

Upon arriving at Gretsch in Gallatin, I immediately starting bringing in the various Chicago-based supplier contacts for printing, graphics, photography, carton design, price list layout etc,. all from my Ludwig association. Cedar Valley Printing jumped in to help with all the color posters designs, price lists and new Techware hardware cartons. Reed Wallace Photography was called upon to assist with product and artist photography,...for example.

We also started development and research into designing a Gretsch Snare Drum Kit for beginners and the school market,... based upon the essentials of the Ludwig UFO Kits that were selling like hot-cakes at that time. I knew if we could capture the beginning drummer's Gretsch brand loyalty with their first snare drum, their first drumset would also be a Gretsch.

While Selmer was intentionally disconnecting with all my marketing and advertising partners in Chicago, I was bringing all that expertise and contacts to the Gretsch product and brand. This was a win-win for all connected to the projects and assignments I was working on from the very beginning, through the end of 1984.

RC: You joined Gretsch in 1983, not too long after big moves by both the offices and the factory.

KD: Yes. The factory had previously been in Booneville, Arkansas. They moved it to an empty piano warehouse that Baldwin owned in De Queen, Arkansas. That happened right before I got there. Production was already back up and running again and all the Gretsch products and Sho-Bud guitars were being produced. I was not even aware of that yet when I arrived in Gallatin, just outside of Nashville. When I got to Gallatin I asked Charlie to show me the factory. He said, "There is no factory here." I asked, "What do you mean there's no factory?" He said, "These are just the corporate offices." I asked where the factory was and he said, "De Queen, Arkansas." Charlie Roy was very aware that this (1983) was an anniversary year for Gretsch, and he wanted to ramp up with speed and style to make Gretsch drums a competitive market force. You only have a 100 year anniversary every 100 years. We didn't have 5-10 years to plan out the celebration. He bought the company in 1982 and immediately started spending money to ramp up to 1983. I give Charlie credit that he knew what needed to be done. Maybe he didn't know quite HOW to do it, but he knew he had to get artists back through unique colors, having first class print material, having first class displays, and to make it look like a bigger company than it really was. He was going up against the Ludwigs, the Sonors, the Yamahas and the Pearls.... He said the summer NAMM show would be my baby– he said make it happen and make it big. So within 60 days I had to come up with a big trade show display while I was guiding product development, the new artist relations program, advertising, and so forth.

RC: Were you working together with the Kustom people on the trade show preparations?

KD: No, that was a separate exhibit that I had nothing to do with, but it was right across the aisle. The Gretsch drum exhibit was 40x40, which was a big space. We had all these huge blowups of the artists up on risers, etc. The display cost over $50,000.00. Charlie had been doing ALL the right things, but the problem as I saw it was that he was under-capitalized. Every dime that came in, he immediately spent on marketing, sales, promotions. We were going to do clinic programs. We were going to put on a percussion symposium, just like I had at Ludwig. Charlie had said to me, "Karl– just do what you did at Ludwig, and go do it." It takes money. Lots of money to do that. And it just didn't happen fast enough. Charlie knew what to do and he knew how to do it, but it cost far more money than he ever expected

it was going to cost. The early-80s was a challenging time for MI.

Projects at the top of the list were to publish a new catalog and to produce a centennial anniversary drum kit.

RC: That was the kit with the special badges and labels, limited to a total of 100 kits in three veneers??

KD: Correct. That was a major project. We didn't have to produce the 100 kits by the time of the NAMM show when they were introduced, but we did have to be geared up and have sets to show.

RC: I've heard suggestions that perhaps not all 100 actually ever got produced.

KD: To my knowledge they did. Previous researchers have asked me if I could document who got them. I've gone through every single piece of paper in my file cabinets and I don't have it. They show up on Ebay from time to time. Tom Shelley from Universal had bought one, he just sold it. Wes Falconer in KC (Explorer's Percussion) bought like half a dozen of those kits sight unseen. He's a Gretsch fanatic.

RC: You got the catalog out in time for the show?

KD: Yes, it was what Gretsch collectors now refer to as the "poster catalog." Tommy Winkler of Nashville loaned us the vintage Gretsch tom-tom for the cover.

So we got through '83 and all the celebrations, the big cake thing... and we rolled in 1984. We were still busy doing neat stuff; clinic programs, artists....

1983 NAMM reception: l-r Wayne Summers (sales manager), Karl Dustman (newly appointed marketing manager), Charlie Roy (Kustom/Gretsch owner and president), Randy Houck (international sales manager)

1983 Gretsch NAMM show exhibit

We actually had an artist contract now, a clinic program with set fees... everything was getting organized so that we were doing things the way the other companies were doing them. Then I went into Nashville and started recruiting every top recording drummer. I hit on every one of them. Clyde Brooks, Jerry Kerrigan, all these top studio guys. The only guy I couldn't get was Larrie Londin because he was tied in so tight with Pearl. Pretty soon everybody in the country music scene was playing Gretsch drums. That had never happened before. It wasn't because I did it, but it was Charlie's vision. We needed to get out of the black jazz drummer's idiom; we got the rock involvement with Phil Collins, we had all the country drummers, we owned a good amount of the jazz market, this is really starting to come together now. You see, in the 1980s, "Made In America" still meant something. Drummers were delighted to be approached by an American drum company. Ludwig has stopped doing much of anything for their artists as a result of Selmer acquiring the firm. Slingerland and Rogers were gone.

Another factor in our association with high-visibility artists was a newly viable clinic program. It was built on the universal success of the Ludwig clinic format that I developed. This was of extreme interest to most artists, as it brought additional earning power and more visibility.

The tremendous inroads that Gretsch made with artists in such a short time was simply because Gretsch DID what we said we were going to do with and for the artists, and soon the word got out. The company was soon swamped with every caliber of drummer, approaching the firm and wanting to play *American* drums.

In terms of product, we were becoming very solid. I oversaw a new line of Gretsch sticks that included signature models for Phil Collins and Mark Herndon. The new Techware line of hardware was well received and we had plans to augment it with a lighter-weight more portable series.

All during 1984, we kept jumping at every opportunity. We provided all the drumsets for the Jazz Educators convention, through my contacts. Then we provided all the sets for the Kool Jazz festival. This was like a dozen drumsets for all the stages, all in a special color, Kool Green, to match the distinctive trademark color of Kool cigarettes. We put gold heads on. This was part of our "equipped convention stages" program like I had done with Ludwig. Another convention we did was the IAJE (International Association of Jazz Educators.) We supplied drums that the hosting organizations loved, and the drummers were delighted to be playing on "cool Gretsch kits."

The first signs of trouble started to show up in about mid-1984 when there were indications that money was getting really tight.

RC: It must have been a real challenge to ramp up what in many ways was a new company in the face of all the very solid competition that you mentioned earlier.

KD: Yes. And Charlie was certainly up for it mentally. physically, emotionally, but not financially. Charlie created an image and a prestige that was expensive. He did the Frankfurt show in the spring of 1984 in a big way. I think Charlie got a company that needed a real infusion of cash in order to bring it up to what it *could* be. Charlie spent money very freely to try and do new catalogs, artist relations, etc. They had hired me and moved me to Nashville. They did all of the right things to really get it going, but it didn't ramp up fast enough to keep the dollars changing hands; coming in, going out, etc. It just didn't pay back fast enough to keep the thing going, or at least that is my assessment. I never got close enough to inspect the books and I didn't know exactly how much he was losing, but as soon as I saw the Baldwin people show up, I smelled trouble. Here comes the bank. Any time the bank shows up, that means trouble. They are not there to say thank you for your business. They can do that with a phone call. I thought "Oh no. I just moved down here and

1984 Frankfurt Music Messe display

the banks show up."

RC: Was it an unsound business plan, or did expected sales not materialize?

KD: It was some of both. There were a number of unintentional errors that blindsided Charlie, but there was also some hoping and dreaming going on at the same time. At one point the demand grew far beyond production capability. The factory down in De Queen could not produce drums fast enough to meet demand. They had excellent people down there and the plant manager Ben Johnson was magnificent, but you can't go from zero to 90 mph in a year. A big factor is that you have to buy the raw materials. We were getting the shells from Jasper down in Indiana and they could not build them fast enough. So now we want to get a Centennial kit out with 14K gold plating on the hardware, 100 limited edition sets... that takes money to build them in all those expensive veneers.

Gretsch position in the marketplace, 1983

Charlie Roy's aggressive plan to increase the visibility of Gretsch began to show results within the first year. The move from Chanute to Nashville with it's easy access to top endorsers resulted in an impressive endorser roster, and the beefed-up ad campaign was succeeding in changing the image of Gretsch as an old jazz drum line.

When asked if this contest response summary from Creem magazine pretty much reflected the position of Gretsch in the marketplace in 1983, Karl Dustman had these insights:

"CREEM Magazine was pretty much a rock-roll readership publication. I know Gretsch advertised in these types of publications, as rebuilding the Gretsch images required visibility and perception that Gretsch was more than a black jazz drummer's drum company. This ranking is fairly accurate for that time,...and the ROCK-minded readers of CREEM Magazine. I am surprised that Rogers and Gretsch appear this "high" on the list.

In the early 1980s the Gallatin, TN team definitely changed that image with the addition of Phil Collins, Harvey Mason, Jerry Brown (Lionel Richie), Mark Herndon (Alabama), Graham Lear (Gino Vanelli)... all the top Nashville recording drummers (except Larry Londin) were now playing Gretsch.

To see Ludwig as the highest ranking BRAND in consumer responses would also be correct. Selmer had acquired Ludwig in November of 1981 and in 1983 had not yet had time to totally dismantle the Rock Artist endorsement roster Bill Ludwig (the third) had built. ALL the top players were still playing and supporting Ludwig in this time frame. Ludwig Artist collage posters were still being put together, but NOT for long.

OCTOBER ISSUE DRUM CONTEST GIVEAWAY

Brand	Responses
Ludwig	695
Tama	371
Pearl	311
Slingerland	285
Rogers	178
Gretsch	123
C.B.	118
Premier	76
Yamaha	68
Sonor	57
Other	871
TOTAL RESPONSES	3,153

Karl Dustman: "I would agree that this CREEM consumer contest evaluation responses and readership audience profile pretty much reflects the market rankings of these brands in the rock marketplace. Gretsch's competition in this marketplace at this time was Ludwig, Pearl, Tama. Those were the brands we felt we were competing with."

Karl Dustman accompanied Modern Drummer's Rick Mattingly to the factory and Gretsch worked with Modern Drummer on the layout of a feature story on Gretsch. Five thousand copies of the article were purchased by Gretsch for promotional purposes.

Inside Gretsch
100 Years of Gretsch
A Visit To The Gretsch Factory

De Queen Manufacturing Pictures and captions here are excerpted from the May, 1984, *Modern Drummer* article *Inside Gretsch*, text by Richard Egart (color photos from the archives of Karl Dustman)

(left to right) National Sales Manager Wayne Summers, International Sales Manager Randy Hauck, Operations Manager Walt Jordan, President Charlie Roy, Marketing Manager Karl Dustman

Plant Manager Ben Johnson inspecting a Centennial shell

The shells are manufactured in 13 different diameters, and except for large bass drums, a number of drums are cut from a single shell. A 14" shell which is 32" long could produce two 14x14 floor toms, or up to six 5x14 snare drums. The cuts are planned carefully, to avoid waste.

De Queen manufacturing: excerpts from *Inside Gretsch*, May, 1984 *Modern Drummer*

The shells are divided according to the visual beauty of the grain. The better looking shells are used for the natural-wood lacquer finishes; the shells of poorer visual quality are used for the drums with pearl finishes. Gretsch emphasized that this is *only* a visual separation, based on the grain pattern. Coverings are not used to hide defects in the wood. If a structural defect turns up, the shell is destroyed.

As we watched shells being cut, trued, beveled and sanded, Ben commented on the touch of the worker. "In woodworking and in musical instruments, there's a lot of feel. If you watch Merle closely while he performs these operations, you'll see that he's not really looking. He's feeling it. That's what it's all about."

After being cut, the shell is given a rough sanding on a belt sander. This removes any glue that may be on the outside of the shell from the manufacturing stage. It also opens up any cracks. Gretsch wants to find any defects as soon as possible, so that time is not wasted on a shell which will not be used.

The final sanding is done by hand, with the shell spinning on a turntable. This is the last step before the shell is either finished or covered. This step is especially important for those shells which will be given a natural-wood finish, because, as Ben explained, "There's a fallacy that the finish will hide and cover everything. The truth is, the finish will highlight every mistake we make. If the drum is not properly prepared, we're going to have a product of inferior quality at the end of the line. That's all there is to it. So the woodworking is critical."

De Queen manufacturing: excerpts from *Inside Gretsch*, May, 1984 *Modern Drummer*

"Everybody makes such a big deal out of sanding, and they go out and get digital readout computers to analyze how much sanding should be done. The real trick is the detailed attention that the employee pays to it. Merle can tell how much he's going to have to sand it by the grain structure."

After being belt sanded, the shell is placed on a turntable which trues the rim. This compensates for the tendancy of a saw not to end up in exactly the same place it started.

After truing, the shell is put on a special machine that cuts the bearing edge, which is so critical to the tuning of a drum. "We shape our bevels on a single-spindle shaper," Ben explained. "The bevel is not controlled by the employee; it's controlled by the configuration of the cutting tool. We purchase the cutting tools to meet our exacting specifications. What we're doing is getting the surface that the head comes in contact with." Both ends of the drum are beveled, making it possible for any shell to become either a single or double-headed drum.

Ben re-emphasized the importance of catching defects early. "Everybody in the system is looking for the defect. We want to stop it before we have all our money in it. We normally don't have a high scrap rate. That's the whole name of the game and everybody is in this building is an inspector. That's a part of everyone's job. All employees inspect their own work, as well as the work of whoever is feeding them, and if they see a flaw anywhere on the line as they're walking by, they'll point it out."

After the sanding is completed, the shells are loaded onto a dolly, and taken either to the covering area or the finishing area. We stopped first at the covering area and watched a bass drum shell receiving a pearl covering. "This is a straight-forward, simple operation," Ben commented. "I'm sure that everybody does it about the same. Both the shell and the covering material are coated with contact adhesive and allowed to dry. I know that some companies use double-face tape, but we have not found that to be adequate. We start it by hand on the top just enough to hold it, and we put it through the pinch roller." After the covering has been applied by machine, the overlap on the ends of the shell is trimmed by hand.

To get from the woodworking shop to the finishing department, we walked down a long corridor and through a heavy door, which is always kept closed. Ben explained the reasons for the separation of these departments. "If you're going to have a class finish, you're going to have to keep the dirt out of it, and the woodworking generates a lot of dust. That's why we've isolated the dust and dirt of woodworking. It adds clarity to our finishing. The booths are cleaned and the floors are mopped daily."

The finishing area seemed warmer than the area we had just left, and I commented on that. Ben replied, "We have to control the humidity in this room. Right now the humidity is a little high, so we're forcing heat in here. If it's 85 degrees outside and the humidity is too high, we still force heat in here to drive the humidity out. Likewise, we have a static problem in finishing if the humidity gets too low. So at that point, we pump moisture back in. We like to maintain about 42% humidity in here. There are days when we can't do that. Mother Nature just does not cooperate at all and equipment can't overcome it. We will not sacrifice the quality of our production just to keep the line going. Therefore, it is possible that we may have to shut down the finishing area completely for a day or two."

De Queen manufacturing: excerpts from *Inside Gretsch*, May, 1984 *Modern Drummer*

The first step in the finishing process is the application of a wash coat, which is merely a colored tint. As Ben explained, "This will show up defects that we have not been able to see in sanding. If there's any glue there, it will jump right out. If there are any cracks, they will show up. We can either block sand them by hand to get the glue off or send them back to woodworking to be started all over again."

After being wash coated, the shells are stained. Depending on the grain structure, a shell may be given from one to three coats of stain. Ben described the process: "In staining, it's a real talent to be able to blend these colors and make them match the control chip. We have to know when to stop. Otherwise we're into a rework situation. We let the coating dry and then recheck it. It it's just a shade light, we put on another coat to make it darker. If it happened to be too dark, we would wash it back with alcohol."

Throughout these operations, the skill of the workers was evident, and Ben commented again on their touch. "In our staining operation, our people can actually tell which one of the woodworking operators finished the shell by the feel of the wood and the way it takes stains. The quality isn't different; it just has a different feel."

"Our next operation is sealing. We wash coat, we stain, we seal. That's it on the first day. Then we shoot one coat of lacquer per day. We sand the second coat, and then apply the final two coats. It takes seven days to put lacquers on because we allow two days' drying after the sixth coat before we go to the buffing. That allows the solvents to get out. Most companies are laying two coats a day. We're putting on one coat, letting the solvents dissipate, and it reduces the shrink. Lacquer will shrink into grain. Sometimes, as on guitars, you can see where the lacquer has shrunk into the grain, and it looks like it's checked. That's what we're trying to eliminate."

After the final coat of lacquer has been allowed to dry for two days, the shell is wet sanded. "We use just soap and sandpaper for this process of removing the lacquer buildup."

De Queen manufacturing: excerpts from *Inside Gretsch*, May, 1984 *Modern Drummer*

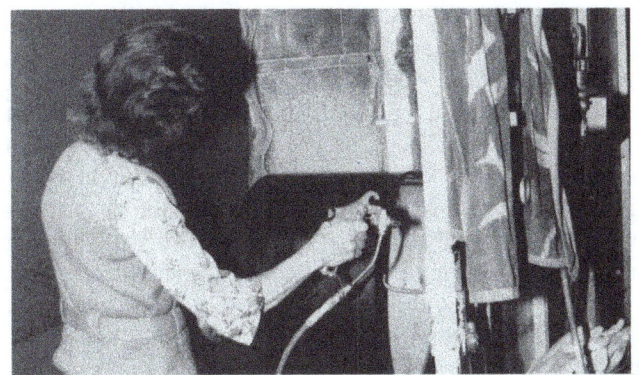

The next step is the application of the "magic coating"- the silver-colored sealer on the inside of every Gretsch drum shell. Again, this process in important to the Gretsch sound, so the company was reluctant to discuss the chemical structure of the sealer, or to have the application process photographed. However, I witnessed the process and can verify that the coating is *not* used to cover up inferior wood. Scratch it away and you'll find high-quality maple. I questioned Ben about the reason for putting anything on the inside of a drum shell. "It seals the wood. In finishing, if you only finish one side of the wood, the wood is not stabilized. Moisture will affect the other side and work one side of the surface against the other.

"You want a protective covering so that the moistures are not attacking the interior. As far as the specific covering that we use, all I can say is that it's "That Great Gretsch Sound." The sealant that we use gives more of a resonator effect to the shell, so that the shell carries the vibration of sound without absorbing it."

The next step is to buff the shell. Ben explained why the wet sanding which was done after the lacquering operation is important. "That makes it easier on the buffer, because the buffing wheel generates so much heat that you can scorch lacquer. We could go directly from the final lacquer to the buffing wheel, but it heats up the lacquer so much that we would have a lot of rejects. So we put that extra sanding in to cut down on the buffing time.

"We have a wet wheel and a dry wheel. The wet wheel has an abrasive, and that takes the wet sanding even further to smooth out the lacquer. Then it's washed off with naptha and goes to the dry wheel. There's no compound at all. You can actually see the lacquer moving and you have to know when you're applying too much pressure so you don't scorch or cut through it. Here again, it's the craftsman's feel that makes it controllable. I have not found a machine that could do it without someone directing it."

"What we do better than anybody is wood finishing, because we start it out properly and we finish properly. We're woodworkers and finishing people. We just do it better than anybody. Nobody can touch us without rushing this process. We could put them out a lot faster, but not any better."

De Queen manufacturing: excerpts from *Inside Gretsch*, May, 1984 *Modern Drummer*

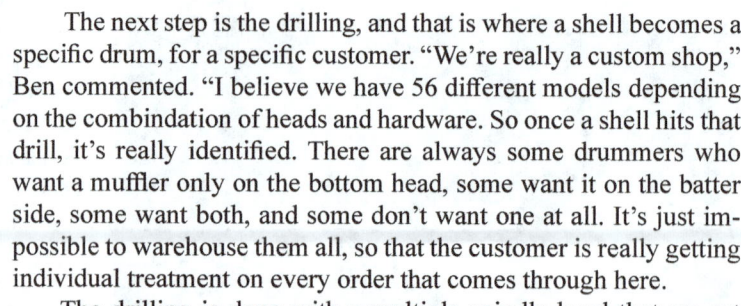

The next step is the drilling, and that is where a shell becomes a specific drum, for a specific customer. "We're really a custom shop," Ben commented. "I believe we have 56 different models depending on the combindation of heads and hardware. So once a shell hits that drill, it's really identified. There are always some drummers who want a muffler only on the bottom head, some want it on the batter side, some want both, and some don't want one at all. It's just impossible to warehouse them all, so that the customer is really getting individual treatment on every order that comes through here.

The drilling is done with a multiple spindle head that we set up per model. We can either drill single or double-headed drums. We've chosen to limit our drilling to one lug station at a time, because that results in better alignment."

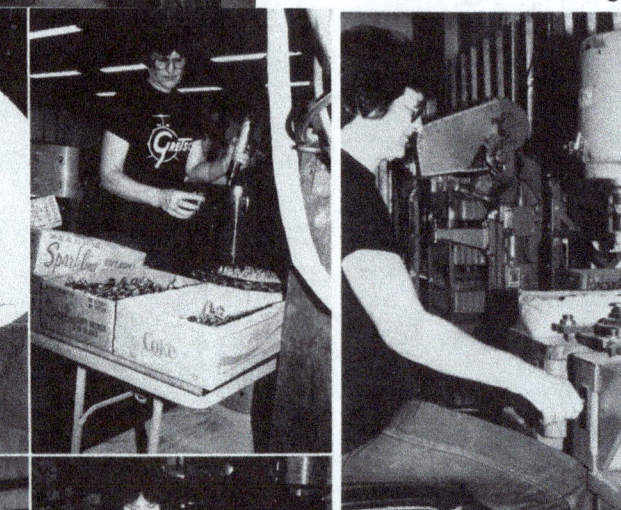
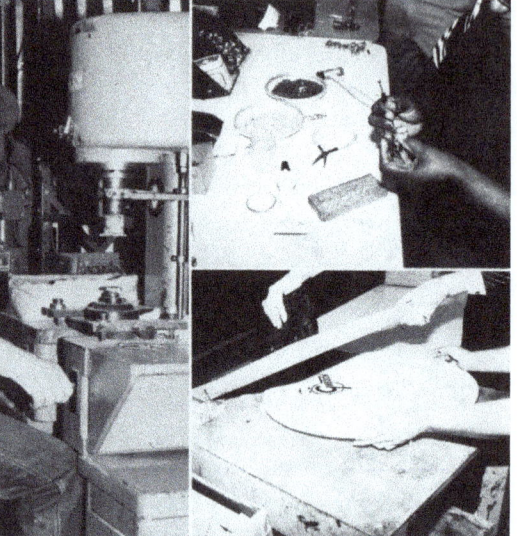

At this point, the shell moves down an assembly line. The Gretsch nameplate it installed, lugs are mounted along with whatever holders and mufflers are required, heads and rims are added, the finished drum is inspected, given a thorough cleaning, put into a plastic bag, and then into a carton. From there it's only a few steps away to the loading dock, where our tour began.

The final "staging area" is for large consolidated shipments for both domestic and international business. Each product has a control tag with the model number, color, serial number, and order number for easy tracking. The control tag is generated in the first production process and stays with the product until it ships from one of the three docks. Shown here are Gretsch drums and Sho Bud pedal steel guitars ready for shipment.

resuming Rob Cook's interview with Karl Dustman:
KD: As I said, the drums being made in De Queen were world class instruments, and we were starting to attract a lot of attention. Gretsch aficionados that are out there (and there are many self-proclaimed) have the common perspective about Gretsch "Quality time-lines." The Baldwin ownership periods were the most turbulent and unsettling. Delivery was very long and the quality was unpredictable and varied from one shipment to the next. Dealers were frustrated about not being able to receive production orders and when they were finally shipped to the stores, the orders, drilling, etc. could be wrong and they needed to start the order all over. Once the De Queen Arkansas factory was taken over by Charlie Roy and Plant Manager Bob Johnson was installed, the whole perception of *Quality is #1* was established with time. Eventually, Charlie was able turn around the Baldwin ownership negative perspectives. The Gretsch products at the 1983 and 1984 NAMM shows were better than anything ever coming out of Brooklyn and the new colors, finishes and hardware were steps in the right direction that Gretsch customers were extremely thirsty to embrace. Ben achieved a greater quality control and finish match perfection then ever before. The work force Ben recruited all came from the furniture-building and finishing industry. They were accessible and affordable to him, and he employed those "quality oriented wood-workers" through the Gretsch factory. (Keep in mind the only other employers around the Gretsch De Queen factory (a former Baldwin Piano manufacturing/finishing operation) were the chicken slaughter house and the gym-shoe manufacturing factory. De Queen had a total population of 600 people at that time.

This "sweeping change" was quickly recognized by the market and *Modern Drummer* wanted to explore *why* and *how* this was all happening. This led to the trip of Rick Mattingly and myself to the De Queen Arkansas plant/factory together. Rick and I worked on the story together, focused on providing factory insights and calling attention to the quality story. The publishing of the *Modern Drummer* article in the May 1984, issue placed Gretsch right in the center of USA manufactured drum business and interest. It was such a favorable article that we ordered 5,000 copies of it as a reprint to use as a promotional tool.
RC: Can you tell me about Charlie's departure from the company?
KD: He was gone by the end of May 1984. It did come as a surprise to me. I was quietly taken aside and told that he was leaving. At the NAMM show the next month, a press release was issued to the NAMM daily. The announcement made no mention of Charlie Roy, or even of Kustom/Gretsch. It simply said that the Baldwin Piano & Organ company was announcing its purchase of the "Gretsch company." Duke Kramer was mentioned as the new general manager of the company.
RC: You didn't discuss it with Charlie?
KD: No, he was gone. His departure seemed deliberately quick and quiet. A representative from Baldwin came in and I helped him get the signatures he needed, the company automobiles, keys to the building, bank account access. This was all done very quickly, following the directives of Harold Smith and Dick Harrison.
RC: Who did that leave you reporting to?
KD: Both Harold Smith, President, and Dick Harrison, Chairman, and Duke Kramer. Duke Kramer arrived on the scene one morning very shortly after that to act as the stand-in manager. He was in charge when he was there, I was in charge when he was not there. I ended up signing my name to most of the Centennial kits, because Charlie was gone.
RC: Had Duke been visible through the Charlie Roy era?
KD: No. Duke was not involved again until Charlie was gone. Baldwin didn't know anyone in Gallatin. They wanted someone they knew and trusted to go in and put the fire out. Duke started commuting, going down there every two weeks; he'd be there a week, then gone for two weeks, etc. from June to the end of the year. There was a lot of restructuring going on at the time in the musical instrument industry, so the development was perhaps surprising, but not shocking. Harold Smith, who was president of Baldwin, reassured all of the Gretsch Gallatin employees that Baldwin was going to continue to own it, everyone had a job, and everyone was to keep doing what they were doing. Meanwhile, it's obvious in retrospect, all they were doing was positioning it to sell it out from underneath everybody.

The last project that they gave me was a license to go crazy on the November 1984, Percussive Arts Society convention at the University of Michigan. Mike Udow was the host. We went in there bigtime, with a lot of equipment and a big display. It was set up in the music building, in a set of rooms. I got a phone call from Duke Kramer that said you need to call me when you can get off the booth. So I went to the pay phone (we didn't have cell phones then) and I called him. He told me the company was going to be sold. I said, *"What?"* He said, "It's going to be sold to Fred W. Gretsch and he will take over Jan 1st, 1985. You need to get back and you need to start getting involved in the transition team, Fred needs to know who you are." This was in the middle of the PAS show. I went back to the booth in a state of shock knowing the company was being sold. I'd just heard at the June show from Harold Smith that nothing was going to change! In fact, he had instructed Duke to find a buyer; they wanted to cash out.

RC: Were you offered a job by the new owner?

KD: Fred W. Gretsch and I did discuss the possibilities. I went to Savannah, we talked, but never came together. My last day was Dec 31, 1984 and I later read that Fred picked up the keys on Jan 1, 1985. People started disappearing like flies and stuff was being liquidated, packed up to be shipped to Savanah.

RC: Did everything go to Fred?

KD: Everything Gretsch, and Sho-Bud. Duke did sell Kustom to another entity.

The preliminary poster for the Gretsch Drummer's Workshop. This poster was released to select Gretsch artists by Karl Dustman in November of 1983 to begin gauging response. The Workshop was modeled on the famous Ludwig Percussion Symposiums that Dustman had been involved with. Baldwin killed this idea as soon as they re-acquired the company in May of 1984.

The Conway, Arkansas Connection

In 1965, the Baldwin Piano & Organ Company built a huge (190,000 square feet) manufacturing plant in Conway, Arkansas.

By 1998, the Conway operation's 270 employees were building 2,200 Baldwin grand pianos per year.

Gene Haugh, who started in Booneville in 1969 and worked in the De Queen facility, was once transferred by Baldwin to Conway for a time. (Haugh later helped establish production in Ridgeland SC and trained Paul Cooper there.)

In late October 1984, Baldwin announced that Gretsch drum production would be moved to the Conway facility and that the De Queen plant would close on December 21st, 1984. That closure and move never happened.

In 2001 the reorganized Baldwin Piano Company was again forced into bankruptcy. This time (2003) Baldwin sold to the Gibson guitar company. When Gibson Chairman and CEO Henry Juszkiewicz announced the letter of intent to purchase Baldwin in November of 2001, the Nashville Business Journal quoted him as saying he intended to build upright pianos in the Truman, Arkansas facility and grand pianos in the Conway facility. Gibson instead used the building to assemble Slingerland drums and Tobias basses for a couple years beginning in 2003, but eventually shuttered the Conway facility.

Fred W. Gretsch had purchased the Slingerland Drum Company in 1986, just a year after buying Gretsch from Baldwin. He sold it to Gibson in 1994. Gibson first produced Slingerland drums in Nashville and halted production with an announcement that a new factory was being built in Memphis, a move that never happened. Slingerland was dormant until reappearing in Conway.

Fred W. Gretsch

Fred W. Gretsch's deal with Baldwin was signed in October of 1984. The terms of the deal called for Baldwin to continue running the business through the year end, and for the family to take over production, sales, marketing, etc. on the first of January, 1985. Fred continued production in Arkansas for 6 months. He convinced Bill Hagner (the person who had moved production from Brooklyn to Arkansas in 1969) to rejoin the Gretsch team to supervise the move to Ridgeland, South Carolina.

John Sheridan conducted this interview with Fred W. Gretsch for *Classic Drummer* magazine on the occasion of the Gretsch 125th Anniversary in 2008.

JS: 2008 is the 125th Anniversary of the Gretsch Company. I want to congratulate you on this occasion and I'm guessing this is a year you've been anticipating for some time now. How do you think your ancestors would feel about their business having this kind of longevity?

FG: Thanks for the congratulations. In each generation there was a lot of dedication to the business so it's a matter of family spirit and carrying on the family legacy. It's happened in the first, second, third and now the fourth generation and I'm glad to say we're getting a lot of interest from both the fifth and the sixth. So I can't help but think they'd be overwhelmed how the world has changed in the last 125 years and be equally amazed to think that the business that they started and fostered has continued. Back in 1883 the concept of a business lasting 100 years, there just weren't examples and models. We're talking about the opening chapters of the Industrial Revolution. What a different day and time that was. But there's no question that the past bears on the present and it's the foundation for our future.

JS: You personally knew some of the key men that were in Gretsch's employ during the innovative '50s & '60s, such as "Duke" Kramer, Phil Grant, Jimmie Webster, and Bill Hagner. Do you find yourself reflecting on them and their past contributions during this milestone year?

FG: I certainly do. In the last couple of years we've profiled key people on our website. [www.GretschDrums.com] So you can look at past stories. They're all there. Obviously Duke Kramer is. There's a profile of Billy Gladstone in the Gretsch House Telegram and also on the Gretsch website. Before that was Phil Grant. We've paid tribute to them along the way. I'm

(l-r) grandfather Fred Gretsch Sr., Fred W. Gretsch, uncle Fred Gretsch Jr.

still in touch with Bill Hagner, still in touch with Fritzie Kramer. Had a message from Ken Kramer over the weekend, that's Duke's oldest son, who's my age. It's all part of our past and how it really informs the present.

JS: Sure. They're part of the family, aren't they?

FG: They absolutely are.

JS: Of course, it all goes back to your great-grandfather, Friedrich Gretsch, who founded the company in Brooklyn during 1883. How did he learn his craft for making musical instruments?

FG: You may recall that he came to the States in 1872 at that age of 16 and lived with his sister, brother and cousin in Brooklyn, and apprenticed at the Albert Houdlett Banjo and Drum Factory. He fell in love with Rosa, who was a wonderful musician, a great piano player. They got married in 1879. So working in a shop apprenticing making instruments and marrying a woman who was a great musician, I think those two things collaborated to further kindle the fires of interest in instrument building.

JS: It must have been traumatic for your ancestors when Friedrich suddenly died in 1895. He was only 39, which was young, even for the time. Your family's company could've ended right then. Did his son/your grandfather, Fred Sr., ever reminisce with you of his resolve to save the company at that time?

FG: The interesting reminiscing comes from his mother Rosa, my great-grandmother, who died in 1936. Here he was a boy of 15 years old. He was in Business College at that point, which was the equivalent of high school. And his dad had founded the business, nurtured it to a point that we were not only making instruments, but we were importing instruments from Europe and selling them, and using those connections to the instrument building centers of Europe. That, I think, was the basic organization that my great-grandfather put in place, plus the mentoring of my great-grandmother. When her husband died, they had seven children. I think it was the unique combination of a very helpful and well-organized mother working with her oldest son and a staff that had been put in place by her husband, those things working together. Of course, Grandpa had a great business skill and moved forward rapidly. In 1914-1915 Williamsburg, there was an opportunity to redevelop a quarter-block and build the Gretsch Building at 60 Broadway. And again it was Rosa and her two oldest sons that collaborated on building that building. We tend to give all the credit to Grandpa, Fred Gretsch Sr. But as a matter of fact, as we look closer at the history books and are able to check the records further, there's no question that my great-grandmother played a very important role in the continuity of the business and in its success in the later years. We view this 125th anniversary year as the first years of our next 100 years. One of the things we've done is added a full-time curator of collections to the Gretsch team, so that we're able to work closely with museums and sources of information to better catalog all the materials that we've gathered over time. One very interesting item is a 1912 Gretsch catalog. I don't know whether you've seen the 1912 catalog.

JS: No, I don't think I ever knew it existed.

FG: It's 184 pages long! 1912 was 17 years after the passing of the founder and four years before the Gretsch Building. The business had progressed so much that the catalog was 184 pages. It's pages and pages of drums and materials, drums of various kinds. And we've been fortunate enough to acquire many of those instruments over the years and have them here in our collection.

JS: When Fred Sr. retired in 1942, your dad, William and your Uncle Fred Jr. ran the company. Sadly, your father passed away in 1948. I imagine your grandfather helped you and your mom through that difficult time?

FG: Well, he certainly did. I saw a lot of him in those years. We've got lots of old pictures of me as a young lad with Grandpa. I was reminiscing with my sister just yesterday about what she remembered about Grandpa. I remember as a young lad spending the night at Grandpa's house. She doesn't have that recollection, she's younger.

JS: Wasn't that Forest Hills?

FG: Yes, Forest Hills. Grandpa built that house at the same time they were building the factory in Brooklyn. It's the house that my dad and his brothers moved to in 1915.

JS: A defining time, for sure.

FG: A challenging time. At the time of the First World War, there was very strong anti-German sentiment. Though the number one immigrant population in the country was German at that point in time, there was still a terrific anti-German sentiment. They obviously navigated those things businesswise, and it's part of the history books.

JS: After World War II, some new products resulted from interviews that Phil Grant & Duke Kramer had with local NYC working drummers; an effort made by Gretsch to help drummers improve their set-up/playing and transport situations, like Jimmy Pratt's idea for an adjustable bass drum tone control and Dave Tough's request for a small (20") bass drum. Do you still get suggestions from today's Gretsch endorsers?

FG: We absolutely do. I think the first high-water mark probably came in the early '30s, right at the depth of the Depression, when Radio City Music Hall opened and Billy Gladstone was the principle percussionist. By the end of the '30s, our collaboration with Billy brought out the Gladstone snare drums, which of course are revered today as some of the best of all time. Radio City Music Hall opened in 1932 so we're talking about 76 years ago. In that same Radio City area, in an adjacent building, was where NBC was headquartered. In the '20s and absolutely in the '30s, radio was the new and primary medium of the day, that and newspapers. Harry Volpe was playing guitar on NBC radio as their staff guitarist. We were collaborating with these fellows to dial in our recipe on Gretsch instruments. For us to have Billy Gladstone and Harry Volpe, a couple of key players in New York City, the music Mecca of world, I think the die was cast for professional instruments well before the War. At that point, professional instruments were a new focus for Gretsch. After the War, the guys came back from the service: Fred Gretsch Jr., and Phil, whom my dad hired, and Duke, whom my dad had hired in Chicago 10 years earlier, got together with my dad and decided that our focus was going to be toward the professional side of the products from then on. So you can see in the post-war years, the collaboration with individual artists, whether it was Jimmy Pratt or Louis Bellson or just so many others – Chico [Hamilton] or Max [Roach] or Elvin [Jones] or Mel Lewis or Art Taylor – all of them worked with Phil, who was a gifted percussionist in his own right, to help us dial in the recipe, and that recipe we essentially dialed in by the early '50s. That's the recipe we're faithful to today, and another example of how our past informs our present, realizing that the recipes that were developed then were really superb and maintaining those recipes are what we're all about today.

JS: You were born in Chicago, near Gretsch's western sales office. When did you move to New York and become active at the factory in Brooklyn?

FG: My dad moved the family back to New York in '48. One of the bittersweet remembrances we have came by way of Ted McCarty – a good friend of the family, who along with his wife, attended my baptism shortly after I was born. There was a group of music people in Chicago. A friend of Ted's ran into dad and my mother and four kids on the way to the station to take the train back to New York and my dad confided in him that he was going home to die. Dad had cancer and fought it for a number of years. By the time '48 came, kind of halfway through the year, he knew he just had a short time left. So he headed home in '48. Dad died in September of '48 and Grandpa – Fred Gretsch Sr. – lived another 4 years; he died in September of '52. So it was in those years that I saw a lot of Grandpa and I'm sure he enjoyed taking his young grandson to the factory in Brooklyn that he built.

JS: Obviously he felt a great deal of responsibility, not only to the business, but to the family. Not all businessmen are like that. It's very admirable that he looked after you like that. It seems greater fortune happened for Gretsch shortly after you started working in Brooklyn. By 1955, color catalogs and many new design options became available; especially Cadillac Green sets with gold-plated hardware, as well as the Progressive Jazz snare drum. Many top jazz guys like Max Roach, Art Blakey, Jo Jones, Mel Lewis, and Shelley Manne, were all playing Gretsch drums. Even early rockers like Elvis and Jerry Lee Lewis had drummers playing Gretsch drums. Despite your obvious youth at the time, did you realize how dramatic the music world was changing and how positive the response was to your line of instruments?

FG: I think if you're talking about the mid-50s, the core of the music business at that point was the accordion and keyboard business. Back in 1954, 75% of the business was pianos, keyboards and accordions. You're talking about a period of time when you had some popular music that was utilizing our drums and guitars. Obviously we were gratified, but no one had slightest idea it was going to build to the point where today the business is very heavily guitar-oriented. Keyboard and string-instruments have flopped – by that I mean flopped percentage-wise – from being heavily string-instruments and keyboards to just a minor player. And all the time there's been good growth in the percussion business, particularly in recent years. I got my first paycheck working the summer of '58. I worked as an office boy that year. One of the things I did was clean out the stationery room. It was quite large and it was full of old catalogs. You're talking about '58 so it was shortly after the first color drum and guitar catalogs had come out. So those catalogs from 1950 and before that were ancient history. I recall personally putting boxes and boxes of those old catalogs in the dumpster.

JS: Which are now worth hundreds of dollars a piece.

FG: Exactly. All the brass plates for printing artwork and likewise. They were obsolete at the time so they went, too. Phil Grant, among other things, was in charge of the office. He was very complimentary about the good job I had done cleaning out the stationery room. (Laughs) So, who knew? And '58, that's the year that Bo Diddly came in and got us to make a rectangular guitar. Billboard's first "hot 100 singles" list came out. The number one record on that first list was Poor Little Fool by Ricky Nelson; RCA released their first stereo LP record. Miles Davis did Milestones. Rockin' 'Round the World with Bill Haley and the Comets. Buddy Holly, Maybe Baby. Summertime Blues, Eddie Cochran, a Gretsch guitar player. The first Grammys were given out in '58. So we've come a long way in 50 years, particularly with music and technology.

JS: Of course by 1964, the British Invasion exploded and suddenly every kid wanted to play drums or guitar. Gretsch's sales skyrocketed. Did you find yourself putting in longer hours and what was it like at the factory back then?

FG: The factory had a big backlog of orders. We were hiring workers. We spread out from 60 Broadway in the early '60s. We were on the 7th floor and half the 9th floor in the building. Plus the basement, where we stored things we were buying in large qualities – like die-cast hoops. You'd run a thousand of a size or 2,000 of a size but you wouldn't use them all immediately. Because there were other tenants, we couldn't get more space in the building. We had to move a couple of blocks away to South 5th Street, another building that was owned by a Gretsch cousin. We moved the drum production over there. That gave us more room to expand drum production there and to expand guitar production at 60 Broadway. Of course, the accordion was just ancient history, or was certainly significantly on the wane. It was a great memory to be part of; when you were making drums and they were going out the door immediately because you had orders for every one. This was the round badge drum sets of the '60s. Primarily, we were making drum sets and secondarily, snare drums. I'd say 95% of the drums in that day and age were covered [in sparkles or pearls].

JS: The building on South 5th Street was owned by a Gretsch cousin?

FG: Right. 109 South 5th Street. We had half of the 2nd floor in that building. It's still there. So much of Williamsburg has turned from manufacturing to being an arty community. The building at 60 Broadway is residential condos now. And the building at 109 South 5th Street is lofts. I've run into people that have practice studios in that building. And I know of one on South 4th Street a block over from where the original factory was located. There are more practice lofts for musicians on South 4th Street, too. Some famous musicians have practice lofts there. So the manufacturing is gone, but the spirit is still there.

JS: So the buildings on South 4th Street and on South 5th Street are two separate buildings. I always assumed it was the same building in the middle of the block.

FG: South 4th Street was the factory up until 1916 when we moved to Broadway, and some years later it was torn down and replaced with a more modern structure that stands today. So that building is lost to time. But the buildings at 60 Broadway and 109 South 5th Street are still there. We were there a couple weeks ago. It's fun to tour the neighborhood, usually with musicians or music dealers, and talk about the various activities that went on in the different buildings and share those stories. And there's always Peter Luger's for a good steak. When we were there a couple weeks ago, we even ate at the Gretsch table. Luger's started in 1887. I think we're the only family who can say, "Our family's been dining here since you guys opened." We have to remind them though because the guys who are there now have been there 10, 15, 20 years. And we've been out of Brooklyn since about 1970 so that's 38 years. Time flies.

JS: In 1966, the Monkees cut a deal with Gretsch to supply them with instruments in exchange for mass television exposure. Was it somewhat surreal to see them playing your instruments on TV every week, knowing that 30 million teenagers were also watching?

FG: I was working at the factory in Brooklyn at the time. I started there fulltime in '65. They came to visit and it was nice to meet them and we were very proud of the fact that the instruments were played on television.

JS: In 1967, your Uncle Fred shocked everyone by selling Gretsch to Baldwin. It's been said that he did so, only as he had no son to leave it to. I know you were very disappointed. How were you told and what did you resolve to do about it?

FG: He took me to lunch at Luger's, which was an unusual occasion. At lunch that day he gave me the news. I told him I wanted to buy the business. He said, "But Baldwin paid cash for it." Of course Baldwin was like Steinway is today, one of the top brands in the industry. A good cash buyer. So we worked for Baldwin after that.

We interrupt the interview at this point to say a few words about Fred W. Gretsch's activities between 1967 when his uncle sold the Gretsch company out of the family and 1984.

In January of 1968, Fred W. Gretsch moved to Dungannon, Virginia to set up a drumstick manufacturing operation called "Dungannon Lumber Company." He knew that in the 1960s Gretsch had always had a tough time getting enough sticks, so the plan was for Gretsch to be his only customer. He purchased machinery for making the sticks from the Goodspeed Machine Company in Winchendon, Massachusetts, because of their reputation for being the top maker of circular back-knife lathes. He located in Virginia to be near the source of the raw material, white hickory.

In September of 1969 he rejoined the Baldwin/Gretsch business in Elmhurst, Illinois, a suburb of Chicago. As a salesman for special accounts, he was working under Duke Kramer. He also started studying business administration as a part-time student at Elmhurst College. He graduated in 1971 and went into business for himself, establishing Fred W. Gretsch Enterprises. Fred imported and wholesaled popularly priced instruments, working with large retailers such as Montgomery Ward and Spiegel.

It was a good time to begin importing instruments, as the Japanese market was exploding. He imported guitars, drums, amplifiers, and band instruments under the names Bandmaster, Concerto, and Chicago. In 1976 Fred bought the tools from the Harmony (guitar) company when it went out of business. That purchase included tooling for making banjos, which he began to build at his Addison, Illinois facility. In 1978 he moved his operations to Ridgeland, South Carolina. (Many midwestern firms were moving to the south and south east, the "sun belt," in that era in search of lower utility bills and an unskilled labor force.) Fred continued his Illinois operation for a couple years, then consolidated his business to Ridgeland. When he bought Gretsch from Baldwin in late 1984, the agreement called for Baldwin to continue operating the division through the end of the calendar year 1984. Fred took control on January 1, 1985, and under agreement with Baldwin he left manufacturing in Arkansas for one year before moving it to Ridgeland in 1986. Bill Hagner had come back into the business and worked on the move with Gene Haugh who had been with Gretsch since 1969. Haugh helped re-establish the drum building in Ridgeland, working there for one year. The staff totaled about 25 at that point.

interview, continued...
JS: Many longtime Gretsch fans were upset at how Baldwin handled Gretsch, especially with their decision to move production out of Brooklyn. In 1984, you & your wife Dinah became the light at the end of the tunnel when you returned the company to family ownership. How did this come about?
FG: It was 17 years of aspiration and work. Over the years, I spoke to the Baldwin people at trade shows and told them I'd like to buy the Gretsch business back. I asked them if it was for sale. Dick Harrison was the Senior Vice President I spoke with most often and the answer was always no. In the intervening 17 years, Baldwin entered financial business, insurance and banking and in 1984 was the Enron of the day; one of the biggest bankruptcies up to that date that anyone had ever seen. They were on the NY Stock Exchange. They were a financial empire with a small music business. The piano guys bought the music business out of the bankruptcy from the judge, and they were only interested in the piano business. They brought Duke Kramer out of retirement to figure out what to do with the Gretsch business. He knew of my interest in buying it back. Dick Harrison, though still there, didn't make the call. Duke made the call. Summer of '84, I traveled to De Queen, Arkansas with Duke, kind of undercover, without announcing who was coming. Duke and I went through the place. I wasn't introduced so I got a chance to look at it from the inside. One of the fellows there recognized me and spread the word in De Queen that I'd been there. So the word was out in inside circles. We signed the agreement in November of 1984 and announced it to the world first business day of January '85.
JS: For the last 22 years, Gretsch drums have been made in your facility in Ridgeland, SC, and Kaman has handled distribution since 2000. How has Kaman's involvement benefited the company?
FG: When we partnered with Kaman we were simply building "original recipe" instruments in Ridgeland, SC, in what today we call the "Custom Shop." It was our desire to expand the international and national distribution. We knew and respected the Kaman people. They had the ability to fill in other series of drums and to offer a complete package of Gretsch instruments in the marketplace. And that's the reason we partnered with them. They had that reputation and had demonstrated ability to marketing and distribution on a worldwide basis. In the ensuing years, the business has increased probably 7 or 8 fold from where it was in 2000.
JS: Yes, Gretsch drums are everywhere now. It used to be that only a dealer here and a dealer there would have them. Now they're much more visible in the marketplace.
FG: And the Custom Shop is as busy as ever. Nice backlog at the Custom Shop. Lots of orders coming in. People want the original recipe instruments and by offering instruments at other price points that are faithful to the Gretsch heritage at another level, we've been able to bring lots more people into the fold.
JS: And now Gretsch is in its 125th year. What special products have you issued to celebrate the anniversary?
FG: We've got 3 anniversary drum sets and 2 anniversary snare drums. Today you've got the internet where you can see all those instruments and almost taste them. (laughs)
JS: Yes, that Cadillac Green is awfully tasty looking.
FG: (laughs) Yeah. That part of the recipe you have to get your drumsticks and sit down with them to really appreciate all that.
JS: When you come up with these new products, how are they chosen? Is it based on what you think is popular from years past, like a reissue type of thing or people's requests?
FG: A key element over the years has always been collaboration with artists, right from the early '30s with Billy Gladstone and Chick Webb. Then later artists. Music goes back and forth and we're able to work with the artists of today. We get good input from music shop owners as well. We utilize all those inputs. Of course we've got a catalog of instruments that we've made for a long period of time. Many oc-

casions we're able to remake something that had success in another era and make it that more interesting for drummers today.

JS: And what special events are going on for the celebration? I understand that Gretsch is having a contest for unsigned and independent bands competing for a spot at a NYC concert event headlined by legendary Great Gretsch Artists. Can you give any details, such as the concert date and venue?

FG: Looks like the date is the 20th of November. We're still negotiating to sign a contract for the venue, but it looks like the Thursday before Thanksgiving, couple of weeks after the election. We had to plot it in there to get it in the end of the year. The contest kicked off May 1st when people could begin to upload their MP3s. So it's coming along fast. We have other events forthcoming, but I'd better not talk about them until all the contracts are signed. But there's an event in the Museum of Making Music in Carlsbad, CA. And we're negotiating with several other museums. There's a dealer reception at the Country Music Hall of Fame. We're also closing in on a date in the Northeast in August. And a couple of dates in Japan in mid-September in Tokyo and Osaka. Atlanta, GA on the 20th of September and it looks like the Northwest in October. That's kind of a general sketch, how the events have been coming along. There have already been 3 dealer events in St. Louis, Memphis and Nashville. Others planned on the west coast coming up probably in July and August.

JS: People should keep tabs on the website.

FG: Absolutely! Gretsch125th.com will have the latest and greatest information. We have a Gretsch MySpace page that you can link from the Gretsch125th site as well. [MySpace.com/Gretsch125th] It came up in mid-January and we're closing in on 10,000 friends. In a little over 3-1/2 months we're real happy to have acquired all those friends.

JS: So how does it feel to be celebrating the 125th anniversary of your family's company?

FG: You know the music business has given us so much, John, as a family. We have a chance now to give back in the form of work that the Gretsch Foundation is doing. And I encourage you to look at a new link – GretschInstitute.org. Our vision of the Gretsch Foundation is to enrich people's lives through participation in music. We've been able to partner with institutions of higher learning in terms of scholarships, been able to initiate learning programs here in Savannah. It feels really good to be able to give back. The realization here in our 125th year is that the music business has been very good to the Gretsch family.

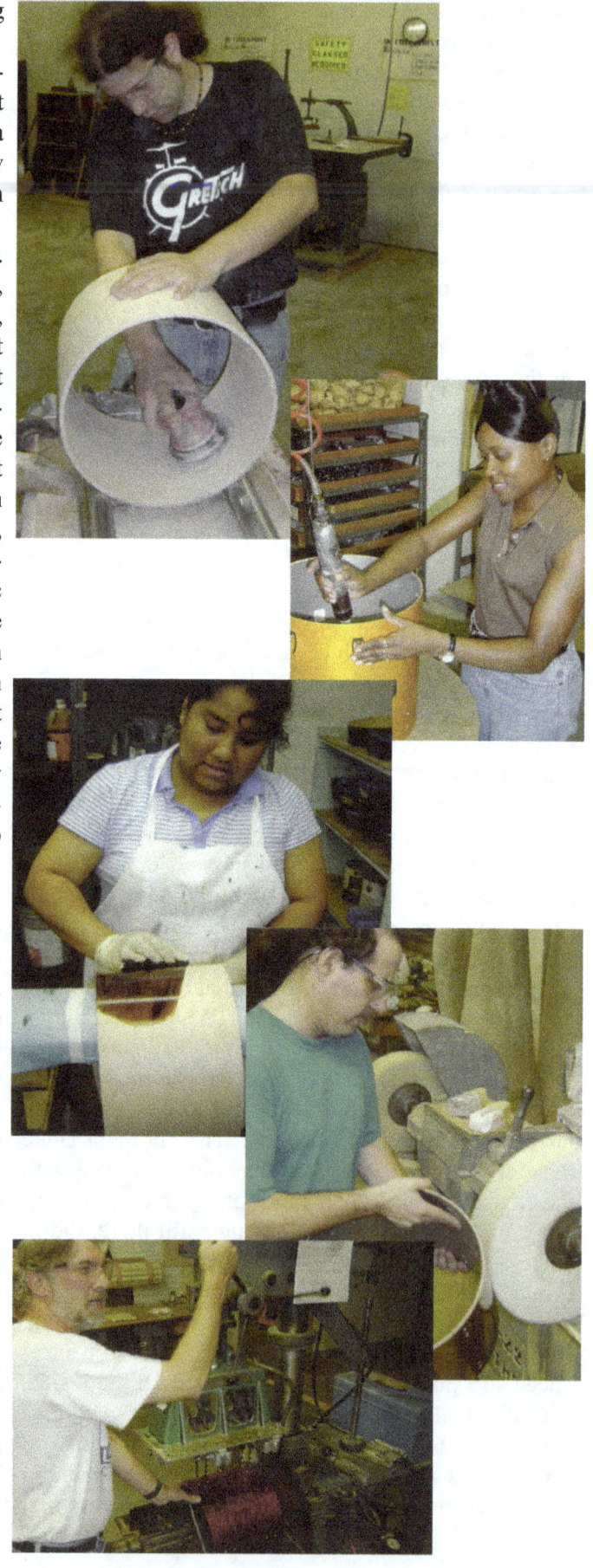

Ridgeland production photos

JS: So, any plans for the 150th Anniversary?

FG: Oh, yes. We absolutely do have a plan for the 150th Anniversary. Dinah and I plan to be there! Obviously there's going to another generation of Gretsch family members running the business at that time. But it's our fondest goal to be there. In June this year, we have a family reunion in celebration on the occasion of my father's brother who will be 100 years old. He's still quite healthy and has 8 children and lots of grandchildren. 15 of our children and grandchildren are coming with us for that celebration in Connecticut.

JS: Oh, God bless him!

FG: At the time when we're celebrating the first years of our next 100 years, we celebrating the birth of Uncle Dick. And Uncle Dick, though he never worked in the music business, he's certainly a big supporter of the business and he's a good cheerleader for us.

JS: Well, God bless you all. I've enjoyed playing your instruments since 1974. I just love the way Gretsch instruments play and sound, the way they actually feel when I play them, it's kind of hard to describe. All I know is that they don't feel like any other drums I've ever played and it inspires me to play better.

FG: Thank you very much, and you put your finger on it. We hear from Rob Bourdon, Charlie Watts, Steve Ferrone, Vinnie Colaiuta, Phil Collins, Cindy Blackman, Stanton Moore. When you talk drums with them, that's the kind of things they're saying. Certainly the unique tonal quality of the instruments, something we call "That Great Gretsch Sound." It's been the innovation and the responsiveness to input from others over the years, the collaboration with key artists along the way. Hand-craftsmanship has been an issue since the beginning and we maintain that today. And family is really the thread that's woven throughout it all that brings us to where we are today.

ERNIE GADZOS (1922-2005)

Ernie Gadzos was born in Windsor, Ontario, in 1922. (Windsor is across the Detroit River from Detroit, Michigan.) At the age of 16 Ernie began playing with local bands and later studied with Jack Ledingham, the principal percussionist with the Detroit Symphony. He moved to the United States in 1948 and began touring as a drummer shortly after his move. Gadzos played with some significant names, including Vaughn Monroe and the Glenn Miller Band.

He settled on Chicago as a home base and continued his career as a professional drummer until 1965 when he married and retired from road life to take a job at Karnes Music Store. He did continue to take occasional gigs. After Karnes Music, Gadzos worked at Franks Drum Shop, Drums Unlimited, and the Slingerland Drum Company, his last Chicago position. When Fred W. Gretsch purchased Slingerland and moved it to Ridgeland, SC, he hired Ernie to join Fred Gretsch Enterprises.

GRETSCH AND SLINGERLAND

In most Fred W. Gretsch interviews of this type including the one conducted by the author, the topic of Slingerland is conspicuous by its absence. Although the complete history of the Slingerland marque is detailed in *The Slingerland Book*, the author feels it is important to give at least a brief overview of the Gretsch-Slingerland sequence of events from 1986 through 1994.

Baldwin was not the only huge corporation that got into the drum business in the 1960s and 1970s, then wanted out of the drum business in the 1980s. The publishing giant CCM (Crowell, Collier, McMillan) was trying hard to divest itself of the Slingerland Drum Company by the end of the 1970s. They did so in 1980, but the new ownership was unable to stop the tailspin the company was in and bankruptcy was declared in 1986. By the end of that year, a deal was arranged to sell the company to Fred W. Gretsch.

Since Leedy was a dvision of Slingerland, Gretsch got the Leedy name as part of the package. All things Slingerland were trucked to the Gretsch warehouses in Ridgeland, South Carolina. The assets included some finished stock, lots of parts, roughly 15 four-drawer file cabinets of records, and manufacturing equipment and machinery from several Slingerland eras. (Some of that old Slingerland production machinery is used in today's Gretsch drum manufacturing.)

Gretsch negotiated a partnership with the HSS company, a large wholesaler of musical instruments. HSS had stood for Hohner-Sonor-Sabian but their distribution deal with Sonor had expired and they needed a drum line. It was convenient that Slingerland started with the same first letter; HSS became known as Hohner-Sabian-Slingerland.

Entry-level Slingerland drums were built to HSS specs, and royalties for the use of the Slingerland name were paid to Gretsch. The premium Slingerland drums were made to HSS specifications in the Ridgeland, South Carolina, Gretsch manufacturing facility. Shells for these American-made Slingerland drums were made by Jasper using molds that were made to HSS specs and purchased by HSS.

In 1994 Gretsch rather abruptly announced the sale of Slingerland to Nashville-based guitar maker Gibson. HSS had a fire-sale and dumped all Slingerland inventory and parts. Most things Slingerland were trucked to Nashville. All items not specifically itemized in the purchase agreement with Gibson remained in the Ridgeland warehouse. Those items included some heavy manufacturing equipment such as the machine used to stretch springs into snappi-snares, shell-making molds and equipment from the Radio King days of the 1930s, barrels of parts, some finished goods, and the shell-making molds and equipment from the 1970s.

When officials at Gibson realized they had not purchased all things Slingerland, they went back to the table with Fred W. Gretsch to negotiate for a few more items they particularly wanted, such as the snappi-snare making machine. (Gretsch retained ownership of the Leedy name, which it still owns at this writing.)

In 2003 Gretsch sold the Slingerland shell-making machinery and equipment at auction. There were two auctions; one for the 1930s equipment, a separate one for the 1970s equipment. Both winning bidders were from Ft. Wayne, Indiana. At this writing the 1930s gear lies in a barn rusting away while the 1970s gear has been reverse-engineered and restored to working condition by Bernie Stone of Stone Custom Drums.

GRETSCH & LEEDY

As mentioned in the previous section, Gretsch obtained the Leedy brand in 1986 as part of the Slingerland purchase. Gretsch retained Leedy when they sold Slingerland, still owns the Leedy trademark and maintains a Leedy website. which includes a company history, dealer listing, and some products which at this writing are no longer available. A custom Leedy outfit was made for endorser Tré Cool.

Fred W. and Dinah Gretsch

In 1979, Fred Gretsch Enterprises in Savannah, Georgia, hired a new office manager, Dinah Murphy. The skill set she brought to the office and the efficiency with which she used it made an immediate impression on Fred W. Gretsch. The two soon found that they had much more in common than office interests and they married in 1984, just before Fred managed to acquire the Gretsch drum and guitar division from Baldwin. The couple worked together at re-establishing family control of the business. Dinah, as CFO of Gretsch, became one of the most prominent women in the musical instrument industry. She worked with George Harrison to create the Traveling Willburys guitar and with Bono on the Irish Falcon. She also secured drum endorsements from Vinnie Colaiuta, Stephen Ferrone, Mark Schulman, and Jack Gavin. Along with husband Fred, Dinah received a Heroes Award from the Atlanta Chapter of the National Academy of Recording Arts & Sciences in 2003, and induction into the Georgia Music Hall of Fame in 2008.

Although she semi-retired from the office in 2010, Dinah has remained very involved. "I still go in for month-end close-outs," she said recently. "I still work with all my artists, and I do PR work. I'm very involved; I just don't have to sit behind a desk every day." 2010 also marked the year in which Dinah created Mrs. G's Music Foundation. The purpose of this foundation is to promote music education and musical activities in rural southern schools. In the first year the foundation funded eight Headstart programs, got the World Drumming program into two schools, and started a guitar instructional program in another. The foundation also converted an old storage room into a music studio, funded teachers, and sponsored appearances by Gretsch artists. "I believe that music has the power to change children's lives for the better," says Dinah, "If we can reach young children with that power, we can set them on a positive path for the rest of their lives."

Since KMC assumed manufacturing, marketing, and distribution duties of Gretsch drums, Fred W. and Dinah have remained *very* busy. Their headquarters are the Fred Gretsch Enterprises corporate offices and museum in Pooler, Georgia, just outside Savannah.

One of the most important activities is the supervision of the Gretsch marque. Fully cognizant of the family business history, Fred and Dinah oversee the trademark and copyright issues related to Gretsch. That is no small task considering the worldwide fame and recognition that Gretsch instruments have enjoyed for over a century. They pay close attention to the use of the Gretsch name by others to prevent unauthorized use. In today's technological age, that of course means monitoring the internet to enforce trademark rights, copyrights and property rights against unauthorized distribution.

There are other trademarks and product lines to manage; Sho-Bud, Leedy, and Bigsby, as well as Gretsch branded merchandise and collectibles such as clothing items.

There is even a retail outlet, Outlet Music, in the same Pooler strip mall that houses the corporate offices.

Fred and Dinah assist Fender and KMC with their marketing and promotional efforts on behalf of Gretsch guitars and drums, often appearing at events such as the 125th Anniversary concert and tour.

Philanthropic activities are conducted through the Gretsch Foundation and include not only general humanitarian assistance such as support of the Salvation Army, Big Brothers/Big Sisters and The Monroe Art Guild, but efforts to enrich lives through participation in music through guitarart.org. The Gretsch Foundation started Guitar Art in 2002 as an art program in which instruments are donated to schools and organizations to assist them with fundraising efforts. Through the program, non-profit organizations have received used guitars and turned them into beautiful and unique works of art that were then sold at auction.

GUITAR ART

The Guitar Art program was followed up with two giving programs for qualified schools and organizations. The first is the "Basic Instrument Program." In this program, the Gretsch Foundation provides up to five guitars to one organization. The second program features non-playable Professional Level instruments meant to appeal to professional artists. Schools and organizations are encouraged to recruit prominent local artsts to decorate the instruments for auctions or fundraising events.

Gretsch Foundation Scholarships and Assistanships to date have included: The Jimmie Webster Memorial Scholarship at Berklee College of Music, the Ernie Gadzos Scholarship in Music at Georgia Southern University, the Duke Kramer MBA Graduate Assistantship at Georgia Southern University, the Duke Kramer Scholarship at Elmhurst College and the Joseph R. Johnson Scholarship at the University of West Georgia.

The Gretsch Foundation provided a $75,000.00 gift to Georgia Southern University in 2012 to establish a Music Education Partnership with the Boys & Girls Club.

for more information about Guitar Art:

**GuitarArt.Org
P.O. Box 2468
Savannah, Georgia
31402**

2009 Gretsch Institute-sponsored Music & Art & Dance camp in Savannah

Lena Thomas

Lena Thomas today continues the tradition of strong and qualified women in the Gretsch family business, following the path of Rosa (wife of founder Fritz Gretsch), and Dinah (wife of Fred W. Gretsch.) As Fred and Dinah's daughter, she started with the company when she was twelve, working in the office part-time after school. This continued until Lena entered Columbia College in South Carolina, where she earned her degree in business administration. Further training as a paralegal allowed Lena to assist Dinah Gretsch on artist relations projects and Fred Gretsch on trademark infringement issues.

Lena started attending NAMM trade shows for Gretsch in 1992, and she came to work at the company's Savannah office full-time in 1994. There she supervised inventory control, purchasing, quality control, and production scheduling for the drum division. She managed Gretsch's Ridgeland, South Carolina drum factory for two years before taking time off to have her son Logan who is a sixth-generation Gretsch family member.

The Gretsch family was recognized as the 2007 Georgia Family Business of the Year in 2007. The Avedis Zildjian company sent their family congratulations with this custom plaque and autographed cymbal.

THE BACK COVER PHOTOS

The portrait above hangs in the museum/offices of Fred Gretsch Enterprises in Pooler, Georgia.
L-R: Fred Gretsch Junior, founder Friedrich "Fritz" Gretsch, Fred Gretsch Senior, and William Gretsch

Dinah Gretsch, Fred W. Gretsch, and grandson Logan Thomas representing the 4th and 6th generations of the Gretsch family preserving their musical business heritage.

GRETSCH WEB SITES

The various corporate entities involved in the 2013 production and distribution of Gretsch-branded products are seamlessly integrated through several web sites. The page frame below is copyrighted by "The Gretsch Company," (Fred W. Gretsch.) Some of the tabs navigate the reader to partnering corporate entities as noted.

HOME GUITARS DRUMS ABOUT BLOG COMMUNITY GRETSCH GOODS BIGSBY

HOME
The "HOME" page uses this template and is copyrighted by "The Gretsch Company." (Fred Gretsch Enterprises)
It features lead-ins to several of the other tabs.

BIGSBY
The "BIGSBY" tab links to a separate site copyrighted by Bigsby Guitars & Vibratos (Fred Gretsch Enterprises)

BLOG
The "BLOG" page uses this template and is copyrighted by "The Gretsch Company." (Fred Gretsch Enterprises)
It features press releases related to all Gretsch products and activities; guitars, drums, Bigsby, Sho-Bud, Gretsch Foundation, etc.

GRETSCH GOODS
The "GRETSCH GOODS" page uses this template, copyrighted by "The Gretsch Company," (Fred Gretsch Enterprises.) It features tabs with links to:
Gretschgear.com (clothing, etc.)
GretschGuitars.com
GretschDrums.com
LeedyDrums.com
Bigsby.com, Sho-Bud.com
GuitarArt.org,
Gretsch eBay Vero page

GUITARS
The "GUITARS" tab links to a separate site copyrighted by "Gretsch Guitars." (Fender Musical Instruments Company.)

ABOUT
The "ABOUT" page uses this template and is copyrighted by "The Gretsch Company." (Fred Gretsch Enterprises)
It features a company history and links to Fred's blog, a company timeline, Gretchen Elsner-Sommer's family history site, and Bigsby & Sho-Bud pages.

COMMUNITY
The "COMMUNITY" page uses this template, copyrighted by "The Gretsch Company," (Fred Gretsch Enterprises.) It features links to forums, Facebook, Twitter, Youtube, & Myspace associated with The Gretsch Company, guitars, drums, & Bigsby.

DRUMS
The "DRUMS" tab links to a separate site copyrighted by "KMC Music, Inc." (a division of Fender Musical Instruments Company)

Home   Gretsch Guitars Site   Gretsch Drums Site   About Us   Blog   Community Sites   Gretsch Goods   Bigsby   Terms Of Use

125th Anniversary Concert
November 18, 2008 Highline Ballroom, Manhattan

GRETSCH DRUM ENDORSERS
Brooklyn, 1936-1967

The first catalog to mention names of Gretsch users was the 1936 catalog which listed some drum corps. When the first drum division catalog was published in 1939, it included an endorser roster and featured endorsers on the front cover. There were very few changes when the 1941 catalog came out other than increasing the number of artists on the front cover.

1939 Catalog Cover

endorser page used in both 1939 and 1941 catalogs

1941 Catalog Cover

Baldwin, 1967-1981

Baldwin demonstrated little interest in an endorser program. They reluctantly maintained a couple of high-profile artists, but by 1971 not one artist was included in the Gretsch drum catalog.

Karl Dustman, 1983-1984

Shortly after Charlie Roy acquired Gretsch from Baldwin, he hired Karl Dustman as marketing director. Dustman relocated to Nashville where he aggressively pursued top drummers and quickly built a leading roster. When Baldwin purchased Gretsch back from Roy, they asked Dustman to keep doing what he was doing, explaining that nothing would change in the way Gretsch was conducting business.

Fred W. Gretsch 1985-2001

When Fred W. Gretsch re-acquired the company from Baldwin at the end of 1984, he remained committed to trying to maintain the momentum and leadership market position Gretsch had attained under Karl Dustman through his artist relations and developing educational programs. He took over the company with an unprecedented stable of Gretsch artists representing every musical art form and the focus on Artist Relations continued in the capable hands of Dinah Gretsch. Many of those artists are still connected with the company in some way today.

KMC Music 2001- present

Kim Graham: "When I started at KMC Musicorp (formerly Kaman Music) 26 years ago, we were in the beginning stages of Gibraltar Hardware and Toca Percussion with very few artists. With endorsement requests coming our way, we started an Artist Relations program, which was new to us. I now manage the Artist Relations for Gretsch Drums and Gibraltar Hardware. When we took on distribution of Gretsch Drums in 2000, we also took on the Artist Relations. Over the past 12 years, our roster has grown and the popularity of the Gretsch drum line grew into markets outside the recording studios. Gretsch drums are now seen on numerous tours with many high-level artists, various late-night and award shows; as well as movies and TV. Additionally, we have placed Gretsch drums into backline/rental companies in the U.S. and internationally to meet the needs of our expanding roster. While we do have a growing roster with artists in many genres of music, we concentrate on quality and not the quantity of artists that we sign each year. Being that we are a small team, all of our signings are important to us and it's instrumental to our reputation and the reputation of the brand to meet our artists' expectations."

This list of Gretsch drum endorsers and dates of affiliation has been compiled primarily from Gretsch promotional literature and advertising through 2012. Dates of Gretsch association are not meant to be precise. In some cases an artist was loosely affiliated with Gretsch for many years but only had their photo published in an ad or catalog in one year. The most likely errors are those of omission. The author apologizes to those who have been omitted from the list or whose tenure as an endorser is incorrect.

		See Page			See Page
Abadi, Yvo	2008-2010				
Adams, Jack	1949-1958	68	Bosarge, Harrell	1984	
Alexander, Pete	2006-2010		Bourdon, Rob	2003-2011	76,79
Anderson, Trent	2006-2011		Boutherre, David	2011	
Apo, Earl	1973		Boyd, Raymond	2003-2011	
Baibai, Yves	2008-2010		Boydstun, Jack	1983	
Bailey, Colin	1984		Bram, Michael	2007-2012	80
Bailey, Dave	late 1950s		Brande, Sherman	1939-1941	
Balbinot, Tony	2008		Braunagel, Tony	1984	
Baron, Dutch	1984		Brazil, Karl	2006-2012	78
Barrett, Creighton	2011		Bridges, Reees	2006	
BayBay, Ives	2008-2010		Brill, Rob	1984	
Beaver	2006-2011		Brock, Tony	1984	73
Beck, Paula Cole-	2008		Brockstein, Herb	1954-1958	68
Beddoe, Rich	2007-2012	80	Brooks, Clyde ('84 clinician)	1984	28,74
Bellerose, Jay	2003-2008	77	Brooks, Philip	2011	
Belleville, Pierre	2006-2011	78	Brown, Gerry	1984	
Belli, Remo	1954-1955	67	Brown, Jeff	early 1980s	
Bellson, Louis	1946-1961	62,63,66,68,128	Brown, Jerry ('84 clinician)	1984	30
Bennett, Alvino	1983-2011	76,80	Brown, Les	2008	
Benson, Bernie	1945	61	Browne, Ian	2003-2011	77
Bey, Sam	2011		Bruno, Jack	1984	
Best, Denzil	1949-1955	128	Bukowski, Nicolas	2011	
Bigay, Danny	1984		Burns, Roy ('84 clinician)	1984	74
Biwandu, Roger	2011		Byrne, Bobby	1941	
Black, James	1984		Byrne, Mike	2012	
Blackman, Cindy	2003-2012	75,77,78	C'Alberon, Alberto	1941	
Blakey, Art	1954-1966	63,67,68,69,128	Cafforio, Franco	2008-2010	
Blanchard, Amaury	2006, 2008		Calderon, Alberto	1941	59
Blane, Dewey	1939-1941	60	Camera, Cesar	1939-1941	
Bode, Frank	1951		Cambre, Herman	2008-2010	
Bomba, Nicky	2010-2011		Campbell, Harry (Eddie Duchin band)	1930s	
Bonner, Fred	1984	67	Caputo, Greg	1984	
Borden, Barbara ('84 clinician) 1984			Carlock, Keith	2012-2013	

		See Page			See Page
Carlson, Peter	2011		Drain, Ish	1939-1941	
Carrigan, Jerry	1984	85	Droubay, Marc	1983	72
Carroll, Charlie	1939-1941		Drummond, Billy	2012	
Carrorio, Franco	2011		Duggins, Dan	2010-2011	
Carter, Lamar	2008	79	D'Auria, Oscar	2006-2011	77
Castka, Joseph	1939-1941		Dyrason, Orri Pall	2008-2011	
Cester, Chris	2006-2011	78	Eckberg, Paul	2006-2011	
Champion, Jared	2011		Edlin, Mike	1983	
Chapman, Steve	1983		Edwards, Dennis	1984	
Christian, Bobby	1984		Ellison, Nathan	2011	
Churilla, Scott	2006		Ellner, Sam	1939	
Clapp, Geoff	2011		Emphrey, Calep	1983	
Clark, Brett	2006-2011	77	Enyard, Ron	1973	71,129
Clark, Terry	1973		Entressangle, Phillippe	2011	
Clarke, Kenny	1949-1958	68	Ernie, Francois	2011	
Clegg, Joe	2011		Esposito, Davide	2008-2011	
Cobb, Jimmy	1963		Etkin, Norman	1939-1941	
Colaiuta, Vinnie	1983-2012	47,77,79,150	Eulinberg, Stefanie	2008-2010	79
Collins, Phil	1983-2011	28,30,72,77,85	Evans, Darren	2010-2011	
Combs, J.C.	1984		Fa, Patrick	2011	
Connors, Norman	1973		Faberman, Leo	1939	
Cool, Tré	2012		Fadden, Jimmie	1983-2013	80
Cooper, Al	1941		Fagan, Aaron	2006-2008	
Coste, Yann	2011		Farro, Zac	2011	
Cottrill, Tony	1984		Farrugia, Daniel	2008	
Clarco, Dave	1984		Fatool, Nick	1941-1949	59
Crahan, M. Shawn "Clown"	2008-2011	79	Fiel, Max	1973	
Craney, Mark (clinician 1984) late 1970s-1984		72	Fein, Paul	1963	
Crosby, Caleb	2009-2013	81	Ferguson, Gary	1984	
Cruse, Will	2006-2008		Ferrone, Steve	1978-2013	47,52,72,78
Cusatis, Joe	1984		Fineo, Mika	2011	
Dam, Kasper	2008-2010		Fink, Herman	1939-1941	60
Damin, Hugo	2008-2010		Fisher, Eddie	2008-2012	79,80
Danielson, Richard	2012		Flores, Chuck	1954-1958	68
Danziger, Zach	2012		Flores, Martin	2006-2011	
Dapper, Frank	2008-2010		Florio, Andy	1930s- ??	65
Davison, Daniel	2011	78	Fogarino, Sam	2008-2010	78
Dawson, Alan	1966		Fontana, D.J.	2003-2006	
Day, Josh	2012		Fonseca, Paulinho	2008-2011	
de Seta, Lucrezio	2011		Ford, Hannah	2008-2013	80
Deakin, Paul	2006-2008		Forte, Nick	1984	
Dennis, Kenny	late 1950s		Frankel, Danny	2006-2011	
Dentz, John	1984		Frasure, Doug	2008-2011	
Derge, David	2006-2011	76	Frazier, Stan	2003-2012	77
dei Lazzaretti, Maurizio	2011		Freire, JJ	2006	78
Delong, Paul	1984		Friday, Johnny	2003-2011	
Dentz, John	1984		Fryar, Chris	2012	
DeRon, Cal	1949		Fryoux, Ray	2008-2011	
Doksausky, Lukas	2008-2011		Fulterman, Harry	1939-1941	
Dolenz, Micky	1966-1967		Gagon, Jeremy	2006-2010	
Donlinger, Tom	1984		Gajo, Dragan Gajic	1983	

		See Page
Galland, Stephane	2008-2010	
Gannon, Sean	2008-2010	
Garibaldi, Alonso	1984	
Garman, Greg	2011	
Gary, Bruce (84 clinician)	1983-2006	77
Gates, Richard (84 clinician)	1984	
Gavin, Jack	1983-2010	47,76
Gladstone, Billy	1939-1941	22,60
Goldberg, Paul	2003-2010	76
Goldman, Dr Edwin Franco	1941	
Gonzalez, Paul Alexander	2006-2010	76
Goodman, Saul	1945	61
Goodwin, Garrett	2008	79
Goossens, Mario	2006-2010	
Grainger, Sebastien	2006-2010	77
Grant, Phil	1941-1963	18,40,61
Graves, Justin	2008-2010	
Grey, Trey	2003	
Grossman, Steve	1983	
Grupp, Dave	1941	
Guiliana, Mark	2012	81
Hamilton, Chico	1958-1978	67,68,69
Hamilton, Jeff	1978-1984	72
Hanna, Jake	1961	
Harris, Eddie	1939-1941	
Harte, Roy	1948-1955	63
Hawkins, Taylor	2008-2013	
Helmecke, Gus	1939-1941	61
Herman, Sam	1939-1941	
Herndon, Mark	1983-1984	30,73
Hervol, Sergio	2011	
Hiraoka, Yoichi	1939-1941	
Hodgson, Nick	2006	76
Holland, Milt	1948-1949	
Honnet, Davy	2011	
Horowitz, Dick	1963	
Horton, Chaun	2012	
Huff, David	2003-2011	77
Hyde, Dave	2008-2011	
Hyndman, Clint	2006-2011	
Ichinose, Hisashi	2010-2011	
Imamura, Mai	2011	
Imbrechts, David	2008-2011	
Infusino, Chris	2012	80
Izumitani, Makoto	2006-2011	77
Jablonski, Kuba	2008-2011	
Jaeger, Rick	1978	
Jansen, Ken	1984	
Jean, Norma	2008	
Jenkins, John	2010-2011	
Jenkins, Phillip	2011	

		See Page
John Jr, Paul "Phinkky"	2006-2010	76,79
Jones, Elvin	1958-1978	67,68,69,128
Jones, Harold	1960s	67
Jones, Jo	1941-1958	18,62,63,68,128
Jones, "Philly" Joe	1941-1963	68,70,128
Judd, Harry	2006-2011	
Kajitani, Masahiro	2010-2011	
Kalafus, Caitlin	2010-2011	
Kamoosi, John	2003-2006	
Keeling, Bryan	2008-2011	78,79
Kelly, Kitty	1950s	64
Kerrigan, Jerry	1984	28
Kerswill, Derek	2008-2011	79,80
Kidd, Chip	1984	
Kiri	2010-2011	
Kirkpatrick, Scott	2011	
Koba, Dean	2006-2011	
Krom, Ro	2008-2010	
Kreutzman, Bill	1973	
Krom, Ro	2008-2010	79
Kutak, Frank	1939-1941	69,61
Labarbera, Joe	1974-2012	76,81
Labovitz, Jesse	2006-2011	77
Lackey, Jim	early 1960s	
Lamond, Don	1949-1966	63,68,69,70,128
Lane, Johnny	1984	
Larsen, Claus Andre	2006-2011	
Lauro, Albert	1984	
Layne, Larry	1949	
Lazzaretti, Maurizio dei,	2008-2010	
Lear, Graham (1984 clinician)	1984	30
Lebrosa, Joe	1973	
Lenailly, Eric	2008	
Lemen, ??	1949	
Lenga, Zeke	1939-1941	60
Lewis, Mel	1949-1978	68,69,72
Mackley, Linda	1983	
MacMillan, Ryan	2008-2011	79
Maher, Mark "KRAM"	2005-2012	
Malen, Phil	1939-1941	60
Mann, Howie	1949	
Manne, Shelly	1948-1955	62,63,67,128
Maronet, George	1939-1941	
Marsh, Mike	2003-2006	76
Martin, Stu	1961	
Marucci, Mat	1983	
Masaki, Garo	2010-2011	
Mason, Harvey (1984 clinician)	1983-2003	30,144
Mason, Nick	1973	
Mason, Paul	2006-2011	
Mason, Tony	2006-2011	

		See Page
Masui, Remio	2010-2011	
Mattinson, Bernie	1939-1941	59
McClanahan, Mary	1941	59,61,64
McClure, Rick	1984	
McDonald, Pat	2003-2012	76
McGlinchey, Cameron	2006-2011	
McHugh, Chris	2006	77
Medeles, Jose	2008-2011	
Meissner, Konrad	2012	
Mela, Francisco	2008-2011	
Mendelsohn, Jules	1939-1941	
Mendolia, Francesco	2008-2011	79
Messina, Louis Jr.	2012	
Mette, Dave	2008-2011	78
Micali, Eric	2006-2010	
Milovac, Joe	1984	
Mitchell, J.R.	1984	
Miyauchi, Kosuke	2010	
Moffatt, Al Sr.	1945	61
Moffett, Jonathan	1983	

(Moffett was required to endorse Yamaha in 1984 as a condition of playing with Michael Jackson, but he agreed to pay for the Gretsch drums he was using because he wanted to keep them.)

Monkees	1966-1967	
Montgomery, Mike	2010-2011	
Morgan, Doug	1984	
Morgan, Barry	1984	
Morgenthaler, Bobby	2010	
Moore, Stanton	2003-2013	76,79
Mossis, Cameron	2010-2011	
Morris, Lee	2006-2010	
Moy, Russ	1973	
Musiate, Oscar	2006-2011	78
Nakamura, Tatsuya	2010-2011	
Neal, Bob	1950s	128
Neblett, Nate	1984	
Negron, Didi	2011	
Norman, Duane	2006-2011	76
Northrup, David	2003-2012	77,80
Norvo, Red	1939-1941	
Oakes, Warren	2008-2011	79
Odman, Ferit	2013	
Owczarz, Radek	2008-2011	
Owens, Ulysses Jr.	2012	81
Palermo, Matt	2008-2011	
Palmer, Carl	late 1970s	71,72
Parolin, Robi	2006-2011	
Parrish, Ryan	2010-2011	
Pasillas, Tiki	2011-2012	81
Payne, Sonny	1958-1966	68

		See Page
Pedersen, Nathan	2003	
Pent, Mark	1973	
Pemberton, Brad	2010-2011	80
Perkinson, Tommy	2010-2011	
Perry, Charlie	1948-1949	67,68
Persip, Charlie	1958-1963	67,68,69,128
Peterson, Debbi	2003-2011	
Petri, Sven	2008-2011	
Phantom, Slim Jim	1984, 2006-2011	72,76,79
Pierce, Ray	1984	
Pillado, Joe	1939-1941	60
Plummer, Kenny	1939-1941	60
Pluta, Jan	2010-2011	
Pontius, Mark	2012	
Pope, Jarred	2008	
Powell, Chris	2010-2011	
Pratt, Jimmie	1954-1958	40,68
Price, Nick	2010-2011	80
Pruitt, Brian	2011	
Pryor, Wesley	2003-2011	77
Ramos, Mauro	2010-2011	
Rausch, Seth	2008-2010	
Receli, George	2008	
Reed, Ted	mid-1960s	
Reid, Frank	2006	
Richmond, Bill	1954-1958	68
Rickard, Tommy	2008-2010	
Riddle, Paul	1978	72
Rieflin, Bill	2003-2011	72
Rickard, Tommy	2006-2010	
Rivera, Anthony	2012	
Roach, Max	1949-1966	63,66,68,69,70,128
Robinson, Forrest	2003-2011	77
Robley, Bart	2007-2012	80
Robson, Paul	1973	
Rodriguez, Alex	2008	79
Romaine, Van	2003-2012	76
Ross, Kent	2006	
Roth, Bob	1939-1941	60
Rottella, Bill	1973	
Russo, Rich	2006-2012	78,81
Ruth, Milton	1984	
Saito, Syuuichiri, Saito	2010-2011	
Sakiyama, Tatsuo	2011	
Sakurai, Masumi	2010-2011	
Salmins, Ralph	2006-2011	
Sanders, Mark	1984	
Sanford, Kevin	2006-2008	
Savage, Scott	2003-2010	76
Saxton, Dusty	2010-2012	
Saxton, Mark	2011	

		See Page			See Page
Scaffidi, Anthony	2006-2010		Vander, Christian	2008-2010	78
Schild, Daniel	2008	78	Vanalli, Northon	2011	
Schulman, Mark	2002-2013	47,77,78,79,80	van den Broeck, Joost	2008-2010	
Seiwell, Denny	1978-2006	77	van Tornhout, Wouter	2008-2010	
Seixo	2011		van Wijk, Wouter	2008-2010	
Senda, Akiharu	2010-2011		Vargas, Paulo	2010	
Seta, Lucrezio de	2006-2010		Vasquez, Roland	1984	
Shanahan, Dick	1948-1955	62	Very, Mike	2012	
Sharp, Lee	1984		Von Ohlen, John	1973	
Shiino, Kyoichi	2011		Waits, Freddy	1973	72
Shlosser, Rick	1984		Walker, Matt	2008-2011	80
Shrieve, Mike	1973		Waltzer, Jack	1939-1941	60
Silverlight, Terry	2003-2011	76	Watson, Sammy	2008-2011	79
Silvio, Andrew	2006-2010		Watts, Charlie	1963-2013	71,72,76
Simmons, Paul	2012		Webb, Chick	1939	59
Simpson, Boomer	2008-2011		Weisbach, Ken	2010-2011	
Sims, Ben	2012		Weiss, Sammy	1939-1941	60
Simms, Zach	2008-2011	78	Wells, Tommy	2001-2012	76,81
Sinai, Joe	1939-1941	60	Wettling, George	1948-1958	62,68
Skinner, Carl	1939-1941	60	White, Lenny	1973	
Sloan, James	2008		White, Noel	2006-2011	
Smith, Aaron	1984		White, Skip	1984	
Smith, Charlie	1954-1955	128	Wilk, Brad	2003-2011	76
Smith, Wayne	1983	72	Williams, Tony	1959-1993	68,72,73,85
Smith, Ty	2011		Wilson, Chris	2003	
Smith, Viola	1941	61,64	Wilson, Damon	2006-2011	
Soule, Kenny	1984		Wilson, Shadow	1949	
Soulier, Francois	2006-2011		Wolf, Teddy	1939-1941	
Spencer, Joel	2011		Wolfe, Jim	1984	
Starosta, Maciek "Slimak"	2008-2010		Wood, Nate	2003-2011	77
Spencer, O'Neil	1939-1941		Woodyard, Sam	1940s-1950s	
Stephens, Michael	1984		Woolstenhulme Jr., Rick	2010-2012	
Stewart, Bill	2003-2011	76	Wolfe, Jim	1984	
Stocki, Gregg	2003-2011	77,78	Worf, Neil	1984	
Stoeck, Martin	2008-2010	78	Wrennell, Jarred	2006-2011	76
Stroud, Keio	2011		Woolstenhulme, Ricky	2008-2010	79
Stroud, Melvin	1984		Wynn, Donnie	1984	
Studer, Fredy	2008-2010		Yagami, Toll	2011	
Tavares, Omar	2012		Yerdon, Ryan	2008-2011	
Taylor, Art	1958-1963	68,69,128	Yoshizawa, Kyo	2011	
Taylor, Daren	2010-2011	80	Young, Brandon	2003-2008	
Teixeira, Cuca	2011		Zhu, Dawn	2006-2010	
Thompson, Tony	1984				
Thomson, Paul	2006-2008	78			
Thornton, Billy Bob	2010-2011	80			
Tough, Dave	1948	62			
Trafton, Casey	2003-2006				
Tribolet, Xavier	2008-2010				
Trucks, Butch	1973				
Ulano, Sam	1954-1958	68			
Underwood, Scott	2006-2010	76			

Chick Webb   1939 catalog cover   Bernie Mattinson

Joe Jones   Nick Fatool   Bernie Mattinson   Mary McClanahan   Alberto Calderon
1941 catalog cover

ACE DRUMMERS FROM COAST TO COAST PLAY AND ENDORSE GRETSCH-GLADSTONE!

1. **FRANK KUTAK** — Edwin Franko Goldman's Band
2. **JOE PILLADO** — Casa Mañana Band, N.Y.
3. **HERMAN FINK** — Leo Reisman's Orchestra
4. **JOE SINAI** — RKO Golden Gate Theatre, San Francisco
5. **PHIL MALEN** — 'Ruby' Newman's Orchestra
6. **DEWEY BLANE** — Hodalki's Orpheum Ball Band, Springfield, Ill.
7. **BOB ROTH** — Bob Grant's Trocadero Band
8. **CARL SKINNER** — S.S. Corinthian Orchestra
9. **SAMMY WEISS** — Radio and Recording Artist (N.Y.)
10. **JACK WALTZER** — Joe Rine's Orchestra (N.Y.)
11. **KENNY PLUMMER** — Denver Theatre Orchestra
12. **ZEKE LENGA** — Radio and Recording Artist (N.Y.)

Endorser page from 1939 and 1941 catalogs

Billy Gladstone

In the anchor position of the new artist roster introduced in the 1939 catalog was the legendary Billy Gladstone. This page (with different text) faced the page above with the rest of the endorsers. Gladstone was not only a great drummer, but also was an inventor with 15 successful patents already to his credit. In addition to six pages devoted to Gretsch-Gladstone drums, the catalog listed a Gladstone remote hihat. Gladstone would be conspicuously absent from post-war catalogs; by that time he was working on his own line of drums. (He continued to buy shells from Gretsch for his drums.)

Carnegie Hall, December 29, 1945

An elite group of percussion world personalities that included manufacturers, executive staff, production supervisors and top endorsers gathered at the venerable Carnegie Hall in late December of 1945 to present a "Drum Demonstration And Clinic" sponsored by the Fred Gretsch Mfg. Co. The event was billed as the first civilian activity for the recently discharged Master of Ceremonies Phil Grant, who was presented as Gretsch's head of the Educational Department. This event marked the first time that a rudimental snare drum solo had been performed in Carnegie Hall.

The Program

The Rudiments of Snare Drumming and Their Application in Music
Frank Kutak and Phil Grant of the Goldman Band
Demonstration of Bass Drum and Cymbal Technique
Gus Helmecke– Formerly of Sousa's Band– America's Foremost Bass Drummer
Ensemble Drumming   Symphony In Drums
Goldman Band Drum Section
Specialty Number
Viola Smith of Phil Spitalny's All-Girl Orchestra
Rudimental Drum Solo   The Downfall of Paris
Al Moffatt– Former Instructor Navy School of Music
The Tympani- Technique and Use in the Symphony Orchestra
Saul Goodman of the New York Philharmonic Orchestra
The Art Of Dance Drumming
James Crawford of Cafe Society Uptown
Accompanied on the Vibraphone by Phil Grant

1940s

SHELLY MANNE

Star pupil of Billy Gladstone, and winner of the Down Beat Poll for 1947, Shelly's superb work with the Stan Kenton Band has skyrocketed him to the top of the drumming world.

DICK SHANAHAN

A thoroughly schooled drummer whose fine work with the Les Brown and Charlie Barnet bands has won him a host of admirers.

JO JONES

Mainstay of the Count Basie rhythm section, Jo's great technique and fine beat make him one of the all-time "Drumming Greats."

LOUIE BELLSON

One of the outstanding drummers of today, Louie's technical skill and brilliant solos have made him a top favorite.

DAVE TOUGH

His solid beat, driving power and crisp technique have been the inspiration behind some of America's top-flight bands.

GEORGE WETTLING

A veteran of the Paul Whiteman, Artie Shaw, Bunny Berigan and Red Norvo bands, now playing the many intricate and difficult radio programs from WJZ, New York.

1940s

Here are the Gretsch Drum Outfits played by winners in the recent Downbeat and Metronome popularity polls

---

SHELLY MANNE

1 ea.—X4247—Gretsch Broadkaster Bass Drum, 22x14	$118.50
1 ea.—X4157—Gretsch Broadkaster Snare Drum, 14x5½	80.00
1 ea.—X4415—Gretsch Broadkaster Tom Tom, 12x8	58.00
1 ea.—X4418—Gretsch Broadkaster Tom Tom, 16x16 w/legs	85.60
1 ea.— 4805—All Height Cymbal Holder	6.50
2 ea.— 4826—Cymbal Floor Stand with built on tilters @ $10.25	20.50
1 pr.— 4960—Disappearing Drum Spurs	4.50
1 ea.— 4955—Floating Action Pedal	21.50
1 ea.— 4840—Hi-Hat Pedal	14.00
1 ea. Buck Rogers Snare Drum Stand	19.00
1 ea.— 4942—Rail Consolette Tom Tom Holder	13.50
1 set—PX4480—Gretsch Timbales	82.50
1 ea.— 4971—Bass Drum Floor Holder	4.50

SHELLY'S CYMBAL SETUP
1 pr. 15" Hi-Hats, 1-15" Medium, 1-20" Medium, 1-22" Medium, 1-19" Crash

---

LOUIE BELLSON

2 pcs.—X4269—Gretsch Broadkaster Bass Drums, 24x14 @ $127.50	$255.00
1 pc.—X4157—Gretsch Broadkaster Snare Drum, 14x5½	80.00
2 pcs.—X4415—Gretsch Broadkaster Tom Tom, 12x8 with holders @ $66.50	133.00
1 pc.—X4418—Gretsch Broadkaster Tom Tom, 16x16 w/legs	85.60
1 pc.—XSpec.—Gretsch Broadkaster Tom Tom, 14x16 w/legs	78.60
1 pc.— 4807—All-Height Cymbal Holder	5.25
3 pcs.— 4826—Cymbal Floor Stand @ $10.25	30.75
2 pr.— 4960—Disappearing Spurs @ $4.50	9.00
2 pcs.— 4955—Floating Action Pedal @ $21.50	43.00
1 pc.— 4840—Hi-Hat Pedal	14.00
1 pc.— 4982—Heavy Duty Drum Stand	7.75
2 ea.— 5436—Pratt Tone Control @ $6.50	13.00
2 pcs.— 4955—Bass Drum Pedal @ $21.50	43.00

LOUIE'S CYMBAL SETUP
1 pr. 15" Hi-Hats, 1-15" Medium, 1-16" Medium, 1-18" Medium, 1-22" Medium

---

MAX ROACH

1 ea.—X4249—Gretsch Broadkaster Bass Drum, 20x14	$100.00
1 ea.—X4175—Max Roach model Snare Drum	72.00
1 ea.—X4416—Gretsch Broadkaster Tom Tom, 13x9	60.00
1 ea.—X4418—Gretsch Broadkaster Tom Tom, 16x16 w/legs	85.60
1 ea.— 4805—All Height Cymbal Holder	6.50
2 ea.—4826—Cymbal Floor Stands @ $10.25	20.50
1 pr.—4960—Disappearing Drum Spurs	4.50
1 ea.—4955—Floating Action Pedal	21.50
1 ea.—4840—Hi-Hat Pedal	14.00
1 ea.—4982—Snare Drum Stand	7.75

MAX'S CYMBAL SETUP
1 pr. 15" Hi-Hats, 18" Ride, 16" Ride, 20" Medium

JO JONES

1 ea.—X4269—Gretsch Broadkaster Bass Drum, 24x14	$127.50
1 ea.—X4153—Gretsch Broadkaster Snare Drum, 14x6½	82.50
1 ea.—X4416—Gretsch Broadkaster Tom Tom, 13x9	60.00
2 ea.—X4418—Gretsch Broadkaster Tom Tom, 16x16 w/legs @ $85.60	171.20
2 ea.—4826—Cymbal Floor Stand @ $10.25	20.50
1 pr.—4964—Giant Bass Drum Spurs	2.50
1 ea.—4956—Heyn Pedal	19.00
1 ea.—4840—Hi-Hat Pedal	14.00
1 ea.—4982—Snare Drum Stand	7.75
1 ea.—4942—Rail Consolette Tom Tom Holder	13.50

JO'S CYMBAL SETUP
13" Hi-Hats, 18" Medium, 15" Crash, 18" Ride

DON LAMOND

1 ea.—X4247—Gretsch Broadkaster Bass Drum, 22x14	$118.50
1 ea.—X4157—Gretsch Broadkaster Snare Drum, 14x5½	80.00
1 ea.—X4416—Gretsch Broadkaster Tom Tom, 13x9	60.00
1 ea.—X4418—Gretsch Broadkaster Tom Tom, 16x16, w/legs	85.60
1 ea.—X4805—All Height Cymbal Holder	6.50
2 ea.—4826—Cymbal Floor Stand with built on tilters @ $10.25	20.50
1 pr.—4960—Disappearing Drum Spurs	4.50
1 ea.—4955—Floating Action Pedal	21.50
1 ea.—4840—Hi-Hat Pedal	14.00
1 ea.—4982—Snare Drum Stand	7.75
1 ea.—4942—Rail Consolette Tom Tom Holder	13.50

DON'S CYMBAL SETUP
1 pr. 14" Hi-Hats, 18" Top, 20" Medium, 20" Ride

ROY HARTE

1 ea.—X4247—Gretsch Broadkaster Bass Drum, 22x14	$118.50
1 ea.—X4175—Max Roach model Snare Drum	72.00
1 ea.—X4415—Gretsch Broadkaster Tom Tom, 12x8	58.50
1 ea.—X4418—Gretsch Broadkaster Tom Tom, 16x16 w/legs	85.60
1 ea.—X4419—Gretsch Broadkaster Tom Tom, 18x16 w/legs	99.50
2 ea.—4826—Cymbal Floor Stand @ $10.25	20.50
1 pr.—4960—Disappearing Drum Spurs	4.50
1 ea.—4955—Floating Action Pedal	21.50
1 ea.—4940—Hi-Hat Pedal	14.00
1 ea.—4982—Snare Drum Stand	7.75
1 ea.—4940—Heavy Duty Tom Tom Holder	8.50
1 ea.—5430—Jimmy Pratt Bass Drum Control	6.50
1 ea.—4971—Bass Drum Floor Holder	4.50

ROY'S CYMBAL SETUP
15" Hi-Hat, 17" Medium, 16" Crash, 21" Medium

ART BLAKEY

1 ea.—X4249—Gretsch Broadkaster Bass Drum, 20x14	$100.00
1 ea.—X4157—Gretsch Broadkaster Snare Drum, 14x5½	80.00
1 ea.—X4416—Gretsch Broadkaster Tom Tom, 13x9	60.00
1 ea.—X4418—Gretsch Broadkaster Tom Tom, 16x16 w/legs	85.60
1 ea.— 4805—All Height Cymbal Holders	6.50
1 ea.—4826—Cymbal Floor Stand	10.25
1 pr.—4960—Disappearing Drum Spurs	4.50
1 ea.—4955—Floating Action Pedal	21.50
1 ea.—4840—Hi-Hat Pedal	14.00
1 ea.—4982—Snare Drum Stand	7.75

ART'S CYMBAL SETUP
15" Hi-Hat, 20" Medium, 18" Ride

Kitty Kelly
Billed in the 1950s as
"The World's Greatest Female Drummer."
One fan commented that he saw her approach the stage in a sequined evening dress like this. The dress was so form-fitting that she had to take tiny steps. When she got to the drum throne, she reached down for a zipper that opened the side of her dress so she could straddle the snare drum. As recently as 2012 she demonstrated she can still play; the youtube video can be accessed at: http://www.youtube.com/watch?v=5sCoBVf485U
kitty kelly 2012

KITTY KELLY and her Escorts
The Worlds Greatest Female Drummer

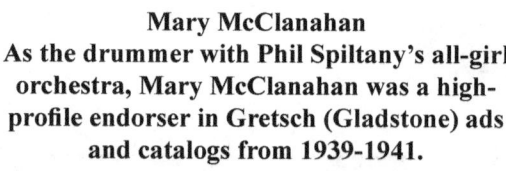

Viola Smith was a WFL/Ludwig endorser for most of her career, but played this Gretsch kit when she was with Phil Spitalny's all-female orchestra. (1942-1944) Her NAMM oral history interview (conducted one month before her 100th birthday) can be accessed at www.namm.org/library/oral-history/viola-smith

Mary McClanahan
As the drummer with Phil Spiltany's all-girl orchestra, Mary McClanahan was a high-profile endorser in Gretsch (Gladstone) ads and catalogs from 1939-1941.

ANDY FLORIO
(1927-1998)

Andrea "Andy" N. Florio, was a big band drummer, inventor, and character actor. He served in the Army at the end of World War II and performed with President Harry S. Truman's Official Air Forces Band. Florio also appeared with the big bands of Benny Goodman, Les Brown, Tommy Dorsey and Lawrence Welk. Because of his musical abilities, Florio landed a number of film roles as a bandleader or drummer. He was also a skilled horseman who often played Indians in westerns. (He was an Indian in the tv series *F-Troop*.)

Florio did some drum equipment design work, with the Buck Rogers snare stand and Gretsch Micro-Sensitive strainer among his proudest accomplishments.

Florio passed away in 1998 at the age of 70.
(additional photos in appendix IV, pages 258,259)

Florio at age 11 playing his first Gretsch set with his older brother's orchestra in Pennsylvania.

RAVEN GREY EAGLE
Andy Florio AKA Raven Grey Eagle

ANDY FLORIO and his ORCHESTRA   MOTION PICTURES-TV-RADIO

MAX ROACH

MAX ROACH—Gretsch Broadkasters are the choice of Max Roach, one of the greatest of the modern drummers. Max says "Those new Gretsch drums are the greatest."

60 Broadway
Brooklyn, N. Y.

FRED. GRETSCH MFG. CO.
Drum Makers Since 1883

218 So. Wabash Ave.
Chicago, Ill.

MAX ROACH—Top Jazz favorite, with his GRETSCH Progressive Jazz Outfit

LOUIE BELLSON

1958:
2 14x22,
2 9x13,
16x16,
5.5x14

Louie Bellson plays Gretsch Drums

You can too. Try an outfit like Louie's or specify your own set at your dealers. Write Gretsch, 60 Broadway, Brooklyn 11, N.Y. for Diamond Jubilee drum catalog. (This is our 75th year.)

Louie's special outfit, finished in Jet Black Nitron, contains: two 22"x14" bass drums; two 13"x9" tomtoms; 16"x16" tomtom; 14"x5½" snare drum, plus exclusive Gretsch Disappearing Drum Spurs, which Louie designed.

SHELLY

SHELLY MANNE: The country's Number One Drummer, according to the DownBeat Magazine annual poll. His work with the Stan Kenton Band is nationally recognized. Shelly uses the Gretsch-Gladstone drum and considers the tone and performance "TOPS."

FRED. GRETSCH MFG. CO.
Drum Makers Since 1883
60 Broadway, Brooklyn, N. Y. — 218 So. Wabash Ave., Chicago, Ill.

REMO BELLI
Top West Coast Recording Artist GRETSCH Drums

Harold Jones

Elvin R Jones — AND HIS GRETSCH DRUMS

Chico Hamilton

Chico Hamilton AND HIS GRETSCH DRUMS

CHICO HAMILTON with his Progressive Jazz Outfit by GRETSCH

Chico Hamilton

Featuring the Drums **FRED BONNER**

Charles Persip

Charles Persip AND HIS GRETSCH DRUMS

ART BLAKEY

GRETSCH ART BLAKEY'S JAZZ MESSENGERS

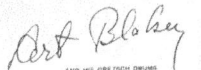

Art Blakey AND HIS GRETSCH DRUMS

CHARLIE PERRY: Although still a youngster, Charlie has done stints with the bands of Benny Goodman, Stan Kenton, Skitch Henderson, and Jimmy Dorsey. Gretsch Broadkaster drums dramatize his spectacular style.

FRED. GRETSCH MFG. CO.
Drum Makers Since 1883
60 Broadway, Brooklyn, N. Y. — 218 So. Wabash Ave., Chicago, Ill.

Tony Williams

1958 Catalog

Elvin Jones | Herb Brockstein | Jo Jones | Don Lamond | Mel Lewis | Sonny Payne

Jack Adams | Louie Bellson | Art Blakey | Charlie Perry | Charlie Persip | Jimmie Pratt | Bill Richmond

Kenny Clarke | Chuck Flores | Chico Hamilton | Max Roach | Art Taylor | Sam Ulano | George Wettling

1963 Catalog

Phil Grant — Paul Fein — Dick Horowitz
The Goldman Band percussion section

Max Roach

Art Blakey

"Philly" Joe Jones

Chico Hamilton

Elvin Jones

Mel Lewis

Art Taylor

Charlie Persip

Don Lamond

Sonny Payne

Jimmy Cobb

1966 Catalog

ELVIN JONES

ANTHONY WILLIAMS

MAX ROACH

ART BLAKEY

DON LAMOND

SONNY PAYNE

CHICO HAMILTON

MEL LEWIS

CHARLIE WAITTS AND HIS GREAT GRETSCH DRUMS

The iconic Charlie Watts of The Rolling Stones is perhaps the most high-profile Gretsch artist of the last five decades. Although he is by definition a top rock star and rather inaccessable, Charlie does maintain many contacts in the world of custom drum makers and Gretsch buffs.

Ron Enyard
Billed as the mid-west's #1 Jazz Drummer, Ron's playing credits include Roland Kirk, Herb Ellis, Barney Kessel, Woody Shaw and many other top names. Officially a Gretsch endorser from 1973 to 1982, he was a part of the NYC Gretsch scene much earlier and still plays Gretsch today. With the change of ownership at the end of the Baldwin era, Ron was told that his official endorsement association was terminating because he was not getting enough MTV play.

Carl Palmer's first professional drum set was a Silver Sparkle Gretsch kit that he purchased from Drum City in London in 1967. It was a 14x22 bass drum with 9x13 and 16x16 toms and a 5.5x14 snare drum. He used that kit to record *The Crazy World of Arthur Brown*, which included his first number 1 U.S. song *Fire (1969.)*

Palmer also used the silver Gretsch kit to record the first two *Emerson Lake & Palmer* albums. By the time ELP went on their first U.S. tour in the spring of 1971, Palmer had switched to Ludwig.

About the time of ELP's last album in 1978, Palmer returned to Gretsch for about a year. (poster at left from 1978.)

0 to 90 in 12 months

The Charlie Roy era of Gretsch witnessed the most spectacular artist roster growth Gretsch had ever experienced.

Thanks to the efforts of Karl Dustman, a world-class roster was assembled in under a year. This "photo G" ad ran in magazines with general Gretsch information in the center area where the non-illustrated artists are mentioned here.

James Black *James Black Ensemble*, **Barbara Borden** *Alive*, **Jack Boydstun** *Jana Jae*, **Tony Braunagel** *Independant*, **Tony Brock** *Rod Stewart*, **Clyde Brooks** *Independant*, **Roy Burns** *Independant*, **Greg Caputo** *Independant*, **Roy Clark** *Himself*, **Phil Collins** *Genesis*, **Jeff Cook** *Alabama*, **Joe Cusatis** *Art Davis Trio*, **Jimmy Day** *Independant*, **Paul DeLong** *Max Webster*, **John Dents** *John Dents Reunion Band*, **Marc Droubay** *Survivor*, **Mike Edlin** *B.J. Thomas*, **Calep Emphrey** *James Cotton Blues Band*, **Gary Ferguson** *Independant*, **Dragan Gajic Gajo** *Foreign Artist*, **Alsonso Garibaldi** *Pat Collins*, **Bruce Gary** *Independant*, **Richard Gates** *Nantucket*, **Lloyd Green** *Independant*, **Jeff Hamilton** *L.A. Four*, **Mark Herndon** *Alabama*, **Ken Jansen** *Tammy Wynette*, **Doug Jernigan** *Independant*, **Chip Kidd** *Fullerton Brothers*, **Scott Kirkpatrick** *Firefall*, **Benjie King** *Independant*, **Graham Lear** *Santana*, **Linda Mackley** *Thrills*, **Mat Marucci** *Independant*, **Harvey Mason** *Independant*, **Tony Mathews** *Independant*, **J.R. Mitchell** *J.R. Mitchell Universal Ensemble*, **Jonathon Moffett** *The Jacksons*, **Charlie Perry** *Independant*, **Slim Jim Phantom** *Stray Cats*, **Ray Pierce** *Traces*, **Mark Sanders** *Tower of Power*, **Rick Shlosser** *James Taylor*, **Kenny Soule** *P.K.M.*, **Michael Stephens** *Independant*, **Melvin Stroud** *Independant*, **Tony Thompson** *David Bowie*, **Buck Trent** *Roy Clark*, **Charlie Watts** *Rolling Stones*, **Skip White** *Commander Cody*, **Jim Wolfe** *John Anderson Band*, **Donnie Wynn** *Robert Palmer*, **Jerry Brown** *Lionel Richie*

"While there were never any endorsement fees paid to artists, we did provide drums ON LOAN during the endorsement contract period. Phil Collins, Harvey Mason, and many others were agreeable to these terms and conditions. We used the same strategy on top educators such as Roy Burns, Jerry Brown, Barbara Borden and others."
Karl Dustman

"We took the awareness BEYOND the "Black Jazz Drummer" image, while not abandoning this foundation that Gretsch had for decades. By approaching artists in all musical forms (country, rock, pop) along with the theme parks like Opryland, Dollywood, Disney, etc. Gretsch made impact on musical styles that had never been approached before."
Karl Dustman

1983 Poster Series (22x28)

ROY BURNS

Tony Williams 1984

CLYDE BROOKS 1984

JERRY CARRIGAN 1984

Phil Collins

I love the Gretsch sound! The warmth, tone, resonance & feel are so rich and they tune to a pure and beautiful note.
Just about all of my favorite drummers played Gretsch- Art Blakey, Max Roach, Philly Joe Jones, Elvin Jones and Tony Williams; So, I was in love with that sound before I even owned a set of Gretsch. Yep, love them & that's why I play them!
Cindy Blackman Santana

Gretsch News

2006 *Gretsch News* Artist Photos

Rob Bourdon
Linkin Park

Charlie Watts
The Rolling Stones

Paul "Phinky" John, Jr.
Alicia Keys

Mike Marsh
Dashboard Confessional

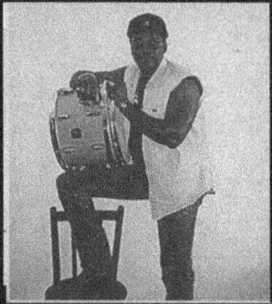
Alvino Bennett
Bryan Ferry/Robin Trower

Brad Wilk
Audioslave

Jack Gavin
Nashville Touring Pro

Van Romaine
Steve Morse

Stanton Moore
Galactic

Scott Underwood
Train

David Derge
Independent

Nick Hodgson
Kaiser Chiefs

Duane Norman
Independent

Pat McDonald
Charlie Daniels Band

Joe LaBarbera
Joe LaBarbera Quintet

Bill Stewart
John Scofield, Pat Metheny

Terry Silverlight
Independent/Studio

Slim Jim Phantom
Stray Cats

Jarred Wrennell
Steriogram

Scott Savage
Jaci Velasquez/Chris Rice

Tommy Wells
Independent/Studio

Paul Goldberg
Independent/Studio

Paul Alexander Gonzalez
Paulina Rubio

2006 *Gretsch News* Artist Photos

Cindy Blackman
Independant/Lenny Kravitz

Phil Collins
Solo Artist/Genesis

Stan Frazier
Sugar Ray

Denny Seiwell
Paul McCartney & Wings

Bruce Gary
The Knack/Studio

Vinnie Colaiuta
Independent/Studio Legend

Mark Schulman
Cher/Stevie Nicks

Bill Rieflin
R.E.M.

Jay Bellerose
Beck/Paula Cole

Nate Wood
Independent

Wesley Pryor
Mark Chesnutt

Brett Clark
SheDaisy

Lucrezio de Seta
Independent (Italy)

David Northrup
Travis Tritt

Sebastien Grainger
Death From Above 1979

Ian Browne
Independent

Gregg Stocki
Marty Stuart

Makoto Izumitani
Gwen Stefani

David Huff
Independent/Producer

Forrest Robinson
India.Arie

Chris McHugh
Keith Urban

Jesse Labovitz
No Warning

Oscar D'Auria
Independent/Studio

2007 Gretsch News Artist Photo Updates

Steve Ferrone
Tom Petty

J.J. Freire
Bacilos

Oscar Musiate
Juan Gabriel

Chris Cester
Jet

Daniel Davison
Norma Jean

Paul Thomson
Franz Ferdinand

Karl Brazil
James Blunt

Sam Fogarino
Interpol

Zach Sims
Day of Fire

Rich Russo
Andrew W.K.

Bryan Keeling
Shooter Jennings

Pierre Belleville
Lofofora (France)

Christian Vander
Magma

Cindy Blackman
Lenny Kravitz

Mark Schulman
Pink

Gregg Stocki
Tracy Lawrence

Martin Stoeck
Pur

Daniel Schild
Blaze

Dave Mette
Laith Al Deen

2008 Gretsch News Artist Photo Updates

Rick Woolstenhulme, Jr.
Lifehouse

Stefanie Eulinberg
Kid Rock

Ryan MacMillan
Matchbox Twenty

Lemar Carter
Joss Stone

Garrett Goodwin
Carrie Underwood

Ro Krom
Kraak & Smaak

Alex Rodriguez
Saosin

M. Shawn "Clown" Crahan
Slipknot/Dirty Little Rabbits

Lucrezia de Seta
Independant (Italy)

Slim Jim Phantom
Stray Cats

Warren Oakes
Against Me

Francesco Mendolia
Elio Volpini

Sammy J. Watson
MT. Helium

Rob Bourdon
Linkin Park

2009 Gretsch News Artist Photo Updates

Derek Kerswill

Eddie Fisher

Vinnie Colaiuta

Stanton Moore

Mark Schulman

Stefanie Eulinberg

Paul "Phinkky" John, Jr.

Bryan Keeling

2010 Gretsch News Artist Photo Updates

Billy Bob Thornton
The Boxmasters

Nick Price
Meg & Dia

Matt Walker
Morrissey

Derek Kerswill
Unearth

Brad Pemberton
Ryan Adams

Eddie Fisher
OneRepublic

Bart Robley
Sam Morrison Band

Alvino Bennett
Dave Mason

Hannah Ford
Peace Love and Drums

Joe LaBarbera
Joe LaBarbera Quintet

Darren Taylor
Airborne Toxic Event

Marl Schulman
Pink

"I have been listening to the sound of Gretsch drums on my classic rock and roll records for my entire life. To be part of their amazing family is a dream come true. A lifetime achievement for me! I am always so excited to play their classic and vintage tones for modern singer/songwriters like Jason Mraz!" **Michael Bram**

"Over the years you just eventually find out some of your heros, although they Happily Endorsed Various other Drum Companies for live performance their recorded sound, the sound that drew you in and connected with you was, in fact GRETSCH drums. (Jeff Porcaro, Vinnie Colauta, JR Robinson, Carlos Vega, Curt Bisquera, etc.) That GREAT Gretsch Sound, Probably the most recorded drum sound ever! It defines my sound!"
David Northrup

"Grestch is home to me. When I finally came to endorse Gretsch, I was like a giddy kid. These drums were always the cream of the crop when I was growing up. When I got hired to do sessions in the 80s and 90s the drum of choice for nearly every producer and engineer was Gretsch. When I had a vision for a signature snare drum, Gretsch made that a reality and we are now celebrating that success together. I also might add that Fred and Dinah have become wonderful friends of my family. I'm a grateful man because I get to play the best sounding drums in the world that have deep roots in the country in which I was born"
Mark Schulman

"We were out in Europe supporting Kid Rock and me Stephanie (kids drummer) just got along great which isn't hard with her as she is such a sweet person and hilarious and a monster behind the drums . She got me in touch with Kim at Gretsch and I was very honored to soon after become an endorsee for them . That was around summer of 2007 I believe . Always wanted to play Gretsch and will always thank Stefanie Eulinberg for getting me on touch with them ! , love ya Steph!! **Rich Beddoe**

Jimmie Fadden,, Nitty Gritty Dirt Band

"Gretsch drums give me the confidence to be myself in all of the music I make." **Mark Guiliana:**

Chris Infusino

"I bought my first Gretsch drum set in 1966 from Jack Adams at Jack's Drum Shop in Boston and have been playing Gretsch ever since. I just love the sound, the feel and the look of these drums".
Joe LaBarbera

"With Gretsch, I feel like I'm a part of a rock solid piece of musical history. I love these drums, and God bless Gretsch!" **Tiki Pasillas**

"Gretsch has always been my ideal recorded drum sound. It is the sound I hear in my head, as well, as the perfect drum sound. I am a Gretsch guy through and through." **Tommy Wells**

Rich Russo

: When I was growing up in Colorado I always considered Gretsch to be the Rolls Royce of American made drums. It truly is an honor to be on their endorsement roster. Rich Russo: Drummer for Andrew WK. I've been a Gretsch endorser since 2006. I am pleased to be a part of the Gretsch Family. **Bart Robley**

: "As soon as I sat down behind a Gretsch kit, I knew it would be my home for a long time. Only the best comes from a legacy like Gretsch" **Caleb Crosby**

"So honored to be apart of the Gretsch family, because it's always been a dream of mine to play drums that the masters play. A true affirmation of my hard work is to be associated with Gretsch, so I am thankful that my musical contribution and hard work has been recognized and affirmed by being able to exclusively play these drums every performance and studio session. "**Ulysses Owens Jr**

DATING GRETSCH DRUMS

The 1959 album cover on this page is well known to many Gretsch collectors because it offers a number of insights into dating Gretsch drums. It is common for collectors to rely on catalogs for production clues, but catalogs were not always printed annually and sometimes used old photos.

John Sheridan's observations and comments on Manny Albam's 1959 "Drum Feast" LP jacket:
This picture seems to present a number of Gretsch features in print for the first time.
These include: -The Gretsch "drum" logo on front bass drum head.   -The finish; Champagne Sparkle.
-Diamond-shaped 4820 floor tom brackets (replacing "Gladstone-tube" style).
-Fully die-cast "beaded" hoops, including 12" tom.
-"Flush-base" hi-hat, cymbal, and snare drum stands with new "disc-shaped" rubber feet.
Other features that we know premiered by September of 1958 but had not been seen much yet:
-"Milled" snare gates on snare-side hoops, not "molded"   -New T-handle rods & claws
It is also interesting to note that the "snap-in" key holder for the snare drum is not there yet.
Its first catalog appearance is on the cover of (& within) the 1961 catalog.

BADGES, LABELS, SERIAL NUMBERS

Gretsch began to use labels and assign serial numbers by about 1962. Date stamps were used inside the shell prior to that, and have been documented as early as 1946 and as late as 1957. Many older drums have no date stamp, it was rather random.

For many years it was accurate to say that Gretsch serial numbers were not useful in determining the age of the drum simply because the Gretsch company itself had no way of making that determination. It was not until collectors began to gather data that patterns become known and the numbers became meaningful.

I will follow the lead of Rick Gier in referring to John Sheridan's rule of thumb for Round Badge drums simply as "Sheridan's Rule." **Sheridan's Rule states that four digit serial numbers are early 1960s, five digit are mid-60s, and six digit are late 60s.** (In his book, Gier refines that rule. Gier's "Sheridan's Rule Refined" is arrived at by overlaying Gier's dating guide onto Sheridan's rule. The result: Sheridan's "early 60s" becomes the years 1962-1963 and involves 9,000 four digit serial numbers. Sheridan's "mid-60s" becomes the years 1963-1968 and involves 90,000 five digit serial numbers. The "late 60s" becomes the years 1968-1969 and involves 17,000 six digit serial numbers.)

Rick Gier has spent five years studying over 5,400 drums and has documented that round-badge drums can be dated with some degree of confidence and the total production quantities can be estimated. Rick's research has been published in a separate booklet published by Rebeats titled *Dating of Vintage Gretsch Drums Based on Serial Numbers: Challenging the Legend, Lore and Lies*. Many notes from that publication appear in this book's dating guide. Gier's book includes a master chart listing all serial number sequences as well as badges and other production clues. I've attempted to credit Rick appropriately wherever he is quoted– watch for comments in italics that are introduced with a bold **GIER:** (an example follows)

GIER: *Gretsch reused serial numbers, with most serial numbers appearing three times from the early 1960s though the 1980s. Restarts occurred in about 1971 and about 1984. It is apparent that Gretsch used serial numbers in roughly numerical order each time it worked through the sequences. When Gretsch changed a physical characteristic like label style, badge style, wrap/finish or type of hardware, those changes are closely linked to particular serial number ranges. With remarkably few exceptions, there are clear and distinct serial numbers which represent the transition points for these changing characteristics. If serial numbers were not issued sequentially, these distinct serial number transition points would not be identifiable. Likewise, original receipts and reports of original purchase dates of drums with known serial numbers track consistently with time. The later the drum sold, the later the serial number is in the orderly sequence. It is important to emphasize that the higher serial numbers are not necessarily indicative of later drums. The use and reuse of serial numbers must be understood to place drums in their proper order.*

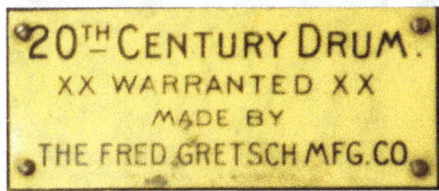

20th Century Badges, the earliest Gretsch badges applied to drum shells, 1912-1920

Gretsch American
Decal and shell engraving are from 1920s drums. This design is also seen in the 1927 catalog.

This badge has been found on drums from the late-1930s to the mid-1950s.

Gretsch Gladstone 1939
This insignia was hot-stamped directly into the pearl covering of some Gretsch Gladstone snare drums. Others had the rectangular badge at right while still others simply had the round Gretsch badge.

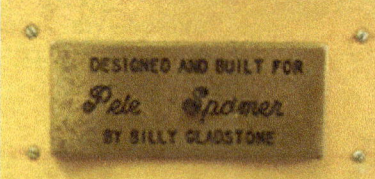

Customized nameplate from a one-of-a-kind gold-plated brass Billy Gladstone drum which evidently was his personal instrument.

Billy Gladstone hand-made drums had personalized name plates for the purchaser and the 3-way key holder.

In addition to the round badge, most (but not all) Max Roach models had this distinctive badge. Lee Ruff estimates that about 70% were fitted with this badge. They were fastened with small nails that did not go all the way through the shell and are often missing.

The Gretsch Round Badge

The famous Gretsch "Round badge" was introduced in the 1930s and was used until about mid-1969. Updated versions began in 2003 with the 120th Anniversary models. Snare drum and bass drum badges were secured with a center grommet providing a vent hole in the shell. Tom-tom round badges were tacked on with (a number of different types of) upholstery tacks. In most eras, a typical Gretsch kit would have had three types of badges for snare drum (with vent), bass drum (with larger vent), and toms (tacked). Most snare drums were fitted with 3/8" brass grommets. Some snare drums, the occasional tom, and all bass drums, were fitted with 17/32" grommets.

A great many variations of the round badge were used in the 30+ year "first round badge era." The only generalization that the author will present here is that the "skinny stick" badges were applied to drums from the 1930s into the early 1960s and that "thick stick" badges were applied to drums from the late 1950s until 1969. Gretsch obtained their badges from a number of different vendors, some of whom are identified by name with an imprint or ink marking on the backside of the badge. Drum historian Rick Gier (with the assistance of Bill Maley and Jim Beebe) at this writing have recently begun a study of the incidence of the various badges and will likely publish his findings when patterns can be better documented.

SKINNY STICK
1930s into early 1960s

Snare Drums

Bass Drums,
some snare drums, some toms
some toms

tom toms
(note the size, spacing, & tighter arc of the "Drum Makers" text)

THICK STICK
late 1950s to 1969

A few of the tacks used over the years, from very rare on the left to most common on the right

Lee Ruff: *"For the most part, starting in the late '50s, the length of badge grommets stayed the same. So the "look" of a grommet when viewed from the inside of a drum, is not always the same. I have seen original drums where the grommet does not completely go through the shell. I have also seen original drums where the grommet is barely flared or not flared at all. Some show a slightly flared edge, and some are rolled over. It all depends on the shell thickness. In the '50s and earlier, there were shorter grommets as well as aluminum and nickel-plated grommets. On many snare drums from the '50s, the grommets do not go completely through the shell. They were simply pressed in. Of course, the metal snare drums used the grommets with the thicker external lip. In the octagon badge era and later, many drums came through with grommets with split ends, that were simply hammered flat from the factory. When authenticating a Gretsch drum with a breather hole, this must all be considered."*

The two badges at left and right have been combined in the center image to demonstrate some of the differences that researchers are considering: size and shape of the drum sticks, the size and style of fonts used for the text, the curvature of the text lines, the distances of various raised impressions from each other and from the badge edge.

Counterfeits

This is an example of a counterfeit round badge, sent to the author by a foreign producer in about 1995. Since that time, unauthorized reproduction badges have become much more sophisticated with "aged" patinas.

Counterfeiters have also gotten much better at grommet work. Not many years ago it was quite easy to spot most grommets that had been replaced. Given the range of different looks that Gretsch grommets have had (see Lee Ruff's comments above), it is harder to be sure with Gretsch than with some other brands. If you have doubts, consult an expert!

Variations

Note the right-side drumstick by the letter H in Gretsch; this is almost always slanted upward rather than down

Copper; most round badges were stamped brass

A skinny stick variation: badge back stamped "Robbins Co Attleboro"

A skinny stick variation; textured "cheesecloth" background

First Gretsch label: OW1   Orange/White with shell guarantee
Gier: *Used on all labeled Round-badge drums and the majority of Stop-Sign Badge #1 drums.*
1962–1975

GIER: Approximate Serial Number Ranges
First Serial Number Sequence
1962   1001 to 6800
1963   6801 to 18400
1964   18401 to 35800
1965   35801 to 55520
1966   55521 to 78720
1967   78721 to 97280
1968   97281 to 111200
1969   111201 to 122800
1970   112801 to 133800
1971   133801 to 136500
Second Serial Number Sequence
1971   00001 to 08300
1972   08301 to 19300
1973   19301 to 30300
1974   30301 to 41300
1975   41301 to 51100

By 1962 (shortly after Gretsch's change from 3-ply to 6-ply shells), the internal orange/white labels began to appear. Rick Gier has documented that Gretsch restarted their serial number sequence two times. The first sequence starts with #1001 in about 1962, continues through 136500 in 1971. The second sequence starts with 00001, continues through 148500.

Model # note: The color of ink used for the model number stamp was, Gier has noted, exclusively black until about 36000 of the first sequence. After that, black and blue seem to have been used interchangeably.

Note that badges and labels did not change styles at the same times.

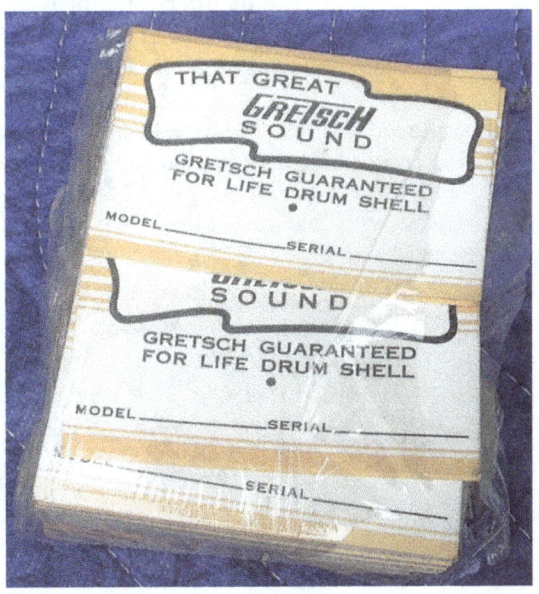

Labels are also counterfeited; this photo is from an April, 2013 Ebay auction.

Gretsch lawyers watch for these violations and aggressively defend their trademarks.

GIER on "leading zeros of first two number sequences:"

Leading Zeros. At times during the early phases of both the First and Second Sequences Gretsch placed zeros in front of the meaningful digits of the serial number. The initial serial numbers of the First Sequence, from about 1000 to about 7000, appeared as four digit numbers without leading zeros. At around number 7000, a leading zero was added, making the serial number appear as a five digit number with a zero as the first digit, i.e.: serial number 9230 became serial number 09230. During the Second Sequence, enough leading zeros were added to make all serial numbers under 10000 five digits long, i.e.: serial number 54 would become 00054 and 706 would become 00706. We do not know if Gretsch did this again in the Third Sequence, as that range of serial numbers is absent from the log.

The presence or absence of leading zeros provides a helpful dating tip. The absence of leading zeros on a serial number less than 7000 indicates a drum from the First Sequence. The presence of leading zeros on a serial number less than number 7000 indicates a drum from the Second Sequence. Unfortunately, the leading zeros on serial numbers from about 7000 to 9999 appear the same whether from the First or Second Sequence.

Other than the way in which leading zeros appeared from 00001 to 07000, the labels used during the early part of the Second Sequence, from 07000 through about 51100, are indistinguishable from those of the First Sequence. They used the same style of paper label. Therefore, from about serial number 7000 through about 52000, one must look to other characteristics to determine is a drum is from the First or Second Sequence.

OW2 photo courtesy of Bill Maley, Classic Vintage Drums, & Rick Gier

Second Gretsch label: OW2   Orange/White
1975–1978

OW2 Serial numbers:
Second sequence, about 51100 to about 75000

The earliest OW2 labels appear to have been cut from rolls of OW1 labels; perforations are still visible below the serial number.

The OW2 labels were used on drums with SSB#1 (Stop Sign Badge #1) and Square badges.

Model # notes: From the first label up until 1973, the model number was machine stamped as seen on the OW1. Rick Gier's research indicates that Gretsch changed to hand-written model numbers at about 22000 in the second sequence. The numbers were for the most part written in green ink with occasional black or blue appearing. Green dominates the second sequence until about number 90000 after which black dominates.

SSB #1

Stop Sign Badge #1   1969-1977
"t-roof" logo above eyelet,
"DRUMS" left of eyelet, "USA" right of eyelet

Serial numbers: (Approximate)
First sequence 117000 to 136500,
Second sequence 00001 to 72000

Introduced in 1969. This marked an end to the era of varying sizes of center holes: all badges were affixed with 3/8" grommets

OW1 with warranty language blacked out
1976–1977
Serial numbers: This label appears in some, but not all, of the range from 61000-67000, second sequence.

Rick Gier's research indicates that Gretsch did not immediately begin blacking out the shell guarantee language when Baldwin purchased Gretsch in 1967 as is commonly thought; this happened about a decade later. Note that the serial number range is within the range of OW2. At this writing only about two dozen are reported.

SQB #1

Square Badge #1 1977-1978
"t-roof" logo with "USA" left of vent, repeated upside down.
Pinkish-copper hue.

Serial numbers: Second sequence,
approximately 72000 to 82000

Badges in the Baldwin era of the early to
mid-1980s were produced by
T & T Label Company of Centerville, Ohio.

Third Gretsch label: OW3 Orange/White 1978–1979

Serial numbers: Second sequence, about 75000 to 90000

Note that this label is very similar to OW2: it is shorter and lacks the thin orange line below the serial number line.

OW3 photo courtesy of Rick Gier

Stop-Sign Badge #2   1978-1979
The rarest of the stop-sign badges. Very similar to SSB#1, except for replacing the slogan under the vent with "Drum Makers Since 1883."

SSB #2 Serial numbers: Second sequence,
approximately 82000 to 92000

SSB #2

Fourth Gretsch label: GW1 (Grey/White)
1979–1983

Fifth Gretsch label: GW2 (Grey/White)
1983–2003

The switch from large stamped number (GW1) to dot matrix small number (GW2) was made at the beginning of October, 1983. The two labels shown here are from the September 1983 internal marketing bulletin announcing the change. The GW1 is the "old version," the GW2 is the "new version."

Serial numbers:
GW1   Second sequence 90000–143000
GW2   Second sequence 143000–148500,
Third sequence 20000 and up.

Model number note: After 2007, the number in the "Model" box refers to the order number rather than the model number of the drum.

SSB #3

Stop Sign Badge #3 1979–1981
"Drop-G" logo, elimination of word
"Drums" left of vent.
Serial numbers:
Second sequence, approximately
98000 to 125000

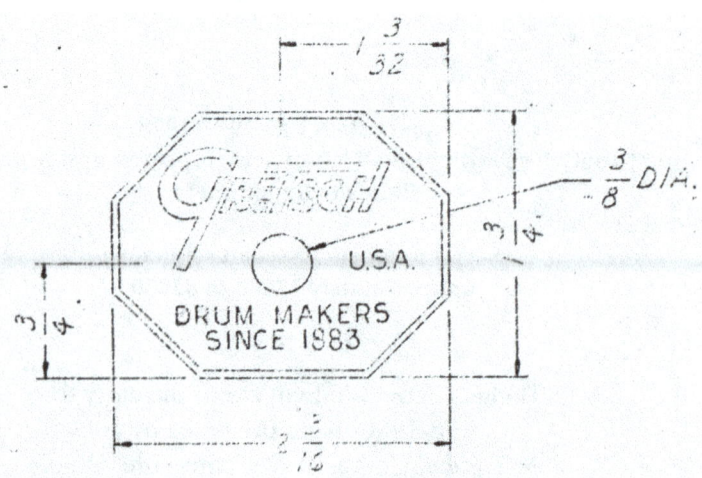

SSB #3 Drawing, from Gretsch archives

Square-badge #2   1982–1998
Serial numbers:
(Approximate)
Second sequence 125000–148500 (1982-1984)
Third sequence 20000+ (1984+)

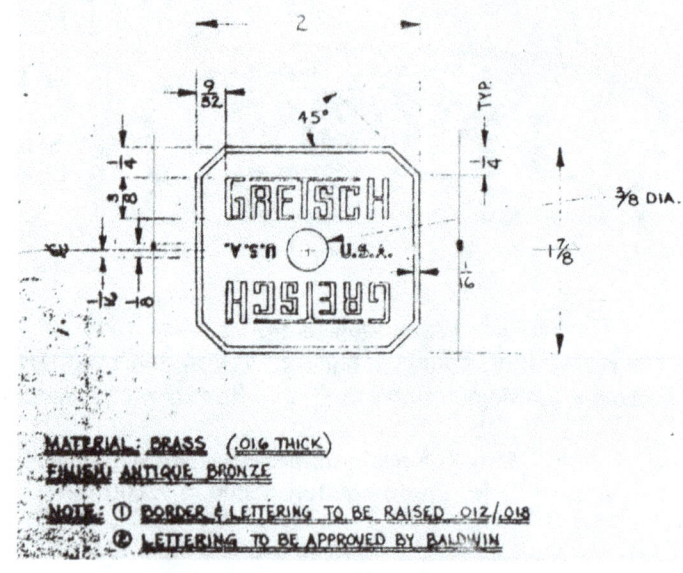

SQB #2 Drawing from Gretsch archives

The 1983 Centennial badge featured the signature of Gretsch owner Charlie Roy until his departure in May of 1984, then the signature of Karl Dustman

This badge is usually referred to by collectors as Square Badge #3, or SQB3

1983 Centennial internal label

Two proposed badge drawings from the Gretsch archives, both dated 1983. Neither went into production.

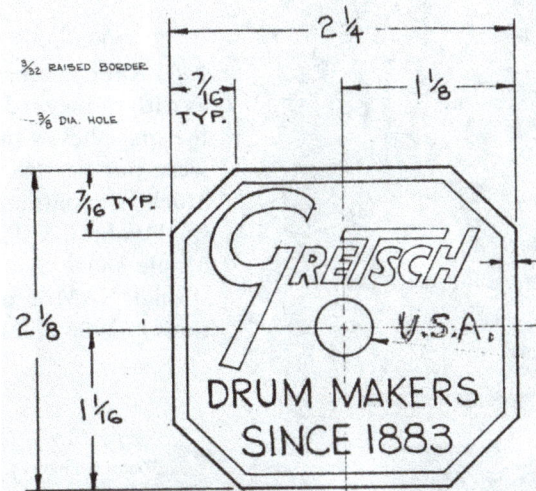

With 4 badge changes in 2 years, it was not unusual for kits to have more than one style of badge within the same set. The back cover of the 1980 catalog showed three types of badges.

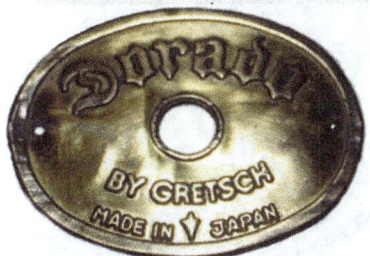

Dorado Series drums, 1973 only

1980s Blackhawk Series

Blackhawk 2003

1998-2005: Square Badge #4 SQB4 Pewter colored, for Broadkaster drums originally, then used on the all-American series Grand Old Flag model, USA Maple drums; American-made shells with import hardware.

Special square badge applied to the Harvey Mason *Grand Old Flag model* 2002 only (Blue version of SQB-5)

SQB5, Square Badge #5: Lighter Sepia finish, more visible circa 1998-2002

2003: 120th Anniversary limited edition drums. First use of the classic round badge since 1969. (3/8" grommet)

Label used on the Vin Yard special models 2006-2007

2006-2007
1983 Anniversary badges with "Vineyard 83" in the space below the vent were put on "New Old Stock" Carpathian Elm, Burl Walnut, & Birdseye Maple snare drums for special NAMM promotions in 2006 & 2007.*

"Drop-G" without USA
Reissue 70s lacquer kits 2004-2005
4000-series snare drums 2004-2012

Only the first two years of New Classics featured the year on the badge; 2004 and 2005.

New Classic limited edition 2005

New Classic Series 2006-2013

SQB6 2006-2008: Square Badge #6
(U.S.A. replaced by "Since 1883")

*note: Gretsch produced 50 one-of-a-kind custom shop snare drums in January of 2006, and 50 more in January 2007. Many of these drums sported vintage badges from the 1979-1983 era.

2002 Gretsch American snare drums

note: The same label with and without the "Gretsch-American" banner was used circa 2003-2006 on many USA Custom Series drums.

2007: Black USA Square Badge, Custom Shop Broadkaster and USA Maple Replacement Badge

Signature Series Harvey Mason 1998-2005

Signature Series Vinnie Colaiuta 1998-2011

2002-2003: Catalina Stage and Elite

2006-2010: Catalina Maple

2010-2013 Catalina Maple

Catalina Club 2003-2013

Renown Maple 2003-2004

Renown Maple 2007-2012
(Renown Maple also used the original '05 Purewood badge 2005-2006.)

Renown Purewood 2006-2013
(Original 2005 badge had "Pure Wood" written below "Renown.")

Revised "drop G" stop sign badge

2004: used in 2004 on the reissue '70s LTD lacquer sets.

2009-2012: Gretsch announced that this "Drop G" badge would be the new spec, updated from Square badge #6.

2003-2012

2008 125th Anniversary label

2009: Gretsch announced that this Grey/White internal shell sticker would be the new spec, though it had already been in use for years. The only difference appears to be that the entire right side is white rather than having a grey border, and the corners are rounded, like a pre-1985 label. Serial number in heavy-type: 2007-2012

2001-2003: Renown Maple, Catalina Stage, Catalina Elite

2001-2013: Badges applied to various "Full Range" snare drums

2010: Special Edition Drop G Badge (Silver/Black) for limited edition Piano Black Lacquer USA Custom kit

Steve Ferrone Series drums 2006-2013

2010-2013: Steve Ferrone signature black brass snare drum

2010-2013: Stanton Moore signature snare drum

2011-2013 Mark Schulman signature snare drum

Renegade series 2011-2013

Energy series 2011-2013

Not pictured: "Free Floating System" badge 2003-2005, "Nighthawk" badge 2005-2013

Black/Pewter Vintage-style re-issue round badge introduced on Brooklyn series drums 2011, with internal label 2011-2013

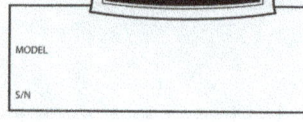

Renown Maple 2013-

The Round Badge Returns to Gretsch USA Custom Drums

In January 2013, Gretsch will reintroduce a round, brass, vent hole badge on all USA Custom drums, including G-4000 Series Metal and G-5000 Series Wood Snare Drums.

The newly designed Gretsch Round Badge shares many of the same characteristics of the original version. Both are made from brass, yet the new version has only the Gretsch name is embossed. (On the original brass badge, all of the graphic elements were embossed.) To enhance the look new badge, a simulated "patina" is applied giving it a textured, rustic appearance. Like the original, the new badge will be affixed to the drums' vent hole using a pneumatically pressed brass grommet.

The Gretsch Round Badge was used on all Gretsch USA-made drums between 1930 and 1970 and grew to become an iconic symbol. Gretsch Drums manufactured during this period continue to be highly collectable and extremely valuable throughout the vintage drum community.

Even though Gretsch has introduced several alternative badge styles since 1970, the Round Badge continued to make periodic comebacks for special commemorative products like the 120th Anniversary Edition Products in 2003 and the 125th Anniversary Drums in 2008. In January 2012, a silver version of the traditional Round Badge was introduced on the newly released, USA-made Brooklyn Series.

"The reintroduction of the Round Badge to our USA-made product is a welcome return to a classic and very emblematic Gretsch Drum design," said John Palmer, Director of Product for Gretsch Drums. "As we approach the company's 130th anniversary, we are very proud to combine key elements of our rich heritage with our continuing advancements in drum making."

Product bulletin October, 2012

The production crew at the factory produced all the new round-badge product for display at the January 2013 NAMM show prior to their Christmas 2012 break. All drums ordered after October 1, 2012 got the new badge because of the normal new-order processing time.

Retro-Luxe snare drums 2012-2013

There were several versions of this label applied to the limited edition 130th series drums depending on how many of the particular model were to be made. (of 30, of 35, etc.)

Taylor Hawkins signature model snare drum badge 2013

The new round badge was joined by a new spec internal label. The first few "new badge" kits (in the 2012 77000 serial number range) still had the Grey/White label but by early 2013 (serial number 79000 range) this new label was used.

GRETSCH CATALOGS

Note: Not all of the documents listed here meet the criteria of what many vintage drum folks think of as a "catalog." There has been a blurring of the lines a bit in certain eras, but certainly the documents listed here are important in that they provided the information generally presented in what most of us today think of as a "catalog," and in most cases provided the only documents from the era represented. Note that in 1954 and 1955, the Gretsch "catalog" was a Downbeat magazine insert. From 1983 to 1997, the only Gretsch "catalog" was a large poster. More recently, the publication "Gretsch News" has morphed into a catalog with just a page or two of endorser "news."

1912-1913 Full-line Gretsch catalog
7.5x10.5, featuring 25 pages of percussion instruments & accessories, most under "20th Century" brand

not illustrated:
1914-1915 Full-line Gretsch catalog
7.5x10.5
Very similar to the 1912-1913 catalog, though the drum section was moved to the front of the catalog.

circa 1916 5.25x7 48 pages
Cover states "Edition 16" but this may be the first stand-alone Gretsch drum catalog; at this writing it is the first to surface that is primarily drum items. (There are a couple pages of brass instruments near the end.)

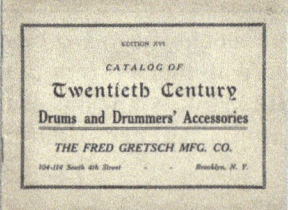

1927 8.5x11
Full line catalog, with yet stronger emphasis on drums

1933 Catalog #33 8.5x11
Full line catalog 160 pages

1936 8.5x11
Full line catalog. *Very similar catalog published in 1937*

1940 Catalog #40 8.5x11, 186 pages
Full line catalog. Pocket inside back cover contained Gretsch drum catalog #39

1939 6x9, 84 pages

Catalog C-82, 1941 6x9, 84 pages (nearly identical to 1939; different cover, updated outfit and mallet instrument sections)

1941 outfit folding poster 18x24

Gretsch & Brenner 8.15x11 215 pages
c. late 1930s

This is not technically a Gretsch Drum Company catalog, but a catalog issued by Gretsch & Brenner Inc. This company was co-founded by Fred Sr.'s brother Walter in 1924. (Walter and another brother, Louis, had worked with Fred Sr. in the family business after the turn of the century. Louis left for a career in real estate. This company, in business until the mid-1950s, distributed instruments manufactured by other firms which were for the most part branded Gretsch & Brenner. All of the drums in this catalog appear to Gretsch-made instruments but are identified as "Rocket" brand drums.

1948 8.5x11 8 pages
"Consumer Price list"
Although this is not a catalog, it is included here because it was pretty much the only drum "catalog" from 1948. It was reprinted in 1950 with the only change being the date at the top of the front cover

1950 8.5x11 8 pages
"Consumer Price List"
Virtually identical to the 1948 publication except for the cover color and date at the top of cover. Printed on front cover of both: "Effective 11 Oct. 1948"

Catalog #50 1949
(All musical instruments that were distributed by Gretsch)
8/5x11 110 pages

Broadkaster flier; 8.75x12, 4 pages
1950

Downbeat Magazine
insert catalog
October 6, 1954, Part Two
7.5x10 32 pages

Downbeat Magazine
insert catalog
Part 2
October 5, 1955
7.25x10, 36 pages

1958 Diamond Jubilee
Edition
7.25x10, 36 pages

Catalog #40 1961
8.5x11 32 pages

Catalog Supplement #41 1961
8.5x11 8 pages

Catalog #42 1963
8.5x11 32 pages

Catalog #43 1966
8.5x11 40 pages

Catalog #44 1968
8.5x11 8 pages

Catalog #45 1971
8.5x11 40 pages

Dorado 1973
8.5x11 16 pages   Only 2 pages are dedicated to drums, a short-lived inclusion in this catalog of imported instruments. The 1972 and 1974 Dorado catalogs include no drums.

1977 8.5x11   10 pages

1980 8.5x11 26 pages

THE LOST GRETSCH CATALOG: DRUM SUPPLEMENT 1973

by John Sheridan   (excerpted from *Classic Drummer* magazine)

The 1973 Gretsch Drum Supplement is easy to miss, as it is almost exactly the same publication as their 1972 supplement. The front cover is virtually the same, as is the interior. The main difference is what's on the 1973 supplement's back cover: a swatch page. Of course, the six classic Sparkles are represented: Gold, Blue, Silver, Red, Green and Champagne, along with the three basic Gretsch pearls: Black, White and Midnight Blue. The slick and long-standing company staple, Jet Black Nitron is also present, as is Gretsch's last surviving Satin Flame finish, Peacock.

Of special note, however, are the "first-time" appearances of wood finishes and Steel wraps on a Gretsch swatch page. A Walnut lacquer set first appeared in the 1968 supplement, catalog #44. (Natural) Maple lacquer finishes were "officially" introduced by the 1970 price list, but were previously made available only for such Gretsch endorsers as Ted Reed. Though both Brass and Chrome Steel coverings are featured on sets in the '72 and '73 supplements, this is the first time they appear on a swatch

1972, 1973 8.5x11, 4 pages

page. It's also interesting to note that the Chrome Steel-covered set is spelled "Broadcaster" in the '72 supplement and "Broadkaster" in the '73 revision. This long-time Gretsch trademark name is traditionally spelled with a "k" and has graced several varied Gretsch products over the last sixty years.

An inclusion considered curious by some is the back cover's advertisement for Sam Ulano's enormous instructional text, *The Professional Drummer's System*. This 590-page hardcover book retailed for $37.50; a hefty sum for any book in 1973! Plugging an instructional manual on Gretsch literature was not a usual practice during Baldwin's 18-year ownership of the company, but Sam Ulano was a very prolific guy. As the ad states, this manual was his latest of over 150! That certainly lent credibility for supplement inclusion, and beyond that, Sam was a long-time Gretsch endorser.

The 1973 Gretsch Drum Supplement has remained largely unknown to most vintage drum enthusiasts and catalog collectors. It's likely been overlooked due to its superficial resemblance to the '72 supplement. With its fifteen varied colors and textures, this eye-catching swatch page is certainly an important chapter in Gretsch drum history.

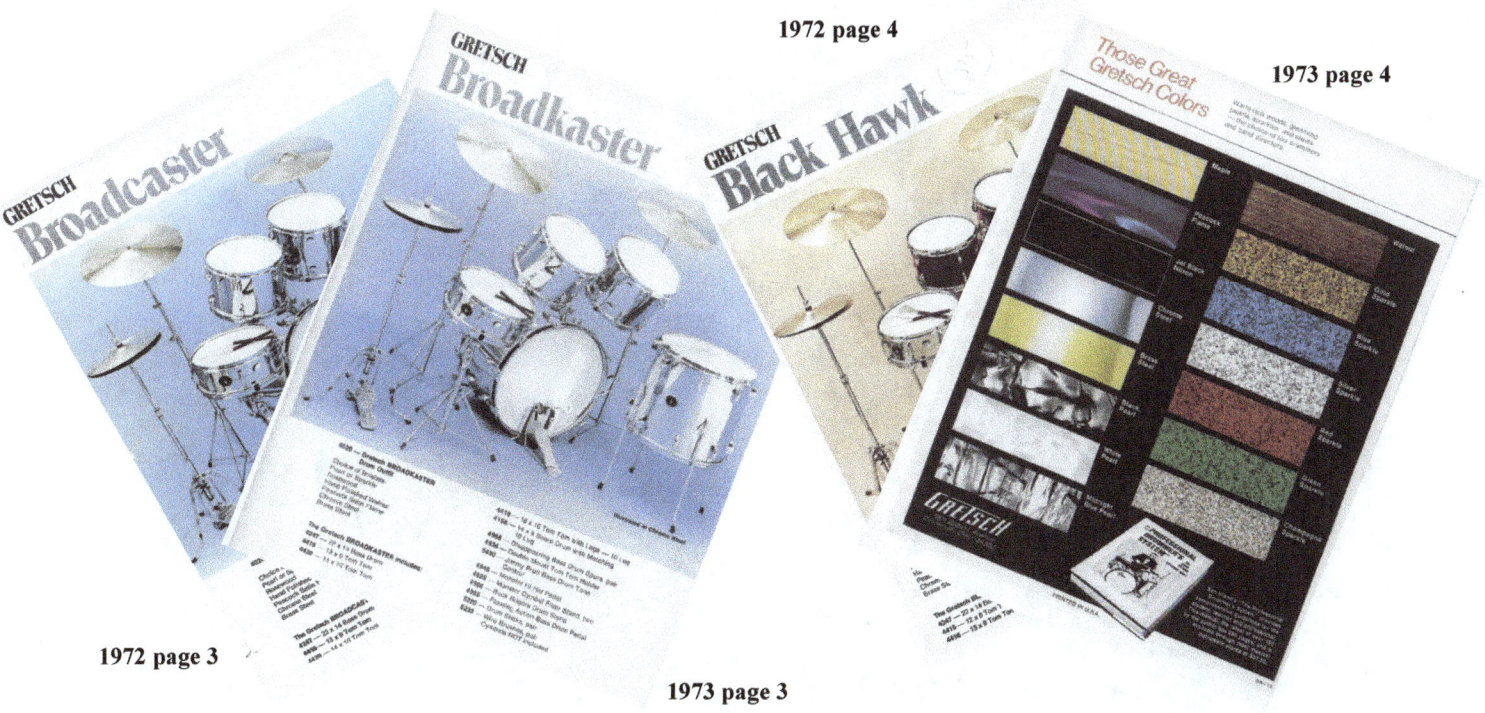

Catalog Poster 22x34

This poster catalog layout was nearly complete when Karl Dustman arrived at the firm in 1983. The vintage tom on the cover was loaned to Gretsch by Nashville's Tommy Winkler.

The poster was changed slightly by Fred W. Gretsch when he purchased the company in 1985 and remained the only Gretsch catalog through 1997.

The changes: Charlies's photo and message were replaced by the photo and message from Fred W. and Dinah, and the endorser photo section was replaced by the text "The World's Finest Drums Are Made In The U.S.A."

Photo of owner Charlie Roy (left) 1983-1984, replaced with photo of Fred W. and Dinah Gretsch (right) 1985-1997

Dinah and Fred Gretsch

Side 1
1983-1997

Side 2
1983-1984
(endorser photos)

Side 2
1985-1997

1998 8.5x11 12 pages

Harvey Mason Broadkaster catalog
1998   8.5x11 4 pages

2001 8.5x11 6 pages

2003 Catalina Elite
double sided single sheet

2003 Catalina Stage
double sided single sheet

2003 Blackhawk
double sided single sheet

2003 Renown Maple
8.5x11, 4 pages

2003 USA Maple   8.5x11 6 pages

2003-2004 120th Anniversary catalog
8.5x11   32 pages

Micro Catalog 2005
5.5x8.5 16 pages

2006 New Classic Series   8.5x11   4 pages

2008 8.5x11   32 pages

2011   8.5x11   40 pages

2011   USA Custom 8.5x11   10 pages

2012 New Products Guide
8.5x11, 12 pages

2013 New Products Guide
8.5x11, 20 pages

2013 New Products Guide
8.5x8.5, 28 pages

Gretsch News, Volume 1   January 2005
8.5x11, 24 pages

Gretsch News, Volume 2   July 2005
8.5x11, 6 pages

Gretsch News, Volume 3   January 2006
8.5x11, 24 pages

Gretsch News, Volume 4   July 2006
8.5x11, 12 pages

Gretsch News, Volume 5   January 2007
8.5x11, 16 pages

Gretsch News, Volume 6   June 2008
8.5x11, 12 pages

Gretsch News, Volume 7   January 2009
8.5x11, 16 pages

Gretsch News, Volume 8   January 2010
8.5x11, 24 pages

Gretsch News, January 2012
8.5x11, 20 pages

Chanute era parts catalog
8.5x11 12 pages
1980

1990 Parts Catalog
8.5 x 5.5   16 pages

KMC era parts catalog 2009
8.5x11, 32 pages
printed in black and white,
with digital color version

The Gretsch House Telegram

Volume 130, #1, 2013
folds out to 17"x27" poster

The Gretsch House Telegram is sort of a newsletter for Gretsch dealers. They have been published at the rate of one or two per year from 1994 to the present. Nearly all have been from 4 to 6 pages and have included Gretsch family news, new model announcements, endorser notes, etc. Because of the inconsistency in the numbering of the issues, a complete list of published issues to date are listed here, exactly as each edition refers to itself. The author feels that in the future the most collectable editions from this list are the Volume 10 #1 from 2004 (because of it's substantive article about Richard Gretsch), Volume 125, Issue #1 of 2008 which unfolds into a poster with a Gretsch company timeline, and Volume 130 Issue #1 of 2013 with an updated timeline. (Note: The italicized issues include *only* guitar-related information.)

#1	*Special Edition 1994*	#8	*Volume 6, Issue 2, Summer 1999*	#15	Volume 10, Issue 1, 2004
#2	Volume 2, Number 2, Summer 1995	#9	*2000*	#16	Volume 11, Issue 1, 2005
#3	Summer 1996	#10	*Millennium 2000 Issue*	#17	Volume 12, Issue 1, 2006
#4	*Winter 1997*	#11	2000 Special Issue	#18	Volume 124, Issue 1, 2007
#5	*Volume 5, Number 1, January 1998*	#12	Volume 7, Issue 1, 2001	#19	Volume 125, Issue 1, 2008
#6	Volume 3, Issue 1, 1998	#13	2002 Issue	#20	"Copyright 2009"
#7	Volume 4, Issue 1, Winter 1999	#14	Volume 9, Issue 1, 2003	#21	Volume 128 #1, 2011
				#22	Volume 130 Issue 1, 2013

GRETSCH COLORS

As with other sections of the dating guide, the dates listed here are for the most part the dates these colors were listed in catalogs. Be advised that exceptions to these color dates abound. Rick Gier: *"Much internet forum discussion and many anecdotal comments put a rough range of availability of a finish three years before it appears and three years after it disappears from a catalog. This range may be even larger, depending upon the frequency of production of catalogs and the supply of particular finishes."*

There were often variations of these colors. Much like dyed fabrics that vary by dye lots, drum covering tints change from batch to batch.

In the case of sparkle finishes, they fluctuated between glass (glitter) and foil (sparkle). A common trend was for some colors to be glitter in the early 60s, change to sparkle, then later back to glitter again– all the while being catalogued as "sparkle;" Gretsch never referred to any covered finishes as glitter. Tangerine Sparkle was always glitter. Champagne Sparkle, Burgundy Sparkle, and Starlight Sparkle were always sparkle. Blue, gold, red, green, and silver varried between glitter and sparkle.

KMC is to be commended for naming their recent glass glitter colors in a manner that identifies them as glass glitter.

The thickness of the coverings varied greatly. The author has measured swatch samples that range from .005" (Black Nitron) to .021" (Tangerine Sparkle) with the latter being so thick that this factor alone can cause poor drum head fitting.

There are many reasons for the fluctuations described above, not the least of which is the fact that Gretsch was constantly shopping for more economical sources of supply and numerous vendors were used over the years.

USA GRETSCH

Color	Dates
Anniversary Sparkle	1958-1962
Antique Maple	1977-1979, 1982-2013
Aqua (Satin) Flame	1965-1972
Azure Gloss	2005-2013
Black Chrome Steel	1977-1978
Black Duco	2004-2013
Black Ebony / Ebony Gloss	1984-2013
Black Glass (Glitter)	2005-2013
Black Marine Pearl	2003-2013
Black ("Diamond") Pearl	1948-1978
(Jet) Black Nitron/Solid Black	1953-2013
Black Sparkle	1992-2013
Blue Duco	2004-2013
Blue Glass (Glitter)	2005-2013
Blue Metallic	1955-1958
Blue Nitron	1992-1999
Blue Oyster (Brooklyn Series)	2013
Blue Sparkle	1939-1978, 2003-2012
Blue Spruce	1977-1978, 1985-1986
Brass Steel	1972-1978
Bright Pink	1986-1990
Burgundy Sparkle	1962-1971
Burnt Orange	1983-2013
Cadillac Green (paint over plastic)	early 1950s-1959
(Steve Ferrone/'08 RB only)	2006-2013
Cameo Coral (paint over plastic)	1953-1959
Candy Red (lacquer)	1984
Caribbean Blue	1984-90, 2000, 2007-2013
Champagne Sparkle	1959-1976, 1993-2013
Chestnut Duco	2011-2013
Chinese Red & Ebony (lacquer) (Harlequin)	1955-1959
Chrome Nitron	1971
Chrome	1992-1999
Chrome Steel	1972-1978
Copper Metallic	1953-1958
Copper Mist (paint over plastic)	1953-1959
Cream Oyster (Brooklyn Series)	2012-2013
Curly Antique Maple Lacquer (125th Anniversary 5x14)	2008
Curly Walnut Maple Gloss	2007-2009
Curly Maple	2009-2013
Curly Millennium Maple Gloss	2005-2009
Curly Maple Rosewood Gloss	2006-2009
Curly Maple Stardust Gloss	2005-2009
Dark Red Nitron	1992-2003
Dark Walnut	1985-2013
Duco Ebony (aka "Full Dress Duco")	1939-1976
Duco White (aka "Full Dress Duco")	1939-1976
Ebony (lacquer)	1985-2013
Ebony (wood grain)	1977-1978
Emerald Green Pearl	1969-1972
Full Dress Duco (White or Ebony)	1939-1976
Gloss Vintage Blonde	2013
Gloss Classic Maple	2013
Gold Glass (Glitter)	2005-2013
Gold Mist Gloss	2005-2013
Gold Sparkle	1992-2013
Gold Nitron	1971-1972
Gold (Satin) Flame (130th Anniversary kits)	1965-1972 (2013)
Grand Piano Black	1986-1999, 2009-2013
Grand Piano White	1986-1999, 2009-2013
Green Metallic	1953-1958
Green Glass (Glitter)	2005-2013
Green Sparkle	1939-1976, 1992-2013
Grey Oyster (Brooklyn Series)	2012-2013
Harlequin (lacquer)	2009-2013
Hot Pink (lacquer)	1983-1986
Ice Blue (lacquer)	1984-1990

Jade Green Gloss	2006-2013
Jade Green Silk	1992-1999
Jet Black Nitron	1953-2013
Kool Green	1984-1986
Light Blue Nitron	1992-1997
Light Blue Pearl (snare only)	1999 only
Lucerne Green	1984-1990
Lustre-Blue Lacquer	1948-1953
Mahogany	1939-1976
Marine (White Pearl)	1950-1953
Metallic Gray	1992-2003
Midnight Blue Pearl	1948-1976
Millennium Maple (Natural)	2000-2013
Mirror Chrome	2003-2005
Mirror Gold	2003-2005
Moonglow Satin Flame	1968-1972
Natural Maple	1970-1999
Olive Satin Flame	1965-1969
Oyster White Pearl	1992-1999
Peacock (Satin) Flame	1970-1974
Peacock (Sparkle)	1955-1958
Pewter Sparkle (130th Brooklyn Kits only)	2013
Piano Black Gloss	2009-2013
Piano White Gloss	2009-2013
Pink Flame	1992-2001

Note: this is a reissue of the late 1960s "Sunset Flame"

Plum Purple (lacquer)	1983-2013
Purple Glass (Glitter)	2005-2013
Red (lacquer)	1985-1990
Red Duco	2009-2013
Red Glass (Glitter)	2005-2013
Red Nitron	1993-1999
Red Oyster (Brooklyn Series)	2012-2013
Red Sparkle	1949-1978, 1992-2013
Red Rosewood	1972-2013
Red Wine Pearl	1969-1972
Salmon Satin Flame	see Sunset Satin Flame
Satin Azure Blue	2002-2013
Satin Burnt Orange	2000-2013
(Broadkaster / 1999-2003)	
Satin Caribbean Blue	2000, 2007-2013
Satin Cherry Red	2002-2005, 2008-2013
Satin Classic Maple	2009-2013
Satin Dark Ebony (Brooklyn Series)	2012-2013
Satin Dark Walnut	2005-2013
Satin Ebony	2000-2013
(Broadkaster / 1998-2005)	
Satin Emerald Green (Brooklyn Series)	2012-2013
Satin Mahogany (Brooklyn Series)	2012-2013
Satin Maple	2000-2009
(Broadkaster / 1999-2003)	
Satin Millennium Maple	2009-2013
Satin Natural (Brooklyn Series)	2013
Satin Purple	2005-2013
Satin Rosewood	2000-2013
(Broadkaster / 1998-2003)	
Satin Sable Black	2002-2005
Satin Sun Amber	2002-2013
Satin Tabasco	2009-2013
Satin Tabasco (Brooklyn Series)	2012-2013
Satin Vintage Blond	2002-2013
Satin Vintage Cherry Burst (130th Anniversary kits)	2013
Satin Walnut	2000-2013

(Broadkaster / 1998-2003)	
Savannah Sunset Duco	2011-2013
Silver Glass (Glitter)	2005-2013
Silver Mist (Lacquer) Gloss	2005-2013
Silver Sparkle	1939-78, '92-2001, '03-13
Silver Satin Flame (130th Anniversary sets)	1965-1968 (2013)
Simulated Rosewood	1977-1978
Sky Blue Pearl Nitron	1998-2013
Smoke Oriental Pearl	1939-1947
Solid Gretsch Orange	2009-2013
Sparkling Blue / Blue Sparkle	1939-1978, 2003-2013
Sparkling Gold/Gold Sparkle	1939-1978, 1992-2001, 2003-2013
Sparkling Green / Green Sparkle	1939-1976, 1992-2013
Sparkling Silver / Silver Sparkle	1939-1978, 1992-2013
Starlight Sparkle	1959-1962
Sun Amber Gloss	2005-2013
Sunset Satin Flame	1968-1970

Note: Sunset Flame was never illustrated in a catalog product photo or color swatch page. The only catalog that even mentioned it by name was the 1968 catalog. Collectors have been known to refer to this as Salmon Satin Flame. This color was reintroduced in 1992 as Pink Flame.

Tangerine Sparkle	1962-1972, 2003-2013
Tri-Tone Blue & Silver (lacquer)	1939-1976, 2003
Tri-Tone Green & Silver (lacquer)	1961-1966
Tri-Tone Sparkles	1966-1976
(usually Blue & Gold or Red & Silver)	
Turquoise Glass (Glitter)	2005-2013
Turquoise Sparkle	2003-2013
Twilight Glass	2012-2013
Two-Tone/Tri-Tone Duco	1939-1976, 2003
Duco: Blue & Silver	
Duco: Blue & Gold (very rare)	
Duco: Red & Gold (very rare)	
Duco: Black & Gold	
Duco: Red & Silver (very rare)	
Duco: Black & Silver	2003
Metallic Lacquer: Green	1954
Metallic Lacquer: Copper	1954
Metallic Lacquer: Blue	1954
Metallic Lacquer: Red	1954
Two-Tone Baroque Pearl	1948
Two-Tone Catalina Green / Ivory (lacquer)	1955-1959
Two-Tone Charcoal Gray / Cameo Coral (lacquer)	1955-1959
Two-Tone Chinese Red / Metallic Gray (lacquer)	1958-1959
Vintage Champagne Sparkle	2006-2013
Vintage Marine (White Marine Pearl Yellowed)	2003-2013
Vintage Oyster White	2009-2013

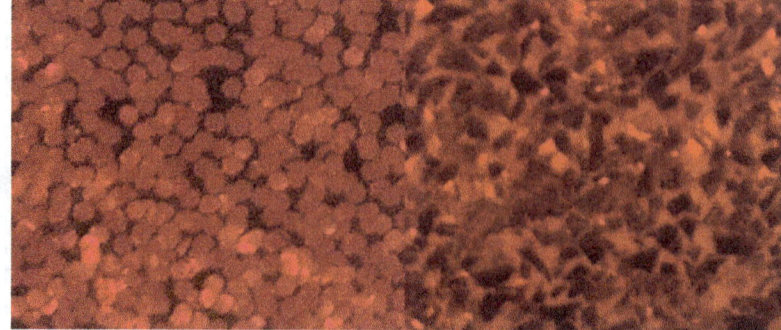

Sparkle (left) vs. Glitter (right)
Sparkle finishes were made with hex-shaped pieces of foil while glitters were made with actual shards of glass.

(Tony Williams) Yellow Lacquer
1985-1995, 2003-2013
Yellow Nitron
1981-1990, 1996-1999
Walnut (Rich Walnut)
1968-2013
White Marine Nitron (White Marine Pearl)   2003-2013
White Marine Pearl
2000-2001   White Marine Pearl Nitron   2002-2003
White Nitron / Solid White
        1977-2013
White Oriental Pearl
1939-1947
White Pearl
1948-1950, 1954-1978
White Tiger Stripe
1996-2001

COLOR CODES

In 1979, Gretsch began listing finish codes in their price lists, which corresponded to the codes on the drum labels. The codes listed for each year here represent colors that were new that year, not all colors available in that year. The codes used are as follows by year and alphabetically:

1979
NB – Jet Black Nitron
NW – White Nitron
WM – Natural Maple
WR – Red Rosewood
WW – Walnut
1981
NY – Yellow Nitron
1982
AM – Antique Maple
1983*
PR – Plum Purple
WO – Burnt Orange
PK – Hot Pink
1984
EB – Black Ebony
CB – Caribbean Blue
GR – Lucerne Green
1985
IB – Ice Blue
KG – Kool Green
BS – Blue Spruce
RD – Red
DKWW – Dark Walnut
TWYL – Tony Williams Yellow
1986
PB – Grand Piano Black
9/1986
PW – Grand Piano White
BP – Bright Pink
1992
AUSP – Gold Sparkle
GSP – Green Sparkle
DRN – Dark Red Nitron
LBP – Light Blue Nitron
JGF – Jade Green Silk
C – Chrome
BKSP – Black Sparkle
RSP – Red Sparkle

CSP – Champagne Sparkle
BN – Blue Nitron
RN – Red Nitron
OWP – Oyster White Pearl
PF – Pink Flame
MG – Metallic Grey
SSP – Silver Sparkle
2000
GMM – Millennium Maple (Natural)
SWW – Satin Walnut
SWM – Satin Maple
SWO – Satin Burnt Orange
SWR – Satin Rosewood
SEB – Satin Ebony
SCB – Satin Caribbean Blue (2000 only)
GWMP – White Marine Pearl Nitron
SBP – Sky Blue Pearl Nitron
2002
ABO – Satin Azure Blue
CRO – Satin Cherry Red (discontinued '05)
VBO – Satin Vintage Blond
SAO – Satin Sun Amber
SBO – Satin Sable Black (discontinued '05)
2003
TGSP – Tangerine Sparkle
TQSP – Turquoise Sparkle
BLSP – Blue Sparkle
VMP – Vintage Marine
BMP – Black Marine
MC – Mirror Chrome
MG – Mirror Gold
WMP – White Marine Nitron
2004
BL – Blue Duco
BK – Black Duco
2005
ABG – Azure Gloss
SAG – Sun Amber Gloss
SMG – Silver Mist Gloss
GMG – Gold Mist Gloss
SPR – Satin Purple
SDKW – Satin Dark Walnut
AUGP – Gold Glass (Glitter)
BLGP – Blue Glass (Glitter)
RGP – Red Glass (Glitter)
GGP - Green Glass (Glitter)
SGP - Silver Glass (Glitter)
BKGP - Black Glass (Glitter)
TQGP - Turquoise Glass (Glitter)
PGP - Purple Glass (Glitter)
CMM – Curly Millennium Gloss
CSD – Curly Stardust Maple Gloss
2006
VCS – Vintage Champagne Sparkle
JG – Jade Green Gloss
CG – 1955 Cadillac Green (Steve Ferrone signature series only)
CWR – Curly Rosewood Maple Gloss
2007
SCB – Caribbean Blue (Satin)
CB – Caribbean Blue
CWW – Curly Walnut Maple Gloss
2008
AM -- Curly Antique Maple Lacquer (125th Anniversary 5x14 only)
CRO – Satin Cherry Red
2009
PWG – Piano White Gloss
PBG – Piano Black Gloss
GOG – Solid Gretsch Orange
SCM – Satin Classic Maple

CM – Curly Maple
STB – Satin Tabasco
HQ – Harlequin (lacquer) (add any finish code)
SN – Satin Natural (New Classic)
VOW – Vintage Oyster White
RD – Red Duco
2011
SAV – Savannah Sunset Duco
CST – Chestnut Duco
2012
TWGP – Twilight Glass
SDE – Dark Ebony (Brooklyn Series)
SEG – Emerald Green (Brooklyn Series)
SM – Mahogany (Brooklyn Series)
ST – Tabasco (Brooklyn Series)
CO – Cream Oyster (Brooklyn Series)
GO – Grey Oyster (Brooklyn Series)
RO – Red Oyster (Brooklyn Series)
BO – Blue Oyster (Brooklyn Series)
*There are no codes for the Centennial finishes – "Birdseye Maple," "Carpathian Elm" and "Burl Walnut" – or 1980s Blackhawk finishes – "Black," "Silver," "Dark Blue", "White", "Burgandy" "Metallics", "Gun Metal Blue", & "Candy Apple Red".

IMPORT COLORS
New Classic Series
BSL – Black Sparkle Lacquer	2011-2013
DC – Deep Cherry Gloss	2006-2008
IMP – Ivory Marine Pearl	2007-2013
MS – Merlot Sparkle	2008-2010
OSB – Ocean Sparkle Burst	2010-2013
SN – Satin Natural	2009-2013
SM – Silver Metallic	2013
VG – Vintage Glass Nitron	2006-2013

Renown Maple Series
BL – Deep Blue Lacquer   2001-2005
BK – Deep Black Lacquer   2001-2003
RD – Deep Red Lacquer   2001-2003
DA – Deep Amber Lacquer   2002-2005
CB – Cherry Burst   2002-2013
CS – Champagne Silk   2002-2006
AB – Autumn Burst   2003-2012
RC – Red Cherry   2003-2006
MP – Magenta Purple   2003-2006
PB – Piano Black   2003-2006
BB – Blue Burst   2006-2008
SL – Slate Silver Sparkle   2006-2010
DIGS – Deep Inca Gold Sparkle 2008-2010
SB – Satin Black   2010-2013
RSF – Ruby Sparkle Fade   2010-2012
CSF – Cobalt Sparkle Fade   2011-2012
MCB – Motor City Blue (Renown '57)
                              2011-2012
MCO- Motor City Onyx (Renown 57)
                              2011-2012
MCR- Motor City Red (Renown '57)   2012
MG - Midnight (Blue) Glass Glitter
                  (only 25 kits) 2012
SW - Satin White   2013
GN - Gloss Natural   2013
SPO - Silver Oyster Pearl   2013
BM - Blue Metal   2013
Catalina Elite
DW – Dark Walnut Lacquer   2001-2003
SB – Smoky Black Lacquer   2001-2003
RR – Ruby Red Lacquer   2001-2003
Catalina Stage
SF – Silver Frost   2001-2003
BK – Liquid Black   2001-2003

107

WR – Wine Red	2001-2003	BS – Black over Silver Sparkle Stripe		AMB – Amber	10/1/10-2013
Catalina Birch			2006-2009	CG – Cherry Gloss	10/1/10-2013
VB – Vintage Burst	2003-2006	SB – Silver Stripe over Black Sparkle		TE – Transparent Ebony	10/1/10-2013
CB – Caribbean Blue	2003-2007		2007-2008	DCB – Dark Cherry Burst	2011-2013
RC – Red Cherry	2003-2006	TAT – Tattoo	2008-2010	SWF – Satin Walnut Fade	2013
DW – Dark Walnut	2003-2007	GT – G-Tube	2009-2010	**Catalina Ash**	
CF – Chestnut Fade	2005-2007	**Catalina Club Mini Mod**		AR – Deep Red	2006-2010
WB – Walnut Burst	2010-2012	BW – Black Widow	2008-2010	AC – Cobalt Blue (UV gloss)	2006-10/1/10
CBB – Cobalt Blue Burst	2010-2012	YJ – Yellow Jacket	2009-2010	LBB – Liquid Black (Wrap)	2008-10/1/10
WP – White Pearl	2010-2011	**Catalina Club Rock**		BCF – Black Cherry Fade (UV gloss)	
SS – Silver Sparkle	2010-2011	BF – Black Flake UV Gloss	2006-2008		2010-10/1/10
EDHB – Ebony Diamond Halogen Burst		SS – Silver Sparkle	2006-2008	**Blackhawk**	
	2011-2012	SS – Silver Sparkle over Silver Lacquer		Black Metallic	1983-1988
BDHF – Blue Diamond Halogen Fade			2008-2009	Dark Blue Metallic	1983-1988
	2011-2012	SB – Silver Sparkle over Black Lacquer		Silver Metallic	1983-1990
SC – Satin Cherry	2011-2012		2008-2010	Burgundy Metallic	1985-1988
SW - Satin Walnut	2012 only	GE – Gloss Ebony	2010-2013	White Metallic	1986-1990
Catalina Club		OT - Ocean Twilight	2013	Candy Apple Red	1989-1990
WP – White Marine (Pearl)	2003-2013	MC - Mirror Chrome	2013	Gun Metal Blue	1989-1990
BP – Black Marine (Pearl)	2003-2006	COS - Copper Sparkle	2013	LB – Liquid Black	2003-2011
SS – Silver Sparkle	2003-2008	GBS - Galaxy Black Sparkle	2013	WR – Wine Red	2003-2011
OS – Onyx Silver	2004-2005	**Catalina Club Classic**		BM – Blue Metallic	2003-2007
SN – Satin Natural	2008-2010	OT - Ocean Twilight	2013	BS – Blue Oyster Swirl	2004-2007
RSP – Rustic Pearl	2008-2010	COS - Copper Sparkle	2013	ES – Ebony Oyster Swirl	2004-2007
RBD – Royal Blue Diamond	2009	GBS - Galaxy Black Sparkle	2013	WD – White Diamond	2005-2007
BP – 1964 Reissue Black Pearl		**Catalina Club Street**		BD – Blue Diamond	2005-2007
(Guitar Center only)	2008-2009	TSS - Silver Sparkle	2013	ED -- Ebony Diamond	2005-2007
WG – Walnut Glaze	2009-2013	TRS - Red Sparkle	2013	MLB – Metallic Liquid Blue	2008-2011
EGF – Emerald Green Flake	2010-2011	**Catalina Maple**		**Energy Series**	
COS – Copper Sparkle	2010-2013	MR – Cherry Red	2006-10/1/10	BLK – Black	2012-2013
GN – Gloss Natural	2010-2013	MA – Deep Amber	2006-10/1/10	GST – Grey Steel	2012-2013
WKP – Whiskey Pearl	2011	TFS –Tobacco Fade Sunburst		WHT – White	2012-2013
WMG –White Mint Green Fade Pearl	2011		2007-10/1/10	**Renegade Series**	
GBS – Galaxy Black Sparkle	2011-2013	EBB–Ebony, Black Hardware		BLK – Black	2012-2013
TS–Teal Sparkle (same as Turquoise Sparkle)	2012		2009-10/1/10	SIL – Silver	2012-2013
Catalina Club Mod		MOF–Mocha Fade		WR – Wine Red	2012-2013
BA – Blue Alien	2006-2008		1/1/10-10/1/10, 2011-13		

The Dixieland snare drum was offered in some unique finishes: Copper, Green, and Blue metallic lacquer. The lacquer was applied directly to the wood. These Green and Copper shells have been mistaken for Cadillac Green and Copper Mist which, along with Cameo Coral, were lacquer applied to clear covering; buyer beware!

Cadillac Green, Copper Mist, and Cameo Coral were lacquer finishes applied to clear pyralin wrap. Some, but not all, drums with this treatment appear to have some type of mesh under the clear pyralin as illustrated here. (see page 208)

Gretsch began to call these finishes "Nitron" finishes in the 1950s. Gretsch used the "Nitron" term on solid-color tinted pyralin coverings through the 1970s, 1980s, and 1990s.

FOR SHOW
JOE LUOMA
GRETSCH

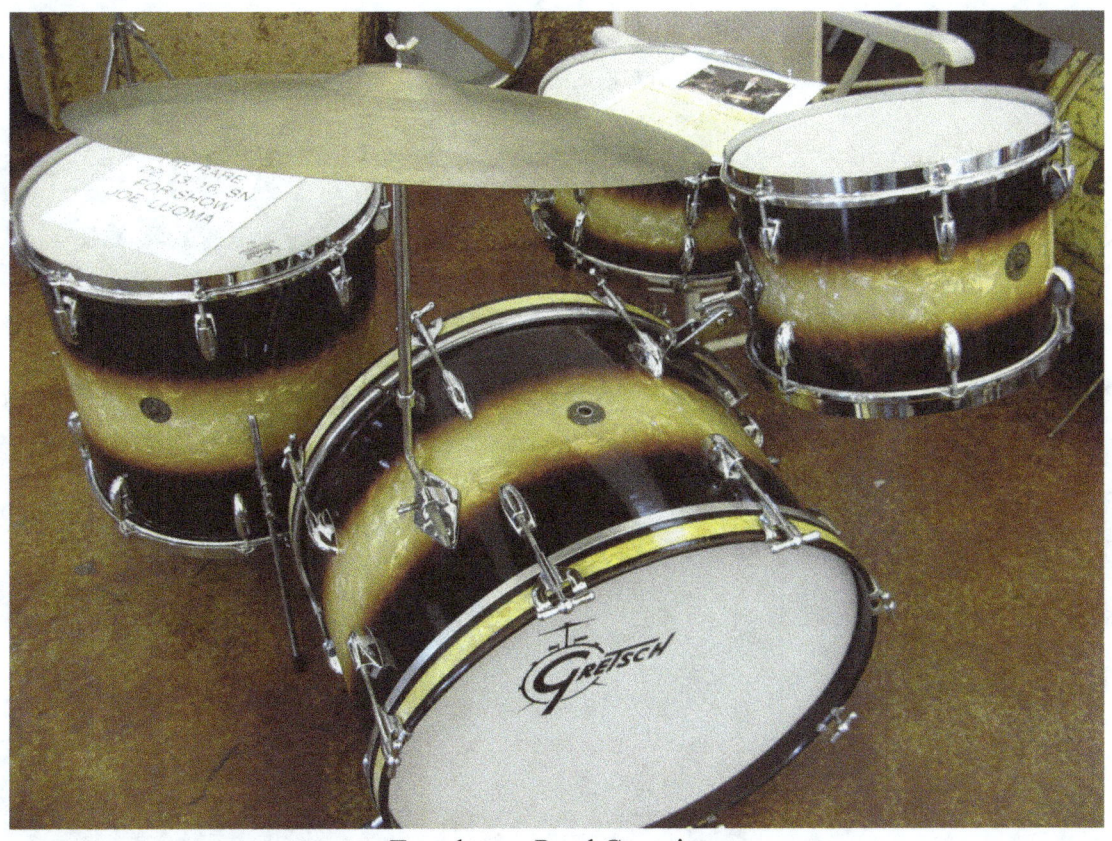

Translucent Pearl Covering

Both the kit here as well as early examples of Midnight Blue were created by applying lacquer (Duco, or dual-color) to the shells, then applying a translucent covering with the design embedded in it.

1958

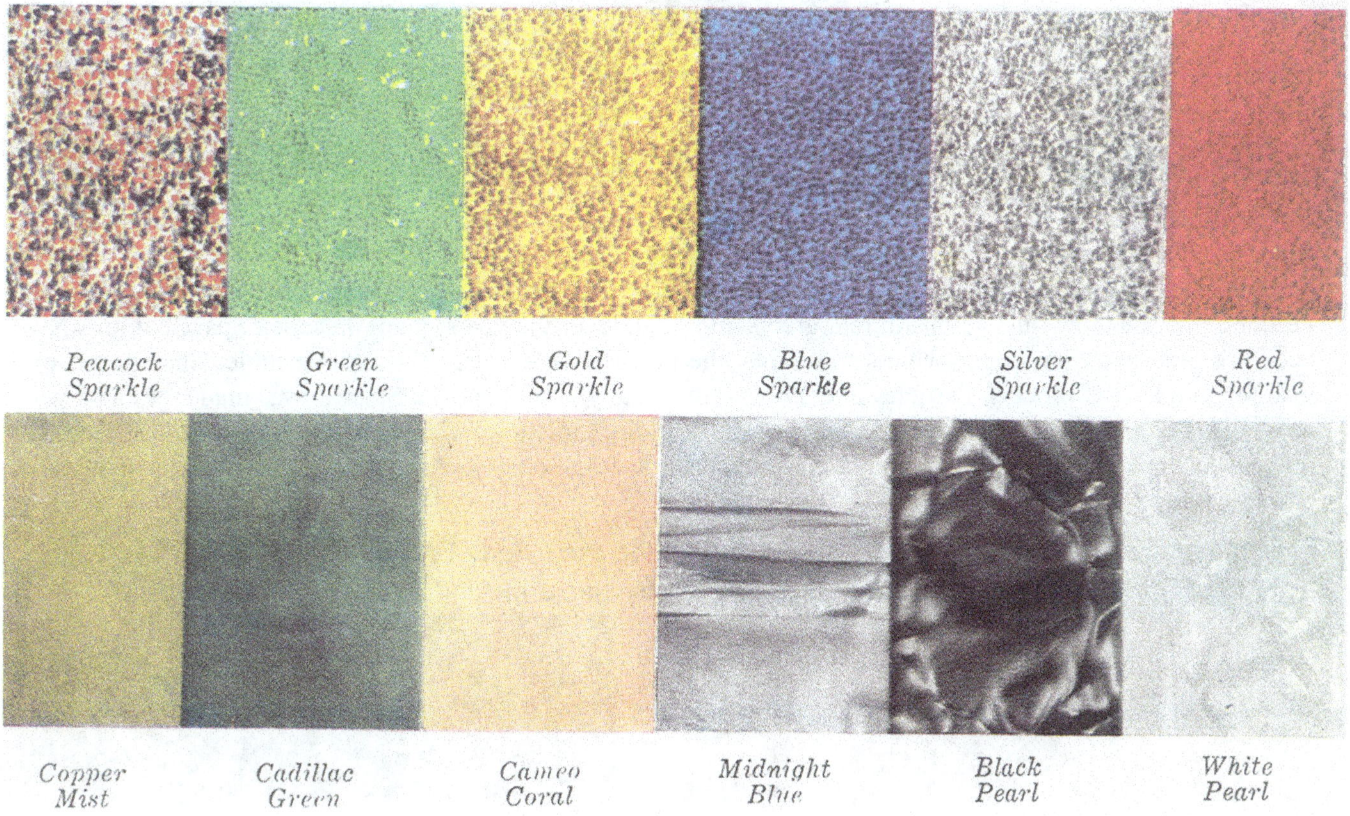
Peacock Sparkle
Green Sparkle
Gold Sparkle
Blue Sparkle
Silver Sparkle
Red Sparkle
Copper Mist
Cadillac Green
Cameo Coral
Midnight Blue
Black Pearl
White Pearl

1961 (Catalog #40)

GOLD SPARKLE PEARL	BLUE SPARKLE PEARL	MIDNIGHT BLUE PEARL
ANNIVERSARY SPARKLE PEARL	SILVER SPARKLE PEARL	BLACK PEARL
WHITE PEARL	RED SPARKLE PEARL	JET BLACK
CHAMPAGNE SPARKLE PEARL	GREEN SPARKLE PEARL	STARLIGHT SPARKLE PEARL

Lee Ruff comment on Champagne Sparkle vs Peacock Sparkle: "The grain in both finishes was very fine, and from a few feet away, they looked almost identical. My first new Gretsch set was Champagne Sparkle, and Gretsch said it was one of the 1st in Champagne. I ordered it in 1960 at Mars Music Store in Elkton, MD. The Peacock Sparkle had "tiny" grains in red, green, and gold. Over the years, many Peacock Sparkle drums have been mistaken for Champagne. Under the lights, the finishes were practically indiscernible. Champagne was made with a unique process. Particles of copper were actually used. Peacock Sparkle was made the same way, using colored particles under clear. The other sparkles and/or glitters were made of silver particles with a tinted translucent layer over top. "Moderately faded" Peacock Sparkle today looks almost identical to Champagne at close scrutiny."

Catalog #42 of 1963: Same colors as above with the exception of Anniversary Sparkle Pearl and Starlight Sparkle Pearl, which were replaced by Tangerine and Burgundy Sparkles below

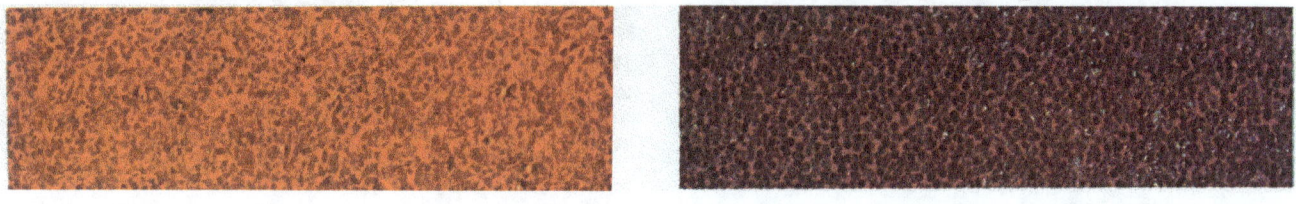

1966

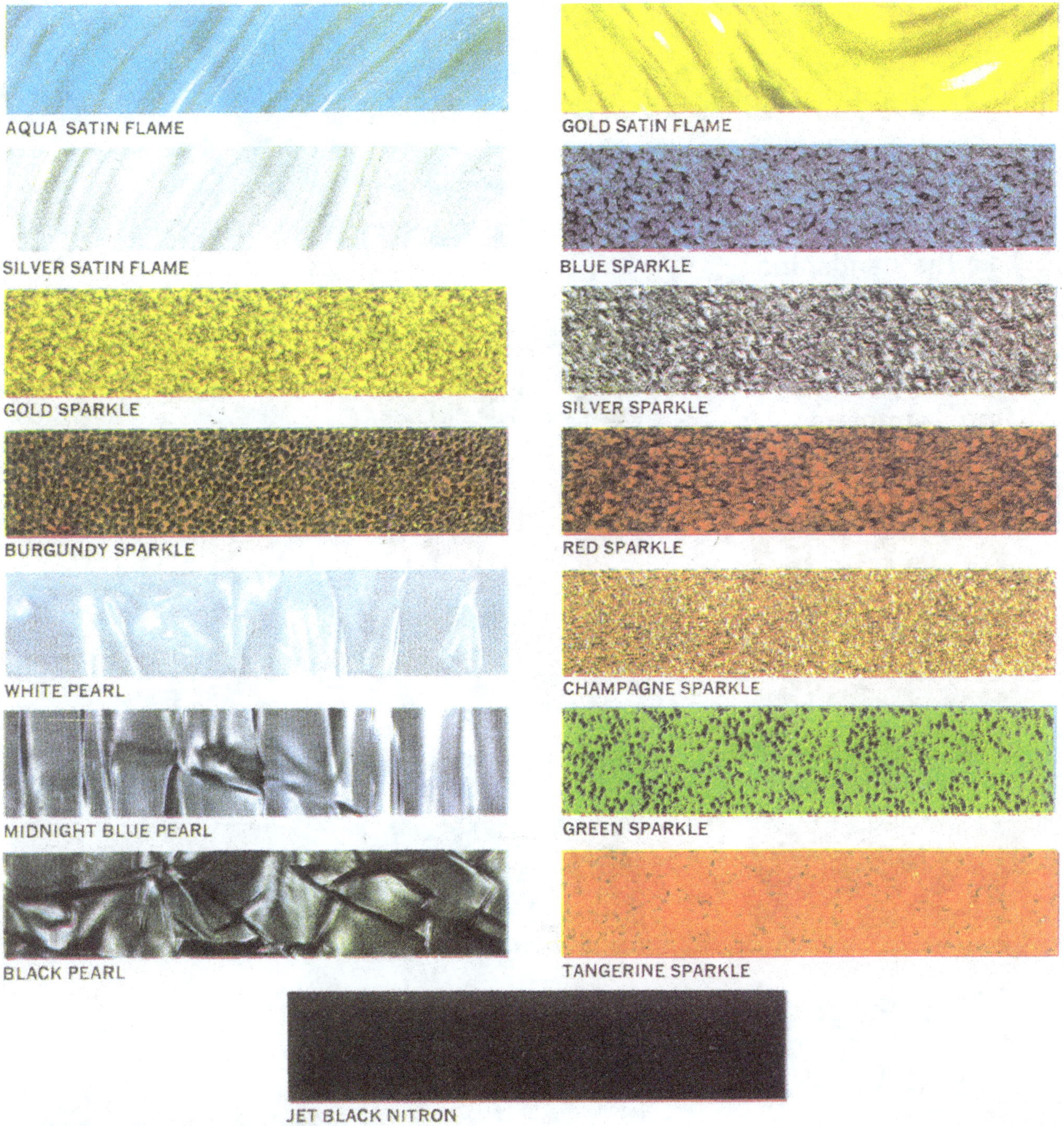

AQUA SATIN FLAME	GOLD SATIN FLAME
SILVER SATIN FLAME	BLUE SPARKLE
GOLD SPARKLE	SILVER SPARKLE
BURGUNDY SPARKLE	RED SPARKLE
WHITE PEARL	CHAMPAGNE SPARKLE
MIDNIGHT BLUE PEARL	GREEN SPARKLE
BLACK PEARL	TANGERINE SPARKLE

JET BLACK NITRON

The snare drum photo at right is from the 2006 *Gretsch News*, presented then as a limited edition (one of 50 drums) of Jade Green Silk. This finish was a standard color from 1992 to 1999, see swatches page 114. A very similar color was produced briefly in the mid-to-late-1960s (floor tom pictured at left is from 1969) but never catalogued or swatched. Our color list includes it as Olive Satin Flame.

1971 & 1973

THE GREAT GRETSCH COLORS

GLEAMING GRETSCH PEARLS, SPARKLES AND SATIN FLAMES — on the bandstand or on parade the choice of America's top drummers.

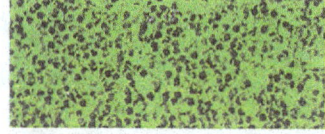
GREEN SPARKLE

AQUA FLAME

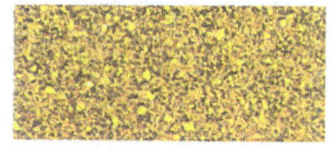
GOLD SPARKLE

TANGERINE SPARKLE

GOLD FLAME

RED SPARKLE

WHITE PEARL

MOONGLOW FLAME

SILVER SPARKLE

EMERALD GREEN PEARL

PEACOCK FLAME

BLUE SPARKLE

MIDNIGHT BLUE PEARL

CHROME NITRON

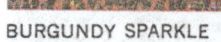
BURGUNDY SPARKLE

RED WINE PEARL

JET BLACK NITRON

CHAMPAGNE SPARKLE

BLACK PEARL

GOLD NITRON

1977

New lacquer finishes, 1984: Kool Green, Candy Red, Ice Blue
Introduced as Candy Red, by the time the next price list was published, the name was shortened to Red.

Gretsch after 1977

No Gretsch drum catalogs were published after 1980 until the 1983 poster-format catalog. That poster had some color swatches, but the tiny slivers of color would serve no useful purpose here. Three new and rather unusual finishes of 1983 were Burnt Orange, Plum Purple, and Hot Pink. The other finishes offered at the time were Natural Maple, Antique Maple, Jet Black Nitron, White Nitron, Walnut, Red Rosewood, and Yellow Nitron. (The Nitron finishes are pearl coverings.)

The author is certain some of these Gretsch colors never appeared in Gretsch catalog color swatch form. This assortment of actual pearl samples is from the 1990s.

Custom/Limited edition finishes

Model GCS-4177SS - 2007 only: Custom Series Square Snare Drum
5x14 USA Custom snare drum with 10 individual square color panels representing the most popular lacquer finishes: Antique Maple, Rosewood, Dark Walnut, Millennium Maple, Purple, Walnut, Azure Blue, Sun Amber, Ebony, Burnt Orange

Steve Maxwell Vintage and Custom Drums special finishes

Mardi Gras The recreation of this finish was accomplished through Steve working with the folks at KMC Music. In January of 2009 Steve and the folks at KMC had their first discussion about this issue. KMC had a desire to re-introduce a vintage finish from the past, and it didn't necessarily have to be a finish that was traditionally associated with Gretsch. Mardi Gras immediately came to Steve's mind and KMC agreed, so the plan was set in motion. There were different versions of Mardi Gras and they varied by drum manufacturer. Slingerland, Leedy and Rogers all had this finish, and each had a slightly different variation of it. Steve provided a pristine example of one of the original Mardi Gras versions and several prototypes of the finish were completed. The intent for the final product was to replicate the concept of the original Mardi Gras finish but with enough subtle differences so as to give this version its own unique character. The final version was approved March 13th, 2010 after almost 15 months of work, and the finish went into production.

Fiesta Pearl (left) is very similar to Mardi Gras, but with a white background instead of black. Maxwell has found combinations of the two finishes very popular; example at right.

Copper Mist
Very similar to the Copper Mist Nitron offered by Gretsch 1953-1959. Maxwell's tint is very similar, but is essentially a stain on the wood. It is offered as a gloss lacquer or a satin finish.

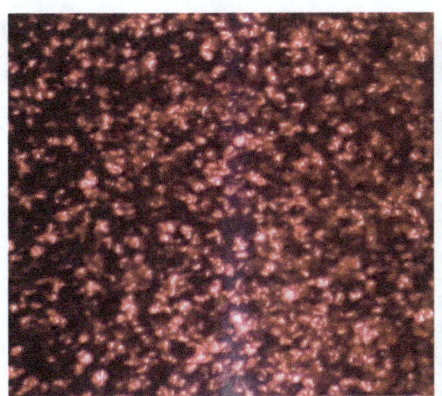

Merlot Sparkle
A close approximation of the vintage Burgundy Sparkle finish.
(Available on the New Classic Series from 2008-2010.)

Espresso Burst
A reproduction of the finish seen on page 109.

July, 2011 USA Custom Finishes

Nitron Covered Finishes — Finish Code "NIT"

Blue Glass - BLGP	Blue Sparkle - BLSP	Champagne Sparkle - CS
Gold Glass - AUGP	Gold Sparkle - AUSP	Green Glass - GGP
Green Sparkle - GSP	Red Glass - RGP	Red Sparkle - RSP
Silver Glass - SGP	Silver Sparkle - SSP	Sky Blue Pearl - SBP
Solid Black - NB	Solid White - NW	Tangerine Glass - TGGP
Tangerine Sparkle - TGSP	Turquoise Glass - TPGP	Turquoise Sparkle - TQSP
Twilight Glass - TWGP	White Marine Pearl - WMP	Vintage Marine Pearl - VMP
Vintage Oyster White - VOW	Vintage Champagne Sparkle - VCS	Black Glass - BKGP
Black Sparkle - BKSP	Black Marine Pearl - BMP	Purple Glass PGP (Not pictured)

Nitrocellulose Gloss Lacquer Finishes — Finish Code "SPL"

Antique Maple - AM	Azure - ABG	Black Duco - BK	Blue Duco - BL	Burnt Orange - WO	Caribbean Blue - CB
Chestnut Duco - CST	Dark Walnut - DKWN	Ebony - EB	Gold Mist - GMG	Gretsch Orange - GOG	Jade Green - JG
Millennium Maple - GMM	Piano Black - PBG	Piano White - PWG	Purple - PR	Red Duco - RD	Rosewood - WR
Savannah Sunset Duco - SAV	Silver Mist - SMG	Solid Yellow - TWYL	Sun Amber - SAG	Walnut - WW	

Nitrocellulose Lacquer Satin Finishes — Finish Code "SAT"

Satin Azure Blue - ABO	Satin Burnt Orange - SWO	Satin Classic Maple - SCM	Satin Dark Walnut - SDKW	Satin Ebony - SEB	Satin Millennium Maple - SWM
Satin Purple - SPR	Satin Rosewood - SWR	Satin Sun Amber - SAO	Satin Tabasco - STB	Satin Vintage Blond - VBO	Satin Walnut - SWW

Satin Caribbean Blue - SCB (Not pictured), Satin Cherry Red - CRO (Not pictured)

Curly Maple Finishes — Finish Code "CM"

Curly Maple features an outer ply of figured curly maple that adds a distinctive appearance to any drum.
All Nitro Cellulose finishes (gloss, satin, Harlequin) are available in Curly Maple.
See size chart for available sizes. Indicate "CM" for Curly Maple Finish.

Harlequin Finishes — Finish Code "HQ"

Gretsch Harlequin finish is a two-toned, triangular patterned finish that combines Piano Black Gloss with the finish of your choice.
AVAILABLE IN ANY GLOSS OR SATIN NITRO CELLULOSE FINISH.
Indicate "HQ" along with finish code when ordering Harlequin finish - ex: HQWR for Harlequin Rosewood

New Brooklyn Series 2012

| Satin Mahogany | Satin Dark Ebony | Satin Tobasco | Satin Emerald | Grey Oyster | Blue Oyster | Cream Oyster | Red Oyster |

GRETSCH OUTFITS

Notes on outfit section of dating guide:

The dates listed in this section for the most part represent the dates that these outfit models were included in published catalogs. Outfits may well have been available for purchase before and after these dates.

Through much of the 1940s-1960s, outfits were given one model number for the basic kit only, another number if cymbals were included. Although the pictures here include cymbals, the model numbers represent the kit without cymbals.

Dealers could (and did) order configurations not represented here. Where options are listed in parentheses, the Gretsch catalog of the era suggested these options.

The most common tradition among American drum manufacturers of the 20th century was to list a drum's size by depth first, then diameter; an 8x12 tom had a shell 8 inches tall with a diameter of 12 inches. In many of Gretsch's earlier catalogs, sizes were listed as diameter first, then depth. The author lists all drums following the industry standard.

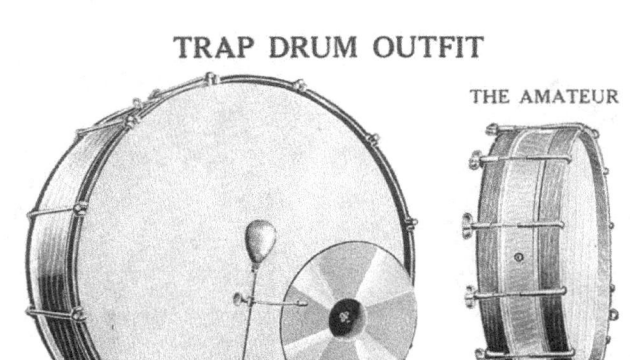

As one of America's oldest makers of musical instruments, Gretsch was making drum sets as soon as there *were* drum sets. The first two known outfits are shown here, as listed in the 1912 Gretsch catalog.

note: In keeping with the pattern set in Gretsch catalogs, sizes are listed by snare drum, bass drum, then toms

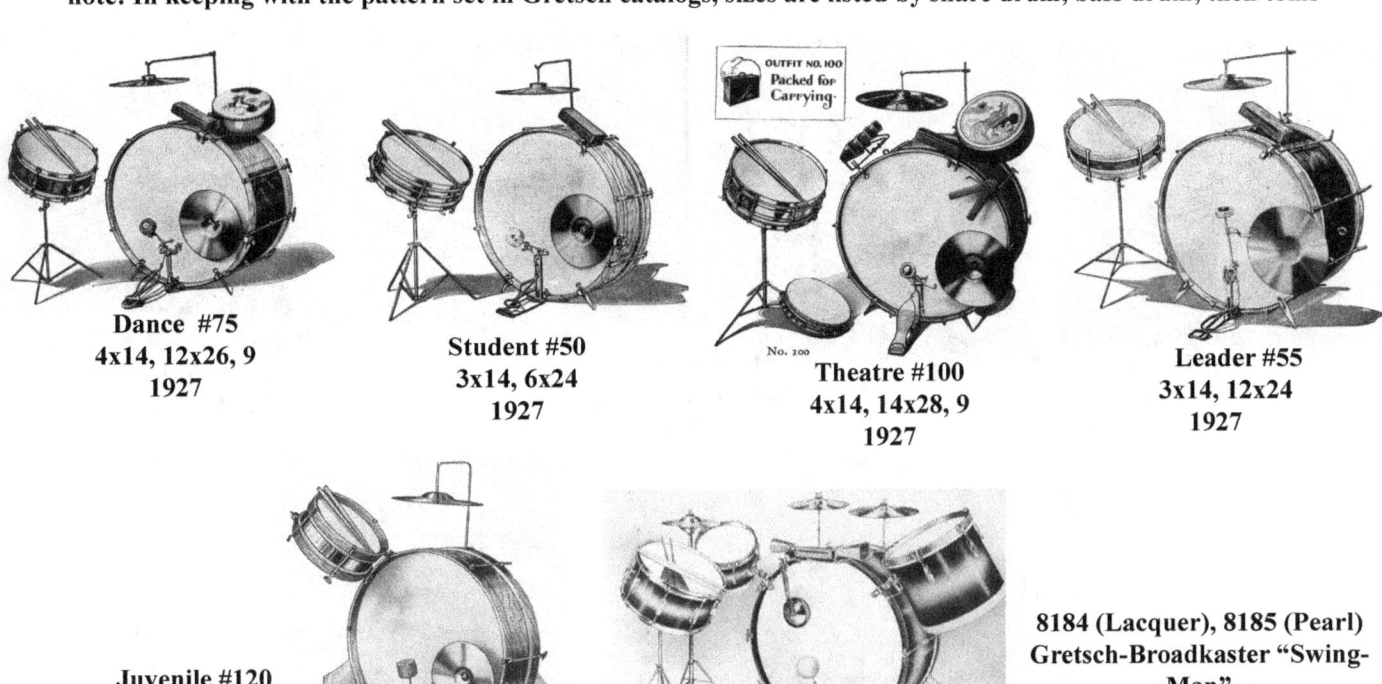

Dance #75
4x14, 12x26, 9
1927

Student #50
3x14, 6x24
1927

Theatre #100
4x14, 14x28, 9
1927

Leader #55
3x14, 12x24
1927

Juvenile #120
3x10, 5x20
1927

8184 (Lacquer), 8185 (Pearl)
Gretsch-Broadkaster "Swing-Man"
6.5x14, 14x28, 9x13, 12x14
1939-1941

8180 (Lacquer) 8181 (Pearl)
Gretsch-Broadkaster "Roll-Away" Outfit
6.5x14, 14x28, 9x13, 12x14
1939-1941

8187 "Times Square" Drum Outfit
6.5x14, 14x28, 4x10 (Chinese)
1939

8190 Gretsch "Catalina"
6.5x14, 14x28, 4x10 (Chinese)
1939

8188 Gretsch Professional Drum Outfit
6.5x14, 14x28, 4x10 (Chinese)
1939

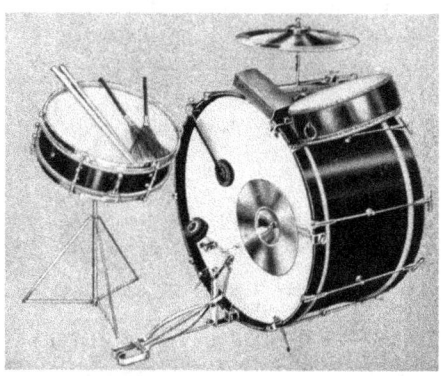

Black And White #65
5x14, 12x26, 4x10"
1936

Professional #90
5x14, 14x28, 4x10"
1936

Our Leader #52
4x14, 12x24
1936

Broadway #85
5x14, 14x28, 4x10"
1936

Young America #45
3.5x13, 8x24
1936

School Days #35
3x13, 6x24
1936

8192 (Pearl), 8193 (Lacquer) "Broadkaster"
6.5x14, 14x28, 4x10 (Chinese)
1939

8191 Improved Gretsch "Catalina"
6.5x14, 14x28, 6.5x10, 9x13
1941

8198 Gretsch "School Days"
3x12, 6x24
1939

8197 Gretsch "Black And White"
5x14, 12x26, 4x10
1939-1941

8195 Gretsch "Leader"
5x14, 12x24
1939

8186 The "Radio Showman"
6.5x14, 14x26, 8x12, 9x13
1941

8194 New Gretsch "Swing-Lane"
6.5x14, 14x26, 8,12, 9x13
1941

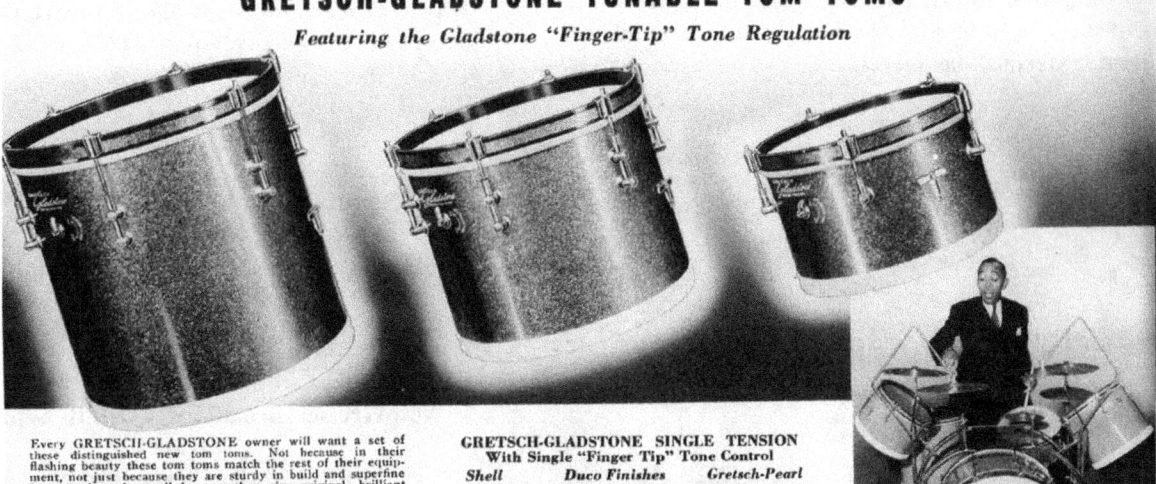

Gretsch did not catalog any Gretsch-Gladstone outfits, just component snare drums, bass drums (single-tension) and tom-toms. They did advertise kits with photos of endorsers; each kit was custom-made to order. Many of the endorser photos show toms that were not catalogued such as toms with tunable heads top and bottom, toms with metal counterhoops, and staggered top and bottom tube lugs. These drums first appeared in the 1939 catalog, were gone by the time of the first postwar catalog.

8196 "Swing" Set
6.5x14, 12x26, 8x12
1941

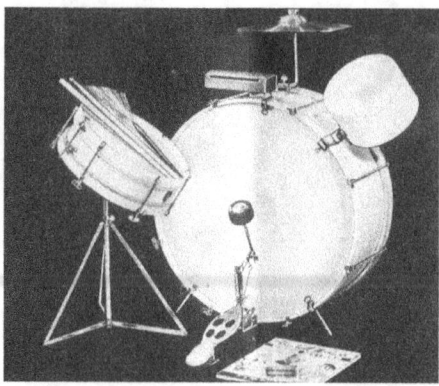
T8198 Improved "Young America"
3x12, 8x22, 5x8
1941

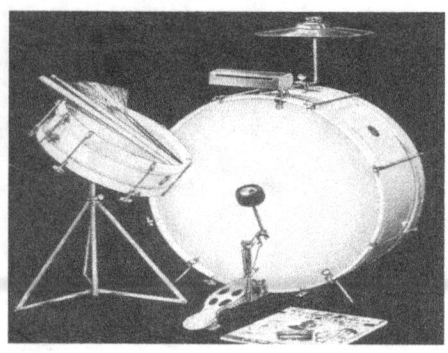
8199N Gretsch "School Days"
3x12, 8x22
1941

Defender 1942-1946
World War II era drums with wooden lugs because the War Production Board had ruled that no more than 10% of the weight of war era drums could be made of "critical materials" i.e. metal.

New Gretsch Broadkaster Outfit- Single Tension
PX4025 (lacquered, nickel), PX4026 (lacquered, chrome),
PX4027 (pearl, nickel), PX4028 (pearl, chrome)
6.5x14 (or 5x14), 14x26 (or 14x24), 8x12, 12x14,
1948

PX4024 Broadkaster Artist Outfit
pearl, chrome
6.5x14 (or 5x14), 14x24 (14x20 optional)
9x13,16x16
1949

New Gretsch Broadkaster Outfit- Separate Tension
PX4020 (lacquered, nickel),
PX4021 (lacquered, chrome),
PX4022 (pearl, nickel),
PX4023 (pearl, chrome)
6.5x14 (or 5x14), 14x24 (or 14x26),9x13, 16x16
1948

PX4023

Catalog numbers listed here are for kits only; Gretsch had slightly different part numbers for kits that included cymbals.

PX4030 Broadkaster Single Tension lacquer, chrome
6.5x14, 14x26 (or 14x24),9x13
1950-1956

PX4011 Broadkaster "Bop" Be-Bop
5.5x14 (or 6.5x14),14x22, 9x13,16x16
1950-1958

PX4075 Student
3.5x13,10x20
1949

PX4010 "Bop"
5.5x14, 14x20, 9x13,16x16
1961-1965

PX4005, Broadkaster "One-Nighter"
6.5x14 (or 5.5x14), 14x22
1949-1958

PX4007 Broadkaster "One-Nighter Plus"
5.5x14, 14x22, 9x13
1950-1974
illustration is from 1950 catalog, with period hardware

**Cocktail drums first appeared in the Gretsch catalog #50 of 1949.
Their introduction was attributed to the Kirby Stone Quartette.**

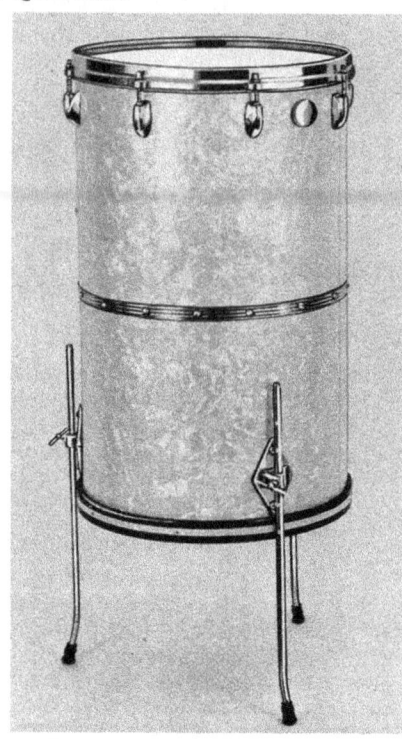

PX4182 Gretsch Broadkaster Cocktail drum
Single headed 14x24 with 5.5x8 side tom
1949-1966
(available as PX4180 without side tom)
earliest versions had "Rocket" lugs, above left

PX4180 Single headed cocktail drum
(no longer called Broadkaster)
PX4181 version included bottom head, pedal
bar, and up-side-down pedal, see below.
14x24 1949-1966

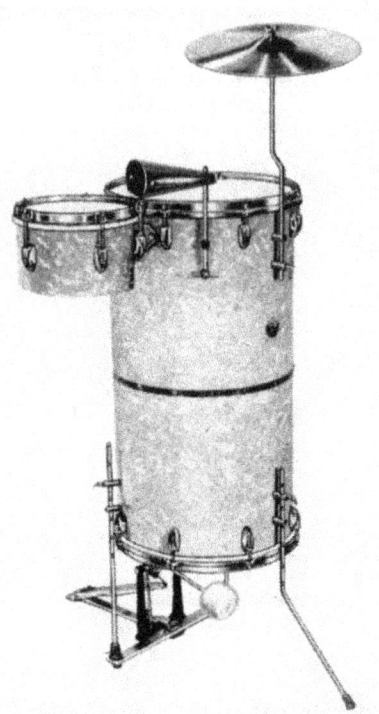
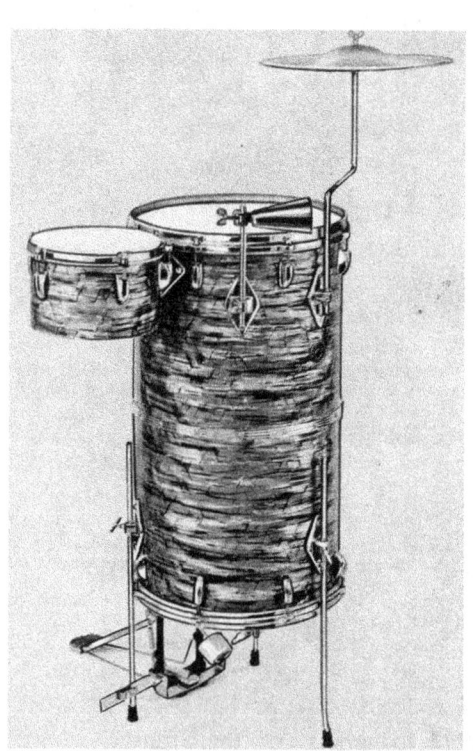

PX4183 Gretsch Broadkaster Cocktail drum
14x28 with 5.5x8
1954-1958

PX4183 Cocktail Drum (no longer called Broadkaster)
14x26 with 5.5x8
1961-1971

Gretsch did not catalog the custom-length bass drums and tom-toms of the 1940s that most associate with Louie Bellson. This kit has two 7x11 toms, 2 9x13 toms, 16x16 and 16x18 floor toms, a 26x18 center tom and two 20x20 bass drums. Although this outfit was made specifically for Louie, some other kits have surfaced, such as the one below.
1946

This (uncatalogued) 1952 kit owned by Ryland Fitchett consists of a 5.5x14 snare drum, 9x13 mounted tom, 24x16 floor tom, and 20x20 bass drum.

Fred W. Gretsch points out that when he began coming to the factory regularly to work in 1955, there were only a few workers building drums on the seventh floor of the 60 Broadway building. Although it was not mentioned in the catalogs, Gretsch was very much a custom shop, building each kit pretty much to order.

PX4055 Renown
6.5x14, 14x24, 8x12
1948-1958

PX4040 Semi Pro
6.5x14, 14x24
1949-1958

PX4070 Dixieland
5.5x14, 14x22
1954: Choice of lacquer colors
1955-1958:
Two-Tone Charcoal Gray & Cameo Coral
1961-1965:
Tri-Tone Green & Silver lacquer

PX4015 BroadKaster Name Band
6.5x14 (or 5x14), 14x22 (or 14x24), 9x13, 16x16,
1950-1961

PX4041 Semi Pro
6.5x14, 14x22
1955-1958

PX4040 Semi Pro
5.5x14, 14x22
1961-1965

PX4055 Renown (4040 without rack tom)
1961-1965: 5.5x14, 14x22, 8x12
1966-1971: 5.5x14, 14x20, 8x12,

"Birdland" outfits

by John Sheridan

In the annals of modern drum production, these are the most significant drum outfits to be offered by the Gretsch Company in the last 60 years.

The "Birdland" model is named after the famous "Birdland" jazz club of New York City in the 1950s. Gretsch built a "house set" for the club in the standard sizes of the day. These were 3-ply shells in Cadillac Green and all parts and stands were plated in 24-karat gold, including the hex key! This combination of appointments was only offered from 1953 to 1959. (They were, of course, priced much higher than standard catalogued kits.) [Ed. note: Gretsch did not catalog "Birdland" outfits. Birdland became a generic term for any outfit configuration in Cadillac Green with gold-plated hardware. The actual Birdland kit that Gretsch provided to the Birdland club was a 22,13,16, 5.5x14]

The kit illustrated here is a Max Roach/Progressive Jazz kit: 4x14, 8x12, 14x14, 14x20. Cadillac Green was an upscale Gretsch "Country Club" guitar model finish.

This kit was purchased by the original owner in 1958 when he was 24. Although it was apparent that the drums were put into storage and played very little if at all after 1959, he kept the drums until his passing in 2003. Gary Folchi of Precision Drum Company acquired the drums in 2003 and brought them to me for assistance with the sale of this kit. The kit was sold in an Ebay auction for the reserve price of $15,000.00. The winner of the auction asked to remain anonymous. From its manufacture in Brooklyn to its delivery to Poughkeepsie Music, it's sale to the original owner who was a resident of Poughkeepsie, and most recent sale to a Long Island resident, this outfit apparently never has left the state of New York.

[Ed. note: This kit more recently sold at Steve Maxwell's shop in New York City for $48,000.00.]

Birdland, jazz corner of world, gives visiting drummers use of its spectacular Gretsch green and gold set

"Most of the drummers playing the club use Gretsch drums anyway," so as a convenience to them, Birdland has a Gretsch outfit on hand at all times. "And what an outfit," says Bob Garrity DJ on WABC's all-night Birdland show. "The Gretsch green and gold drums alone are worth the price of admission." The Birdland Model drums are finished in Cadillac Green pearl with gold plated metal parts. If you're in New York City, be sure to drop in to Birdland for some of the country's finest sounds — for more details about these drums and other favorite Gretsch models played by consistent top winners in national drummer popularity polls, write: FRED. GRETSCH, Dept. DB7144, 60 Broadway, Brooklyn 11, New York.

A few of the star drummers who regularly play Birdland. They all agree "Gretsch Broadkasters, greatest drums I ever owned."

Louie Bellson

Denzil Best

Art Blakey

Birdland MC Pee Wee Marquette, DJ Bob Garrity and Gretsch Drums.

Jo Jones

Don Lamond

Shelly Manne

Bob Neal

Charlie Persip

Max Roach

Charlie Smith

Art Taylor

Gretsch's affiliation with the iconic New York City night club Birdland began in the year it was founded, 1949.

On April 25, 1960, a live recording of "Drum Night" was captured. It was released on two albums in 1960 and 1961.

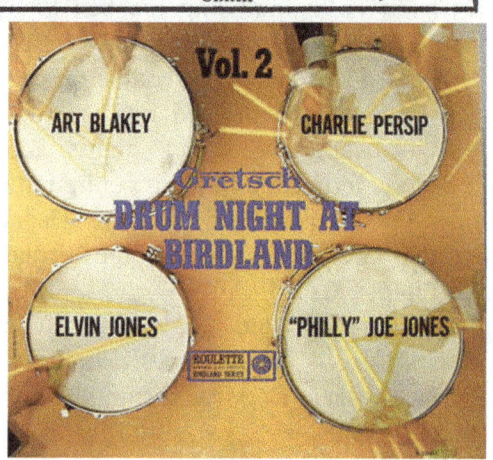

16 Inch Bass Drum

Elvin Jones with his 12x16 bass drum

The 12"x16" bass drum was not catalogued, so suspicions are often voiced that these drums are modified floor toms. The kits on this page are very well documented. An additional famous Gretsch 12x16 bass drum was part of the kit that Art Blakey used with the all-star group "Giants of Jazz" in late 1971 and early 1972. The kit can be seen in the DVD from that tour titled *Live In Prague 1971*. The group included Dizzy Gillespie (trumpet), Sonny Stitt (alto sax), Thelonius Monk (piano), Al McKibbon (bass), and Blakey. Another DVD showing the 12x16 is Elvin Jones playing on the Jazz Icons DVD *John Coltrane, Live in France, 1965*. Art Blakey is seen with his Satin Flame 12x16 in the September, 1984 issue of *Modern Drummer*.

Lee Ruff: *"In 1965, Ron saw John Coltrane's quartet in a live concert in Indianapolis. Elvin Jones was playing a Starlight sparkle covered set with a 12x16 bass drum. Ron, who was teaching at Stradd Music at the time, had the store owner order a set with the little bass drum. Gretsch replied that they had no model number for such a thing. Ron, who had previously visited the Brooklyn factory and met Phil Grant, had the dealer get Phil on the phone. Phil explained that the little bass drums were not catalogued, they were special-order items. Ron ordered the set in Burgundy Sparkle with a Jimmy Pratt tone control but without spurs or rail consolette. (Ron always used the Ludwig rail mounts and Slingerland spurs on his bass drums.) A few months after receiving his set, Ron ordered a second set like it in Starlight sparkle. Gretsch told him they had just enough Starlight sparkle left to do his little set. Ron also has an '80s set with a 12x16 he ordered through Harry Cangany."*

Lee Ruff: *"Down the road, a friend of Ron's ordered a set with a Jimmy Pratt, factory rail, and factory spurs in black diamond pearl. After a time he sold the set to a Scandanavian drummer, Ed Vandenburg, who had migrated to Cincinnati. Years later, an aging Ed Vandenburg sold the drums to Brett Walmsley and I purchased this set from Brett."* (Ed. note: the rack tom mount was fitted with a height extension. These bass drums were not fitted with lifts to raise them off the floor.)

12x16 bass drums usually either had no label, or a label with the model designation "Special," like this one from Lee Ruff's drum.

Since 2009, the Gretsch USA custom shop has been offering 16" bass drums, in 14" depth only.

VARIABLES

The 16x16 and two 14x14 floor toms below demonstrate some of the production inconsistencies seen on Gretsch drums. All of these floor toms are from the late 1960s. These variables are found on other sizes, but are most noticable on floor toms.

-Note that the lugs on the drum at left are positioned quite close to the hoop while the lugs on the other drums are much farther down with longer tension rods.

-Note the positioning of the badge. Most commonly, the badge was positioned a little above center like the one on the center drum. The drum on the left has a badge mounted nearer the top of the drum. The drum on the right actually has it's badge mounted slightly above center as the photo with the measuring tape illustrates; the angle that the photo of the complete drum was taken from creates the optical illusion that the badge is below center. Sometimes the badge actually *was* positioned below center.

-The drum on the right is a glass glitter finish. Drums made earlier and later with the same catalogued finish are "sparkle" as oppoosed to the "glitter."

-Silver sealer appearance can vary from a smooth opaque to a very translucent finish.

-All three of these drums have the larger (5474) lugs. More often, 14x14 floor toms were fitted with the smaller (5473) lugs. The smaller lugs were never found on 16" floor toms until KMC's involvement with Gretsch in 2000; since then all Gretsch floor toms have featured the smaller 5473 lugs. All other factors being equal, a drum with larger lugs is going to produce a slightly brighter tone than one with smaller lugs.

-Shell thicknesses and reinforcement rings are discussed in the shell chapter; variations abound.

1960s Bass Drum Comments by Lee Ruff

"The most rare bass drum size of the 1960s (other than the 16"), is the 24". Many people, if you asked them, would answer that it is the 18". I feel that 18s are hard to find because people rarely part with them. I believe 24s were omitted in some early 1960s catalogs, but Gretsch obviously did not altogether discontinue making this staple size. 20" bass drums were the most common of this era.

18" bass drums made with 3-ply shells were not the same as the 6-ply shells. The 3-ply 18s that I have personally seen I would consider questionable in terms of originality and they sound quite different, more like a Ludwig. To a jazz player, a 3-ply 18" bass drum with reinforcement rings would not be desirable at all. All of the star endorser drummers played 6-ply 18" bass drums."

PX4015 Name Band
5x14 (or 6.5x14), 14x22 (or
14x20) 9x13,16x16,
1961-1976

4002 (4007 with 22" kick)
One Nighter Plus
5.5x14, 20x14, 8x12
1963-1974

4012 Playboy (4013 less floor tom)
5x14, 14x20, 8x12, 14x14
1965-1971

PX4077 Jazz Combo
5x14, 14x20, 8x12
1954-1971

PX4025 Progressive Jazz
4x14, 14x20 (14x18 optional by 1959)
8x12, 14x14
1955-1976
(standard snare drum 5x14 by 1966)

For the first few years, the bass drum-mounted cymbal holder was located at the top of the drum.
By 1966 it had been moved to the right side as pictured.
"Side" placement of cymbal holder is randomly seen on Gretsch bass drums as far back as 1948.

#4026 Progressive Jazz
5x14 brass (5.5x14 wood optional),
14x20, 8x12, 14x14
1977-1979

4029 Avant Garde
1968-1971   5x14, 14x20 (2), 8x12 (2), 16x16
1971-1976   5x14, 14x22 (2), 9x13 (2), 16x16

4027 Rock N Roll
5x14, 14x20, 8x12, 8x12, 16x16
1965-1976

4028 Black Hawk
5x14, 14x22 (or 14x24)
8x12, 9x13, 16x16,
1968-1976

133

4035 Monster
5x14, 14x22, 8x12, 9x13, 10x14, 10x15, 16x16, 16x18
1972-1976

note: 18" floor tom counterhoops sourced from Slingerland; see hoops section of dating guide.

4020 Broadcaster/Broadkaster
5x14, 14x22, 9x13, 10x14, 16x18
1972-1976
spelled with a "c" in 1972, with a "k" 1973-1976

note: 18" floor tom counterhoops sourced from Slingerland; see hoops section of dating guide.

1973 Dorado Series (Imported from Japan)
Dorado was a name applied to a series of guitars, drums, and banjos imported from Japan. Several Dorado catalogs were distributed, but only the 1973 included drums. There were three configurations available in four colors.
#3950 Top Rock Outfit (pictured) 5.5x14, 14x22, 8x12, 9x13, 16x16
#3940 Concert Rock 5.5x14, 14x22, 9x13, 14x22
#3930 Mini Rock 5.5x14, 14x20, 8x12, 14x20
Colors: Jet Black, Blue Sparkle, Red Sparkle, Silver Sparkle

#4031 Concert Rock
6x14 brass (6.5x14 wood optional), 14x24 (2), 5.5x6, 5.5x8, 6.5x10, 8x12, 9x13, 10x14, 12x15, 14x16, 16x18
1977-1979
#9231 1980-1982

#9239 Concert Rock II
24" bass drums
1980-1982

notes: 6", 8", 10" toms had triple-flanged hoops from 1977 until May 1981, then die-cast hoops. New in 1981: 10-hole 18" triple-flanged hoop, replacing outsourced Slingerland 8-hole 18" triple-flanged hoops.

#4034 Monster Plus
6x14 brass (6.5x14 wood optional), 14x24,
5.5x8, 6.5x10, 8x12, 9x13, 10x14, 12x15, 16x16, 16x18
1977-1979
#9234 1980-1982

4032 Jazz Rock (concert toms)
5x14 brass (5.5x14 wood optional), 14x22 (2),
8x12, 9x13, 10x14, 12x15, 16x16
1977-1979,
#9232 1980-1982 (classic toms)
#9240 Jazz Rock Concert (concert toms)
1980-1982

#9241 Nighthawk II Concert
5x14, 14x22, 8x12, 9x13, 10x14, 12x15, 16x16
#9243: double headed toms
#9242: 6x14, 14x22, 9x13, 10x14, 12x15, 14x16, 16x16
1980-1982

4043 Studio
5x14 aluminum, 14x20, 8x12, 9x13, 16x16
1977-1982

Variations of these kits listed in price lists of the era but not illustrated in the catalogs:		
Disco Rock outfit #4033 5x14 brass (5.5x14 wood optional), 14x20 (2), 8x12 & 9x13 classic toms, 16x16 1977-1979	**# 4038 Nighthawk** 5x14 brass (5.5x14 wood optional), 14x20, 8x12, 9x13, 10x14, 12x15 concert toms, 16x16 1977-1979	**#4036 Monster II** 5x14 brass (5.5x14 wood optional), 14x22, 8x12, 9x13, 10x14, 12x15 concert toms, 16x16, #4036, 1977-1979 #9235 1980-1982

4019 Broadkaster II
6x14 brass (5.5x14 wood optional),
14x24, 9x13, 10x14, 16x18
1977-1979
#9219
1980-1982

4021 Grand Prix
5x14 brass (5.5x14 wood optional),
14x22, 8x12, 9x13, 16x16
1977-1979
Model # changed to 9221: 1980-1982
9222 Grand Prix Concert (concert toms)
1980-1982

4042 Recording
5x14 aluminum, 14x22, 8x12, 9x13, 14x16 concert toms,
1977-1982
Catalog photo above shows 20" bass drum though catalog specifies 22" drum. Early versions featured single-headed bass drums.

9252 Jazzette
5x14 metal (5.5x14 wood optional),
14x18, 8x12, 14x14
1980-1982

Variations of these kits listed in price lists of the era but not illustrated in the catalogs:

#9216 Pro Jazz 5x14, 14x22, 9x13, 16x16
1980-1982

#4016 Name Band II
5x14 brass (5.5x14 wood optional), 14x22, 9x13, 16x16
1977-1979

#4017 Big Band
5x14 brass (5.5x14 wood optional), 14x24, 10x14, 16x18
1977-1979

9220 Broadkaster II Concert same as #9219, with 9x13 and 10x14 concert toms
1980-1982

9227 Rock II (shown here)
5x14 metal (5.5x14 wood optional), 14x22 (2) 8x12,
9x13, 16x16, 16x18
1980-1982

9248 Blackhawk III Concert
6x14 brass (6.5x14 wood optional), 14x22, 8x12, 9x13,
10x14 concert toms, 16x16,
1980-1982

OPTION - NAME BAND (Double headed toms)
Finish shown: Maple
Cymbals not included.

#9226 Pro Jazz   1980-1982
5x14 brass (5.5x14 wood optional), 14x20, 8x12,14x14
Also offered with 14x22, 9x13, 16x16 as the "Name Band"

9244 Player
5x14 metal (5.5x14 wood optional),
14x22, 8x12, 9x13, 14x14, 16x16
1980-1982

9215 Renown II
5x14 Aluminum, 14x20, 8x12,14x16
1980-1981

Variations of these kits listed in price lists of the era but not illustrated in the catalogs:

9228 Rock II Plus
6x14 metal (6.5x14 wood optional), 14x24 (2)
9x13,10x14,16x16,16x18
1980-1982

9249 Blackhawk III Plus: double headed toms

9250 Blackhawk IV Plus: 24,13,14,15,18

9251 Black IV Concert: same as 9250, with concert toms
1980-1982

#4023 Blackhawk II
5x14, 14x22, 8x12,9x13,16x16
(8-lug snare and lighter hardware package)
1977-1979

9245 Player Concert: same as Player, with concert toms

9246 Player II: 13 and 14 rack toms, 16 and 18 floor toms

9247 Player II Concert: 13 and 14 concert rack toms, 16 and 18 floor toms
1980-1982

POWERDRUMS 1981-1982
9400 Nighthawk II Plus w/ Power: 16x22, 8x14, 10x12,11x13,12x14,14x15,16x16
9401 Nighthawk II w/ power: same, with concert toms
9402 Broadkaster II w/ power: 16x24, 8x14, 11x13,12x14,16x18
9403 Power Grand Prix 16x22, 8x14,10x12,11x13,16x16
9404 Power Jazzette 16x18, 8x14, 10x12,14x14
9405 Contemporary Jazz 16x18, 8x14, 8x10,10x12,14x14
9406 Jazz Revisited 16x18, 8x14, 8x8, 8x10,10x12,14x14
9407 Session 16x20, 8x14,10x12,11x13,16x16
9408 Fusion 16x22, 8x14, 8x8, 8x10,10x12,11x13,16x16
9409 Fusion II 16x24, 8x14, 8x10,10x12,11x13,12x14,16x18
9410 Fusion Concert 16x22, 8x14, 8x8 concert tom, 8x10 concert tom, 10x12 concert tom, 11x13 concert tom, 16x16
9411 Fusion II Concert 16x24, 8x14, 8x10 concert tom, 10x12 concert tom, 11x13 concert tom, 12x14 concert tom, 16x18
(5x14 Chromed brass 10-lug snare drum optional on all of these outfits.)

Cannon Bass Drums
Catalogued from 1987 to 1999, the Gretsch Cannon bass drums were not a new concept (see page 123). A prototype of a cannon style bass drum was shown at the 2013 NAMM show. From 1987 to 1999, the drums were listed in the following sizes:

18" Depth, by 18, 20, 22, 24
20" Depth by 18, 20, 22
22" Depth by 18, 20, 22
24" Depth by 20, 22, 24

OUTFIT CONFIGURATIONS 1983-1997

As explained elsewhere in this book, Gretsch went through some major changes between the first printing of the "poster catalog" in 1983 (distributed with few changes until 1997) and the next catalog in 1998. The fact that the poster was the only catalog distributed for some 14 years certainly does not mean that all the kits shown on the poster were readily available from 1983 through 1997. The price lists published during the poster era are of some help, but for much of that era, Gretsch drums were rather difficult to obtain. In spite of the increased variety of kits listed in the price lists, they were pretty much made to order, and orders often took over 6 months.

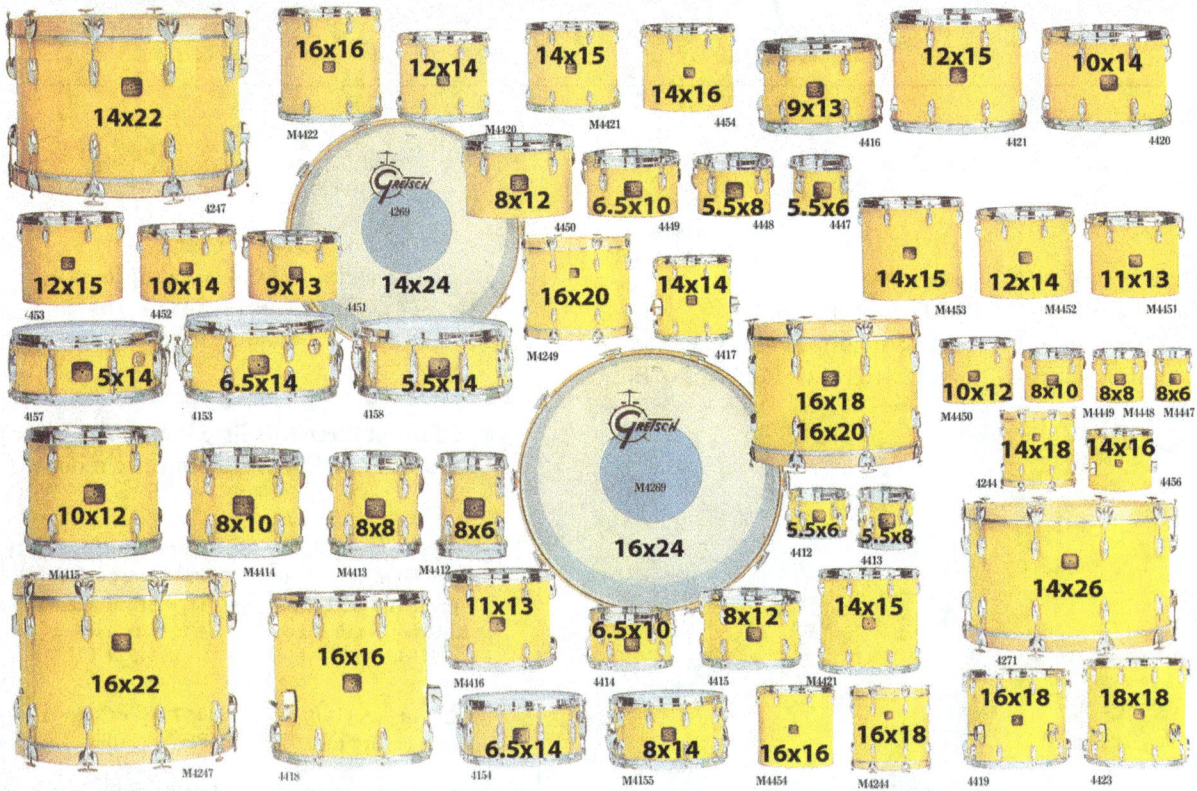

Outfit building blocks, from 1983 catalog poster

Karl Dustman: Production Factory Manager Ben Johnson took pride in building inventory of finished shell-banks in all colors and sizes, ready and able to accomodate the new order model number and respective shell-drilling requirements for shell-mount hardware, holders, etc. This was also the beginning point of the "suspension rings era" where toms were NOT drilled for the chrome plated Gretsch tom bracket but were added to the Gauger Rims product by the end-user/buyer.

Price List Outfit listings: Each of these configurations were listed with 2 to 8 different stock numbers based on bass drum and tom size options. (The only size configurations pictured here are those shown on the 1983 poster catalog.) Of all these configurations, only the Jazz, Grand Prix, and Player series kits remained in the 1998 catalog.

Power Jazzette 9502
5x14, 16x18, 10x12, 14x14
1983-1997

Power Grand Prix   9507
5x14, 16x22, 10x12, 11x13, 16x16
1983-1997

Player 9 9572
6.5x14, 16x22,
8x10, 10x12, 11x13, 16x16
1983-1989

Fusion 12 9571
5x14, 14x22, 8x8, 8x10, 8x12,
9x13, 16x16
1983-1990

Fusion 2 9523
6x14, 16,22, 8x8,
8x10, 10x12, 11x13, 16x16
1983-1997

Fusion 10 9531
16x22, 8x14,
8x10, 10x12, 11x13, 14x15, 16x16
1983-1990

Fusion 6 9527
5x14, 6x18, 8x8, 8x10,
8x12, 9x13, 14x14
1983-1990

Nighthawk 7 9570
8x14, 16x20, 16x22, 8x8, 8x10,
10x12, 10x14, 16x16
1983-1990

Monster Plus 4 9547
8x14, 16x22,
8x10, 10x12, 11x13, 12x14,
14x15, 16x16, 16x18, 18x18
1983-1990

Zenith 9551
6x14, 8x14, 8x6, 8x8, 8x10, 8x12, 9x13,10x12,10x14,11x13,12x14,12x15,14x15,16x16,16x18,18x18, 16x22,16x24
1983-1990

Artist 3 9550
8x14, 16x24 (2), 8x6, 8x8, 8x10,10x12,11x13,
12x14,14x15,16x16,16x18,18x18
1983-1990

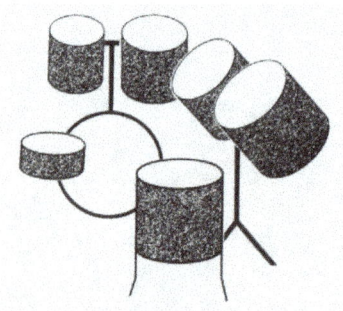

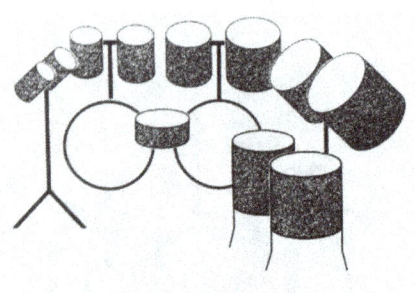

"CONCERT 7" SERIES #9553
8x14,16x22,10x12,11x13,
12x14,14x15,16x18
1983-1986

"CONCERT 10" SERIES #9557
8x14, 16x22,
8x10,10x12,11x13,12x14,
14x15,16x16,16x18,18x18
1983-1986

"CONCERT 13" SERIES #9561
8x14, 16x22 (2), 8x6, 8x8,
8x10,10x12,11x13,
12x14,14x15,16x16,16x18,18x18
1983-1986

1983 Centennial Outfit

The 100th Anniversary kit was the centerpiece of the 1984 NAMM convention

The kits were regular 6-ply shells that were enhanced with "Centennial Only" finishes of Birdseye Maple, Carpathian Elm, or Burl Walnut. Stands, hoops, and tom holders were gold-plated and reflective gold mylar heads were standard. Production was limited to 100 outfits. The August 1, 1983 press release explained that a special badge on each drum would bear the signature of Gretsch President Charlie Roy. When Roy left the company, marketing director Karl Dustman took over the badge signature duties; there were still about 35 Centennial kits to be badged. Other extras with the kit included a certificate of authenticity and a personalized embroidered Gretsch Centennial satin jacket. It was announced that a future promotion was planned listing the 100 Centennial kit owners but company fortunes precluded such a promotion and company archives do not include those names.

The special Centennial kit ended up going far over budget and taking much longer to put together than planned. There were lengthy delays due to problems with the gold plating as well as the extra labor to bookmatch the exotic veneers. Eventually the overstocked shells were finished with chromed hardware and sold at much lower prices.

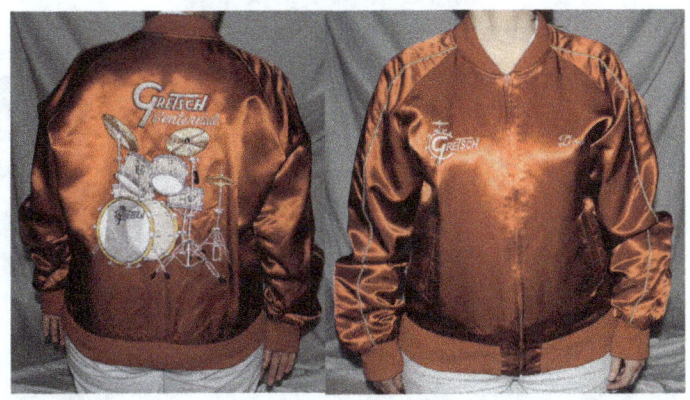

Dana Bentley's 8x14: Carpathian Elm. Dana's is from the 2006 NAMM "50 one-of-a-kind snare drums" that were made from "Vinyard" shells; an original 1983 Carpathian Elm shell that was finished & badged for 2006 NAMM.

Customers who purchased the Centennial kit were presented with a customized jacket with their name embroidered on the front. The jacket offer had to be discontinued before all 100 were supplied.

Gretsch first introduced electronic drums (right) in 1984. They considered stepping up into the professional series of electronic drums to compete with companies such as Simmons and even showed some prototypes, but stepped back and never brought them to market. Orders taken for this series were cancelled shortly after the convention.

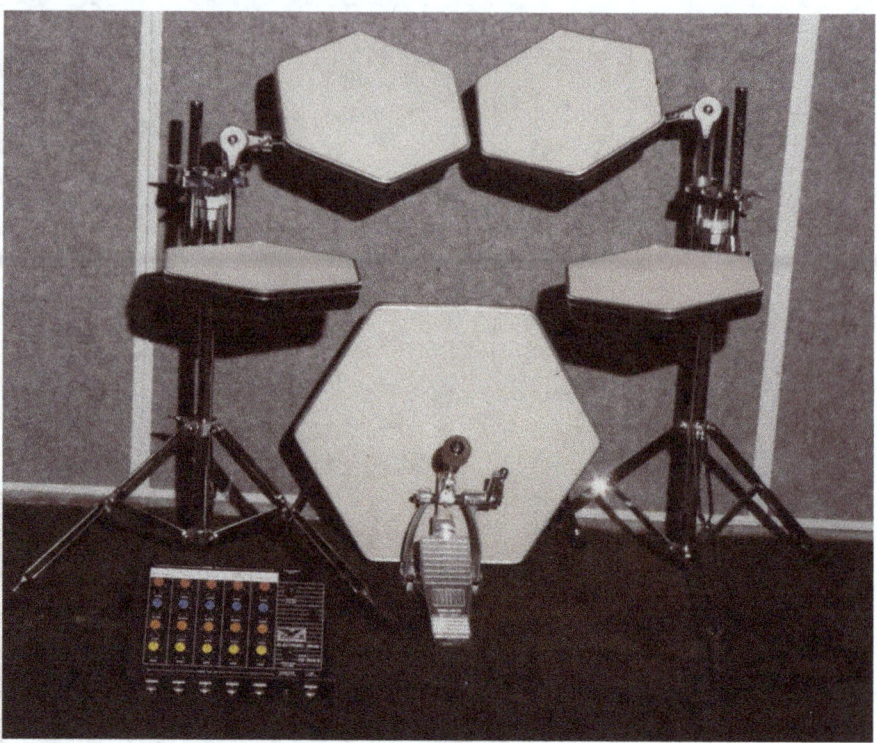

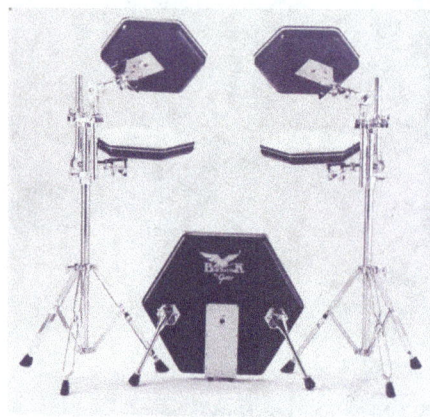

(left) Photo of the first "Blackhawk by Gretsch" low-end "starter" electronic drum kit which they declared an immediate success right after the 1984 NAMM show where it was introduced. Within 120 days of it's introduction, lawyers for the Simmons Group advised Gretsch that their multi-sided drum podules stood in violation of the Simmons trademark. The Gretsch pads were changed to a round shape, below.

Gretsch's biggest success with electronic drums was the Synsonics drum synthesizer. Developed by the toy maker Mattel, Fred Gretsch Enterprises became the exclusive distributor.

THE TONY WILLIAMS SET UP
MODEL No. G9533

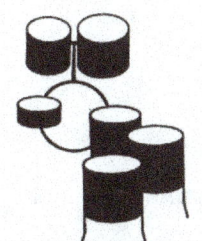

Tony Williams Set Up #9533
6.5x14, 14x24, 9x13, 10x14, 14x14, 16x16, 16x18
1983-1995

SOUND SHUTTLE SERIES

Sound Shuttle #G9573
8x14, 18x22 (2), 8x6, 8x8, 8x10, 10x12, 11x13, 14x14, 16x16, 18x18 (first Gretsch production outfit to include bass drums in 18" depth)
1986-1990

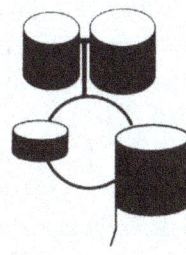

GIG RIG SERIES

Gig Rig #G9575
6.5x14, 16x22, 10x12, 12x14, 16x16
1986-1995

"CALIFORNIA" SERIES
CALIFORNIA SERIES

California Series #G9576
8x14, 16x22, 8x10, 10x12, 12x14, 14x16
1986-1997

Player 1998 (only)
6.5x14, 14x22, 8x10, 8x12, 14x14, 16x16

Broadkaster 9510
6x14, 14x24, 9x13, 10x14, 16x18
shown on the 1983 poster catalog, but not included in the 1983 price list

Jazz 1998-2002
5x14, 14x18, 8x12, 14x14

Grand Prix 1998-2002
5.5x14, 14x18, 8x12, 9x13, 14x14 or
6.5x14, 16x22, 10x12, 11x13, 16x16 or
5.5x14, 14x20, 8x10, 8x12, 14x14

Although 1998 stands as the year in which Gretsch stopped cataloging a dizzying number of outfit configurations (now down to the Jazz, Grand Prix, and Player Series), it more importantly marks the year that Gretsch began to really offer some substantially different drum series. The Broadkaster series was reintroduced, with some distinctive new features. Soon after, in 2000 when the KMC partnership began, new series and limited edition kits would begin to show up at every NAMM show.

BROADKASTER SERIES
Maple shells, satin lacquer finishes, die cast hoops, gun-metal plating

BROADKASTER NOTES
2002: Jazz, Grand Prix, and 4 Fusion configurations
2003: Listed as individual drums and six shell-packs, available only by special order with a minimum 120-day delivery time

Broadkaster Harvey Mason Signature
2 configurations:
5.5x14, 22x22
8x10, 8x12, 8x13, 14x14, 14x15
5.5x14, 22x18,
8x10, 8x12, 13x13, 14x14
1998-2005

Broadkaster Grand Prix
6.5x14, 16x20,
8x10, 8x12,14x14
1998-2002

Broadkaster Fusion
6.5x14,16x22, 9x10,10x12,12x14
1998-2002

Broadkaster Jazz
5x14, 14x18, 8x12,14x14
1998-2002

IMPORT LINES

It should be noted that these import lines often had features that were rather generic and were often nearly identical to other brands in the marketplace. They were included in the Gretsch offerings in order to complete the line with a budget drum set so as not to exclude the student drummer.

Blackhawk 560, 1982 (Gallatin, TN)
5.5x14, 14x22,
8x12, 9x13, 16x16
Also catalogued: 760 (7-piece) and 960 (9-piece)

1983-1990
6.5x14, 16x22, 10x12, 11x13, 16x16
Gretsch continued to offer an even more generic Blackhawk in the 1990s.

Blackhawk GBHS625
5.5x14, 16x22, 9x12, 10x13, 16x16
matching snare, low-mass lugs
Black or Wine Red only
1991-2001

Fusion: BH-F625
5x14, 16x22,
8x10, 9x12, 11x14

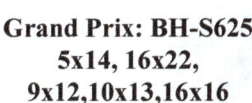

Grand Prix: BH-S625
5x14, 16x22,
9x12, 10x13, 16x16

(KMC) Blackhawk Series, 2003

KMC reintroduced the Blackhawk series in 2003. These drums were offered in "Shell pack" packages which means drums only, with no hardware except the tom holder. Purchasers of these shell packs or other Gretsch series shell packs were offered a variety of Gibraltar brand hardware packages to complete their kits. These drums were 6-ply Mahogany shells witth 45-degree bearing edges, low-mass mini Gretsch lugs, 1.6mm hoops. Offered in Liquid Black, Wine Red, and Blue Metallic.

Blackhawk Series 2005

Changes to the Blackhawk drums in 2005 included a shift to 30-degree bearing edges, and the introduction of kits with Mini-GTS tom suspension hardware in three new finishes: White Diamond, Blue Diamond, and Ebony Diamond. The new kits were dubbed the EX series, the old series was referred to as the SX series.

Nighthawk Series 2005-2013

At the same time the Blackhawk series was being nudged up a bit in quality and features, the Nighthawk series was introduced as the Gretsch entry-level kit; 6-ply mahogany shells, sold with hardware packages, in only two finishes, Liquid Black and Wine Red Metallic. This series was in the January 2005 price list, but discontinued by the time of the July 2005 price list because it was distributed by KMC Music from that point forward and is still available in 2013. Currently, 9-ply "cross-laminated select hardwoods" – 15x22, 9x12, 10x13, 16x16, 5.5x14 matching snare. A few Nighthawks were wrapped in "Blue Metallic" (BM) and "Vanilla Cream Pearl" (VCP).

Blackhawk Series 2006

Change from 6-ply to 9-ply shells.

Blackhawk Series 2008-2011

The EX series was discontinued, and the "SX" prefix was dropped from the remaining offerings. Bass drum hoops were changed from metal to wood with inlay. Shells were changed from 9-ply mahogany to 6-ply Basswood/Poplar. (8-ply for bass drums.) Only the three original colors were available: Liquid Black, Wine Red, and Blue Metallic.

**Renown Maple/Renown Series
2001-2013**

A "premium" import line with triple-chrome plated hardware and high-gloss lacquer finishes.

6-ply all-maple shells with 30-degree bearing edges except for snare drums, which were 10-ply with 45-degree bearing edges.

GTS Suspension systems. Die-cast hoops on all drums, Gretsch Silver Sealer inside all shells.

GRMF825 – 5x14, 8x10, 9x12, 11x14, 18x22 – late 2001 only
GRMS825 – 5x14, 9x12, 10x13, 16x16, 18x22 – late 2001 only
GRMF805 – 5x14, 8x10, 9x12, 11x14, 18x20 – late 2001 only
RM-F805 – 5x14, 8x10, 9x12, 11x14, 18x20 – 2002 only
RM-F825 – 5x14, 8x10, 9x12, 11x14, 18x22 – 2002 to 2004
RM-F824 – 8x10, 9x12, 11x14, 18x22 – 2003 to 2006
RN-M024 – 6.5x14, 9x12, 16x16, 18x22 – 1-1-06 to 3-1-06
RN-E825 – 5x14, 8x10, 9x12, 14x14, 18x22 – 2006 to 2009
RN-M024 – 6.5x14, 9x12, 16x16, 20x22 – 3-1-06 to 2009
RN-F605 – 5x14, 8x10, 9x12, 14x14, 16x20 – 2008 only
RN-R643 – 9x13, 16x16, 16x24 – 2009 to 2012
RN-E824 – 8x10, 9x12, 14x14, 18x22 – 2009 to 2012
RN-E604 – 8x10, 9x12, 14x14, 16x20 – 1-1-09 to 5-1-09
RN-F704 – 8x10, 9x12, 14x14, 16x20 – 5-1-09 to 2012
RN1-E8246 – 7x10, 8x12, 14x16, 18x22 – 2013 -
RN1-E823 – 8x12, 14x16, 18x22 – 2013 -
RN1-E604 – 7x10, 8x12, 14x14, 16x20 – 2013 -
RN1-R643 – 9x13, 16x16, 16x24 – 2013 –

RENOWN '57
RN57-E825 – 8x10, 9x12, 16x16, 18x22, 6.5x14 – 2011 to 2012
RN57-J484* – 9x12, 14x14, 14x18, 6.5x14 – 2012 only
*Many late 2012 Renown 57 "Be-Bop" kits included an 8x12 instead of a 9x12.

**RENOWN PUREWOOD SERIES
2005 –**
silver sealer, matching bass drum hoops, 30-degree bearing edges, die-cast hoops

2005 - limited to 100 kits in each configuration
RP-F826-WL - Renown Purewood Walnut – 6-ply
18x22, 8x10, 9x12, 11x14, 13x16, 5x14
RP-E826-CH - Renown Purewood Cherry – 6-ply
18x22, 7x10, 8x12, 12x14, 14x16, 6.5x14

2006 - Renown Purewood African Mahogany
6-ply – limited quantity
RP-R644-MH - 16x24, 9x13, 16x16, 6.5x14
RP-E826-MH - 18x22, 8x10, 9x12, 14x14, 16x16, 5.5x14

2007 - RP-E826-RW - Renown Purewood Rosewood
– 9-ply – limited quantity
18x22, 8x10, 9x12, 14x14, 16x16, 5.5x14

2008 - RP-E826-BBG - Renown Purewood Bubinga
9-ply- limited quantity 18x22, 8x10, 9x12, 14x14, 16x16, 6x14

2009 - RP-E826-OAK - Renown Purewood Oak
– 6-ply – limited quantity
18x22, 8x10, 9x12, 14x14, 16x16, 6.5x14

2010 - RP-E826-BCH - Renown Purewood Beech
– 7-ply – limited to 45 kits
18x22, 8x10, 9x12, 14x14, 16x16, 6.5x14

2011 - RP-E826-WEN - Renown Purewood African Wenge
– 7-ply – limited to 100 kits 18x22, 7x10, 8x12, 12x14, 14x16, 6x14

2012 - Renown Purewood 100% American Hickory
– limited to 35 kits in each configuration
RP-E605-HCK - 16x20, 7x10, 8x12, 14x14, 5.5x14
RP-E826-HCK - 18x22, 7x10, 8x12, 12x14, 14x16, 6x14

Catalina Elite (lacquer)
6-ply Mahogany shells with 30-degree bearing edges, lacquer finishes. 1.6mm hoops with GTS suspension systems, Millennium lugs. Maple bass drum hoops with high-gloss lacquer.
GCEF825 – 5.5x14, 16x22, 8x10, 9x12, 11x14 – July 2001 to 8-1-03
GCES625 – 5.5x14, 16x22, 9x12, 10x13, 16x16 – July 2001 to 2002
GCFS605 – 5.5x14, 16x20, 8x10, 9x12, 14x14 – July 2001 to 8-1-03
Add-Ons – GCE0708 7x8 and GCE1316 13x16 (2002-2003)

Catalina Stage (wrap)
Covered with "Nitron" wraps. Millennium lugs. Metal bass drum hoops, powder-coated.
GCSF625 – 5.5x14, 16x22, 8x10, 9x12, 11x14 – July 2001 to 8-1-03
GCSS625 – 5.5x14, 16x22, 9x12, 10x13, 16x16 – July 2001 to 8-1-03
GCSS605 – 5.5x14, 16x20, 8x10, 9x12, 14x14 – July 2001 to 2002
Add-Ons – GCE0708 7x8 and GCE1316 13x16 (2002-2003)

Catalina Club
6-ply Mahogany shells with 30-degree bearing edges, 1.6 mm hoops, center-mounted lugs and GTS suspension systems
GCE-S684 – (wrap) 5x14, 8x12, 14x14, 16x18 – 8-1-03 to 2005 (w/ mini lugs – 2006)
GCE-S665 – (wrap) 5x12, 6x8, 7x10, 13x13, 16x16 – 8-1-03 to 2005
Catalina Club '64 Reissue in Black Pearl (Guitar Center exclusive) 14x22 with rail consolette, cymbal arm holder 9x13, 16x16, 5.5x14 (2009)

Catalina Birch
6-ply 100% Birch shells with 45-degree bearing edges, 1.6 mm hoops, low mass ("mini") lugs & GTS suspension system. High-gloss translucent lacquer finishes
CA-S605 – (lacquer) 5x14, 8x10, 9x12, 14x14,16x20 – 8-1-03 to 7-1-05
CA-S825 – (lacquer) 5x14, 9x12, 10x13, 16x16, 18x22 – 8-1-03 to 2006
CA-F825 – (lacquer) 5x14, 8x10, 9x12, 11x14,18x22 – 8-1-03 to 7-1-05
CA-E825 – (lacquer) 5x14, 8x10, 9x12, 14x14, 18x22 – 2005 to 2006
Add-Ons – CA-0708 7x8 (2003-2006), CA-1316 13x16 and CA-1618 16x18 (2003-2005)
Birch Shells with natural interiors, GTS suspension systems, 30-degree bearing edges, mini Gretsch lugs, 1.6m hoops
BRT-E8256 (UV Gloss) – 5.5x14, 8x10, 9x12, 16x16, 18x22 – 2010 to 2012
BRT-S825 (UV Gloss) – 5.5x14, 8x12, 9x13, 16x16, 18x22 – 2010 to 2012
BR-E8256 (wrap) – 5.5x14, 8x10, 9x12, 16x16, 18x22 – 2010 to 2012
BR-S825 (wrap) – 5.5x14, 8x12, 9x13, 16x16, 18x22 – 2010 to 2012
Add-Ons – BR/BRT-0708T 7x8, BT/BRT-0710T 7x10, BT/BRT-1013T 10x13 (2010-2012)

Catalina Club Roll-Away Set (lacquer)
Roll-away set. 6-ply Mahogany shells with 30-degree bearing edges, 1.6 mm hoops, mini lugs and GTS suspension systems
GCE-G485 – 7x8, 8x10, 10x13, 14x18, 5x13 – 2005 only

Catalina Club Rock
6-ply Mahogany shells with 30-degree bearing edges, 1.6 mm hoops, mini lugs and GTS suspension systems
GCE-R665 – (lacquer or wrap) 10x14, 16x16, 16x18, 16x26, 6.5x14 – 1-1-05 to 7/1/05
CC-R665 – (wrap) 6.5x14, 9x13, 16x16, 16x18, 16x26 – 2006 to 2007
CT-R845 – (lacquer) 6.5x14, 9x13, 16x16, 16x18, 18x24 – 2008 to 2009
CT-R844T – (lacquer) 6.5x14, 9x13, 16x16, 18x24 – 2010 to current
CC-R444 – (lacquer) 6.5x14, 9x13, 16x16, 14x24 - 2013

Catalina Club Jazz
6-ply Mahogany shells with 30-degree bearing edges, 1.6 mm hoops, mini lugs and GTS suspension systems
CC-J484 – (wrap) 5x14, 8x12, 14x14, 14x18 – 2006 to current
CT-J484 – (lacquer) 5x14, 8x12, 14x14, 14x18 – 2008 to current
Add-Ons – CC-0710T (wrap) 7x10 (2008-2013), CT-0710T (lacquer) 7x10 (2009-2013)

Catalina Club Funk Jazz
Mahogany shells in Blue Alien wrap, 30-degree edges, natural interiors, mini lugs, 1.6 mm hoops
CC-J884-BA – 5x14, 18x18, 7x10, 12x14 – 2012 (limited to 50 kits)

Catalina Club Mod (wrap / mini lugs)
2006: Blue Alien, Black and Silver Sparkle Stripe
2008: Black Stripe over Silver Sparkle, Tattoo, G-Tube Graphic
CC-M024 – 6.5x14, 8x12, 14x16, 20x22 – 2006 to 2009

Catalina Club Mini Mod (wrap)
6-ply Mahogany shells with 30-degree bearing edges, 1.6 mm hoops, mini lugs and GTS suspension systems
CC-MO-0412T – 6x13, 8x12, 12x14, 20x20 – 2008 to 2009

Catalina Club Maple (lacquer)
Thin Maple shells with natural interiors, GTS Suspension systems, 2.5mm hoops, die-cast claw hooks, mini Gretsch lugs, UV Gloss finishes, and pro tom holders. From 2006 to 2010 all shell packs included free matching 16x16 floor tom.
MC-E825PT – 6x14, 8x10, 9x12, 14x14, free 16x16, 18x22 – 2006 to 10/1/10

Catalina Ash (lacquer)
Thin Ash shells with natural interiors, UV Gloss finishes, GTS suspension systems, die cast claw hooks, 2.5mm hoops, mini Gretsch lugs, pro tom holders. In 2006 all shell packs included free matching 7x8 mounted tom
AC-E826PT – 5x14, free 7x8, 8x10, 9x12, 14x14, 18x22 – 2006 to 2010
AC-E825PT6 – 5x14, free 7x8, 8x10, 9x12, 16x16, 18x22 – 2008 to 2010
Add-Ons – AC-1013T 10x13 (2009-2010)

Catalina Maple
New in 2010: 7-ply 7.2mm shells, "Gretsch Classic" features and hardware including mini-lugs, 30-degree bearing edges, ball & socket tom holder with 12.7mm tom arms, 9020 mounting brackets and 5-lug configuration on 10 and 12 toms. Multi-step lacquer process and Evans heads.
CMT-E825 – 6x14, 8x10, 9x12, 16x16, 18x22 – 10-1-10 to 1-1-11
CMT-E8262 – 6x14, 8x10, 9x12, 14x14, 16x16, 18x22 – 10-1-10 to 1-1-11
CMT-E825P – 6x14, free 7x8, 8x10, 9x12, 16x16, 18x22 – 2011 to current
CMT-E826P – 6x14, free 7x8, 8x10, 9x12, 14x14, 16x16, 18x22 – 2011 to current
Add-Ons – MC-0708T 7x8 and MC-1013T, 10x13 (2009-2010); CTM-0708T 7x8, CTM-0710T 7x10, CTM-1013T 10x13, CTM-1620B 16x20 (2010-2013)

Catalina Club Street (wrap / mini lugs)
Introduced in the USA in January of 2013, this kit (without the extending bass drum) appeared in the Japanese catalog several years earlier. Extending the bass drum expands it by two and a half inches, converting the 12"x16" kick to a 14.5"x16" kick with a more focused and punchier tone with more depth.
CC-S264X – 5x13, 6x10, 11x13, 12x16 (expandable to 14.5x16) – 2013 to current

Catalina Club Classic
6-ply Mahogany shells with 30-degree bearing edges, 1.6 mm hoops, mini lugs and GTS suspension systems
CC-J404 – 5x14, 8x12, 14x14, 14x20 – 2012 to current

Renegade Series   Energy Series   Nighthawk Series
Two new series replaced the Blackhawk marque in late 2011. (The entry level Nighthawk series has been available since 2005.) **Renegade**: double-braced hardware, Gretsch Renegade pedal boards. Brass cymbals included.
All shells 9-ply poplar with 45-degree bearing edges, ball-style tom holders
Energy: a step up from the Renegade series. Sabian SBR cymbals. Double braced hardware, stylized Gretsch Energy pedal boards. All Poplar shells have 30-degree bearing edges, and feature 5 lug configuration on 10" and 12" toms with Gretsch style lug that draw from the rich Gretsch lineage
Nighthawk: Entry-level series. 100% Mahogany shells, matching 8-lug snare drum, two size configuration kits;

Renegade RG-E625
5.5x14, 7x10, 8x12, 14x16, 16x22

ENERGY GE-E8256PK - 5.5x14, 7x10, 8x12, 14x16, 18x22 w/ hardware and SBRs (2012-2013)
ENERGY GE-38265S - same set without hardware or cymbals (2012 only)
ENERGY GE-2828 - 5.5x14, 7x8, 8x10, 9x12, 12x14, 14x16, 18x22 (2) (2012 only) Not available in white.

NH-525PK - 9x12, 10x13, 16x16, 15x22, 5.5x14 w/ hardware and brass cymbals
NH-S505 - 8x10, 9x12, 14x14, 15x20, 5x14. (2004-2005 only)

NEW CLASSIC

In 2006, the New Classic Series was described as the first completely new designed set for Gretsch in more than 50 years. Series Features:
- Proportionate Maple blend shells with Silver Sealer   -Low profile ITS suspension systems
- Low mass vintage styled tube lugs   -Die Cast toms and snare hoops
- New 9025 Hinged tom brackets   -Die Cast claw hooks

Integrated Suspension System

Vintage Styled Tube Lugs

Tom and Floor Tom Brackets

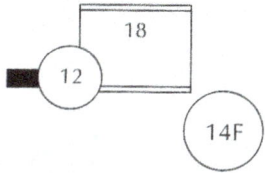

NC-S843 "Bop" 2007 only
NC-S483 "Bop" 2008-2012
NC1-S483 "Bop" 2013-
(shell pack)
14x18, 8x12, 14x14

NC-E824 2006-2012
NC1-E824 2013-
(shell pack) 18x22
8x10,
9x12
14x14

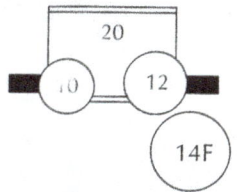

NC-F604 2008-2012
NC1-F604 2013-
(shell pack)
16x20, 8x10, 9x12, 14x14

NC-M823
(shell pack)
2006-2007
18x22
9x12,
16x16

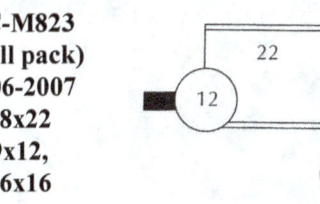

American-made lines

USA CUSTOM SERIES LIMITED EDITION KITS

2003 – Champagne Sparkle or Dark Walnut Lacquer in 120 sets only
RB20-S484 –
8x12, 14x14, 5x14, 14x18
RB20-S484R –
8x12, 14x14, 5x14, 14x18 with rail mount tom holder

USA CUSTOM SERIES LIMITED EDITION KITS

8/1/03 – Black/Silver Duco or Blue/Silver Duco totally 120 sets only
DC-S404R – 8x12, 14x14, 14x20 w/ rail mount tom holder, 5.5x14
DC-S484R – 8x12, 14x14, 14x18 w/ rail mount tom holder, 5.5x14

2004-2005 – Walnut Gloss or Antique maple, totaling 100 sets only
70s LTD C7-S603 – 8x12, 14x14, 16x20 (no mount), matching 5x14 sold separately
70s LTD C7-S623 – 8x12, 16x16, 16x22 (no mount), matching 5x14 sold separately

7/1/05 – Millennium Maple or Stardust Maple, both with highly figured Curly outside ply
C-E826-CMM – 8x10, 9x12, 14x14, 16x16, 18x22, 5.5x14 in Curly Millennium Maple
C-E826-CSD – 8x10, 9x12, 14x14, 16x16, 18x22, 5.5x14 in Curly Stardust Maple

2006-2007 – Walnut Series – 100% 6-ply American-Made Walnut Shells
CW-484WRSP-GW – 8x12, 14x14, 14x18 with rail mount tom holder, 5x14
CW-484SP-GW – 8x12, 14x14, 14x18 (without rail mount), 5x14

2008 – 125th Anniversary editions, only 125 kits of each for 2008
RB125-RL625-GMM – "Rock Legend"
16x22, 8x12, 14x14, 16x16, 6.5x14 in Millennium Maple Gloss
RB125-J404-CG – "Progressive Jazz"
14x20, 8x12, 14x14, 4.5x14 in Cadillac Green with Gold Hardware
RB125-B484-CG – "Progressive Bop"
14x18, 8x12, 14x14, 5x14 in Cadillac Green with chrome hardware

2009 - USA Custom Red Duco with Satin Chrome Hardware (20 kits worldwide)
18x22, 6.5x14, 8x10, 8x12, 14x14, 16x16
Harlequin Curly Sun Amber with gold hardware, limited to 25 kits worldwide
MB-J684-HQG – 16x18, 8x12, 14x14, 5.5x14 8-lug snare

2010 – Piano Gloss finishes with Sparkle inlays limited to 30 kits each worldwide
GR-E8256-PBS – 18x22, 8x10, 9x12, 16x16, 6.5x14 Piano Black w/ Silver Sparkle inlay
GR-J484-PWG – 14x18, 8x12, 14x14, 5.5x14 Piano White w/ Gold Sparkle inlay and gold hardware

2013 – 130th Anniversary kits January to March, 30 kits global

CUSTOM/AMERICAN CUSTOM/USA Custom 1991-2013
Same drum series, different names:
1991-2001 Custom
2003-2004 Custom Series
2005 American Custom Series
2006-2007 Custom Series
2008-2011 USA Custom Series
2012-2013 USA Custom

USA MAPLE SERIES
2002 – 2005
Maple shells, satin oil finishes, Millennium hardware, 2.3 mm hoops

2002
One Jazz, one Grand Prix and 3 Fusion kits
US-S683 - 8x12, 14x14, 16x18
(changed to UD-S683 from 2003-2005)
US-S604 - 7x10, 8x12, 14x14, 16x20
(changed to UD-S604 from 2003-2005)
US-F804 - 8x10, 9x12, 11x14, 18x20
(changed to UD-F804 in 2003 only)
US-F824 - 8x10, 9x12, 11x14, 18x22 (changed to UD-F824 from 2003-2005)
US-F825 - 8x10, 9x12, 11x14, 13x16, 18x22 (changed to UD-F825 in 2003 only)

2003 only
UD-S603 - 16x20, 8x12, 14x14
UD-S824 - 18x22, 8x10, 9x12, 14x14
UD-S825 - 18x22, 8x10, 9x12, 14x14, 16x16
UD-S826 - 18x22, 7x8, 8x10, 9x12, 14x14, 16x16
UD-F826 - 18x22, 7x8, 8x10, 9x12, 11x14, 13x16

GRETSCH USA CUSTOM 125th ANNIVERSARY DRUMS   2008

Limited Edition Custom Series
RB125-B484-CG Progressive Bop
5x14, 14x18, 8x12, 14x14
2008 only

Limited Edition Custom Series
RB125-J404CG Progressive Jazz
4.5x14, 14x20, 8x12, 14x14
2008 only

Steve Ferrone photo by Deboorah Arlook

Steve Ferrone Signature Series
2006-2013
-"Legendary Gretsch 6-ply shells"
-GTS Suspension system
-1955 Cadillac Green gloss lacquer
-Die Cast hoops
-Steve Ferrone signature badges
Listed as component drums: Bass Drums 14x22, 18x22, 14x24, Toms 8x10, 8x12, 9x13, Floor Toms 14x14, 14x16, 16x16

Vinnie Colaiuta Signature Series
1999-2010
1999: kit GVSO622K
White Wash with Black hardware
5x14, 18x22, 7x10,
8x12, 14x14, 16x16
New in 1999, these drums were expanded into an entire line in 2002: 3 suggested kit configurations and four snare drum models.
From 2003 forward, only the signature kit configuration above was listed, along with component drums of most sizes.
GVS0522 - 18x22, 8x12, 9x13, 16x16, 6.5x14 - 1999-2002
GVS0318 - 16x18, 7x10, 14x14 - 1999-2002

Limited Edition Custom Series
RB125RL625-GMM - Rock Legend
6.5x14, 16x22, 8x12, 14x14, 16x16
2008 only

2009 Limited Edition (20 kits worldwide)
USA Custom, Red Duco with Satin Chrome hardware
18x22, 6.5x14, 8x10, 8x12, 14x14, 16x16

Limited Edition: Duco Custom Kits   August, 2003
A total of 120 kits in two configurations: each available in Black/Silver or Blue/Silver

DC-S404R-BK Center Mounted Lugs
Rail-mount holder, 5x14, 14x20, 8x12,14x14

DC-S484-BL Separate Mounted Lugs
Rail Mount Holder, 5.5x14,14x18, 8x12,14x14

Limited Edition: Custom Series '70s LTD Sets   2004-2005
A total of 100 kits in two configurations, each available in '70s Walnut Gloss or Antique Maple Gloss
drop G stop sign badge, t-rods on bass drums, bearing edges cut to exactly match '70s era edges

C7-S603 16x20, 8x12,14x14

C7-S623 16x22, 8x12, 16x16

Limited Edition Custom Walnut Series
CW-484WRSP-GW - 14x18, 8x12, 14x14, 5x14 w/ rail mount
CW-484SP-GW - same but without rail mount
2006-2008 (Introduced with announcement that production would be limited to 2006, but the series was still listed in 2008.)
100% 6-ply vertical grain Walnut shells, die-cast hoops, silver sealer inside shells, custom 1883 badges, 30-degree bearing edges

USA CUSTOM LIMITED EDITION (30 kits each) 2010

GR-E8256-PBS - 18x22, 8x10, 9x12, 16x16, 6.5x14 - Piano Black with Silver Sparkle inlays

GR-J484-PWG - 14x18, 8x12, 14x14, 5.5x14 - Piano White with Gold Sparkle inlays

Limited Edition 2012 Outfits

2012 Catalina Club Limited Reserve
CC-J404-WMR
5.5x14, 14x20, 8x12, 14x14
White Marine Ripple wrap,
touched with subtle light blue hue
limited to 100 kits in North America for 2012
As of 2013, this configuration was made available as
a regular product offering (though not in this color).

2012 New Classic Limited Reserve
NC-E824-STS
limited to 30 kits in USA for 2012
6.5x14, 18x22, 8x12, 14x16
Turquoise Sparkle Delmar Wrap
chrome tube lugs, low-mass tom suspension system,
12.7 mm tom arm and 12.7 mm floor tom legs,
Evans USA heads.

2012 Renown Maple Limited Reserve
RN-E605-MG
limited to 25 kits in North America
Midnight Blue Glass Glitter
matching 5x14, 16x20, 7x10, 8x12, 12x14

2012 Renown Purewood Hickory
Natural finish inside, exteriors finished in gloss lacquer
production limited to 35 kits each configuration:
RP-E605-HCK 5.5x14, 16x20, 7x10, 8x12, 14x14
RP-E826-HCK 6x14, 18x22, 7x10, 8x12, 12x14, 14x16

Limited Edition 130th Anniversary Outfits, 2013

All 130th Anniversary sets come with Certificates of Authenticity signed by
Fred W. Gretsch, Paul Cooper and John Palmer.

130-E605-BSM
6-ply Gretsch formula maple shell with exotic Birdseye
Maple exterior veneer, Satin Nitrocellulose lacquer finish,
30-degree edges, silver sealer, die cast hoops
5x14 (8-lug), 16x20, 7x10, 8x12, 14x14
production limited to 30 kits worldwide during the period
from January to March, 2013

130-J484-SSF
6-ply Gretsch formula maple shells covered in Silver
Satin Flame Nitron, 30-degree edges, silver-sealer,
die cast hoops, satin black bass drum hoops with
matching Nitron inlay
5x14 (8-lug), 14x18, 8x12, 14x14
production limited to 35 kits worldwide during the
period of April to June 2013

130-E826-VCB
6-ply Gretsch formula maple shells in Satin Cherry Burst
Vintage Nitrocellulose lacquer, 30-degree edges, silver
sealer, die cast hoops
6x14, 18x22, 7x10, 8x12, 12x14, 14x16
production limited to 30 kits worldwide during the period
July to September 2013

130-J484V-GSF
6-ply Gretsch formula maple shells covered in Gold
Satin Flame Nitron, 30-degree edges, silver-sealer interior, die-cast hoops, vintage style hardware, special
anniversary logo heads
5x14, 14x18, 8x12, 14x14
October to December 2013 only, production limited
to 35 kits worldwide

Brooklyn Series 130GB-E824-PS 2013
6-ply Gretsch formula maple/poplar shells covered
in Pewter Sparkle Nitron, 30-degree edges, "302"
3.0mm double flanged hoops, anniversary logo heads
5.5x14, 18x22, 8x12, 14x16

Catalina Club Street   CC-S264X TSS Silver Sparkle or TRS Red Sparkle

Introduced in the USA in January of 2013, this kit (without the extending
bass drum) appeared in the Japanese catalog several years earlier

The bass drum expands by two and a half inches, converting the 12"x16"
kick to a 14 1/2"x16" kick with a more focused and punchier tone with
more depth. 5x13, 12x16, 6x10, 11x13

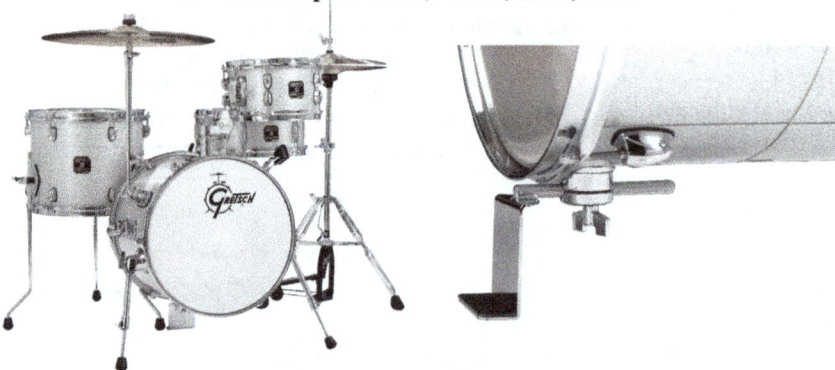

New Classic Silver Metallic
A new finish in 2013 made up of silver glass flakes combined with silver sparkle flakes.
Available in three configurations:
NC1-E824-SM 18x22, 8x10, 9x12, 14x14
NC1-F604-SM 16x20, 8x10, 9x12, 14x14
NC1-S483-SM 14x18, 8x12, 14x14

Catalina Maple Satin Walnut
A new finish for Catalina Maple in 2013.
Available in two configurations:
CMT-E825P-SWF   6x14, 18x22, 7x8, 8x10, 9x12, 16x16
CMT-E826-SWF   6x14, 18x22, 7x8, 8x10, 9x12, 14x14, 16x16

GRETSCH SNARE DRUMS

The earliest Gretsch catalogued snare drums were presented under the brand name "20th Century."
Marching drums and children's models are not included in the listing here

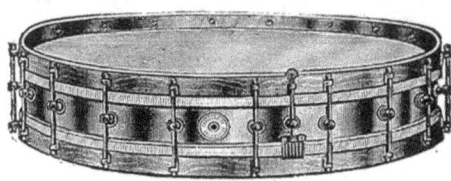

Orchestra Models
#1 5x15   #3 5x16
5-ply rosewood shell,
birdseye maple veneer hoops, 15 lugs

#4 Single head version: 14",
Birdseye maple 5-ply shell, 14 lugs
1912-1915

Semi-orchestra models
(for street or orchestra)
6x16 16-lug
#5 5-ply rosewood shell,
#6 Corrugated nickel-plated shell
1912-1915

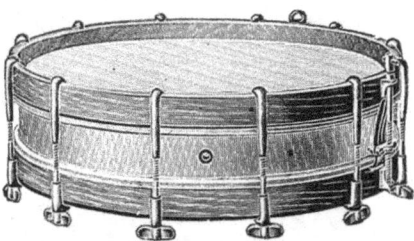

Professional Drums
Maple, Mahogany,
or Nickel-Plated metal shells
#1258 3x14 9-rod   #1259 3x15 10-rod
#1260 5x16 12-rod
#1261 3x15 12-rod
(nickel capped hoops)
1912-1915
"Thoroughbreds" 1914-1915:
#1300 3x14 5-ply oak, #1310 3x15
#1362 3x14 5-ply walnut #1364 3x15

20th Century Professional Drums
Solid Rock Maple shells,
throw-off strainer
#1262 3x14 12-rod
#1264 3x15 14-rod
#1265 5x16 16-rod
#1267 3x15 14-rod
1912-1915

Prussian Style Tenor Drum
Mahogany or maple
veneered shell
#188 4x14   #194 5x16
#196 5x16 w/ scrolled hoops
1912-1915

Prussian Style Tenor Drum
Nickel plated corrugated shell
#224 5x16
1912-1915

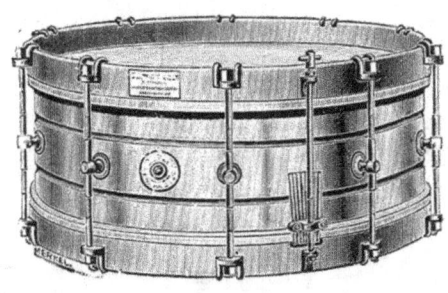

**20th Century
Prussian Style Drum**
#8 5x16 Nickel Plated
corrugated shell
#9 5x16 Walnut shell
1912-1915

Orchestra Drum
Maple or mahogany shell,
plain or scrolled hoops
#242 5x12   #248 5x16
#254 (scrolled) 5x16
1912-1913

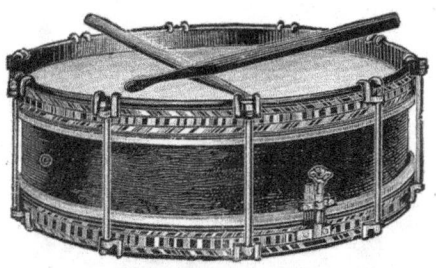

"Extra Narrow Model"
Maple, rosewood,
or metal shell
#258 3x14   #259 3x15
#260 5x16
#262 5x16 w/ capped hoops
1912-1915

At the time of this writing, no Gretsch catalogs or other archives between 1915 and 1927 are known to exist. It is difficult to ascertain the exact years in which the models listed here were introduced and/or discontinued.

Gretsch-American "Orchestra"
3-ply shell: mahogany, maple, or Duco Ebony
Nickel Plated Hardware:
#17 4x14,   #19 4x15,
#18 5x14,   #20 5x15
Silver plated hoops,
Gold plated hardware:
#17 4x14, #19 4x15,
#18 5x14, #20 5x15
1927

Gretsch-American All-Metal Drum
seamless brass shell,
8-rods, new strainer
Nickel-plated shell and hardware:
#12 4x14, #13 4x15,
#14 5x14, #16 5x15
Silver-plated shell,
gold-plated hardware:
#12 4x14, #13 4x15, #14 5x14,
#16 5x15
1927

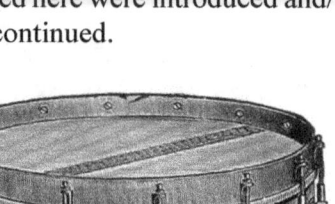

Single Header Orchestra
#268 14-inch maple shell
1912-1915

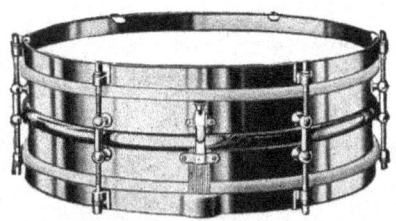

Orchestra Model
#10 4x14, brass shell,
nickel-plated
1927

"Big Value" 1927
3-ply shell, mahogany, maple, or Duco ebony
#1258 3x14, 8 rods, #1259 4x15 10 rods

"Leader" 1927
brass shell, 6 rods
#1213 3x14

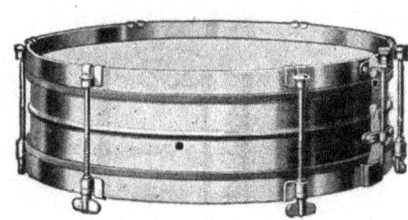

All Metal 1927
budget drum; brass shell, 6 rods
#5 3x14

Gretsch "Standard" Broadkaster Snare Drums of 1936
One-piece brass or 3-ply wood shell finished in Mahogany, Duco White or Duco Black. Hardware plated in nickel, chrome, or "Klondygold"
#14 5x14 metal, #15 6.5x14 metal,   #18 5x14 wood,   #19 6.5x14 wood

Utility Snare Drum 1936
#9 5x14 3-ply shell, Mahogany or Duco Ebony

Utility Snare Drum 1936
#8 5x14, all metal

Junior Professional 1936
#5 5x14

Junior Professional
#6 5x14 Mahogany or Duco
Ebony
1936

Professional All Wood Snare Drum
3-ply shell, 16 thumb-rods,
mahogany or natural maple finish
#70 4x14, #71 5x14, #72 5x15
1936

"Old Favorite"
3-ply, Mahogany or Maple
#1257 3x13, #1258 4x14,
#1259 5x14
1936

Junior
#3 3x13 Wood Shell
1936

Junior
#4 3x13 Metal Shell
1936

Missouri
brass shell, rosewood hoops
#80 4x13, #81 5x14
1936

Economy
#8100 brass shell, 5x14
1939-41

Economy
#8102 3-ply laminated mahogany,
5x14
1939-41

Junior Professional
#8105 3-ply laminated mahogany,
5x14
1939-41

Junior Professional
#8104 solid brass shell, 5x14
1939-41

Junior
#8108 all metal shell, 3.5x13
1939-41

Junior
#8107 3-ply laminated mahogany,
3.5x13
1939-41

 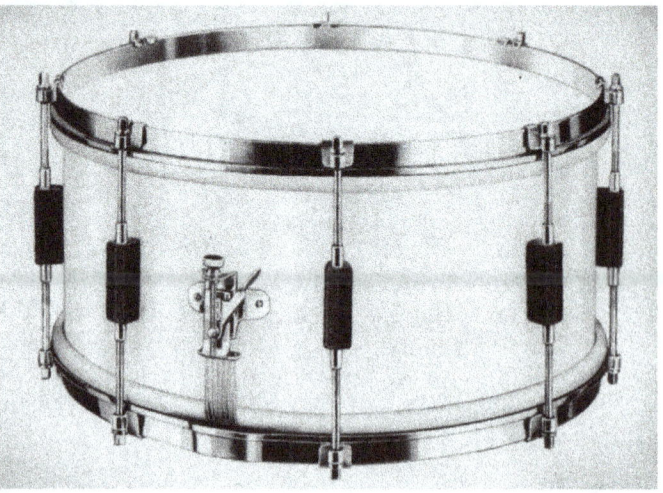

Catalina 1939-1941
3-ply shell, 6.5x14, Bakelite center brackets
#8095 White Duco with black brackets, #8096 White Duco with red brackets,
#8097 Duco-Ebony with white brackets, #8098 Duco Ebony with red brackets
Renown (above left) or #1950 (above right) strainer

 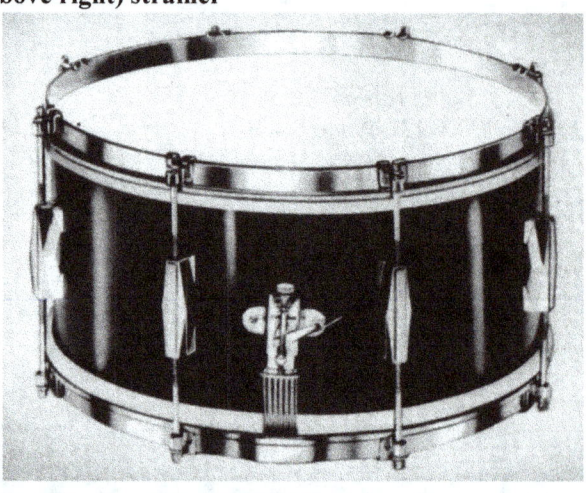

Renown
Brass shell with center bead or 3-ply laminated wood shell "Modernistic" lugs
#8085 5x14 nickel plated, #8087 5x14 chrome plated, #8086 6.5x14 nickel plated, #8088 6.5x14 chrome plated
#8090 5x14 wood/nickel hardware, #8092 5x14 wood/chrome hardware,
#8091 6.5x14 wood/nickel hardware, #8093 6.5x14 wood/chrome hardware
1939-41 (reduced to only #8093 by 1949)

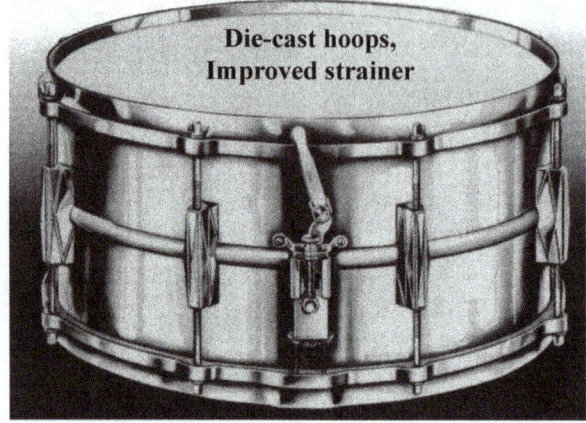 

Broadkaster 1939-41
#8060 5x14 nickel, #8061 6.5x14 nickel,
#8062 5x14 chrome, #8063 6.5x14 chrome
gold plating on special order

Broadkaster 1939-41
#8070 5x14 nickel, #8071 5x14 chrome,
#8072 6.5x14 nickel, #8073 6.5x14 chrome
White or black Duco, two-tone Duco, Mahogany
gold plating on special order

ROCKET DRUMS

For many years, the lugs at the bottom of the facing page have been referred to in the vintage drum community as "Rocket" lugs. There is no evidence that the Gretsch Drum Company ever used that term. Usage of the term probably stems from the "Rocket" brand which was applied by the Gretsch & Brenner company to Gretsch drums that they distributed.

As mentioned in Gretchen Elsner-Sommer's family background section (page 7), Walter Gretsch (Fred Sr.'s younger brother by 1 1/2 years) and another Gretsch employee, William Brenner, left the Fred Gretsch Manufacturing Company in 1924 to start their own musical instrument distributing company. Fred W. Gretsch points out that Gretsch & Brenner distributed Avedis Zildjian cymbals while the Fred Gretsch Manufacturing Company was heavily invested in the importing and marketing of the K. Zildjian line. "We have to guess that the family was trying to keep some separation in its marketing," says Fred. "There was some competition between them and each was looking for good lines to sell. While it is possible that Gretsch & Brenner's Rocket drums were made by a mystery maker, our guess is that the Fred Gretsch Manufacturing Company made the Rocket drums for Gretsch & Brenner."

It is evident that Gretsch did in fact make drums for other companies; all of the snare drums in the 1938 Rogers catalog pages shown here are Gretsch drums.

Gretsch-Gladstone 3-way tension
6.5x14 Mahogany, Black or White Duco, 2-tone Duco, Pearl coverings
1939-41 (discontinued some time before 1948)

Gretsch-Gladstone 2-Way tension
6.5x14, Mahogany, Black or White Duco,
2-tone Duco "Dress Parade",
Gretsch-Pearl "Dress Parade"
1939-1949

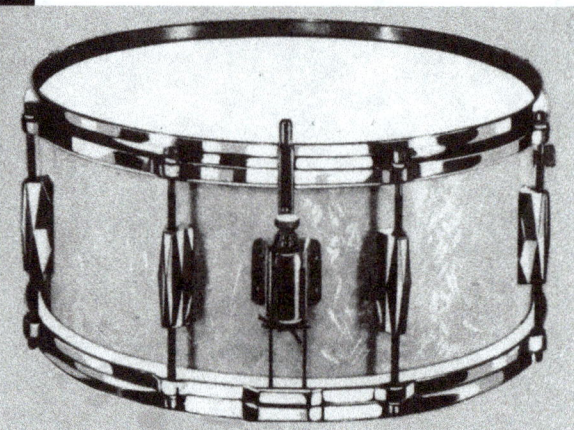

Broadkaster Standard
X4151 lacquer finish, X4153 Pearl covering
6.5x14
1948-49

Broadkaster Concert
X4190 7x14 Mahogany, X4191 7x14 Pearl
X4192 8x15 Mahogany, X4193 8x15 Pearl
1949-1953

Broadkaster "Narrow Model"
X4155 lacquer finish, X4157 Pearl
5x14
1949

Gretsch Concert Snare Drum
(same stock numbers and sizes as Broadkaster Concert)
1954-1967

Concert Snare Drum
(same stock numbers and sizes as Broadkaster Concert)
1967-1974 with Lightning throw-off as shown
1974-1976 with newer Lightning throw-off

Broadkaster Standard - 1950
(Renamed) Broadkaster Floor Show 1958
(Renamed) Floor Show 1961-1966
6.5x14
X4151 mahogany or lacquer (discontinued 1966)
X4153 pearl as pictured until 1967

Floor Show
6.5x14 4153 Pearl, 4153W wood finishes
1967-1974
This model was last referred to as the "Floor Show" by Gretsch in 1971. From about 1975 to today, this model has remained in the line with the updated Lightning throw-off. The internal USA label identified this model as the 4153 and G4153 from 1987 to 2007.

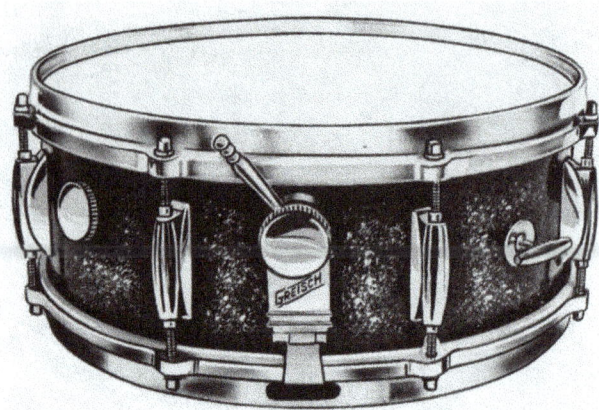

Broadkaster New Narrow Model - 1950
Renamed Broadkaster Name Band 1958
Renamed Name Band 1961-1966
5.5x14
X4155 mahogany or lacquer discontinued 1966
X4157 as pictured until 1967

Renown
X4102 6.5x14
1954-1958

Lee Ruff collection

In recognition of their Diamond Jubilee Anniversary in 1958, Gretsch introduced a special color, "Anniversary Sparkle Pearl," and an anniversary snare drum that was basically a Name Band model with the special finish and an anniversary name plate. Lee Ruff: "*The first ones had the one point butt end, 3-ply shell, stick chopper hoops. Then they evolved to 6-ply with either one or 4-point butt end and stick chopper hoops. Then 6-ply shells with 4-point butt end and the flanged diecast hoops. I have seen some of each with or without the Anniversary name plate. Some say the 1st design 1958s were the only ones w/anniversary name plates. This is not correct. Installation of the anniversary plates seems to have been at random.*" John Sheridan: "*These same plates were also used on the headstocks of Gretsch Anniversary guitars.*"

Name Band
4157 Pearl 4157W Wood
5.5x14
1967-1976
"Name Band" designation last used in 1971.

Renown
5.5x14
X4102 Mahogany or lacquer 1950-1968
X4103 Pearl 1961-1968

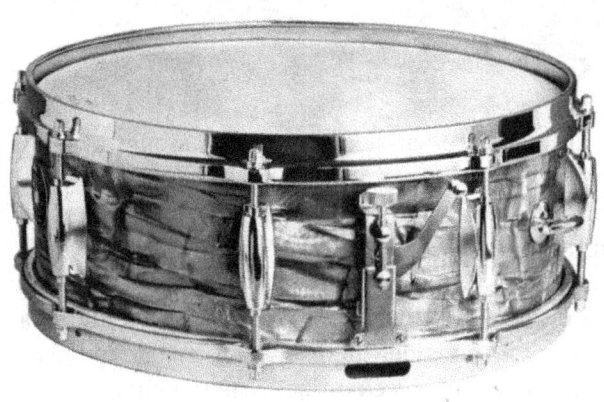

Renown
5.5x14
4102 Mahogany or lacquer 1969-1974
4103 pearl 1969-1979

Dixieland
5.5x14 X4104 lacquer
1954-1966

Dixieland
5.5x14, X4105 Pearl
1958-1968

4105 Dixieland
5.5x14 #4105
1969-1979

The Max Roach Model   From 1949 into the late 1950s

Lee Ruff Collection

The Max Roach model was an uncatalogued snare drum. There has been a certain amount of confusion surrounding this model because of the similarly named X4175 Broadkaster Max Roach model. It can be documented, however, that the Max Roach Model snare drum continued to be produced well after the introduction of the X4175 Broadkaster Max Roach snare drum. What little information we have about this model has been primarily derived from examination of these drums. Much of the information in this section must be credited to Lee Ruff, who probably has personally examined more examples of this model than anyone except the factory personnel who built them. While many serious Gretsch collectors consider themselves fortunate to have come across one or two of these drums, Lee owns a whole rack of them and has examined many others.

The Max Roach model was built in the late 1940s to accommodate the request of Max Roach for a drum this shallow. A 4-inch deep shell presented design problems for Gretsch. Their standard Broadkaster lug was too long for such a drum, so Bill Hagner created a new tube lug specifically for this drum.

The Max Roach Model nameplate is rarer than the Max Roach model snare drum because not all of the drums received such a nameplate. The plates that *were* attached were secured only by two very small pins that did not penetrate the shell; they were never bolted on. Many therefore have fallen off or were easily pried off. When that happened, two very small holes were left. There are drums without these holes which never had the nameplate installed. Note: This style of nameplate was never installed on the X4175 Broadkaster Max Roach model snare drum.

Lee Ruff with a small part of his Gretsch collection. Top row: Progressive Jazz snare drums, Middle Row: Gold 4160, Max Roach and Progressive Jazz snare drums, Bottom Row: Max Roach snare drums.

Nearly all of the Max Roach model snare drums that have surfaced to date are fitted with the Micro-Sensitive strainer. The Micro-Sensitive was designed by Gretsch endorser Andy Florio (see page 65). Florio submitted to Gretsch the designs for three versions of the Micro-Sensitive; the two that were actually produced (see page 214) plus a third, shorter, version specifically designed for drums like the shallow Max Roach model. In the photo at left, the strainer on the right represents Andy's concept for the third Micro-Sensitive. This strainer was never made; the photo is a photoshopped fabrication. The failure of Gretsch to produce this shortened Micro-Sensitive greatly vexed Florio. The shorter of the two Micro-Sensitives actually produced (left side of photo at left) was just a little too big to work properly on the Max Roach snare drum which led to Gretsch deepening the shell by a quarter inch.

Lee Ruff Collection

This model was the first to switch from the "flanged" bottom counterhoop to the milled-gate style. Every Max Roach model that Lee has ever seen has had milled snare gates. Eventually all Gretsch snare drums were converted to this type of hoop. Note: All Max Roach Model snare drums were equipped with die-cast "stick chopper" hoops made of zamack, a zinc alloy.

Some Max Roach model drums positioned the Gretsch badge and Max Roach nameplate as seen in the top photo, others as seen in the bottom photo. This was an arbitrary placement; there are examples of both styles in different eras.

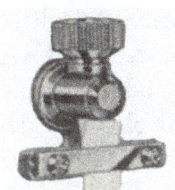

The 5381 butt assembly was also created by Bill Hagner using the same center post that he used for the Max Roach tube lugs. This became standard equipment for all snare drums fitted with the Micro-Sensitive strainer.

The strainer used on the first few Max Roach models was the "Feather Touch" Broadkaster strainer with cowel.

MUFFLER, SHELL, SOUND

Most Max Roach Model drums were fitted with the single-pad mufflers, later Max Roach Model drums had the early two-pad mufflers.

Most Max Roach Model snare drums had the traditional 3-ply Gretsch shell with inner and outer plies of maple. Some were made with plies of mahogany.

Lee Ruff: *"These drums are for decoration. They sound horrible. I have calf heads on most of my examples. They do not tune up crisp and responsive. The wires always splash back when disengaged. Gretsch cut the snare beds too deep on these drums. The deep snare beds and the oversized Micro-Sensitive (for this particular drum), cause this unwanted splash back. I have tried heads with high collars, medium collars, etc. They simply do not work well. It's obvious why Gretsch deepened their 4 x 14s to 4 1/4 x 14s in the '60s."*

The Broadkaster Max Roach Progressive Jazz

Introduced as the:
X4175   Broadkaster "Max Roach" Model   4x14
1954-1960

Name change to:
X4175   Progressive Jazz   4x14
1961-1971

Lee Ruff Collection

Lee Ruff Collection

THE PROGRESSIVE JAZZ SNARE DRUM
By John Sheridan

The Gretsch Model 4175 Progressive Jazz snare is a highly sought-after drum. It was modeled on the Max Roach model snare drum, so it was first given the name "Broadkaster "Max Roach" Model." Unlike the Max Roach model which had tube-style lugs, the X4175 had new Streamlined double-bossed piccolo snare lugs. They offered better stability for tuning and were exclusive to this model. Hardware on this 3-ply 4x14 shell was: Micro-Sensitive Strainer; Fast Tension Bracket; "stickchopper" rims; tone control and Responso 12-strand or 16-strand snare wires.

By 1960, a few modifications were made. First was the change from 3- to 6-ply shells. Also, the true 4" deep shell was extended to 4-1/4" to better accommodate the Micro-Sensitive Strainer and eliminate excessive buzzing. The one-point Fast Tension Bracket was retired in favor of a four-point butt plate, providing better stability, and new die-cast rims replaced those stick-eating "stickchoppers." Another Gretsch "first" was the introduction of an exclusive Snap-In Key Holder with a newly designed key. A few years later, the Responso snare wires were replaced by the 42-Wide Power Snares (which required Gretsch to cut wider snare beds.)

Internal shell model/serial number guarantee labels were introduced on Gretsch drums by 1962, yet many (perhaps most) '60s Model 4175s never had them. Though it's not at all unusual to find the occasional '60s Gretsch drum missing an internal label due to factory oversight, it is extremely commonplace for this particular model.

When Baldwin purchased Gretsch in 1967, changes were made on certain instrument appointments to save money at the point of manufacture in Brooklyn. The most notable change in Gretsch drums was the introduction of the new Lightning Throw-off. As former Gretsch executive Duke Kramer explained: "The Micro-Sensitive Strainer had become too expensive to buy anymore. We were getting killed on the housing. We had to use something else." Inflation had become rampant by 1968. It was decided to take a cue from Gretsch's past. Some 20 years earlier, the Gretsch Gladstone snare drums utilized a simple drop-away strainer based on a cam. The Baldwin version would be smaller and '60s-cost-effective, as it featured no fine-tuning device as on the Micro-Sensitive. Snare tension would only be adjusted at the four-point butt plate (then referred to as a Rear Snare Bracket.)

After the debut of the new Lightning Throw-off, Gretsch's stockpiles of remaining Micro-Sensitive Strainers were mostly assigned to their entry-level Model 4109 aluminum snare drums until depletion in the early '70s. This infuriated Andy Florio, who designed the Micro-Sensitive for Gretsch in 1949. He stated, "I simply gave Gretsch the Micro-Sensitive idea with all my love."

Though the Lightning Throw-off was small, it was apparently not small enough. The new throw-off was too long to properly function on the Progressive Jazz's comparatively shallow 4-1/4" depth, so Gretsch kept using the Micro-Sensitive on the 4175.

Ultimately, Gretsch resolved to simply and quietly drop the 4175 Progressive Jazz from the line some time before 1972.

**Gretsch 24-K Gold Plated
Metal Snare Drum
4160G 5x14 8-lug
identified as 4161
on internal labels
1968-1972**

The earliest models are round-badge until 1970, then Stop-Sign Badge #1 through 1972. A 10-lug version premiered in a 1972 price list and was also mentioned in 1973 price lists. While offered for over a year, it is quite possible that there was no demand for the 10-lug version and none were produced. The authors have not seen examples, and there are no known published illustrations.

Lee Ruff collection

**From John Sheridan's *Classic Drummer* article
"Gretsch Engraved Snare Drums"**

Earliest examples of these prestigious snare drums originated just after Baldwin purchased the Gretsch Company in 1967.

Touted as "the most beautiful drum in the world," the Gold Engraved Snare Drum was Gretsch/Baldwin's first foray into the early "boutique" drum market. With it's elegantly hand-engraved brass shell and all parts plated in 24-karat gold, this was an exercise in unbridled extravagance, much in the same way the opulently gold-sparkle-bound White Falcon was to Gretsch's equally successful guitar line. The company even issued exclusive concurrent post cards to spread the word of these two exceptionally-appointed instruments.

Although this drum was catalogued as #4160G, the labels state the model number as 4161. This is because it was common Gretsch practice when offering a standard guitar model in a different finish to alter the model's last digit. With only "numbered" stamping tools (no letters), the factory sequenced from 4160 to 4161 because they had no way of stamping 4160G.

Gretsch's in-house plating capability for guitar parts allowed them to plate virtually all of it's component parts. (This plating procedure had previously been used in the 1950s for the rare and legendary Cadillac Green/Gold Plated "Birdland" drum sets.)

At it's original retail price of $250, the 4160G was more than double the 4160, its $105 chrome-plated, non-engraved counterpart. Aside from the obvious cosmetic flourishes, it was essentially the same drum, right down to the 5x14's centered knurl. It's a sure bet this *high* ticket item had *low* production totals.

Subsequent price lists show an evolution in the Gretsch Gold Engraved's relatively short life span. The 8-lug 4160G first appeared in 1968's Catalog #44 and was last seen in 1971's Catalog #45. They were "round-badged" drums in their first few years until Gretsch badges were updated to the "Stop-sign" style by 1970.

The 8-lug 4160G was only available from 1968 until mid-1972 when the 10-lug 4165G replaced it, remaining in the line until 1974. With that relatively short life span, it's fair to say that the 10-lug version is considerably rarer than the 8-lugger. So rare, in fact, that there is even speculation that the drum may not have been produced at all since to date no examples have surfaced. The 4165G never appeared in any catalog supplements between 1971 and 1977, it's only the period's biannual price lists that reveal it's brief existence.

John Sheridan collection

Lee Ruff Collection

Gretsch Metal Snare Drum
X4160 5x14 8-lugs
1961-1967

All Gretsch 4160 snare drums had chrome-over-brass shells. Earliest models had the plain shell with no center decorative knurled markings. Rick Gier's research indicates that the plain shells started before or very early in the paper label era and continued through about serial number 55000. As with many Gretsch features, exceptions abound. Gier: "It should be noted that some later model 4160, 4165, and 4166 chrome snares, particularly in the square badge era, vary on whether they have knurled bands."

Metal Snare Drum
4109 5x14 Aluminum Shell 8-lug
1968-1977

Offered with or without the tone control in 1971 & 1972. This drum was discontinued at about the same time as the Micro-Sensitive strainer.

X4106 Dixieland Chrome-Over-Brass,
5.25x14, 6-lug, Renown strainer - 1965-1966
4106 5x14 6-lug Aluminum Shell, Renown strainer
1966-1979

Offered with or without the tone control 1971-1976.

Gretsch Chrome Plated Metal Snare Drum
5x14 8-lugs
updated 4160: Lightning throw-off (5378)
1967-1974

The "Fishtail Butt Plate" began to appear as early as 1971.

4108 5x14 8-lug Aluminum Shell, Renown strainer
1971-1982

Offered with or without the tone control 1971-1976.

4165 5x14, 10-lug
brass shell, die-cast hoops, lightning strainer
(5378, then 5375 by 1975)
1972-2001

1972 and 1973 price lists mention a gold-plated version, #4165G, but to the date of this writing no examples have been located.

Not pictured:
4100 5x14 Recording Snare in Walnut or Maple, 1972-1976
4101 Recording Snare in Chrome, 1972-1976.

4157 5x14, 8-lug
6-ply, die-cast hoops, lightning strainer
1977-2013

Note: After 2007, designation on all USA Gretsch wood drums was that of the order number (as instituted by KMC in 2002) rather than the model number.

4158 5.5x14, 10-lug
6-ply, die-cast hoops, lightning strainer
1972-2013

Earliest models had the early Lightning throw-off; current Lightning Throw-off was in use by 1975. It should be noted that Gretsch made NO 10-lug until 1972. That includes snare drums as well as outfit bass drums. The acceptance of 10-lug drums seems to have been Baldwin's effort to join the status-quo.

4153 6.5x14, 16-lug
6-ply, die-cast hoops, lightning strainer
1974-2013

4154 6.5x14, 10-lug
6-ply, die-cast hoops, lightning strainer
1977-2013

4155 6.5x14, 20-lug
6-ply, die-cast hoops, lightning strainer
1979-2013
not pictured: M4155 8x14 20-lug 1983-1999

4160 5x14, 8-lug
brass shell, die-cast hoops, lightning strainer
1974-2001, 2004-2013

Gretsch halted production of metal snare drums between 2001 and 2004 because of an inadequate source of shell materials.

#4167 10 lugs 1977-1982
see article below

THE UNKNOWN GRETSCH SNARE DRUM – MODEL 4167
By John Sheridan
reprinted from *CLASSIC DRUMMER* magazine

Since 1975, Gretsch aficionados have well been aware of Gretsch's top-of-the-line metal snare drum, model 4166. But how many have heard of model 4167? Not many, and there's good reason for its relative obscurity.

Unlike the common 4166, the 4167 was only available from roughly 1977 through 1982. Both drums feature 6x14 chrome-over-brass shells, center-handle Lightning strainers, "fishtail" butt plates, batter-side tone controls, snap-in key-holders and 10-hole die-cast rims. The only difference is the 4166 has 20 small tom lugs (mounted in doubled, "split-lug" fashion), while the seldom seen 4167 is equipped with 10 standard snare lugs. One has to wonder why Baldwin (Gretsch's owner from 1967 through 1984) would abandon the more efficient 10-lug version in favor of the superfluous 20-lugger. The 4166 requires twice as many lugs, making it a something of a "tank" and a full pound heavier, and the resulting marginal clearance between the head's collar and close-fitting tom lugs can be somewhat dicey, tolerances notwithstanding. (Had they made it six-and-a-half inches deep – like virtually every other drum manufacturer – this would not be an issue.)

From a marketing point-of-view, the 20-lug 4166 looks more substantial, while the 4167 simply appears to be a slightly deeper version of the 10-lug 5x14 model 4165 (which it is). Also, if a half-inch of brass could be saved in the course of manufacturing multitudes of shells, it adds up to a lot! Interesting to note is that the 4166 and 4167 both lack the traditional "center-knurl" found on most other Gretsch chrome-over-brass snare drum shells.

The brief history of the 4167 is something akin to a "comedy of errors" that effectively sealed its fate as that "lost" great Gretsch snare drum. According to company literature, the 4166 first appeared in the August 22, 1975 Gretsch price list at $199.50. It was described as a "10 Lug" drum in price lists until identified as a "20 Lug" by August 1, 1979.

The first catalog to include the 4167 was the 1977 catalog. For its only catalog picture, it's included with a matching "Broadkaster II" drum set on page 4. Unfortunately, the 4167 is mistakenly designated as "4165 5x14" in the set's profile, though its availability was listed correctly on page 7. The 4167 didn't make an appearance in a price list until June 27, 1980. With a retail of $286.00, the 4167 was six bucks less than the 4166 (by then $292.00). Though available through the release of the 1980 Gretsch catalog, the 4167 was not illustrated, or even listed! The February 25, 1981 price list saw the 4167 inflate to $306.00. Exactly three months later, it jumped to $320.00 and remained at that price until its last mention in the May 30, 1982 price list. By June 1983, Gretsch's Centennial poster catalog was released and only three chrome-over-brass snare drums remained: the classic 8-lug 5x14 4160, the brighter 10-lug 5x14 4165 and the beefy 20-lug 6x14 4166.

In the end, the 4167's lack of visibility and proper designation in company literature led it to sell poorly and be subsequently discontinued. But this was no fault of the drum, itself. The failure lies with the bumbling ineptitude that Baldwin was so famous for during their tenure of Gretsch ownership. In retrospect, their cluelessness is compounded by the fact that the drum was only shown in one of two catalogs within a four year period and misrepresented at that. Plus, dropping it from the line just as Gretsch's centennial year was approaching, when the company would surely enjoy a higher-than-normal profile in the industry, killed any shot the drum could have had.

Sales aside, there were also practical considerations that Baldwin could have benefited from by maintaining the 4167 in the Gretsch line. The 4166 was a 6x14 brass shell with 20 small tom lugs. The 4167 was the same shell, but with only 10 snare lugs. From a production standpoint, it was less labor-intensive as it only required 20 lug-holes to be drilled instead of 40! Not to mention, the savings of parts and assembly time to apply half as many lugs. Doubling those lugs likely inhibits the shell's resonance, as well as allowing only marginal clearance between them and the head's collar rim. Though the 4166 is still highly sought after, in summation, the 4167 is likely the superior drum. And at a full pound lighter, think of what could've been saved in shipping costs.

The short-lived 4167 is the rarest production model snare drum Gretsch has made in the last 35 years. A bold statement to be sure, but it's also certain that this drum was practically unheard of until now. Who knows? Maybe if someone like John Bonham played one, things might've turned out differently... had he known about it!

Not pictured: 4166 6x14 10 lug 1975-1976
The 10-lug 4166 is very rare and is mistakenly identified as a 4165 in the Broadkaster II photo caption in the 1977 catalog.

**4166 6x14, 20-lug
brass shell, die-cast hoops, lightning strainer
1977-2001**
This model actually began as a 10-lug drum in 1975 but evolved into the 20-lug version by 1977.

BROADKASTER
Gunmetal Grey lugs and rims

GB4157 5x14 8-lug
1998-2003

(not pictured) GB4156 5x14 10 lug
1998-2003
This model was the first Gretsch snare drum to use the model number 4156. It was the first-ever wood Gretsch 5x14 10-lug drum.

GB4154 6.5x14 10-lug
1998-2003

BROADKASTER BRASS
Gunmetal Grey lugs and rims

GB4160BB 5x14 Black Brass
1998-2003
GB4166BB 6x14 Black Brass
1998-2003
GB4160GB 5x14 Gunmetal Brass
1998-2003
GB4166GB 6x14 Gunmetal Brass
1998-2003
GB4160WB 5x14 White Brass shell
with gunmetal lugs and rims
1998-2003

GB4166WB 6x14 White Brass shell
with gunmetal lugs and rims
1998-2003

All Broadkaster snare drums came with a Lightning Throw-off, though Nickelworks strainers were an option by 2002. Though not included in the 2003 catalog, Broadkaster drums were still readily available as of the 2-28-03 price list. They made their last appearance in the 8-1-03 price list and were available only by special order. Broadkaster parts last appeared in the 1-1-05 price list.

Satin finishes started as early as 1998 with the Broadkaster series and became available on the Gretsch Custom series (known as USA Custom Series starting in 2007) by 2000 as well as the USA Maple series by 2002

Broadkaster Series snare drums post-2000

2002: Nickelworks or Lightning throw-off, 5x14 8-lug, 5x14 10-lug, 6.5x14 10-lug
Brass shell series: 5x14 8-lug or 6x14 10-lug in Black, White, or Gunmetal
2003: Special-order only. Lightning throw-off. 5x14 8-lug, 5x14 10-lug, 6.5x14 10-lug
Brass shell series: 5x14 8-lug, 6x14 20-lug in Black, White, or Gunmetal
note: John Sheridan also has a non-catalogued GB4165GB 5x14 10-lug, all-gunmetal drum.

5.5x14
C-55141S

4x14
C-04148NS
2002-2009

8x14
C-08142S

CUSTOM SERIES WOOD SNARE DRUMS 2002-2013
Choice of Nitron covering, satin or gloss lacquer.
Die-cast hoops, Nickelworks (until 10-1-10) or Lightning throw-off
Dunnett throw-off option added in 2008, Micro-Sensitive option added in 2012

4x14 8-lug (discontinued 2009), 5x14 8-lug, 5.5x14 10-lug, 6.5x14 10-lug, 6.5x14 16-lug, 6.5x14 20-lug, 8x14 20-lug,
5x13 6-lug (2009-2013) 6x13 6-lug (2009-2013) 5.5x14 8-lug (2009-2013) 4.5x14 - 8-lug (2006-2013) 6.5x14 8-lug (5/09 -2013)

Vinnie Colaiuta Signature
GVS04157SWN Millennium wood-shell
5x14 8-lug (Satin Natural)
2003-2011

This model had its genesis in the "Custom Plus" series which means the shell is 25% thicker than a standard Gretsch shell and has more "attack."

Vinnie Colaiuta Signature (black hardware on all)
GVS4160 5x14 8-lug chrome 1999-2001
GVS4157 wood shell 5x14 8-lug 1999-2011
GVS4155 wood shell 6 1/2 x 14 20-lug 1999-2011
GVS4160 5x14 White Brass 8-lug 1999-2004
GVS4166 6x14 White Brass 20-lug 1999- 2004

4108 5x14, 8-lug
aluminum shell, die-cast hoops, renown strainer
1977-1982

Limited Edition 100th Anniversary
1983

There were 3 exotic veneers used on the anniversary drums in 1983; Birdseye Maple (pictured here on John Sheridan's 5x13), Burl Walnut (the most rare), and the most common, Carpathian Elm.

John Sheridan collection

G4173 Piccolo
4x13 12-lug
1992-2001

Steve Maxwell collection

G4176 Piccolo
4x14 16-lug
1992-2001

G4166BC
6x14 polished brass finish 20-lug
1983-2001

not pictured:

G4165BC
5x14 polished brass 10-lug
1983-1987 1998-2001

G4160BC
5x14 polished brass 8-lug
1998-2001

Note: In August of 1983, Gretsch announced that for the first time they were making available their brass-shell drums with reflective gold-tone brass plating. They were offered with either chrome-plated hardware (at a lesser price) or with hardware plated to match the shell.

In November of 1983, a marketing bulletin was released which indicated Gretsch was struggling to resolve all problems related to the shipping of the Centennial kits and the brass-plated snare drums. The bulletin stated that they had decided to convert all brass-plated hardware to 24-karat gold plating. This policy was for existing orders only and staff was advised to accept no more orders for Centennial sets or snare drums requiring gold plating.

In February of 1984 a marketing bulletin was released, advising sales staff that the "BB" version had plating problems and would not go into production.

Harvey Mason Signature
GB4158SEB 5.5x14 Maple shell 10-lug
1998-2005
GB4157SEB 5x14 Maple shell 8-lug
2002-2005

G4166BB   6x14 black brass 20-lug   1998-2004
not pictured:
G4160BB 5x14 black brass 8-lug   1998-2004

GRETSCH AMERICAN SNARE DRUMS

2002 only, to commemorate the 75th anniversary of Gretsch's 1927 "Gretsch American" musical instrument line

Gary Asher collection

Custom "Stars And Stripes"
GA4158SAS
5.5x14 10-lug
Lightning Throw-off

Gary Asher collection

Vinnie Colaiuta "God Bless America"
GAV4157GBA
5x14, 8-lug,
Lightning Throw-off

Broadkaster Harvey Mason "Grand Old Flag"
GAB4158GOF
5.5x14, 10-lug, Lightning Throw-off

Not pictured: 2002 only limited editions

Custom Plus Snare Drums
Traditional Gretsch maple shell, but 25% thicker.
Millennium gloss finish,
choice of Lightning or Nickelworks throw-off.
4x14 (Nickelworks throw-off only: P-04148NS), 5x14 (Lighting: P-05148S, Nickelworks: P-05148-NS), 5.5x14 (Lightning: P-05514S, Nickelworks: P-05514NS), 6.5x14 (Lightning: P-65146S, Nickelworks: P-65146NS), 8x14 (Lightning: P-08146S, Nickelworks: P-08146NS)

Solid Ply Wood Snare Drums
5.5x14, Die Cast Hoops,
Maple, Oak, Walnut, or Rosewood
Maple S-5514-SSM, Oak S-5514-SSO, Walnut S-5514-SSW,
or Rosewood S-5514-SSR

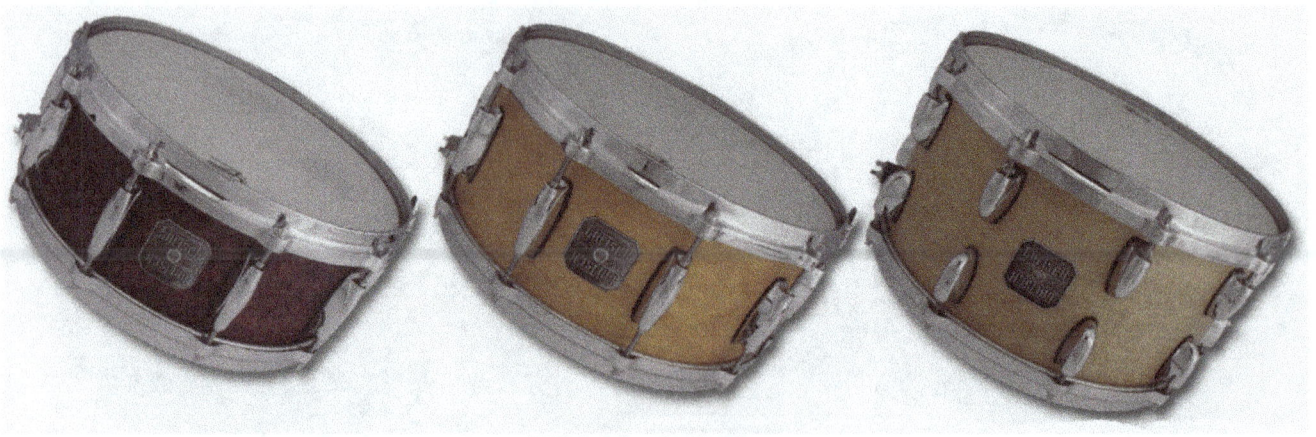

USA Maple Series
2002: Nickelworks throw-off, choice of 2.3 mm or die-cast hoops   4x14, 5x14, 6x14, 7x14
4x14 (2.3 mm hoops: U-04140S, die cast hoops: U-04140DS), 5x14 (2.3 mm: U-05140S, die cast: U-05140DS), 6x14 (2.3 mm: U-06140S, die cast: U-06140DS), 7x14 (2.3 mm: U-07142S, die cast: U-07142DS)

2003-2005: Drop Throw-off, die cast hoops   5x14 10-lug, 6x14 10-lug, 7x14 20-lug
5x14 10-lug (UD-0514S, above left), 6x14 10-lug (UD-0614S above center), 7x14 20-lug (UD-0714S, above right)

Crystal Tone Metal Snare Drums
Die Cast hoops
2002: Hammered Brass or Copper 5.5x14 or 6.5x14
Hammered Brass 5.5x14 10-lug (S-5514-HSS) or 6.5x14 20-lug (S-6514-HSS)
Copper 5.5x14 10-lug (S-5514-SCP) or 6.5x14 20-lug (S-6514-SCP)
2002: Hammered Stainless Steel or Black Chrome Over Steel 4x14 or 5.5x14
Hammered Stainless Steel 4x14 10-lug (S-0414-HSS) or 5.5x14 10-lug (S-5514-HSS)
Black Chrome Over Steel 4x14 10-lug (S-0414-SBS) or 5.5x14 10-lug (S-5514-SBS)
2003-2005: Hammered Brass 5x13 or 5.5x14, Smooth Black Chrome Steel 4x14 or 5.5x14
Hammered Brass 5x13 8-lug (S-0513-HBR, above left) or 5.5x14 10-lug (S-5514-HBR, center left)
Smooth Black Chrome Over Steel 4x14 10-lug (S-0414-SBS, right center) or 5.5x14 10-lug (S-5514-SBS, right)

10-Ply All Maple snare drums 2002 only

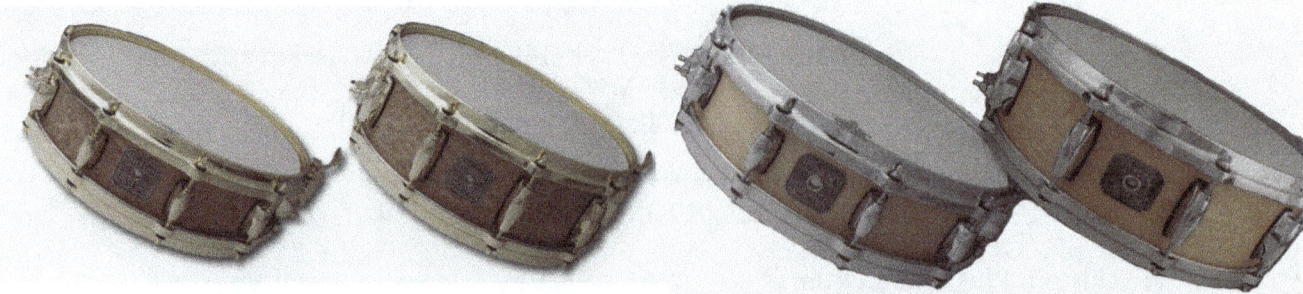

Red Camphor with Brass Hardware
4x14, 5x14, 6.5x14, all with 10 lugs, die-cast hoops
4x14 (S00414-RDC, 2002-2004, above left), 5x14 (S-0514-RDC, 2002-2004, center left), 6.5x14 (S6514-RDC, 2002 only)

Natural gloss with chrome hardware
7x12 2.3 mm hoops 16-lug,
4x14 & 5x14 die-cast hoops 10-lug
Note: the 7x12 had 2.3mm hoops because the 12" Gretsch die-cast rims are 5-hole and not suitable for snare drum use.
16-lug (S-0712-GMP), 4x14 (S-0414-GMP, right center) 5x14 (S-0514-GMP, right)

"Legend" Free Floating Maple Snare Drums
10-ply all maple shell, 2.3 mm hoops 2002-2004;
5.5x10 6-lug (S-5510FMP),
5.5x12 8-lug (S-5512FMP), 5.5x13 8-lug (S-5513FMP),
5.5x14 10-lug (S-5514FMP, above left),
6.5x14 10-lug (S-6514FMP, 2002 only)

2x4 Maple-Brass-Maple: 2" 10-ply maple top and bottom, 2" brass insert in middle, die-cast hoops
2003-2005
6x13 8-lug (S-0613-FMB),
6x14 10-lug (S-0614-FMB, above right)

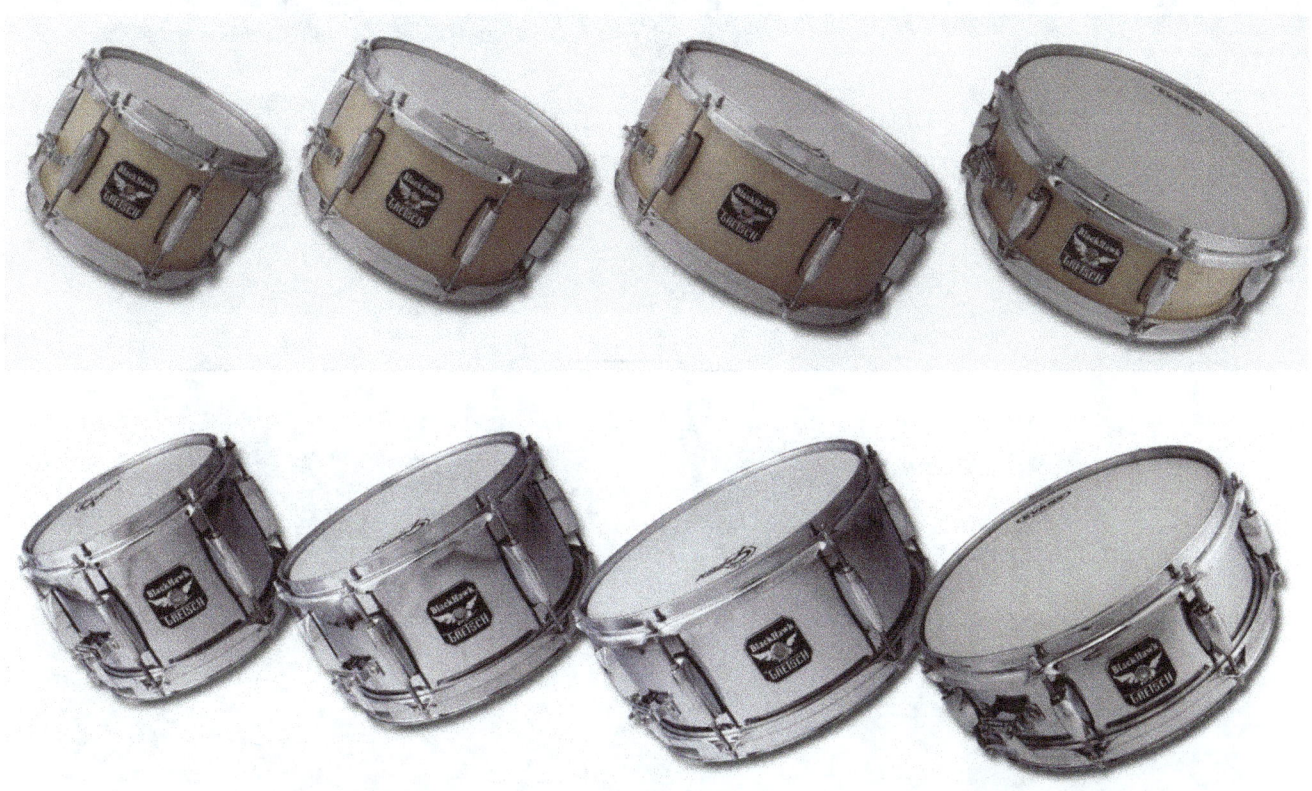

BLACKHAWK MIGHTY MINI AUXILIARY SNARE DRUMS
1.6 mm hoops, steel or basswood shells
with mounting bracket, L-arm, and multi-clamp
2002-2006:
basswood shells 6-lug – 5.5x8 (S-5508-BWD), 5.5x10 5.5x12 (S-5512-BWD) (top left 3, respectively)
or steel shells 6-lug - 5.5x8 (S-5508-SST), 5.5x10 (S-5510-SST), 5.5x12 (S-5512-SST) (bottom left 3, respectively)
2003-2006: 4x13 8-lug basswood (S-0413-BWD, top right) or steel (S-0413-SST, bottom right)

2003 120th ANNIVERSARY LIMITED EDITION CUSTOM ROUND BADGE SNARE DRUMS
not included in the 2003 catalog, a separate sheet was printed which featured these drums.
The black Duco pictured here belongs to John Sheridan.

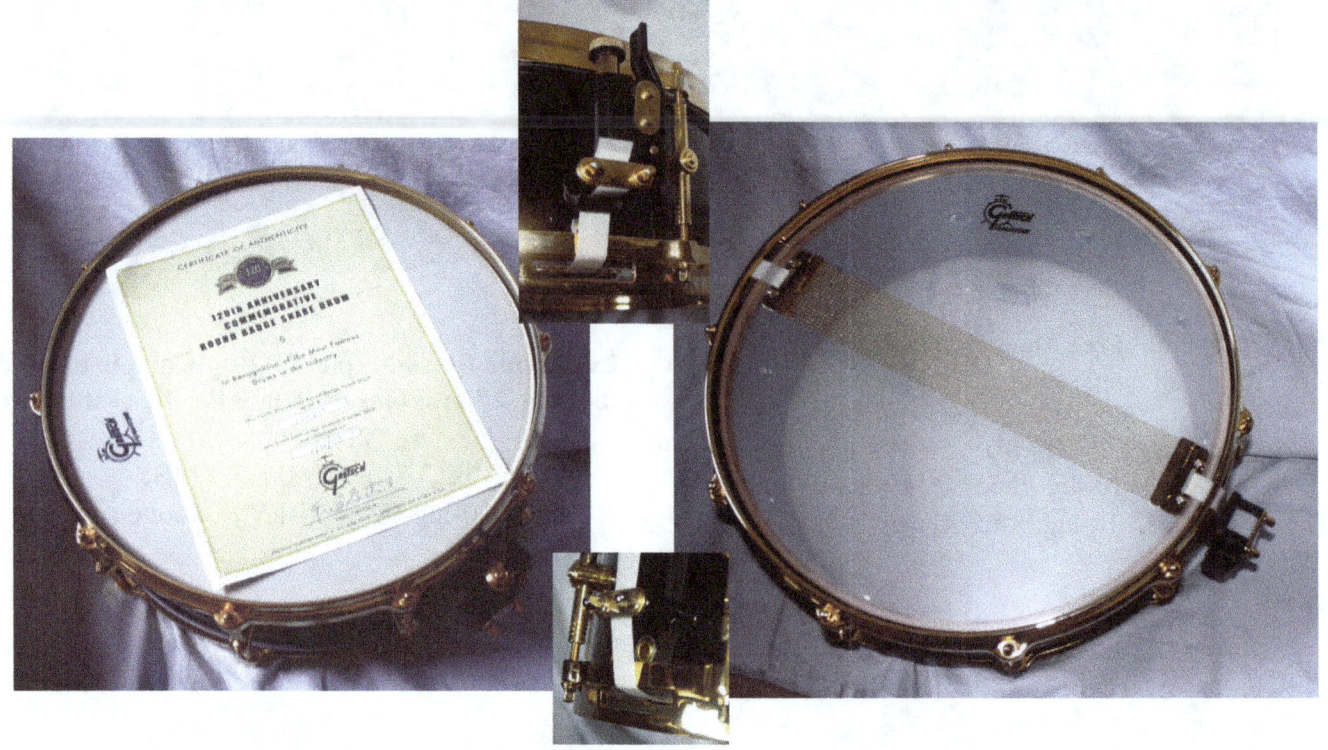

5x14 10-lug Black Duco (RB20-0514-BDG), Nickelworks throw-off,
Gladstone-styled center post tube lug, die-cast hoops, all hardware finished in gold

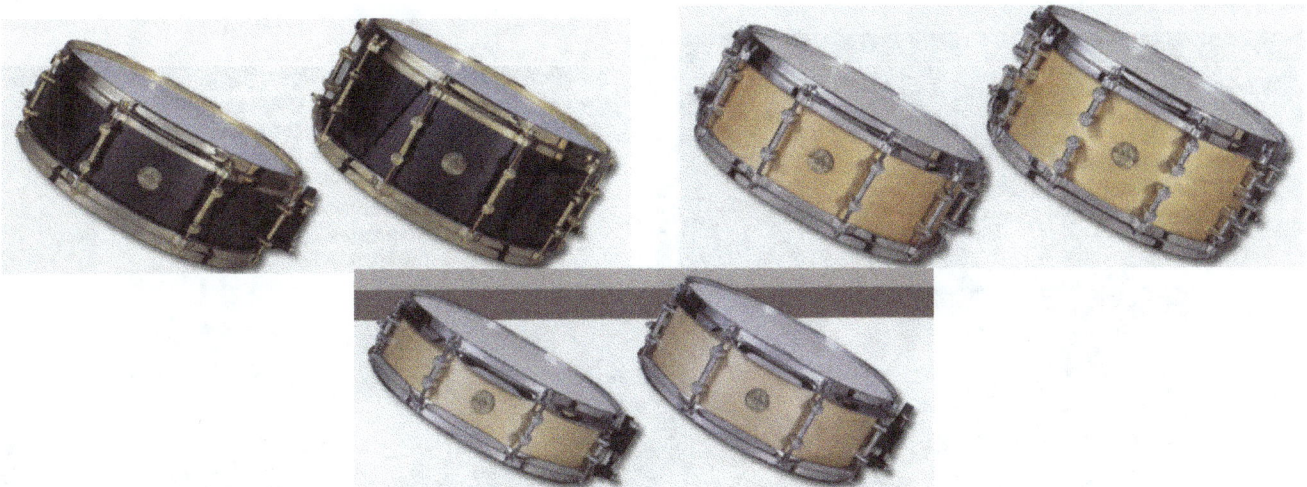

NEW CLASSIC SNARES
tube lugs, 6-ply "thin" 5.33mm shell or "thick" 9.52mm shell or black brass shell, Nickelworks throw-off
2004-2006:

Black Brass shell die-cast hoops, gold accented hardware
5x14 8-lug (NC-0514-BG, upper left)
6.5x14 10-lug (NC-6514-BG, upper center left)
(In 2006, the same Black Brass models were also offered with chrome hardware; NC-0514-BC or NC-6514-BC.)

Custom Light 8-lug 5.33mm shell in natural satin lacquer 2.3 power hoops,
4x14 (NC-0414-CL, lower left) or 5x14 (NC-0514-CL, lower right)

Custom Plus 10-lug 9.52mm shell in natural gloss lacquer, die-cast hoops,
5x14 (NC-5514-CP, upper center right) or 6.5x14 (NC-6514-CP, upper right)

**6x13 New Classic
Hammered Bronze
2004**
This was a prototype that never went into production,
from the John Sheridan collection

NEW CLASSIC 2005 LIMITED EDITION MODELS
Curly Maple models with traditional Gretsch shell & outside veneer of figured curly maple.
Each drum numbered with production date and produced only in 2005.
Chrome over brass models based on the vintage 4160 model. Total of 200 drums produced worldwide, 30 pieces of which were produced with gold accented hardware
5.5x14 10-lug Curly Maple shell, die-cast hoops, Nickelworks throw-off, in Curly Stardust Maple (NC-5514-CSD, above left) or Curly Millennium Maple (NC-5514-CMM, center left)
5x14 8-lug, chrome over brass, die cast hoops Nickelworks throw-off, with all gold hardware accents (NC-4160CG, center right) or with all chrome hardware accents (NC-4160CC, right)

CHROME OVER BRASS RE-ISSUE SNARE DRUM
2004-2013
Re-issue of the classic 4160. 5x14, 8-lug, die-cast hoops, Lightning throw-off, stop-sign logo badge
2007-2013: New brass metal shell (the source for all metal snare drums changed in 2007) and more sizes: 6x13 6-lug & 6 1/2x14 10-lug (G4168 & G4164, respectively)

2007 only: Custom Series Square Snare Drum 5x14 USA Custom snare drum with 10 individual square color panels representing the most popular lacquer finishes: Antique Maple, Rosewood, Dark Walnut, Millennium Maple, Purple, Walnut, Azure Blue, Sun Amber, Ebony, Burnt Orange

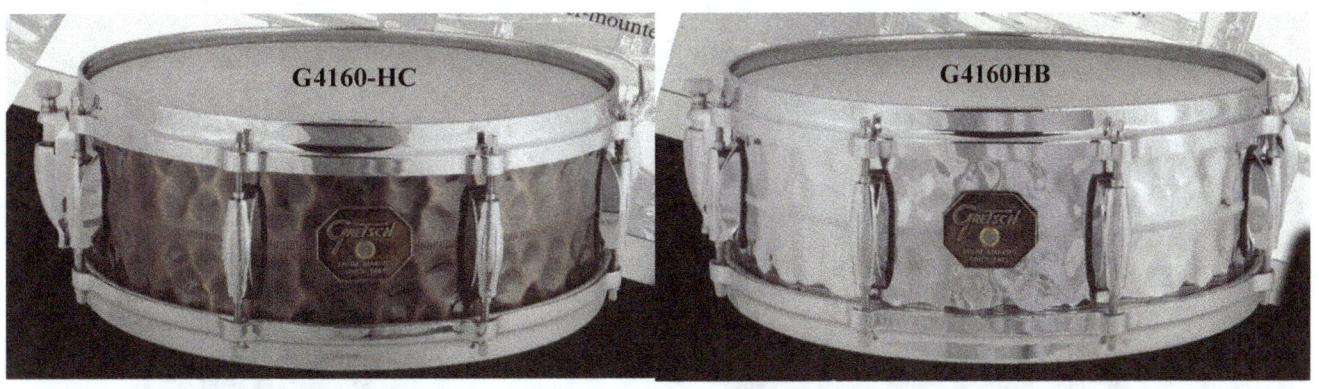

Hammered Antique Copper Shell 5x14
8-lug, die-cast hoops
2006-2013
sizes added in 2007: 6x13 6-lug and 6.5x14 10-lug

Hammered Chrome over Brass 5x14
8-lug, die-cast hoops
2006-2013
sizes added in 2007: 6x13 6-lug & 6.5x14 10-lug

Hammered Black Steel & Polished Brass
1.2mm shell, die-cast hoops
Black Steel - April 2006-2012:
5x14 10-lug (S-0514-BSH), 6.5x14 10-lug (S-6514-BSH),
8x14 20-lug (S-0814-BSH)
Brass - April 2006-2013:
5x14 10-lug (S-0514-BRH), 6.5x14 10-lug (S-6514-BRH),
8x14 20-lug (S-0814-BRH)

John Sheridan collection

Hammered copper 6x13 2007-2013

125th Anniversary Snare Drums
2008: Limited production 125 of each model for 2008 only
6-ply shells, round badge, serialized Vintage internal shell labels.

6.5x14 Silver Mist Lacquer, gold hardware

**5.5x14 Curly Antique Maple Lacquer,
chrome tube lugs**

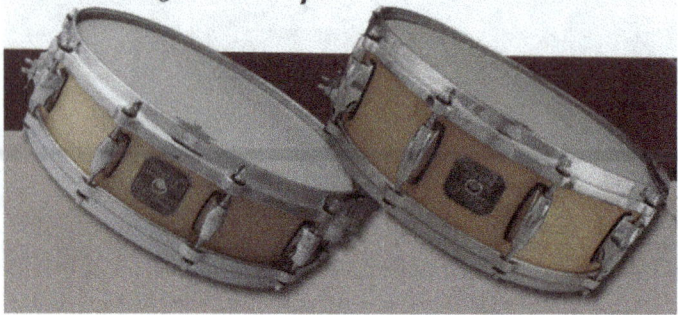

10-Ply Maple Snare Drums
100% Maple 8mm shell with 30-degree edges, Gretsch silver sealer,
die-cast hoops, adjustable throw-off, gloss lacquer
4x14 10-lug (above left, 2001-2002: GRM414D-NM, 2003-2005: S-0414MAP),
5x14 10-lug (above right, 2001-2002: GRM514D-NM, 2003-2005: S-0514MAP,
2006-2013: S-0514-MPL), 6.5x14 10-lug (April 2006-2013: S-6514-MPL), 8x14
20-lug (April 2006-2013: S-0814-MPL)

2010-2013: Satin Ebony finish added in same sizes: Ebony stain with multi-step satin lacquer, so grain is visible.

SOLID STEEL SHELL
Black Chrome finish, lightning throw-off, die-cast hoops
5x14 8-lug (G4160SS),
6.5x14 10-lug (G4164SS, above)
2007-2013

Stanton Moore Signature
4.5x14 8-lug solid ply maple shell (SM-45148DS)
2010-2013

STEVE FERRONE SIGNATURE SERIES
Traditional 6-ply shell, 1955 Cadillac Green lacquer
Lightning throw-off: 2006-2013
4.5x14 8-lug (SF-4514CG),
5x14 8-lug (SF-0514CG),
5.5x14 10-lug (SF-5514CG),
6.5x14 20-lug (SF-6514CG),
8x14 20-lug (SF-0814CG)
Nickelworks throw-off:
4x14 8-lug (SF-0414CG)
2006-2010

G5000 Series Solid Wood Snare Drums
2009-2013

G5-5514SSM 5.5x14 Solid Maple 10-lug (top left)
G5-0613SSM 6x13 Solid Maple 6 lug
G5-0713SSW 7x13 Solid Walnut 6 lug
G5-6514SSW 6.5x14 Solid Walnut 10 lug (bottom left)

Choice of Lightning or Dunnett strainer

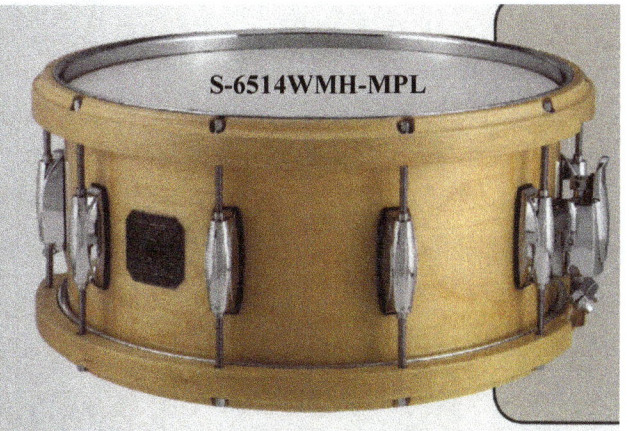

MAPLE SNARES WITH CONTOURED WOOD HOOPS
6 1/2 x 14 10-lug 10-ply maple shell
first two models (wood hoop, wood hoop with metal insert) introduced in 2010
5.5 depth models introduced in 2011 with options: ebony finish, walnut or black satin hoops.
12 models in all: 2011-2013

**G-4000 Series
Phosphor Bronze**
2009-2013
G4160PB 5x14 8-lug,
G4164PB 6.5x14 10-lug,
G4168PB 6x13 6-lug

**STEVE FERRONE SIGNATURE
SERIES BLACK BRASS**
beaded brass shell in polished black
nickel with gold hardware, tube lugs,
2.3mm hoops, adjustable throw-off
6.5x14 8-lug (S-6514-SF)
2009-2013

SOLID ALUMINUM SHELL
lightning throw-off, die-cast hoops
2006-2013: 5x14 8-lug (G4160SA)
added in 2010: 6.5x14 10-lug (G4164SA, above left),
6x13 6-lug (G468SA, above right)

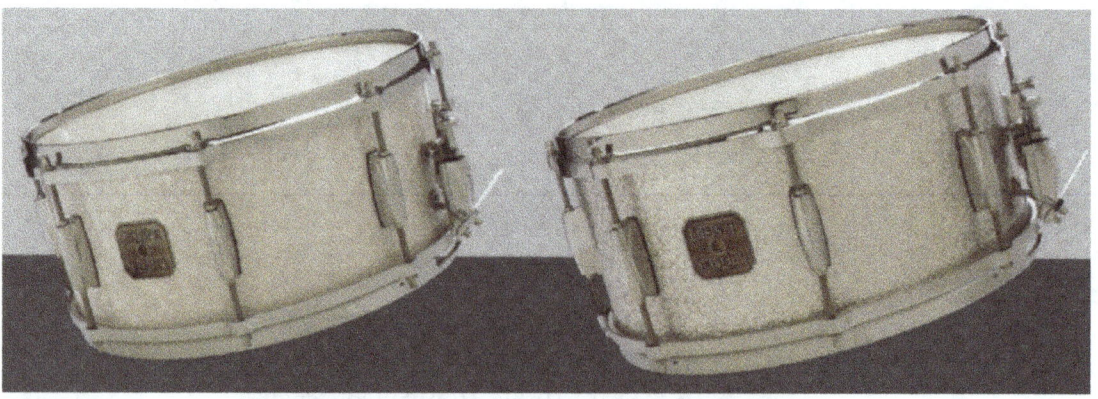

RETRO MAHOGANY SNARE DRUMS
8-ply mahogany shell, die-cast hoops, "adjustable" throw-off
7x13 8-lug (CC-0713S, above left in WMP), 6.5x14 8-lug (CC-6514S, above right in SS),
both sizes available in White Marine Pearl (WP) and Silver Sparkle (SS)
2008-2010

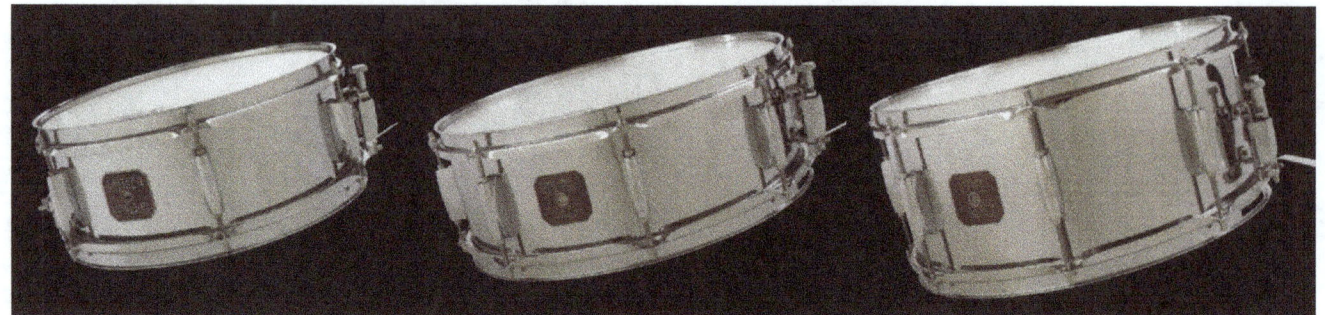

CHROME OVER STEEL SNARE DRUMS
straight-sided 1.0mm steel shell, "adjustable" throw-off
5x12 6-lug (CC-0512S-CRM), 5x14 8-lug (CC-0514S-CRM), 6.5x14 8-lug (CC-6514S-CRM),
triple-flanged hoops
2008-2013

SOLID SPUN BRASS SHELL
lightning throw-off, die-cast hoops
5x14 8-lug (G-4160SB), 6.5x14 10-lug
(G-4164SB, pictured)
2007-2013

ROSEWOOD SNARES 2009-2013
9-ply 100% rosewood shell, "adjustable" throw-off
5.5x14 10-lug (S-5514-RW, above left),
6.5x14 10-lug (S-6514-RW, right),
8x14 20-lug (S-0814-RW, center)

ASH SIDE-SNARE
10-ply ash shell with 45-degree edges, black hardware, 2.5mm hoops, GTS mounting system, 6-lug
6x10 (S-0610-ASHT, above left), 6x12 (S-0612-ASHT, right) 2010-2013

Renown Snare Drums
10-ply maple shells with 45-degree bearing edges, die-cast hoops and "adjustable throw-off"
5x14 8-lug (RN-0514S, lower 2 left),
6.5x14 10-lug (RN-6514S, upper 2)
2009-2013

Also, 5x13 8-lug (RM-0513S) with 2.3 mm triple-flanged hoops (2003-2004), and 5x14 8-lug (RM-0514S) with die-cast hoops and drop throw-off (2003-2005).

Brooklyn Series Black Nickel over Brass
6x14 10-lug, rolled 1.1mm brass shell with center knurl pattern, 302 3mm hoops, 30-degree bearing edge
2013

GB4166B

Pewter/Black
S-6514RLX-PB

Pewter/White
S-6514RLX-PW

Retro-Luxe Snare drums
6.5x14, 16- lug, Maple shell, "fully adjustable throw-off,"
30-degree edges, 2.3mm hoops
2013

Full Range Walnut Snare Drum
6.5x14
S-6514W-MI , 10-lug, 8-ply mahogany gloss natural finish with maple inlays, 2.3 mm hoops, 30 degree edges, "fully adjustable throw-off"
2013

Full Range Walnut Snare Drum
7x13
S-0713W-MI , 8-lug, 8-ply gloss natural finish with maple inlays, 2.3 mm hoops, 30 degree edges, "fully adjustable throw-off"
2013

Swamp Dawg
S0814SD-MAH 8x14,
6-ply mahogany satin finish, 30 degree
edges, 2.3 mm hoops, 8 tube lugs
2013

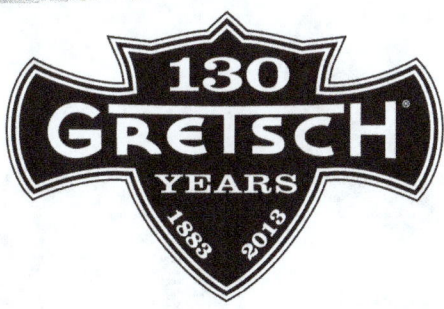

130th Anniversary Limited Edition
130-65146S-SN
6.5x14 6-ply maple with Satin nitrocellulose lacquer
Birdseye veneer
Silver sealer with Anniversary interior shell label, 30-degree edges, Lightning throw-off and butt, batter side muffler, 16-lug, snap-in key holder, 42-strand snares,
Round Badge
2013 only

130th Anniversary Limited Edition
130-7142S-SBB 7x14
Flat black powder-coated aluminum shell
Black hardware, 45-degree edges, Anniversary label
Black lightning throw-off and butt, black suede
ambassador batter head, 20-lug, 42-strand snares,
Round Badge
2013 only

130th Anniversary Limited Edition
130-65141S-CW 6.5x14
Solid Claro walnut with Claro walnut reinforcement
rings, finished in Satin nitrocellulose lacquer
natural interior with 130th Anniversary shell label,
30-degree edge, Lightning throw-off and butt, 10-lug,
20-strand snares, Round Badge
2013 only

Note: All three 130th Anniversary snare drums are limited to 30 pieces each.

MARK SCHULMAN SIGNATURE SNARES
2011-2013
9-ply, 8.6mm maple shells with double Bubinga inlays
and 45-degree edges. Die-cast hoops,
adjustable throw-off, signature badge,
42-strand snares.
S-0612-MS: 6x12, 6-lug
S-0613-MS: 6x13, 8-lug

Cherry 6.5x14 Stave snare drum
S-6514SSC-SN, 20-lug, satin natural lacquer finish, 3.0 mm hoops,
45 degree edges,
"Fully adjustable" throw-off
2013

Oak 6.5x14 Stave snare drum
S-6514SSO-SN, 20-lug, satin natural lacquer finish,
3.0 mm hoops, 45 degree edges,
"Fully adjustable" throw-off
2013

Bell Brass 6.5x14
S-6514BB-BR, 10 lug, natural finish, 3.00 mm hoops, bell-brass shell, 30-degree edges,
"Fully Adjustable" throw-off
2013

Taylor Hawkins Signature Series Snare Drum
6.5x14, S-6514-TH 10-lug
Black nickel over steel (1mm rolled). 2.3 mm hoops
custom badge
2013

NOT ILLUSTRATED

GRETSCH LEGEND BRASS SNARES – 2011-2013
1.0mm beaded brass shell
with 2.3mm triple-flanged hoops.
Adjustable throw-off, lacquered shell and gasketless lugs.
S-0612GL-PBR: 6x12, 6-lug
S-0613GL-PBR: 6x13, 8-lug
S055146L-PBR: 5.5x14, 8-lug
S06514GL-PBR: 6.5x14, 16-lug

BRUSHED BRASS SNARES – 2011-2013
1.0MM beaded brass shell
with 2.3mm triple-flanged hoops.
Vintage patina finish. Adjustable throw-off.
S-5514-BB: 5.5x14, 10-lug
S-6514-BB: 6.5x14, 10-lug

GRETSCH LUGS

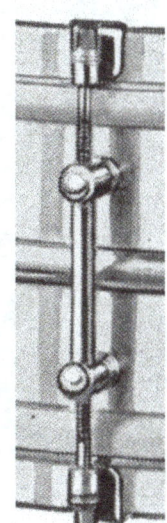

1930s Broadkaster tom lug, preceded Rocket lug

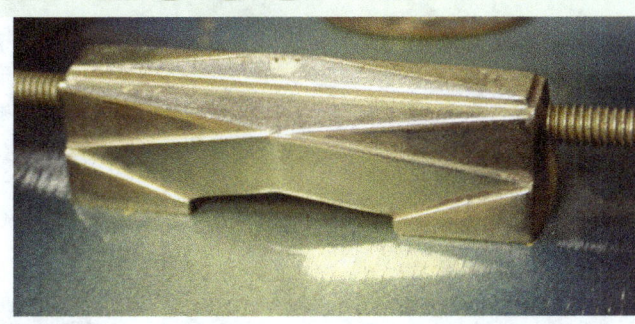

Often called the "Rocket" lug by collectors, this lug first showed up in the 1939 catalog and was referred to by Gretsch as the "Modernistic Center Bracket." It probably got the "Rocket" name because it was used on the Rocket branded Gretsch drums distributed by Gretsch & Brenner. (See page 161)

Earliest Broadkaster kits had these lugs on snare drums, toms, bass drums, and even bongos, so collectors sometimes refer to this as the Broadkaster lug.

Earliest lug, early 1900s most drums in the first Gretsch catalogs either had this post lug or were single-tension. **1912-1927**

First tube lug circa 1927

Tension rods threaded into brass inserts of the Rocket lug. These lugs had no internal springs; the inserts were held in place by internal cast ridges.

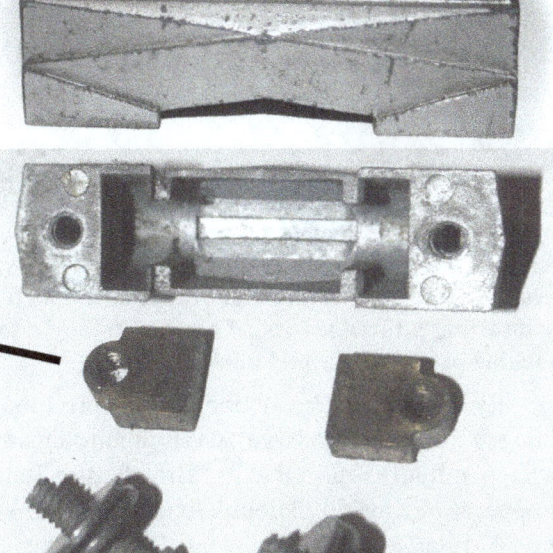

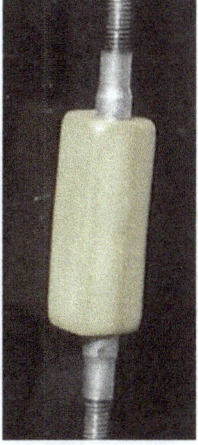

Catalina Lugs 1939-1941 Used on Catalina series snare drums, referred to by Gretsch as "modernistic center brackets." Red or white Bakelite. (Bakelite was a synthetic resin similar to plastic, developed in 1907.)

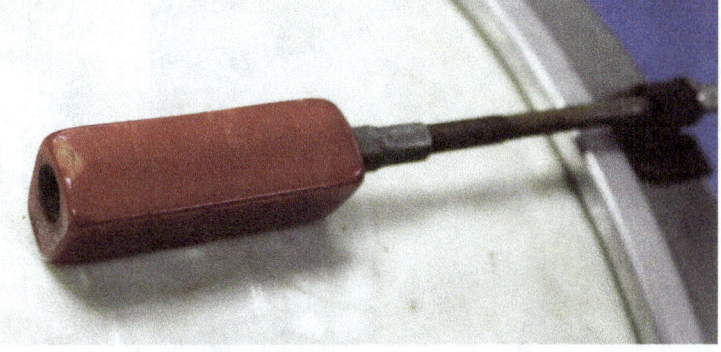

Wooden (World War II era) lug
Resembles Catalina lug, but wood instead of Bakelite

Gretsch Gladstone
small toms
1939-1941

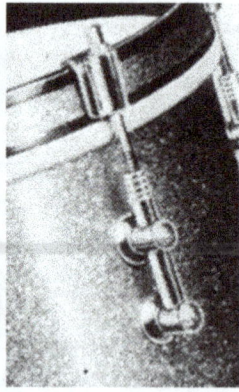
Gretsch Gladstone
large toms, bass drums
1939-1941

Gretsch Gladstone
Center post lug
1939-1941

Max Roach
Model
Center post lug
1949-1959

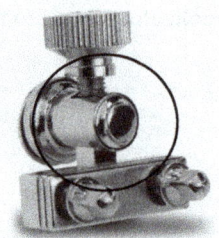
left: "Fast Tension Snare Bracket", 1950-1959
right: reissue 5381, 2011-2013

Former Gretsch plant manager Bill Hagner says they used the same post for the first Max Roach 4-inch lugs by inserting a threaded rod. They had to buy a screw machine part to make this work.

patented Gladstone
"3-way tuning" lug

By 1950 (apparently about the same time the muffler knobs were changed from small to large), Gretsch introduced their die-cast tension rod casings, initially referred to as "Broadkaster Tension Rod Casings." First to appear were the 5472 double-ended lug, 5473 (small) single-ended lug, and 5474 (large) single-ended lug. By 1954 they added the 5471, a smaller double-ended lug. The 5471 was only used on the #4175 4x14 snare drum which was discontinued by August of 1971; the other 3 lugs continued through this writing in 2013 with very minor and subtle changes.

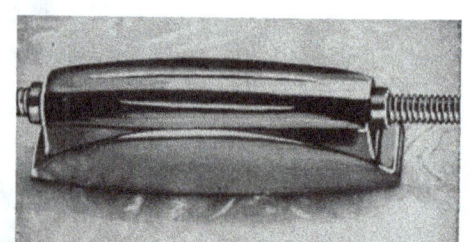
#5472   1950-2013

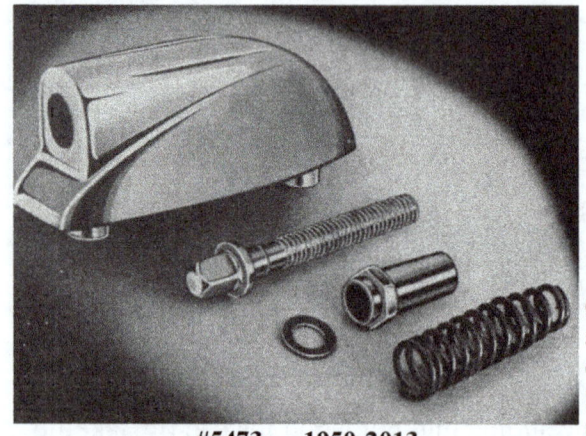
#5473   1950-2013

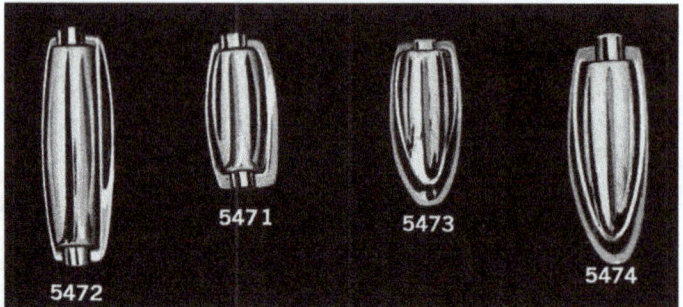

(It is not clear why some 14x14 floor toms received small 5473 lugs and others received larger 5474 lugs.)
GS-5471 Piccolo Snare lug: after a nearly 30-year absence, Gretsch brought back the piccolo lug as part of their new Millennium hardware introduction. It is still in use as of this writing in 2013.

Some of the subtle differences in the lugs are illustrated here not so much to date the reader's drums, but to point out that there *are* some differences. This knowledge is helpful when combined with other dating information to determine if it is original or has been tampered with.

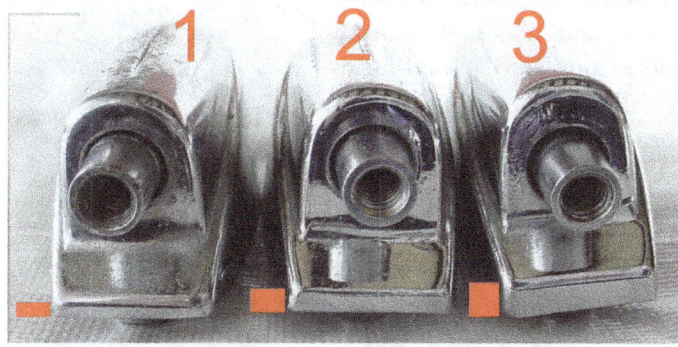

The earliest version of the 5473 is #1. Lee Ruff: "*I first noticed lug #2 in the mid-to-later '60s shortly before the change to hex-head mounting screws. I first noticed lug #3 around 1971-1972. The same applies to the larger 5474 lug.*"

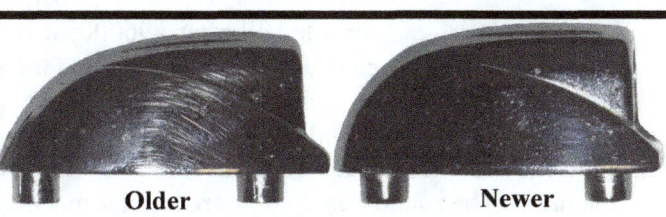

A difference often overlooked: earliest versions of the 5473 and 5474 were slightly lower profile (about 1/16") than later ones.

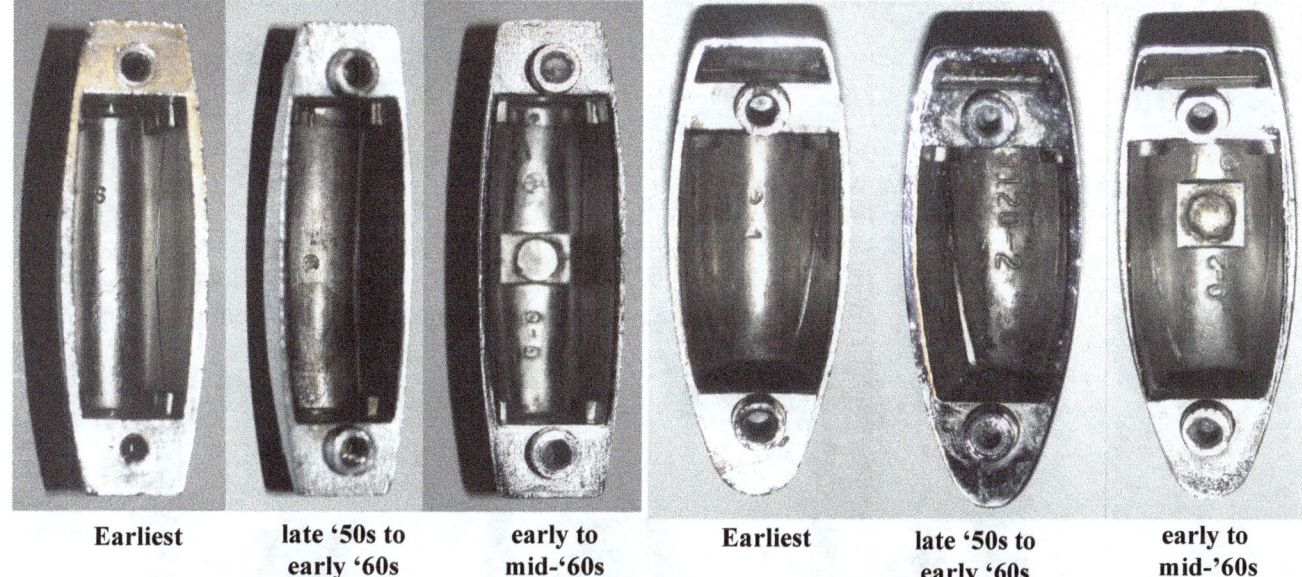

| Earliest | late '50s to early '60s | early to mid-'60s | Earliest | late '50s to early '60s | early to mid-'60s |

There are also some differences on the insides of the lugs over time. These differences are obviously more difficult to detect and the changes do not line up chronologically with the changes mentioned above.

'60s 5472 on left, early '70s 5472 on right

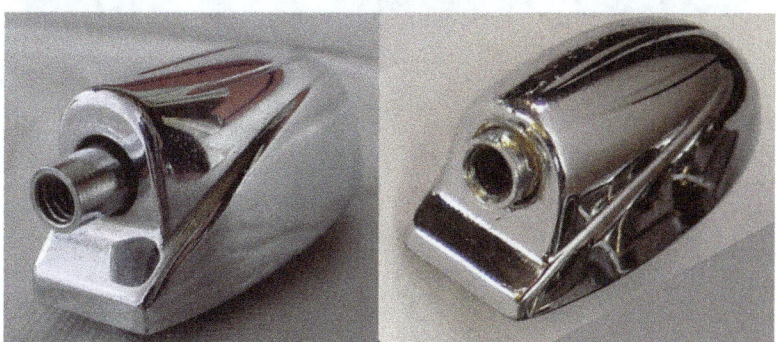

Insert lengths have varied over the years with no pattern or relationship to dating. These two lugs are the same model; apparent differences other than the insert length are optical illusions resulting from the different angles the photos were shot from.

 Gretsch first used round-head machine screws to attach the lugs to the shells. The switch to hex-head machine screws (right) was made in the 1960s. Rick Gier has narrowed the change-over date down to around the 96000 serial number range in the first sequence which would be 1968. Examples of hex-head screws prior to #96000 exist, as do examples of round-head screws well after #96000; it is clear there was not an instant changeover. Gier notes that the screw head type on other hardware appears to have changed at a different time than on lugs.

Neither style always used flat washers, both styles were usually used with flat washers. When used without flat washers, the star washers usually dug into the inner ply of the drum. The round-head type were regular machine screws. The hex-head type were self-tapping threads

Subtle but detectable differences in the hex head screws over time; earliest to newest from left to right. (1960s - 2000s)

Oldest washers (left) were very thin. Washer at right (chrome plated) was used with the diamond-plate mounts.

Variety of lengths for use with various shell thicknesses. It was not unusual for longer screws to be used with thinner shells; washers were sometimes doubled up.

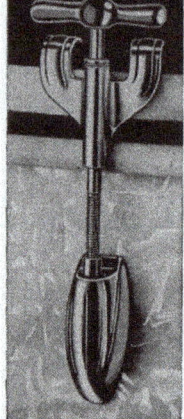

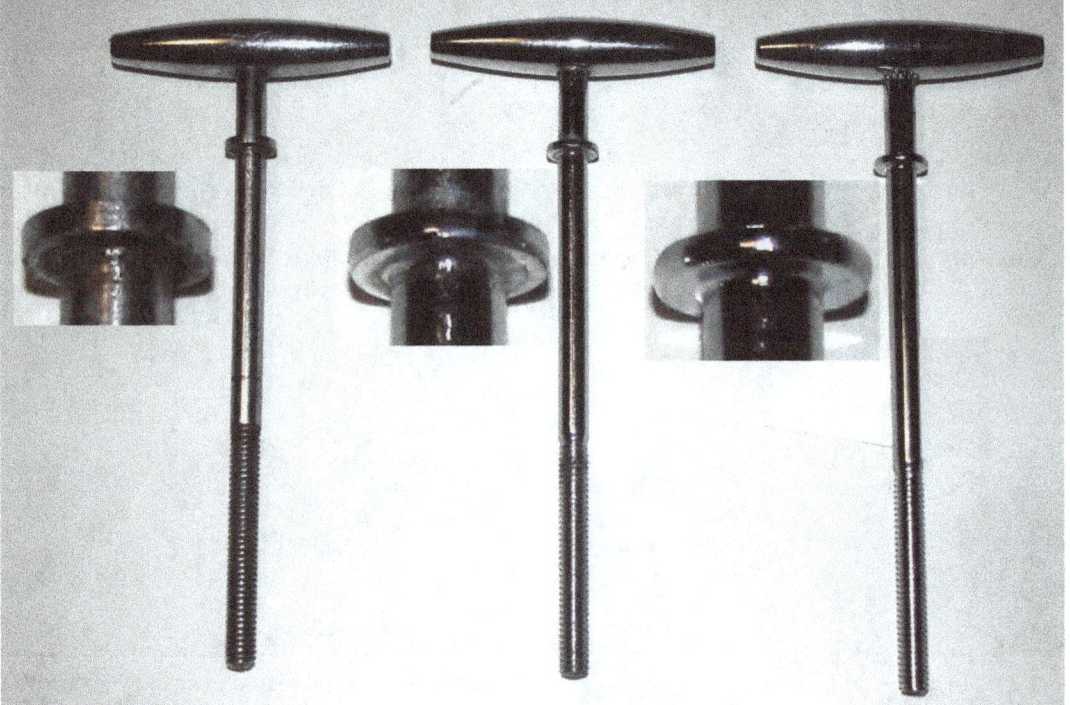

Gretsch referred to the bass drum t-handle at left as the "Tympani handle rod." This was a generic design used by many drum companies of the era. They were catalogued in a variety of lengths for use on dual or single tension bass drums of different depths.

The #5454 distinctively Gretsch t-rod has been in use since 1958. The changes have been very subtle, but there are differences. Pay close attention to the ring on the shaft. The earliest is flattened, the next is more rounded, and the newest t-rods have a very rounded ring.

5477   5472

The 2001-2006 #5477 is shown below left. It is not interchangeable with the #5472, shown below right. The lugs used on Catalina series drums from 2003 to present have all been identified as part #5477 but from 2001-2006 were as shown below left, from 2007 forward have been identical to the 5472 below right.

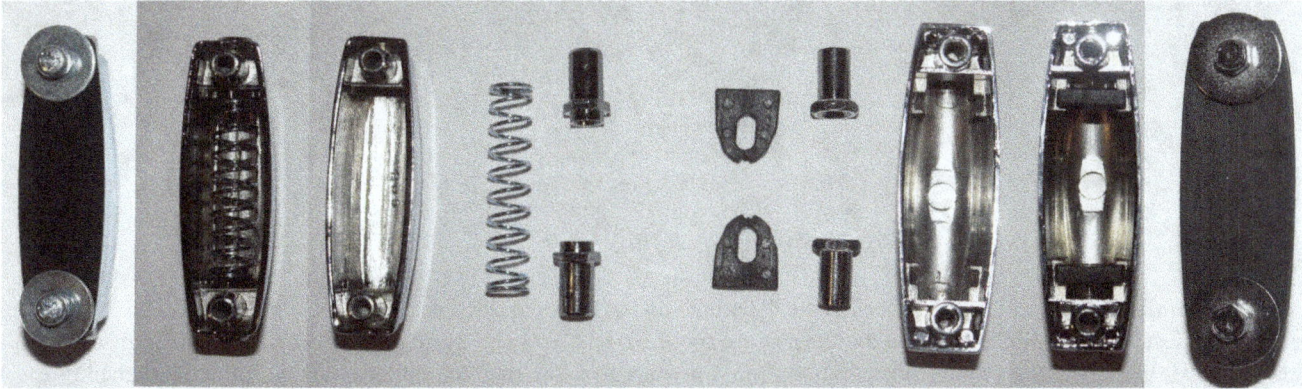

phillips-head screws, spring-loaded, different inserts
Length: 2 7/16"   Width: 11/16"
Hole spacing: 2"

hex-head screws, no springs, different inserts
Length: 2 5/8"   Width: 13/16"
Hole spacing: 2 1/8"

John Sheridan: *"The transition from lugs loaded with springs to lugs with tabs (referred to by Gretsch as "Millennium" lugs) was in 2001 with the appearance of the first drums that were sourced from overseas by KMC. American-made drums continued to have spring-loaded lugs until the Ridgeland assembly operation began using these "Millennium" lugs in 2003. The American-made spring-loaded lugs remained available as replacement parts at least through 2006. [Ed. note: Broadkaster gunmetal lugs were never converted to tab type.] The spring-loaded 5471 piccolo lugs were discontinued by the early 1970s when Progressive Jazz snare drums were discontinued. They re-emerged after KMC re-tooled for most of Gretsch's common parts. During the brief period when both types (spring-loaded and tab type) were available at the same time (from 2002 to 2006), the American-made lug part numbers were prefaced with a G while the "Millennium" part numbers began with GS. Over the last several years, most "Millennium" hardware part numbers (including all tabbed lugs) have come to begin with G."*

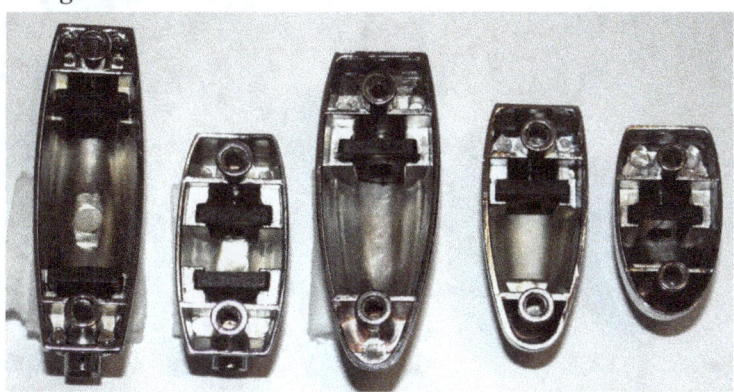

G5472   G5471   G5474   G5473   G5476   G5476 disassembled

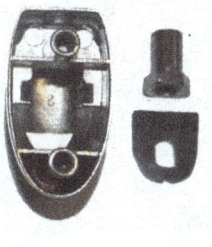

The G5476 Mini-lug appears on all Catalina (2003-2013), Blackhawk (2003-2011) and Retro-Luxe (2013-).

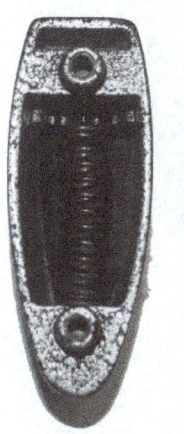   

All Broadkaster gunmetal parts (prefaced with "GB") were spring-loaded American-made lugs.

The gunmetal spring-loaded Broadkaster lug was the last lug to have the area (highlighted in red) completely solid. Note that the Millennium series lugs above have space in this area. There is also a significant difference in the thickness of the side walls. The wall thickness of the lug at right is .086 inch, the sidewalls of the lugs above range from .0415 to .0595

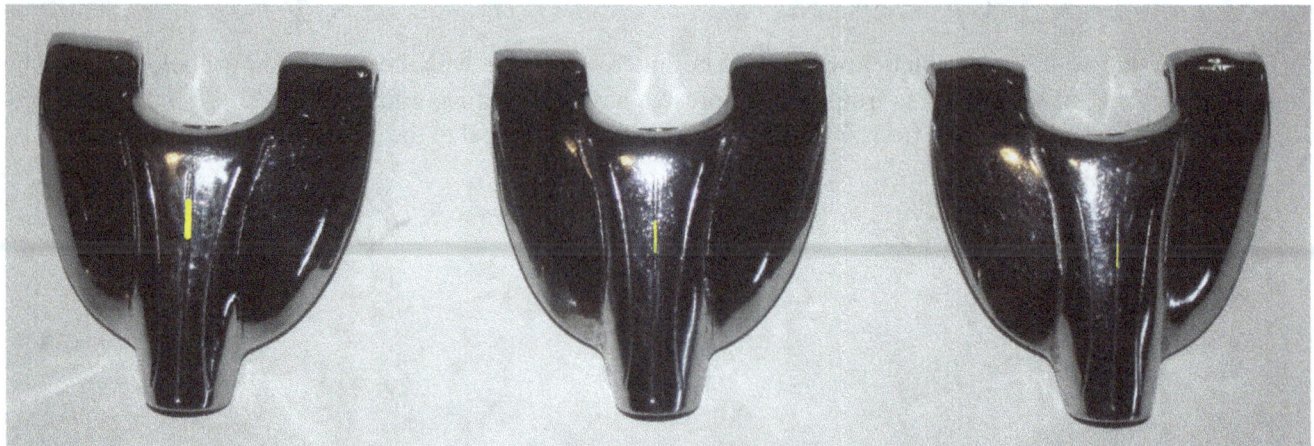

There are subtle but noticeable differences in the "etching" on the claws of different eras. The earliest claws have the deepest and widest lines while the lines on the newest are the thinnest. To help the reader detect this, sections of each era's claws shown here have their center lines partially filled in with a yellow line that matches the width of the etched line.

1970s Claw (left) made specifically for bass drums with metal hoops. Shown with wood-hoop claw to illustrate the difference. These claws should not be considered interchangable.

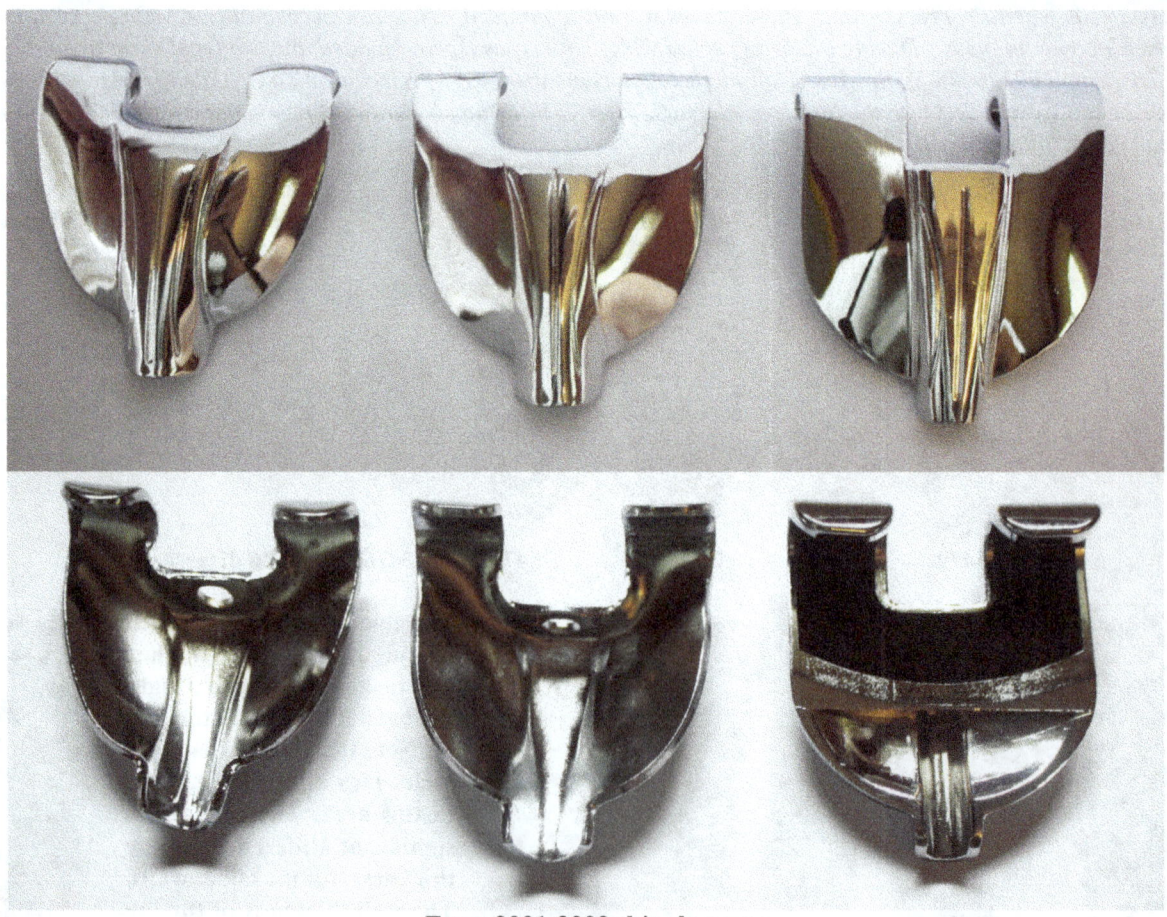

G5462 Claw
1958-2005

From 2001-2009 this claw was identified as the Millennium GS-5462
From 2010-2013 it was identified as the G5472 Classic Claw

G5463
Padded Claw
2011-2013

2003-2013 "Low-Mass" or "mini-Gretsch" lugs first appeared on Catalina and Blackhawk drums. (The earlier Blackhawk drums used a generic non-Gretsch looking lug. 2001-2002 Catalina drums used premium "Millennium" lugs.)

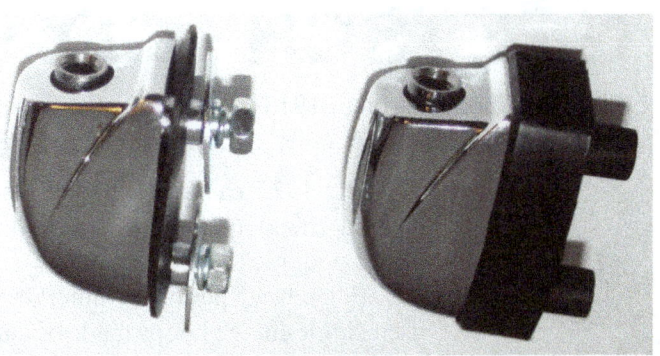

GS5476 mini-lug

GS5476B mini-lug for bass drum same as GS5476 except for the black "lift"

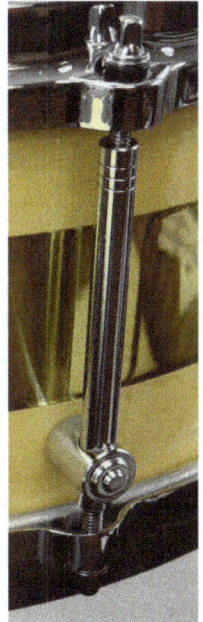

GS-FFL2x4
2x4 (3 piece maple/brass/maple shell)
2002-2006

GS-FFL
Free-floating Legend lugs
2002-2006

New style hex screws
Prior to 2003, the hex screws were standard thread 8/32 with a length of 7/16" with a 5/16 hex head. The change then was to metric M4 with .7 thread pitch and length of 10mm with a 7mm hex head.

2003: 120th Anniversary Limited Edition Custom Round Badge Snare Drums: Gladstone Styled Center Post Tube Lug
Appeared on only two 120th Anniversary snare drums in 2003. There also was a rarely seen piccolo version (chrome only) (bottom left). These lugs were never available from Gretsch as replacement parts.

NC-5471
(Same part number as double-post tube lugs at right.)
New Classic single-post piccolo tube lug
2004-2012

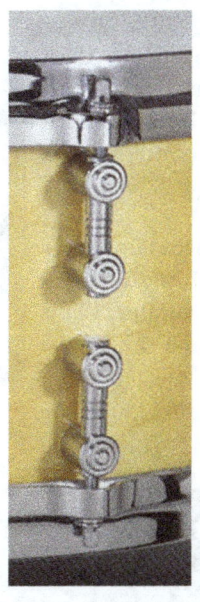 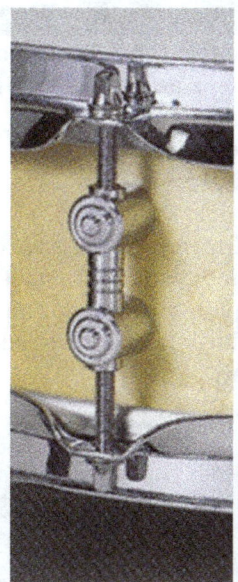 

2004-2012: New Classic Double-Posted Tube Lugs NC-5471
These lugs appeared on many New Classic series drums, the 8x14 "Swamp Dog" released in 2013, and some U.S. Custom Shop drums. These lugs were never available from Gretsch as replacement parts.

GRETSCH COUNTERHOOPS

All counterhoops through 1915 were made of wood and there was a wide variety of materials including: Birdseye maple veneer, solid maple, oak veneer, nickel-capped maple.

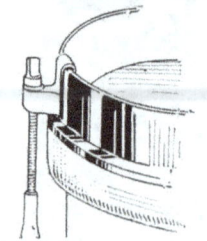

Notice the broad extension rim on this improved counterhoop. It positively prevents the flesh-hoop from turning under.

The 1927 catalog included single-flanged metal (seamless brass) hoops plated with nickel or silver.

For a brief period of time Gretsch used single-flange hoops made of aluminum; there are "Super Structure" drums with aluminum hoops.

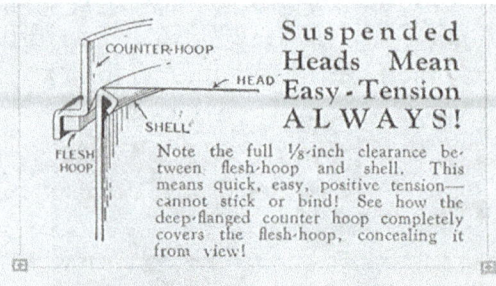

Late-'20s double-flange hoop: "new style deep flanged extension metal counter hoops"

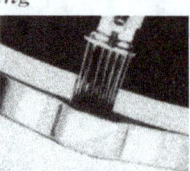

Early snare gates were either notched (on the wood hoops, right) or simply bent (metal hoops, left)

Gretsch counterhoops evolution in the early 1940s: The hoop shown here first appeared in the 1941 catalog on the "Tournament" model parade drum and was described as the "Flanged-Base Polished Metal Hoop." Because of the relatively sharp edge that chewed up sticks with every rimshot or rimclick, they came to be referred to as "stickchoppers." This style of hoop (made of roll-formed plated steel or brass) would become standard on 12", 13", 16", & 18" Gretsch toms by 1950 and continue through 1958.

In that same 1941 catalog, Gretsch introduced (on their Gladstone and Broadkaster snare drums) the heavier die-cast "stickchoppers," described by Gretsch as "Deep-Flanged Metal hoops." These hoops were used on all premium snare drum models from 1950-1958 and on 14" floor toms from 1954-1958.

According to Fred W. Gretsch, Gretsch die cast hoops since the earliest days have been made of Zamack 7, a zinc alloy with elements of aluminum, magnesium, and copper. This and several other zinc alloys were developed in 1929 by the New Jersey Zinc Company.

Snare gates on the earliest die-cast snare-side counterhoops were cast. The switch to milled snare gates (below) began in the mid 1950s, first on the Max Roach Model, then on the X4175 Broadkaster Max Roach model, then on nearly all snare drums by the late 1950s.

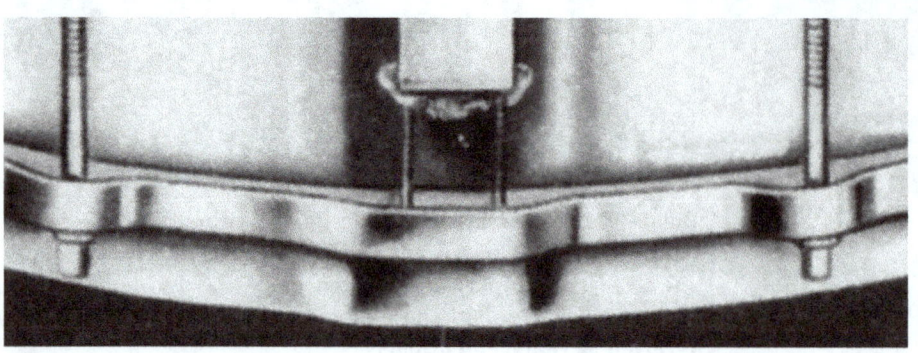

These hoops are often rather rough-looking today. Lee Ruff: *"Pot metal is rather tricky to chrome plate. To do it right, it must be plated with copper first. The old timers always refer to the process as a "copper strike." This helps "seal" the metal in a sense, which makes for a durable chrome plating. In the Max Roach days I do not believe Gretsch did the copper process, which resulted in plating that appeared pitted or flaky. It didn't take long for the chrome to get ugly or even disappear. This resulted in the pewter look. Antique juke boxes have a lot of pot metal parts that are chrome plated. Many collectors and restorers send these parts to other parts of the world for proper plating due to EPA regulations in the USA."*

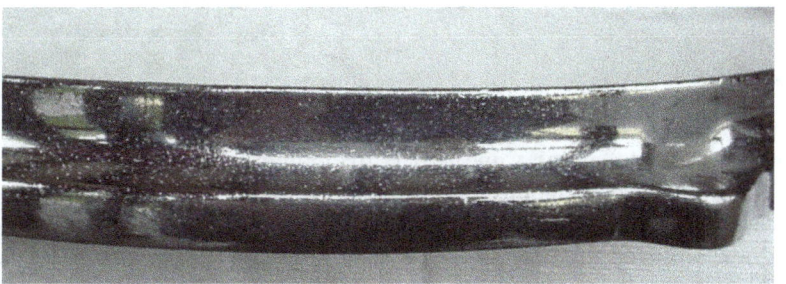

Milled-out snare gates appear in a variety of widths that do relate to different eras; they are shown here from earliest (left) to latest (right)

The second-generation die-cast hoops which first appeared in 1959 had a bead at the top to ease stick damage. Used from 1959 through 2002 when they were replaced by the imported Millennium series versions.

Round-badge era (zinc) die-cast hoops:
- 5485   12" 5-hole
- 5486   13" 6-hole
- 5487   14" 8-hole
- 5488   15" 8-hole
- 5489   16" 8-hole
- 5490   18" 8-hole
- 5491   14" 6-hole

Note: When Gretsch made the change from die-cast stick choppers to "beaded top" die-cast hoops, sizes ranged from 12 to 16. 18" hoops were probably outsourced from Slingerland, as the only known examples resemble Slingerland as opposed to Gretsch. 18" floor toms were converted from 8-lug to 10 lug in the very early 1970s. 8-lug 18" floor toms are in demand by drummers who want to convert them to bass drums; they have become very scarce.

Presented on Ebay as Gretsch 1960s round badge bass drum counterhoops, which was a misrepresentation. The inlays are too narrow and Gretsch did not use staples

Correct width Gretsch inlays are easy to spot at a glance; Gretsch has always used 13/16" inlays

Gretsch installed inlay on the bass drum hoops before they were painted, then covered them with masking tape, painted the hoops black, then removed the tape. This frequently resulted in unpainted wood visible at the inlay seam as well as paint on the inlay. Portions of the painted inlay in this photo have been marked with yellow.

Gretsch first offered 6, 8, and 10 toms by 1977. They were fitted with generic triple-flanged hoops: 6-inch 4-hole, 8-inch 4-hole, and 10-inch 6-hole through 1980. (Commonly referred to as "pre-die-cast" drums.)

In about 1981, die-cast hoops were made available for these small drums, with slightly different configurations on the 6 and 10-inch drums: 6-inch 4-hole #5482, 8-inch 5-hole #5483, 10-inch 5-hole #5484. The five-lug configuration was unique to Gretsch and carried over through the "Millennium Era."

In the KMC era (2000 forward) conventional triple-flanged hoops continued to be standard on Blackhawk, Catalina, many Full-Range snare drums and other economy drums. The thickness of the triple-flanged hoops was either 1.6mm or 2.3mm depending on the series. A new generation of die-cast hoops appeared in 2001 as part of the "Millennium Series" imported hardware. They first appeared on two Gretsch Auxiliary Maple snare drums in 2001 while all the other models featured 2.3mm "power hoops" triple flanged hoops. All Renown series drums were fitted with Millennium diecast hoops beginning in 2002 and these hoops were supplied on all USA Maple and Custom Series beginning in 2003.

triple flanged 1.6mm hoops first catalogued as replacement parts in 2003:
8" 4-lug GS-0804BH
8" 6-lug snare GS-0806SH
10" 6-lug GS-1006BH
10" 6-lug snare GS-1006SH
12" 6-lug GS-1206BH
12" 6-lug snare GS-1206SH
13" 6-lug GS-1306BH
14" 8-lug GS-1408BH
14" 8-lug snare GS-1408SH
16" 8-lug GS-1608BH

Wood counterhoops
Maple, Walnut, Ebony finishes,
all wood or metal-lined wood (right)
2010-2013

Gretsch introduced their 302 series hoops on the Brooklyn Series drums in 2012, and made them available as aftermarket parts. The hoops are 3mm thick and double flanged. Gretsch introduced them describing them as reminiscent of the hoops used up until the mid-1950s with the same height profile as the classic die-cast hoops for a playing experience that feels the same as traditional Gretsch USA Custom drums.

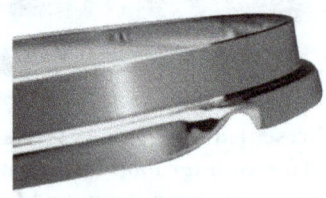

GRETSCH SHELLS

If the reader is unfamiliar with the basics of wood-shell drum design and construction, he is encouraged to reference Appendix 1 near the end of this book. Written by woodworker and drum builder Joe Partridge, the appendix includes a discussion of woods, shell designs, and how these factors affect drum tone.

3-Ply and 6-Ply

As far as many Gretsch fans are concerned, there have been two basic eras of Gretsch shells; the older (1920-1959) 3-ply shells with "roundover" bearing edges and the newer (1959-today) 6-ply shells with beveled bearing edges. This is true to an extent, but certainly there is a great deal more to the Gretsch shell story.

The Gretsch catalogs of 1912-1915 included drums with a wide variety of shell materials: nickel-plated metal, corrugated metal, solid maple, mahogany, and walnut.

All wooden drum shells prior to 1920 were made of solid planks of wood that were bent into a circle and glued. The earliest brass shells had seams, and were listed as seamless by 1927.

The angle turned rim and the heavy beadings in the rim give extra strength to the shell.

1927 Metal shell diagram, caption

According to Gretsch, they were the first company, in 1920, to introduce a new and improved process for drum shell construction; multi-ply lamination. Laminated shells were rounder and lighter than steam-bent solid shells. In 1941 Gretsch proclaimed that since 1920 many of their competitors had also begun to offer laminated shells. The Gretsch shells, however, were declared to be superior because of their exclusive method of keeping the shells under pressure during the laminating process. There was a much more significant difference.

COMPETITORS BENT PLYWOOD

Companies like Ludwig bent plywood that had already been glued together. The plywood was heated by large steel rollers with open gas flames inside. One roller rotated slightly faster than the other, so the plywood bent as it exited the rollers. The ends of the plywood would then be tapered so the shell could be glued together with a scarf joint.

1927 Catalog
The 1927 catalog listed 3-ply maple, 3-ply mahogany. By 1936 Gretsch was using poplar (much cheaper) for the inner ply and charging extra for the 3-ply maple as a special-order option. The bass drums were 5-ply; inner, outer, and middle plies of maple.

GRETSCH BENT PLIES OF WOOD

What Gretsch did was start with 3 separate sheets of wood cut precisely to size. For many years, according to former superintendent Bill Hagner, the 3 sheets were two sheets of maple 1/16" thick and one sheet of poplar 1/8" thick. The sheets would be inserted into a steel chuck which was the same size as the outside diameter of the finished drum shell. Gretsch promotional material pointed out that the 3 individual plies were separately lapped 120 degrees apart. After the plies were all in place, another steel chuck was inserted into the middle. This inner chuck had wedges that would put pressure on the plies of wood. The chuck (wedge) was driven in with a sledge hammer, putting the glued plies under pressure. It was not only this pressure, but the fact that the three plies were jointed in three separate places that made Gretsch shells stronger than the competitors.

WARTIME

Like all the American drum companies, Gretsch stopped manufacturing metal-shell drums during the second World War due to restrictions imposed by the War Production Board. (No metal-shell drums reappeared in Gretsch catalogs until the 1961 catalog when they again catalogued a 5x14 spun brass snare drum.)

Also like all the other American drum companies, Gretsch had to develop drums that used less than 10% (by weight) metal. The Defender series had wooden lugs and hoops.

3-PLY PRODUCTION AND THE CHANGE TO 6-PLY SHELLS

The Gretsch fan consensus has traditionally been that the change from 3-ply to 6-ply happened within a 1958-1959 window. It is more complicated than that. Either Gretsch began to experiment with many different production standards in the postwar years of the 1950s, or they began to purchase shells from a number of different suppliers. There were a couple of reasons for this. One was that Gretsch was having a hard time keeping up with demand using their existing methods of manufacturing. Another reason: structural concerns. In spite of the laminated-ply hype, Gretsch was worried about their drums staying in round.

from Rick Van Horn's 2012 interview with Bill Hagner, courtesy of Fred Gretsch Enterprises:

"The process we used in my early days was not the same as is used today. Today several thin veneers are bent and glued into a mold. Back then we formed them in a chuck. The original Gretsch ply shell was very thin, with an outer ply 1/16" thick, a center ply 1/8" thick, and an inner ply 1/16" thick. The outer and inner plies were maple; the center ply was usually poplar. We formed the shells using a process that employed heated rollers and metal panels. It made great drums, but it didn't lend itself to mass production. One day in 1948, Bill Gretsch brought in a drum shell and laid it down on the floor. Then he had two guys hold him up while he stepped on the shell, and he said, 'See? It doesn't bend.' That's when we determined to use molded shells. But you don't make those types of molds every day of the week. It was more cost-effective to get somebody else to do it. The deal wasn't done until shortly after Bill Gretsch died, but we ultimately started using shells sourced from Jasper Wood Products in Indiana. Of course, we had to buy shells in every drum size that we sold. We weren't making shells to order anymore; we were stocking raw shells from which to create drums. But that was okay, because we needed more shells to meet the exploding demand for drums in the 1950s and '60s."

The shells that Jasper made for Gretsch were proprietary; Gretsch owned the dies that Jasper used; they were on loan to Jasper for nearly 50 years. Jasper did produce shells for other companies, presumably using different dies. Customers included Rogers, the George Way Drum Company, and Camco. (Jasper also made guitar tops and backs for Gretsch.)

MANUFACTURING PROCESS DIFFERENCE BETWEEN 3-PLY and 6-PLY

3-PLY (Gretsch in-house method.)

The three sheets of wood veneer were passed through heated steel rollers to make them easier to bend. They were then placed in a steel cylinder that had an inside diameter equal to the outside diameter of the finished drum. The sides of the plies that would be touching each other were coated with animal glue before being placed in the cylinder. When the plies were all in place, a steel chuck was placed in the middle. The wedges of the chuck were forced outward by the force of a top wedge that was driven in with a sledge hammer. This put tremendous pressure on the plies from the inside outwards against the cylinder and the whole assembly would be left for a day to dry.

6-PLY (Outsourced method.)

The method was similar to that described above, but the cylinders were much longer, making several drum shells at a time in one long tube. Instead of the steel chuck being driven in by hand, a flexible bladder was inserted into the middle. It not only inflated to put pressure on the plies, but was also heated to speed the curing of the glue. This process was referred to as molding.

SHELL THICKNESS

Lee Ruff: "The shells for the most part did not remain the same thickness from the 3 ply to the 6 ply change. That was the time of the most pronounced change in thicknesses. The later 3 ply were mostly that very thick shell, while the earliest 6 ply drums without stickers had much thinner shells. They were also true 5 1/2" depth. Both the thinner and thicker versions also varied in thicknesses within themselves. Gretsch shell thicknesses in these decades were "always" all over the place."

4-ply snare drum circa 1950
3/8" thick

3-ply snare drum circa 1957
inner ply 1/8"
5/16" thick

BEARING EDGE EVOLUTION

The basic bearing edge evolution has been from the "roundover" edge (diagram A below) of the early days (1920s into the 1950s) to the 30-degree bevel of the other two diagrams. Throughout the 1950s, and into the early 1970s, it was common for tom-toms (only) to have a "reverse bevel" as shown in diagram B below. By the late 1970s, and through 2002, the near universal Gretsch bearing edge for all drums was the 30-degree bevel shown in figure C below.

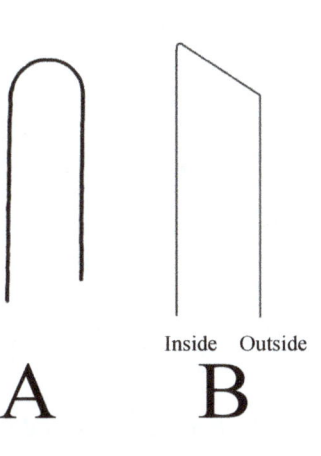

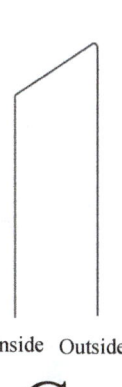

Exceptions to these generalizations of course abound; "roundover" edges are sometimes found on drums produced well into the 1950s. Nearly flat bearing edges are not uncommon, particularly among the 2-ply, 3-ply, and 4-ply drums. Into the 1960s they varied around the 30 degree angle. There are rare examples of thin shells with roundover edges in the 1960s and significantly more very thin shells with roundover edges in the mid 1970s.

Also the reader is cautioned that bearing edges are frequently "tweaked" by drum restorers. Speak to nearly any expert drum restorer/customizer and they will tell you about Gretsch drums they have repaired and restored. Often their work includes not only recovering and refinishing, but recutting of bearing edges. Their work also frequently involves modifying individual Gretsch drums to match an existing Gretsch kit, or even modifying other brands of drum shells to match a Gretsch kit. The reader is cautioned to seek expert counsel if you are trying to determine the authenticity of a Gretsch drum or outfit.

REINFORCEMENT RINGS

For the most part, Gretsch did not find it necessary to install reinforcement hoops after they began using 3-ply shells in the 1920s. (Gretsch engineers were reported to have indicated that they felt such rings interfered with the resonance of the drum, degrading its tone.)

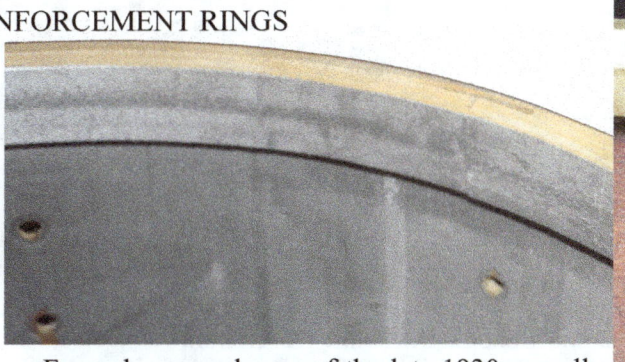

There have been many exceptions. Four-ply snare drums of the late 1930s usually had reinforcement hoops. Most 18" 3-ply tom toms (and 18" 3-ply shells made into bass drums) had reinforcement rings. The author has documented numerous other models with reinforcement rings: Very small 3-ply drums (bongos), Gretsch Gladstone snare drums of the late 1930s to early 1940s. An internet forum visitor reported having a 1937 Gretsch American 3-ply snare drum with reinforcement rings, another has a 1939 Broadkaster 4-ply with rings and reports having seen 12", 13", 14" and 16" Gretsch drums with rings. Those drums were the exceptions, not the rule.

Gretsch Gladstone (3-ply)
internal ply mahogany, maple reinforcement rings

Look **inside** a Gretsch drum shell. It's a smooth **unmarred cylinder**—the only absolute guarantee a drummer has of clean, distortion-free drum tone. No extra reinforcing rings (which actually distort drum tone) are needed inside a Gretsch shell. Shell strength and perfect roundness (for the life of the drum) are guaranteed through the use of 6-ply construction.

Gretsch Warrantry card of the early 6-ply era, suggesting that reinforcement rings distorted the tone of a drum. By 1941 Gretsch began a policy of providing a written guarantee with each wood-shell drum sold. The original guarantee was that the wood shell and hoop would hold their perfect roundness throughout the service life of the instrument. The warranty offered with the 6-ply shells was a 5-year warranty against manufacturing defects.

Numbers stamped inside shells

Apparently predating the silver sealer era, numbers pressed into reinforcement rings have been spotted on a number of drums. This example is on a maple reinforcement hoop of a drum with an internal ply of mahogany, believed to be a late-'40s to early-'50s snare drum with round badge, die-cast stick chopper hoops and rocket lugs.

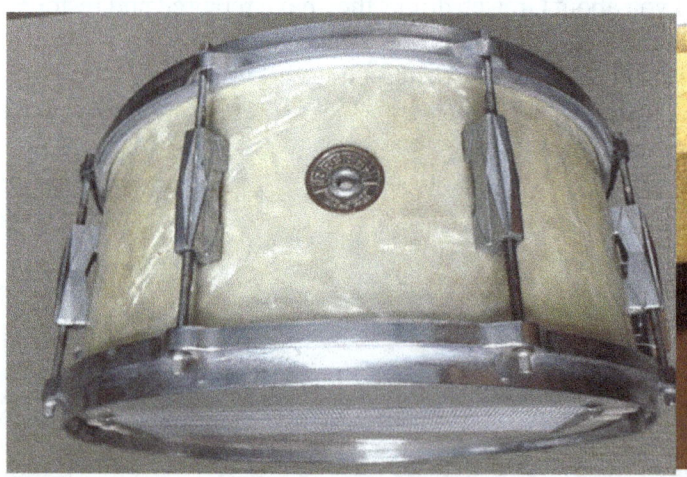

At this writing, little is known about the 3 and 4-digit numbers that have been observed ink-stamped inside shells of the 1950s. Rick Gier: *"All that I have seen to date have silver interiors and predate the labels. This would tend to point to somewhere in the post 1953, pre-1963 time frame. I do not know what the code means, but it does not appear to follow the old month-year or year-month type of logic. It could have been a type of serial number. The numbers I have recorded are: 817, 1196, 1213, 1236, 1585, 1761, 1838, 1946, 3146, 3259, 3266, 3876, 4327, 4774, 4804, 5016, 5184"*

Gretsch Super Structure

The "Gretsch Super Structure" stamp was applied to (some, not all, of) the inside of Gretsch guitar bodies and drum shells of the 1940s and 1950s. To date the author has documentation of the stamp appearing in a number of different models and shell types from 1952 to 1957. In the guitar world, the date range is earlier, beginning in the early 1940s on specific models and continuing into the early 1950s. Guitar historians have theorized that these dates align with an era of outsourced guitar tops evidenced by contour and sound hole differences from tops known to be made by Gretsch. Since Jasper Wood Products of Jasper, Indiana, was known to have sold guitar tops to Gretsch prior to their becoming a supplier of drum shells to Gretsch, there is speculation that perhaps Super Structure shells were the first drum shells supplied to Gretsch by Jasper. This speculation has been fueled by the fact that many of the Super Structure drum shells do not match either the traditional 3-ply Gretsch manufacturing methods or what most consider the "usual" Jasper 6-ply shells. There are many differences in the woods, thicknesses, and method of manufacture.

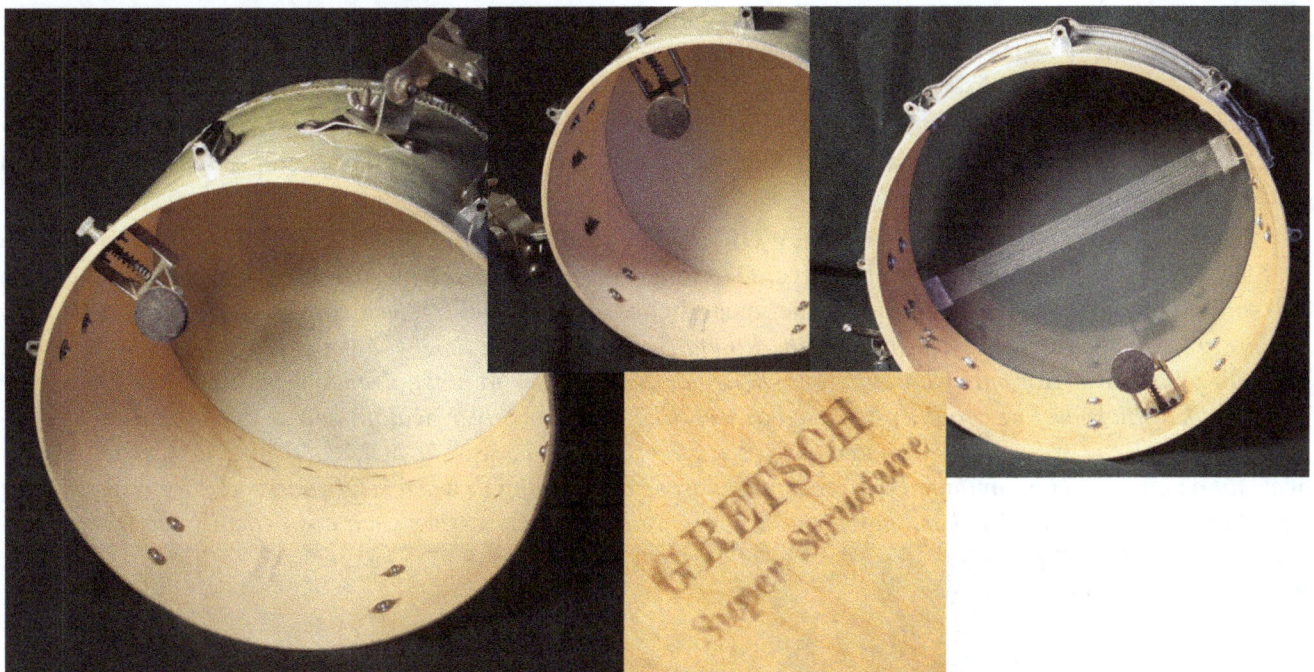

From the Will Tillman collection: a rare Super Structure outfit. All plies of all drums are maple. The snare drum is a 6.5x14, 3-ply drum: 1/16" inner, 1/8" middle, 1/16" outer. The 8x12 and 14x14 toms (both with tacked bottom heads) are both 2-ply drums with 1/8" outer and 1/16" inner plies. The bass drum is 2 plies, both 1/8".

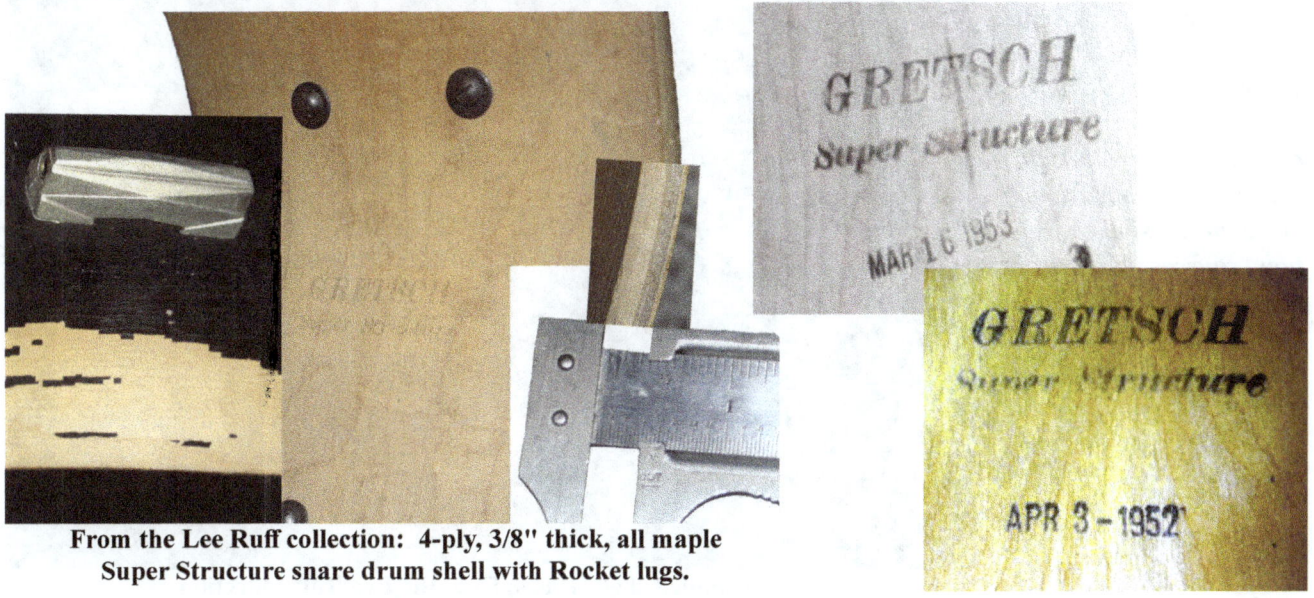

From the Lee Ruff collection: 4-ply, 3/8" thick, all maple Super Structure snare drum shell with Rocket lugs.

SILVER SEALER

In the 1950s, Gretsch began to paint the insides of the shells with the famous "silver sealer," which quickly became a Gretsch unofficial trademark. There are 3-ply drums in the marketplace from the late 1950s with silver sealer. Lee Ruff: *"I have no hard evidence, but I believe this started around 1956-1957. The Max Roach models never had silver sealer. My D J Fontana copper mist drums from 1957 did have the silver. It seems that the later 50s drums which had the thick 3-ply shells, did have the sealer. I do not recall seeing a thin 3-ply shell with the sealer. Most 3-ply drums with the silver sealer have the 1st version of the two-pad tone controls. Again.......no hard evidence."*

As with many things Gretsch, the exact dating of silver sealer application will probably remain unknown. Rick Gier owned a cocktail drum with silver sealer and has a photo of it being played in 1955. A Super Structure parade drum with unfinished inner ply is date stamped November 14, 1957. These drums make it clear that while some drums began receiving silver sealer by the mid-1950s, other Gretsch drums from the late 1950s well into the 1960s did not receive the silver sealer. Rick Gier has at this writing recorded 17 Round Badge drums with serial numbers between 72000 and 76000 (1966) that do not have the silver sealer. Not all drums in that range lack the silver sealer.

Dave Gordon (drum marketing director in the Baldwin era, working under Duke Kramer in Cincinnati), tried updating the paint in the late 1970s, but there was an immediate uproar about the "sound change" so they quickly changed back to the original sealer. Gretsch is of course reluctant to give specifics regarding the brand and type of paint.

PATCHWORK SHELLS AND PLIES

The shells provided by Jasper were delivered as long (approximately 60 inch) tubes. Chunks of leftover tube too short to produce another drum were sometimes patched together. John Sheridan: *Gretsch drums made from scraps are quite common, especially from the Round Badge-era. At a time when most drums were wrapped, it was not a concern. Not only were different shells bonded together to make deeper drums, but ply scraps (for overall shell thickness) were quite often used as well. The interior Silver Sealant actually "highlights" the adjoining seams! But everyone used coated heads back then and no one saw the inside of their drums, so again, this was not a concern. This continued until recently. Jasper left nothing to waste! Of course, as Gretsch got more into translucent lacquer finishes, they generally reserved shells possessing such cosmetically pleasing outerface plies for that purpose. However, I did once own a Burnt Orange 16x18 that had an external seam that went right around the exact center of the shell. I wound up selling it to a guy who ultimately had it wrapped. Over the years, I've seen other examples of this, so while it was not a common occurrence at Gretsch, it did happen occasionally. Of course, since Gretsch now sources their proprietary formula shells from Keller, and with master drum builder Paul Cooper at the helm, this just doesn't happen at Gretsch anymore.*

Coupled shell (1960s) from the Lee Ruff collection

Jasper shells were not always made up of plies that were each one sheet of wood per ply, but rather a patchwork as can be seen on this Jasper shell. This is why one of the first jobs in Gretsch drum production was to sort the Jasper tubes and decide which sections of which tubes would be acceptable for drums that would show the grain.

OVERSIZED GRETSCH SHELLS

It is common for both vintage Gretsch drums and vintage Slingerland drums, both of certain eras, to be slightly "oversized," making it very hard to fit standard heads on the drums. Lee Ruff points out that Gretsch's oversized shells varied, as did the thickness of the coverings which results in head fits that are "all over the place." Aquarian released a series of heads in 1996, the American Vintage series, that accomodates those slightly larger shells better than most other standard mylar heads.

Roy Burns, Aquarian Drum Heads:

It has been my experience that most problems associated with "oversized" drums are with either Slingerland or Gretsch shells. In the days that a lot of the so-called "oversized" drums were made, head fit was not much of an issue because with calf heads, it was easier to simply make heads to fit specific drums. The introduction of mass-produced plastic heads changed the situation because they are less forgiving of shell variances. Part of the reason for the "larger" drums was that many of them were made the same size as the catalogued dimension; a 12" drum was made exactly 12", etc. Today most drums are slightly undersized. There were other factors as well. Some of the coverings used in those days were thicker than others; they varied. And quite often the problem was shell inconsistency; I saw a drum that a head fit on one side but not the other. That tells us that the problem is not so much with size as with uniformity; one side has gone a little bit out of round. It doesn't take very much. We decided to produce a head to address this and introduced the American Vintage series in 1996. The heads were oversized by fifty thousandths. They were really received well. Another goal we had with that series was to come as close in tone and feel as we could to calfskin. We began to get requests for that same skin in standard sizing, so we did just that and called them the Modern Vintage series because they are sized for modern drums but have the vintage calf tone and feel.

Lloyd McCausland, BJ Percussion (retired from Remo after 40 years):

Remo fought with Gretsch from the very beginning about making drums that our standard heads would fit, but it didn't do any good. Between their thick coverings and large shell sizes, standard heads would often not fit their drums.

John Sheridan:

[Current Gretsch shell sizing is] actually one sixteenth of an inch (a 1/16") undersized (like Jasper, Keller only does this for Gretsch, as 1/8" undersized is Keller's normal standard). For the most part, post-'60s-era

Gretsch shells do not seem to have "fit" issues with contemporary heads. However, many of their '60s 6-ply shells do. (From my personal experience, I'd estimate approximately a quarter up to a third!) Conversely, I rarely, if ever, have had problems with contemporary heads fitting on '50s Gretsch 3-ply shells. Though Gretsch 3-ply shells are not as plentiful as their 6-ply shells (made mostly in the post-Beatlemania era), it's common knowledge among vintage collector/dealers that many '60s-era Gretsch drums are problematic in this regard.

Ed. note: According to Dave Gordon, it was during his tenure at Gretsch in the late 1970s that Jasper shells were adjusted from full size to undersized.

SNARE BEDS, SNARES

Snare beds cut into Gretsch snare drums were relatively narrow and deep from their beginnings all the way up until about 1962. This was about the time of the introduction of the wide (42-strand) wire snares. Presumably to react more appropriately to these wider snares, the depth of snare beds was lessened and widened to the point that they nearly stretched all the way between the lugs on each side of the snares.

Some, but certainly not all, shells from the late 3-ply era and into the early 6-ply era had what appears to be a linen cheesecloth mesh between the outer ply and the pearl covering. The shell in the photo is a six-ply.

SCARF JOINTS

While most Gretsch plied shells were made with butt joints on the plies, some were made with scarf joints. Like the butt-joint shells, the joints are in different positions. These photos are of a Progressive Jazz 4-ply shell circa 1950 showing the inner ply scarf (right) and a middle ply scarf (left.)

An unusually clean scarf joint on a 3-ply drum; note that the outer ply blends very smoothly into the inner ply.

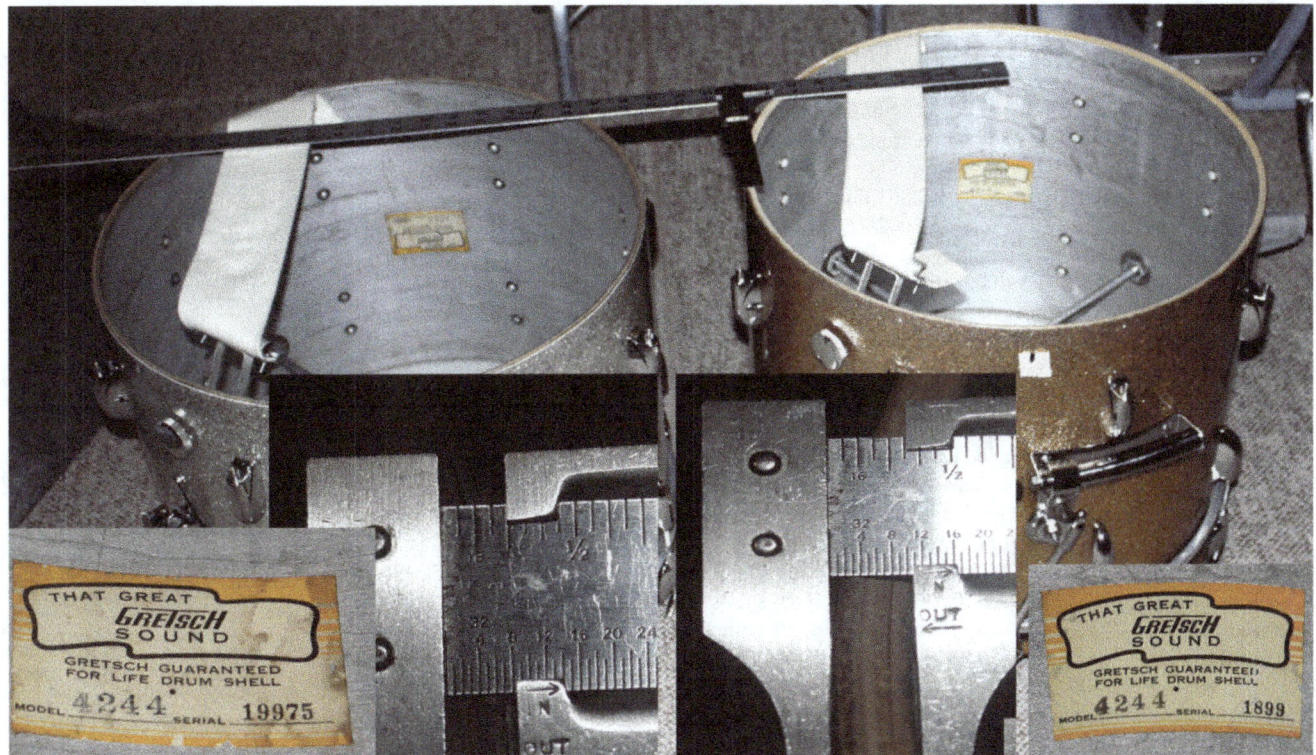

There are thin 3-ply drums and thicker 3-ply drums, there are thin 6-ply drums and thicker 6-ply drums. This photo collage illustrates two 18-inch bass drums from the Lee Ruff Collection. The one on the left is a 6-ply drum with a quarter-inch shell thickness. The one on the right is a 6-ply drum with a 5/16" shell thickness. The shell below, also from the Lee Ruff collection, is a 6-ply tom shell from the 1960s with "roundover" bearing edges, outer and inner plies of mahogany, and is only 3/16" thick.

Lee Ruff: "*The most defined variation in shell thickness was the transition from 3-ply to 6-ply. The end of the 3-ply era is where the very thick shells appeared. The beginning of the 6-ply era is where the true 5 1/2" snares appeared with the short, shallow snare beds and the extra thin 6-ply shell. This carries over to other sizes of drums and thicknesses are random part of the time.*"

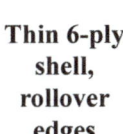

Thin 6-ply shell, rollover edges

Jasper Wood Products, of Jasper, Indiana, went out of business in January of 2002. A former employee of Jasper, responding to an inquiry on an internet forum, explained that their formula had been hard maple inner and outer plies with inner plies of Sweetgum. The hard maple they used was also referred to as Sugar Maple and they purchased it from mills in the upper parts of Wisconsin and Michigan; areas that grew lots of nice white color maple that the drum companies wanted.

Duke Kramer phoned John Sheridan and asked him to recommend another shell supplier. He explained that Jasper was going out of business and were returning all the tooling (drum molds, dies) that Gretsch owned. Sheridan told Kramer that for the kind of quantities Gretsch required, Keller was pretty much the only game in town. To this day, Gretsch representatives are reluctant to discuss who manufactures their shells. They *do* make it very clear that today's Gretsch shells are identical to the traditional Jasper-supplied shells; the same maple/sound gum blend of woods, the same thicknesses and diameters.

SINCE 2001

Gretsch snare drums in the years since 2001 have been produced with a great variety of shell materials, origins, thicknesses and bearing edges. While the shell materials, thicknesses, and edges are often identified for marketing purposes, origins are often difficult to determine. The reader is cautioned not to assume that any Gretsch drum not specifically identified as "American made" is imported, nor to assume that "imported" should be construed as inferior.

Auxiliary Maple Snare Drums   2001 only   100% U.S.A. Maple 10-ply shells
All Maple Snare series   2002 - 2005   10-ply all-maple shells
Blackhawk 2003-2004   6-ply mahogany shells with 45-degree edges and mini-lugs
Blackhawk EX & SX series' 2005-2006   9-ply mahogany with 30-degree edges and mini-lugs.
Blackhawk 2007-2011   6-ply basswood/poplar snare and tom shells, 8-ply bass drum, steel snare drum.
Nighthawk 2004-2005   6-ply mahogany with 45-degree edges and mini-lugs.
Nighthawk 2006-2013   generic imported drum features included 9-ply cross-laminated Select Hardwoods
Renown 2001   6-ply 100% maple shells, 30-degree edges, 10-ply snare drum with 45-degree edges, triple-flanged hoops.
Renown 2002-2006   same as 2001, but now with die-cast hoops.
Renown 2007-2013   upgraded to Gretsch-formula maple shells with new bass drum options
Renown '57 2011-2012 same Renown Gretsch formula shells with 1957 classic car appointments including 2-tone Motor City Blue (& white), chrome chevrons, and Gretsch metal-stenciled nameplates on each drum instead of badges, matching throne. Motor City Black option added in mid-2011, Motor City Red added in 2012.
Catalina Stage & Elite   2001-2003 6-ply mahogany shells with 30-degree edges. Stage series = wrapped, Elite series = lacquered.
Catalina Birch   2003-2006 2010-2013   6-ply birch shells with 45-degree edges
Catalina Club   2003-2013   6-ply mahogany shells with 30-degree edges
Catalina Maple   2006-2010, 2010-2013   "thin" maple shells. 7-ply maple shells with 30-degree edges as of October 2010
Catalina Ash   2006-2010   (Discontinued by October of 2010.) "Thin" ash shells with 2.5mm triple-flanged hoops..
Custom Plus series snare drums and Vinnie Colaiuta snare drums   2002
     8-ply instead of 6-ply, making them 25% thicker than U.S. Custom Shop snare drums.
Legend Free-Floating Snares   2002-2005 10-ply maple. Free floating snares meant the shell "floated" in the middle of all the hardware, was not attached directly to the shell at any point.
10-ply Gloss Maple Snares   April, 2006 -2012 100% Maple 8mm shell with 30-degree edges & Silver Sealer
New Classic Series   2006-2013
     American maple blended drum shells The 2004 and 2005 New Classic snare drums were U.S. made. The rest of the drums in the series were "American maple blended drum shells." In May of 2007 the descriptive verbiage was adjusted to "proportionate Gretsch formula maple shells." These outfits have proportionate shell thicknesses, while the U.S. Custom Shop shells do not. This means that as the drum's diameter increases, the thickness of the shell ply increases (to maximize the tone of each drum). All toms are 6-ply shells. 8" & 10" are 4.8mm thick. 12" & 13" are 5.7mm thick. 14" & 15" are 6.6mm thick. 16" & 18" toms & 18" bass drums are 7.5mm thick. 20", 22", & 24" bass drums are 8-ply shells & are 9.1mm thick. All 14" snare drums are 12-ply shells & are 12.5mm thick. All drums have 30-degree edges and silver sealer.
Limited Edition Custom Walnut Series   2006-2008
Renown Purewood Series   6-ply 100% Walnut or Cherry shells, 2005 only
Curly Maple Exotic Veneer shells   July 2005- 2013
New Classic Black Brass   2004-2006

G-4000 Series

Hammered Polished Brass 2006-2013, Chrome-Over-Brass 2004-2013
Hammered Chrome-Over-Brass 2006-2013, Hammered Antique Copper 2006-2013,
Solid Aluminum June 2006 - 2013, Solid Steel July 2006 - 2013, Solid Spun Brass 2007-2013,
Solid phosphor bronze 2009-2013

Retro-Mahogany/8-ply snare drums   2008-2010
Beech Limited edition Renown Purewood series: Beech 7-ply, 30-degree edges; production limited to 45 kits for distribution in the USA. 2010
Limited edition Renown Purewood series: 30-degree edges in limited numbers of kits for distribution in the USA. 2005 Walnut – 6-ply, Cherry – 6-ply (100 kits each), 2006 African Mahogany – 6-ply, 2007 Rosewood –9-ply, 2008 Bubinga – 9-ply, 2009 Oak– 6-ply, 2010 Beech – 7-ply (45 kits), 2011 African Wenge – 7-ply (100 kits), 2012 Hickory (35 kits)
G-5000 Solid Wood Series: USA Custom shop: solid single ply, 30 degree edges and maple reinforcement rings 2011-2013
Solid plywood snares: Solid ply shells with 3-ply sound support rings. Maple, Oak, Walnut, Rosewood, 2002
Crystal tone metal snare drums: Hammered Stainless Steel, Copper 2002 only:
Hammered Brass, Smooth Black Chrome Steel   2002-2005
Full Range Snare Series: Hammered Brass, Black Chrome Over Steel, 10-ply Gloss Maple, Blackhawk Mighty Mini Auxiliary in chrome over steel or basswood, "Legend" Free Floating Maple
Limited Edition Custom Walnut Series: 6-ply 100% Walnut, vertical grain 2006-2008
New snare drum series 2013:
     Black powder-coated Aluminum, Solid Claro Walnut, Cherry Stave Construction, Oak Stave Construction, Bell Brass

GRETSCH DRUM HEADS

Like most of the major drum companies of the early part of the 20th century (Rogers, Ludwig, Slingerland, Leedy), Gretsch had their own tannery facility. It is not clear when they began to outsource their calfskin head; probably during or shortly after the second world war.

By 1955, catalogs mentioned that Gretsch drum heads were made from selected skins that represented the "cream of the great Chicago hide market." During this era they branded their calf skins to match their flagship drum line, the Broadkaster.

Gretsch began the shift from calfskin to mylar drum heads with the rest of the percussion industry in the late 1950s when they introduced the Perma-Tone series. These heads were made for Gretsch on an OEM basis by Remo. Gretsch catalogs indicated that the Perma-Tone heads were mounted on metal flesh hoops until the mid 1960s. They shifted to the synthetic flesh hoops (pictured below), for a brief period, then went back to aluminum flesh hoops. The "No further Tensioning" stamp shown below first appeared in the very early 60s with the aluminum flesh hoops. The first stamps were done in blue ink, later ones were done in black ink as shown.

GRETSCH STRAINERS

Early post-type tensioner
1912

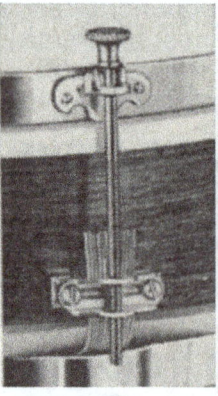
#5390 "Economy"
1936-1966

Parade Model
#2150   1935
Junior Strainer
#5396 1954-1958

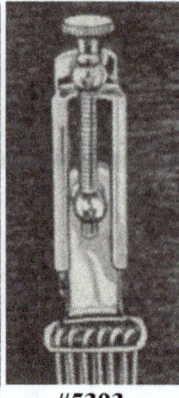
#5393
Parade Drum
1954-1963

First throw-off type strainer
1927-1936

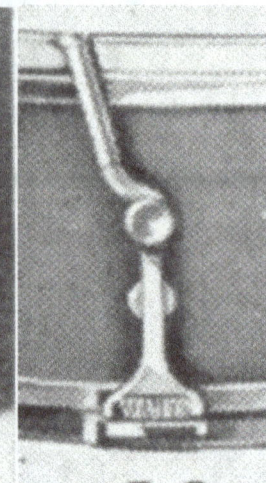
Broadkaster strainer
1936

stamp on rear,
Made In England

Improved snare strainer
1939

#1950 Throw-off strainer
1939

Gretsch Gladstone
1939-1941

"Feather-Touch"
Broadkaster & early Max Roach Model
1947-1950

The Feather Touch strainers have the same mounting bolt spacing as the Renown shown on the next page. Lee Ruff has observed that the difference is in the metal. Lee: "The Feather Touch was made of much stronger, rigid metal. It felt solid and worked well. The Renown was always very flimsy and draggy."

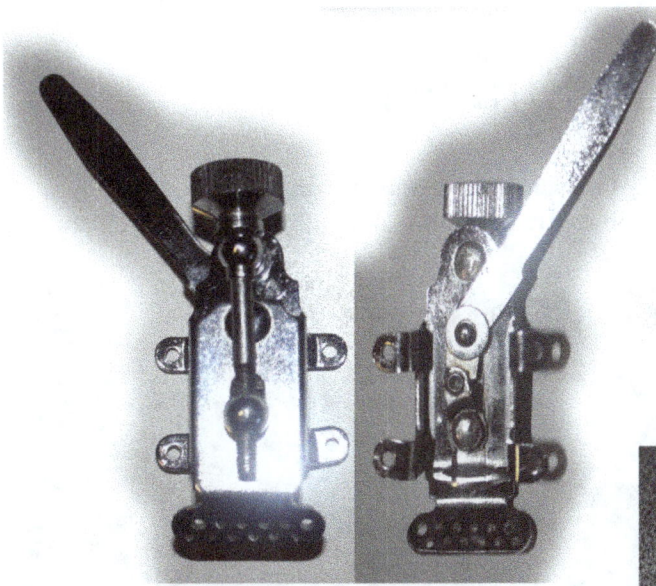

#5385 Renown 1950-2001
Lee Ruff: "The knobs are different (from the Renown) on the Feather Touch models. The Renown was simply a cheap copy of its predecessor the Feather Touch. The cover plate transition probably occurred when the construction of the strainer changed."

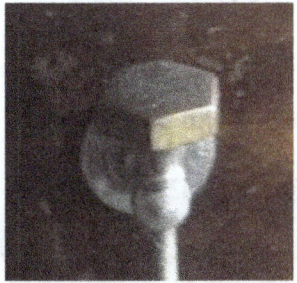

Hex knob on the Renown & Junior Strainers, early 1950s

#5386 Renown Rear Snare Bracket, commonly referred to as "towel rack" design 1950-1979

1954 catalog illustration showing hex-knob

Gretsch snare wires of the 1940s, 1950s, and 1960s tended to be rather stiff and wider-coiled than those of some of their competitors such as Slingerland. According to Ron Enyard, most of the big-name Gretsch endorsers of the jazz glory days of the 1950s in New York would replace their Gretsch wire snares with Slingerland wire snares which were softer and more tightly coiled.

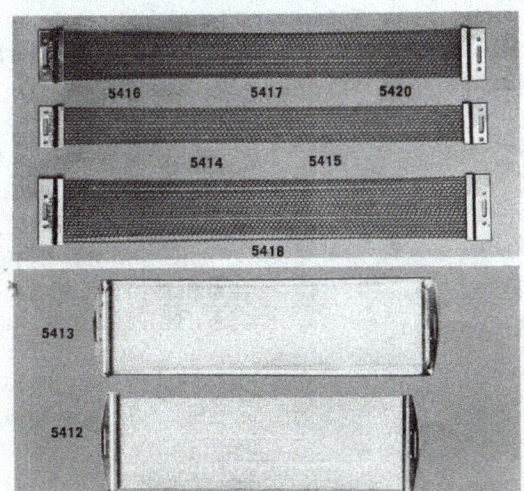

GRETSCH RESPONSO SNARES
Every strand lies flat and hugs the Head to give instant response.
5414 — Responso 12 strand snares for 14" drum Set $ 3.00
5415 — Responso 12 strand snares for 15" drum Set 3.00
5416 — Responso 16 strand snares for 14" drum Set 3.50
5417 — Responso 16 strand snares for 15" drum Set 3.50
5420 — Responso 16 strand snares for 16" drum Set 3.50
5418 — Responso 20 strand snares for 14" drum Set 4.00

GRETSCH WIDE-42 POWER SNARES
WIDE-42 power snares provide extra-power, extra-snap and extra-response resulting in better and more outstanding player performance.
5412 — WIDE-42 power snares for 14" drum Set $10.00
5413 — WIDE-42 power snares for 15" drum Set 10.00

GUT AND SILK WIRE-WOUND SNARES
To fit drums 13" to 16" shell diameter. Made up in 12 strand sets with fibre snare butt.
5422 — Gut Snares, med. gauge for orchestra drum (not illustrated) Set $4.50
5423 — Gut Snares, heavy gauge for concert or parade (not illustrated) Set 5.00
5410 — Silk Snares, silvered wire wound (not illustrated) Set 1.25

1966 Catalog snare listings

Micro-Sensitive Strainer
1950-1977   2012-

The Micro-Sensitive strainer is one of the most distinctively Gretsch components. It was designed by Andy Florio, a Gretsch endorser (and sometimes actor) who was constantly designing and building drum hardware.

Although Florio wanted Gretsch to produce three versions of the Micro-Sensitive, they only did two, one for drums 4" to 5.5" deep, the other for all deeper drums. (The third would have been for short-depth drums such as the Progressive Jazz.)

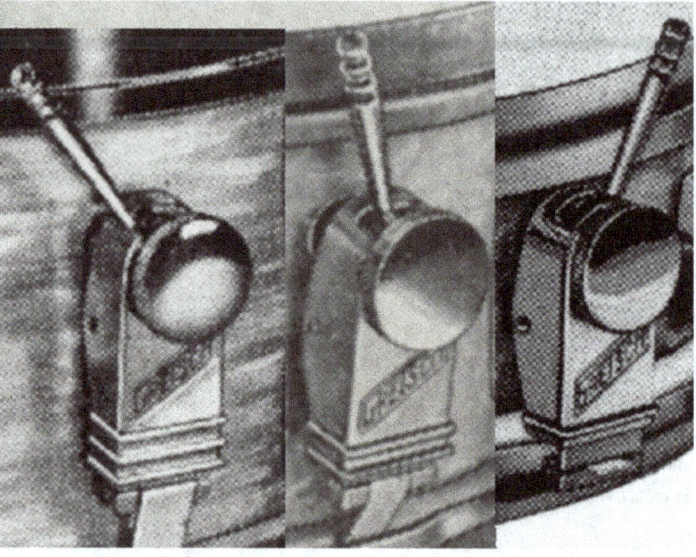

Gretsch catalog representations of the three styles of Micro-Sensitive strainer. The representation at right appeared only in the 1958 catalog on the Max Roach Progressive Jazz snare drum but was never in fact produced; this was an artist's rendering.

8/32"   10/32"

The earliest Micro-Sensitive strainers (about 1950) had an 8/32" threaded hole for the throw-off lever to screw into. The size of this hole was later increased to 10/32".

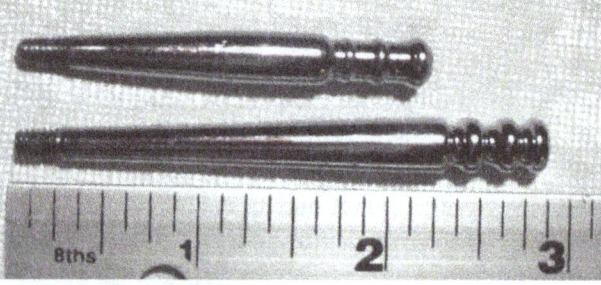

There were 4 different Micro-Sensitive throw-off levers; long and short 8/32" thread on older strainers, long and short 10/32" thread on newer strainers. The shorter levers were used on 4" and 5.5" depth snare drums, the longer levers were used on all deeper drums.

Micro-Sensitive mounting screws

The "roller" inside the Micro-Sensitive was originally brass, later was changed to steel

Holes to secure the individual snare strands, early Micro-Sensitive. Parade drums only.

The bottom section attached to the strainer with two screws like the bar style, but the hole spacing is different so they are not interchangeable.

214

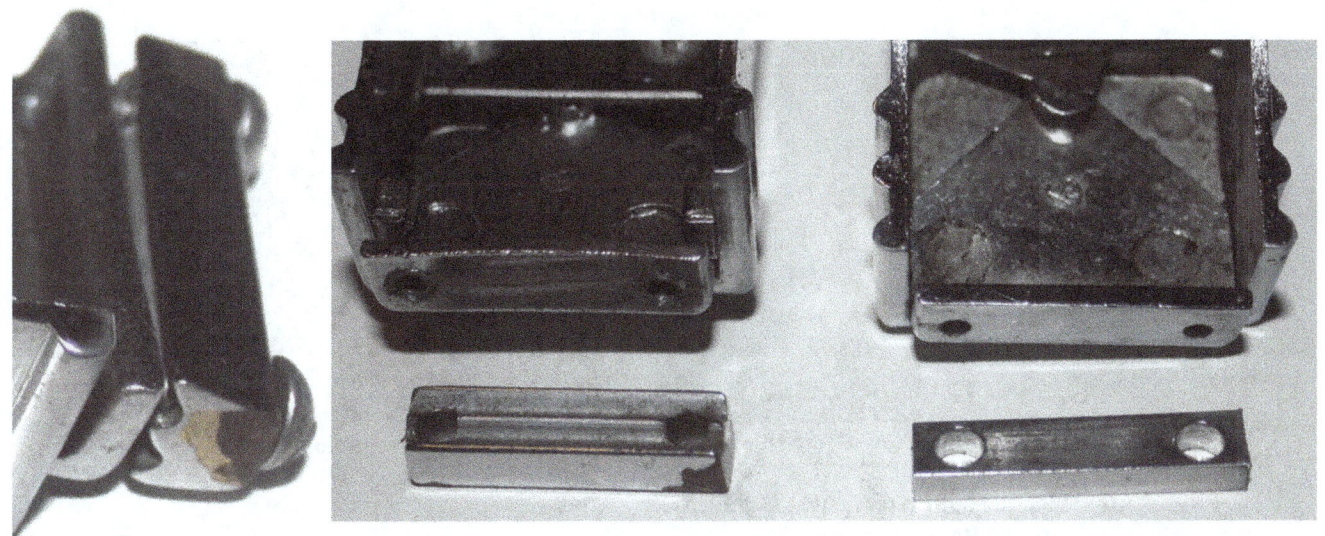

The block that secures the snare tape in early days was concave on one side with a "tooth" to prevent slippage. (Left)

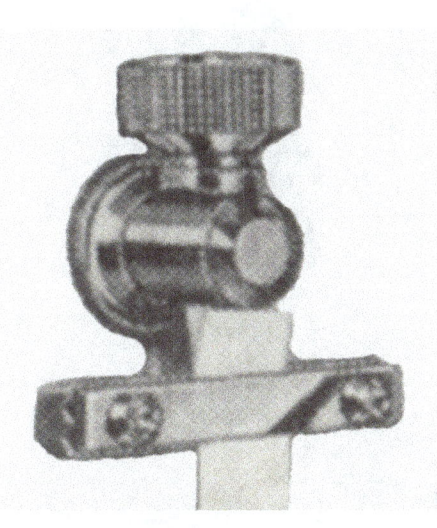

#5381 Fast-Tension Snare Bracket, or "single point butt plate," supplied with #5380 strainer 1950 to around 1960 (replaced by the 4-point 5381)

Micro-Sensitive strainers, from the back. Note the greyish cast block near the top that the throw-off lever screws into. The one on the left is loose because the grommet that holds it in place has detached. These castings occasionally strip or break also.

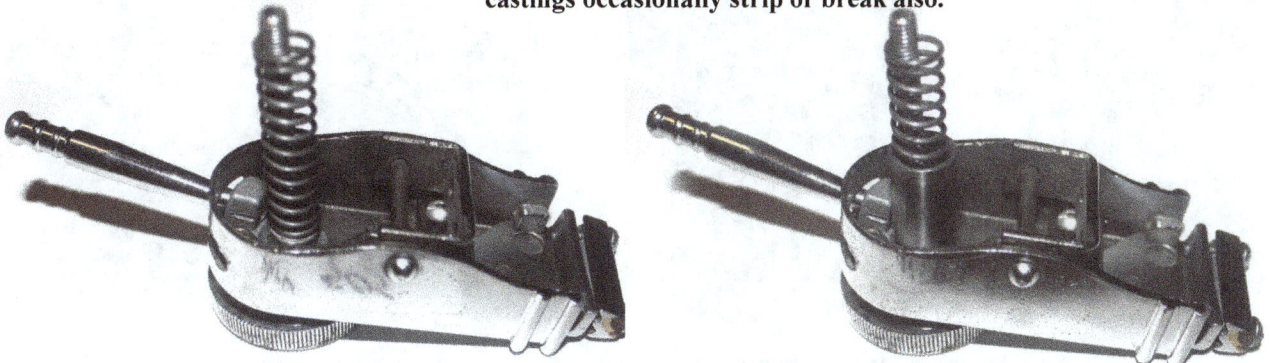

Through the 1950s, the Micro-Sensitive spring stood alone in the strainer (left). A metal cylinder was then added to protect and control the spring (right.)

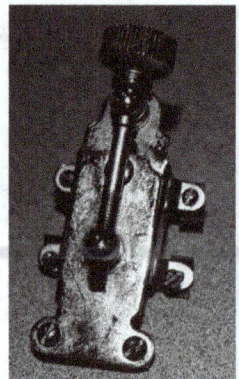  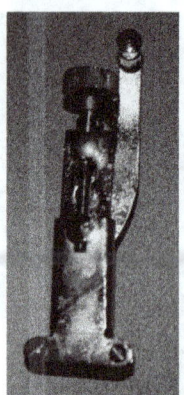 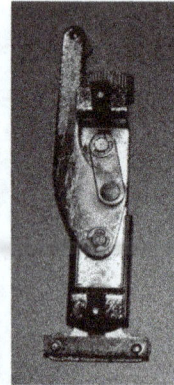

4-point version of #5381
circa 1960-1977
by 1966, the 5381's name was changed to the Rear Snare Bracket.

1970s version of #5385
Renown throw-off
1971-1979

The 5380 and 5381 were reissued as the G5380 and G5381 in 2011 These parts will retrofit into original drill holes of any vintage Gretsch drum that was drilled for the original 5380 and 5381.

  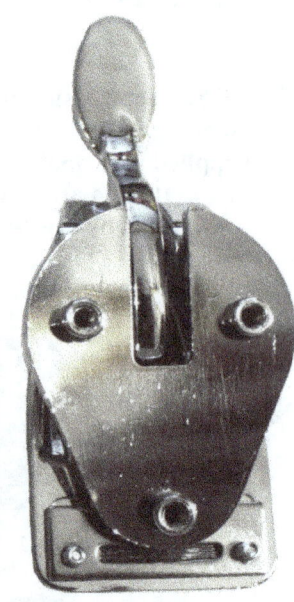

Lightning Throw-off #5378 1967-1974
When the Lightning throw-off was introduced in 1967 as the premium throw-off for upper line drums, the Micro-Sensitive was relegated to the 4109 aluminum snare drum.

Lightning Throw-off #5375
1975-2013
Lever in center, smaller footprint

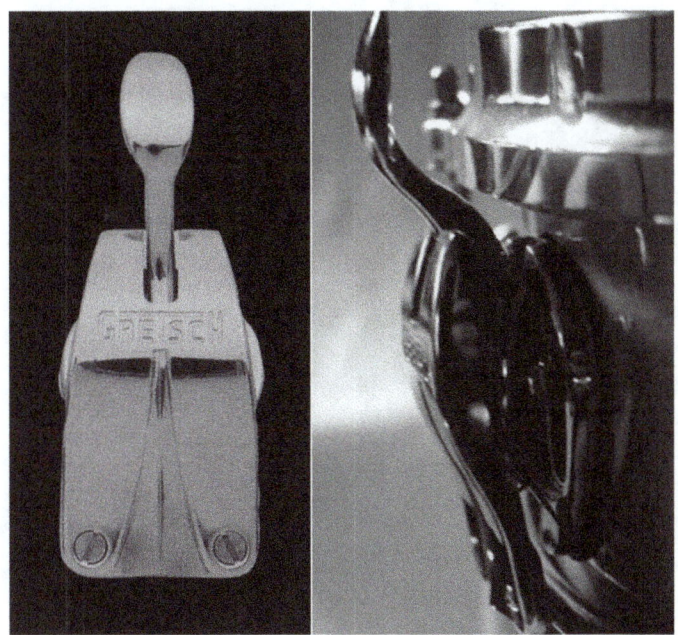

John Sheridan: "I believe the first drums issued with this revised Lightning were made as early as 1975; possibly 1974. One must recall that Gretsch went a good 6 years without issuing a full-line drum catalog, so it's quite likely this strainer appeared sooner than 1977 which is the first catalog to feature this strainer."

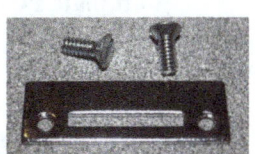

5375-22 Snare Mount Back Plate

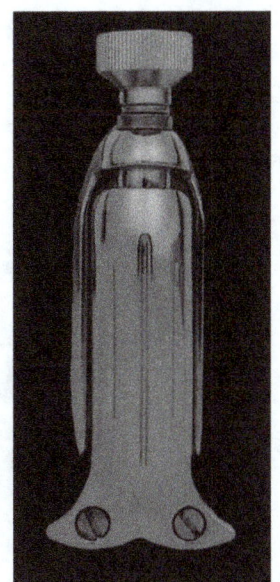

1971-2013
The #5379 Rear Snare Bracket was first paired with the 5378 Lightning, then the replacement 5375. It first appeared in the 1971 catalog. It is commonly referred to by collectors as the "Fishtail Butt Plate," while Gretsch began to refer to it as the "Strainer Butt End" by 1989. In 2002 that name changed to the "Lightning Strainer Butt Plate," and in 2009 to the "Lightning Butt Plate."

5379-13 Plate For Rear Bracket

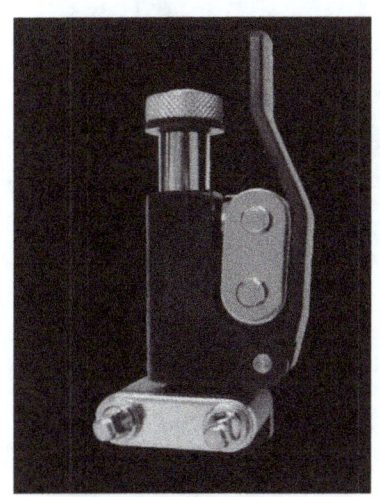

Nickelworks Throw-off
In 2004 Gretsch introduced the New Classic snare drums that featured the Nickelworks throw-offs and butt plates.
2002-2010

GS-DSTO (New Classic)   **butt plate GS-DSBP**

2006-2013
In 2006 the New Classic line expanded to kits and this strainer/butt premiered on the New Classic snare drums. Also utilized on all the higher end "Full Range" snare drums, 2007-2013.

"Drop-Style" Throw-off
all "Full Range" snare drums 2002-2005 except for the "Mighty Minis"

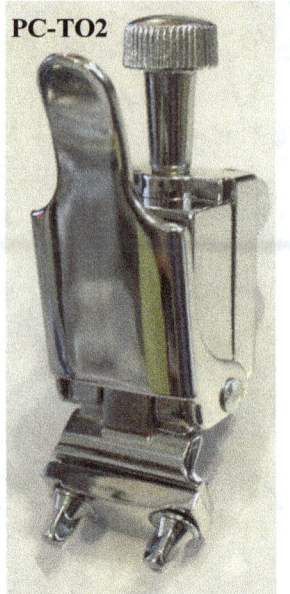

PC-TO2

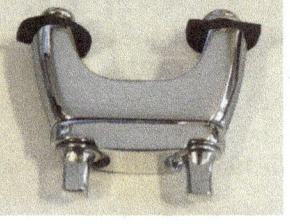

PC-TO2B

PC-TO2 Catalina Birch (2003-2006),
Catalina Maple (2006-2010),
Catalina Ash (2006-2010),
Blackhawk (2003-2010)
butt plate PC-BP1
PC-TO2B (black nickel) 2008-2010
butt plate PC-BP1B
(replaced by PS-DLSTO in 2011)

PC-TO1 2001-2003
Catalina Stage, Catalina Elite

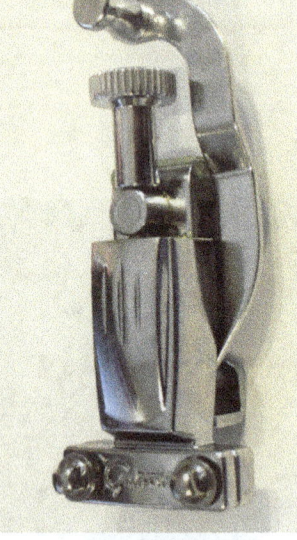

GS-DLSTO
New Classic & Full Range Snare Drums (2006-2013)
Catalina/Catalina Club Jazz (lacquer)/
Blackhawk /Renown
2011 Replacement

PS-TO1 Catalina Maple (2010-2013), Catalina Birch (2010-2012)
butt plate PS-BP1, aka GS-DBDS

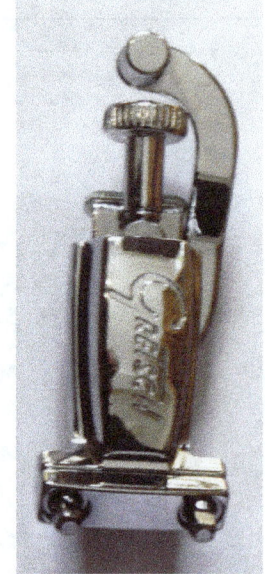

GS-CCT01
Catalina Club Mini Mod (2008-2009),
Club Jazz (wrapped) (2003-2013)
butt plate GS-SBSC
All Catalina, 2003-2013.

Dunnett Throw-off and butt plate 2008-2013

butt plate GS-DBDS
2001-2009

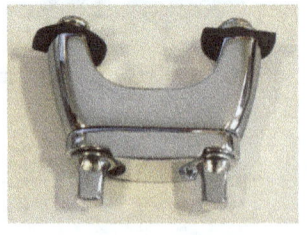

MUFFLERS/TONE CONTROLS

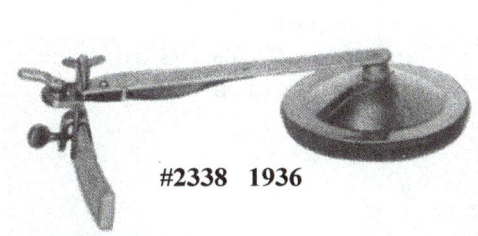

#2338 1936

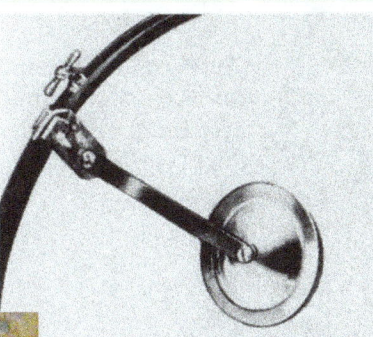

#9161 1941

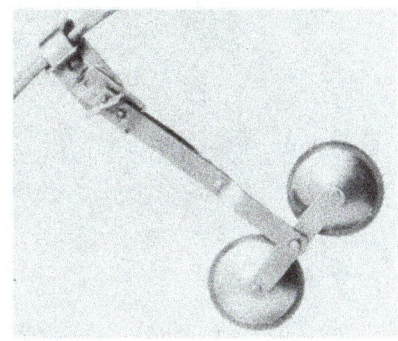

#9164 1941

Three-Way Muffler #5435
1949-58

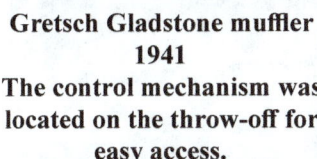

**Gretsch Gladstone muffler
1941**
The control mechanism was located on the throw-off for easy access.

**"Jimmie Pratt" Bass Drum muffler 5430
1950-2012**

The brilliant concept for this internal bass drum muffler was suggested by Gretsch artist Jimmie Pratt. It allows varying degrees of internal bass drum muffling by simply turning the external knob. The external knobs were initially a small hex shape, but were changed to the distinctive large round knob by 1955.

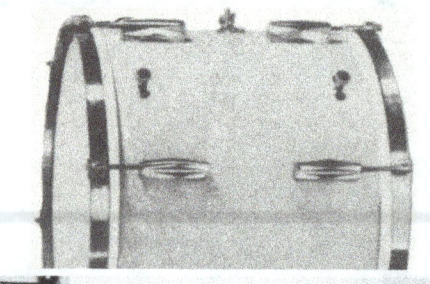

The first internal muffler (other than the Gladstone tone controls) showed up in the late 1940s. Gretsch was the first company to install mufflers both top and bottom. Early versions had small round knobs.

The next muffler knob was the hex-knob, followed in 1950 by the larger round knob. The muffler pad itself through all of these eras was the single round disc, changed to the rectangular pair of pads (below) in the early 1950s.

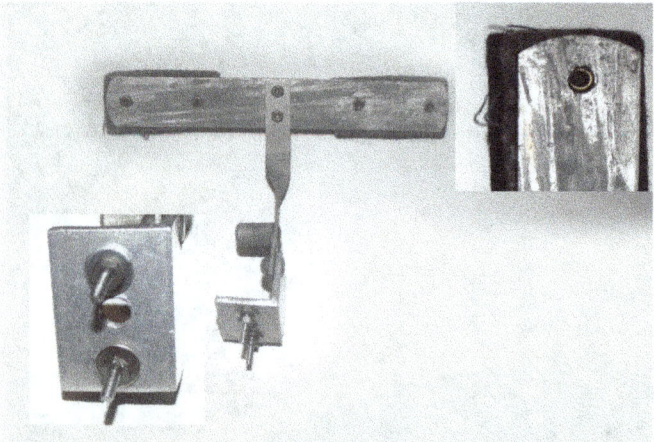

Earliest rectangular 5540 muffler assembly, 1950s. Note that the ends of the support plate (which the felt pads are riveted to) are rounded. Also note that the muffler is mounted to the shell with bolts, washers and nuts.

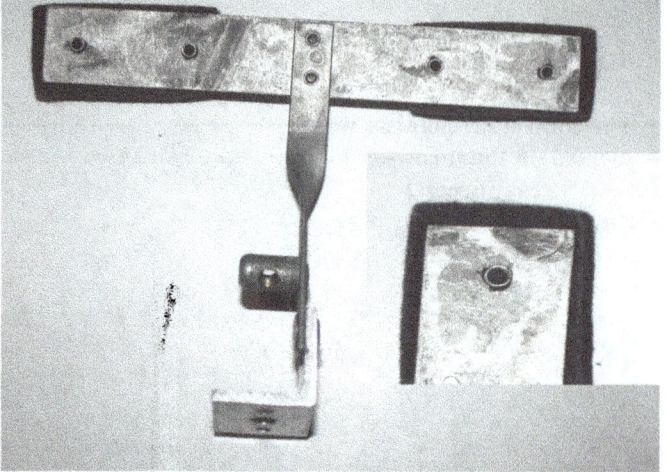

Second generation rectangular muffler plate from early 1960s

Sporadically throughout the 1950s and 1960s, Gretsch would substitute a pair of round cymbal felts for the rectangular felts.

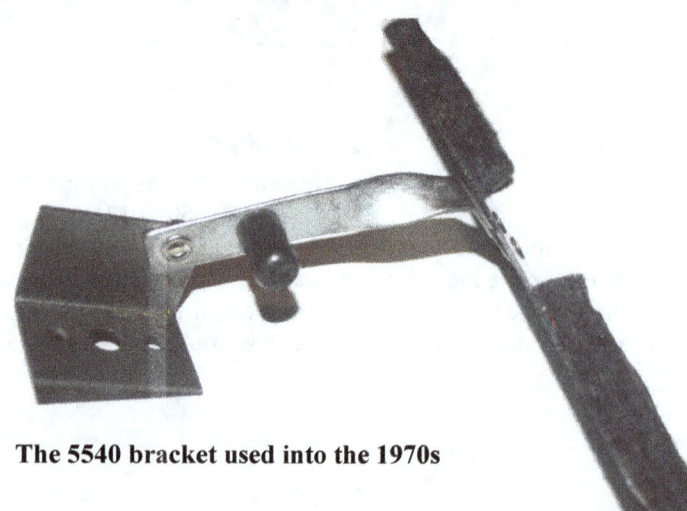

The 5540 bracket used into the 1970s

1950s bracket frames were thicker

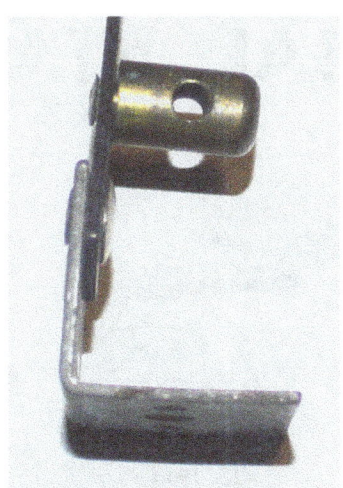
Early-to-mid 1960s: thinner bracket frame with brass cylinder.

Later '60s and '70s: thinner bracket frame and steel cylinder.

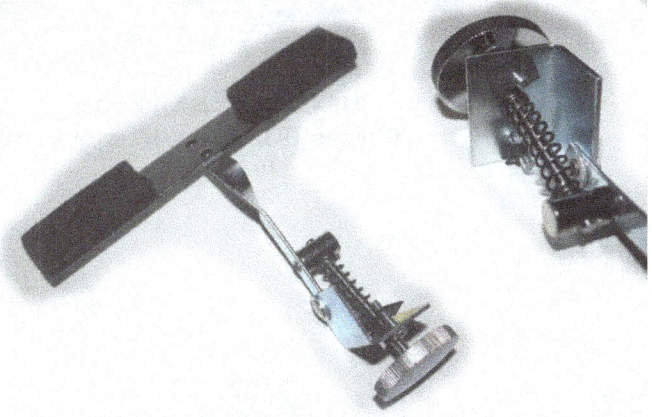
The newest (and current) version of the 5540 bracket; essentially the same design for over 60 years.

G4880 external tone control 1982-2001

Occasionally in the '60s, '70s, and '80s Gretsch used small knobs on their mufflers; they are most often found on inexpensive snare drums.

Mounting screws & speed nuts for various Gretsch hardware: tone controls, butt plates, etc. The smaller versions lasted from circa 1960 through circa 1980. The larger versions were used on #5430 Bass tone controls from circa 1950 through 2013 and on the #5540 Tone controls from about 1980 through 2013. (The bass drum tone control mounting screws had to be countersunk to avoid catching on the head.) Hex nuts were originally used; speed nuts have been widely used since about 1960.

Original large muffler knob

Knob #3 Late 1960s to early 1970s; peaks in the center

Knob #2: Round flat area in middle

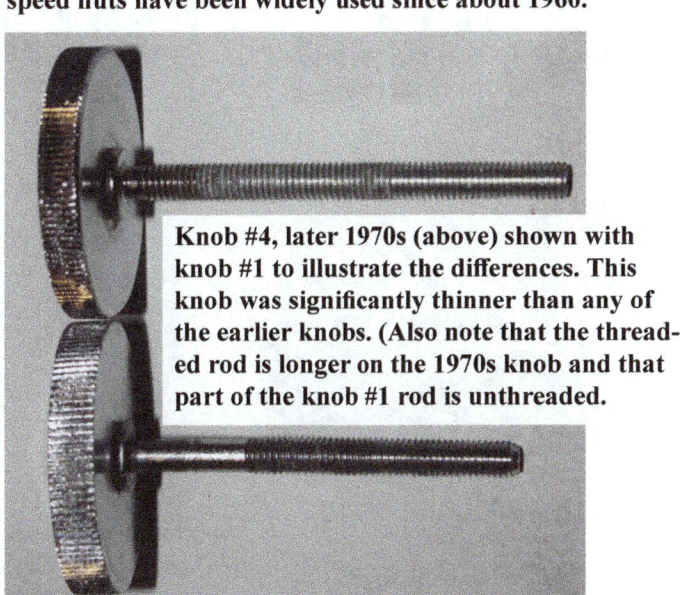

Knob #4, later 1970s (above) shown with knob #1 to illustrate the differences. This knob was significantly thinner than any of the earlier knobs. (Also note that the threaded rod is longer on the 1970s knob and that part of the knob #1 rod is unthreaded.

CYMBAL STANDS

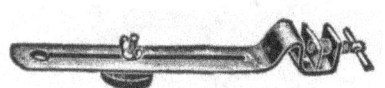

#25   1912–1936
The first cymbal-holding hardware was the "side-cymbal holder." It clamped to the hoop of the bass drum and supported a cymbal to be played either with sticks or the little beater that attached to the bass drum pedal beater shaft.

#23 1914

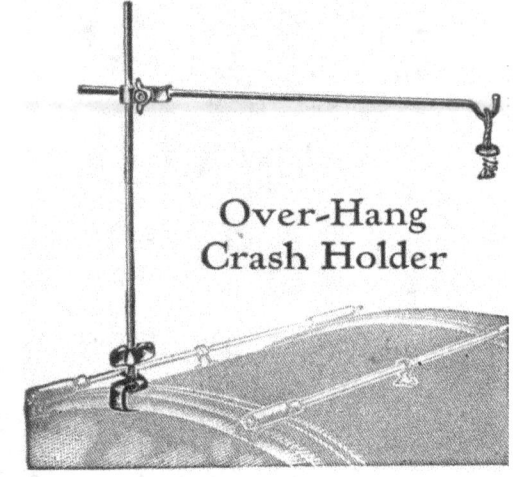

#48 Crash Cymbal holder
also listed in 1936 as #48-1/2 with 2 arms
1914–1936

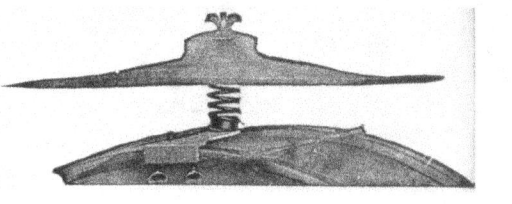

Crash cymbal holder #24
1914–1936

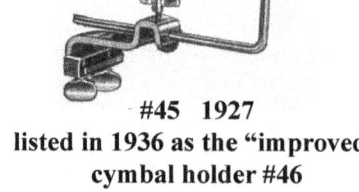

#45 1927
listed in 1936 as the "improved" cymbal holder #46

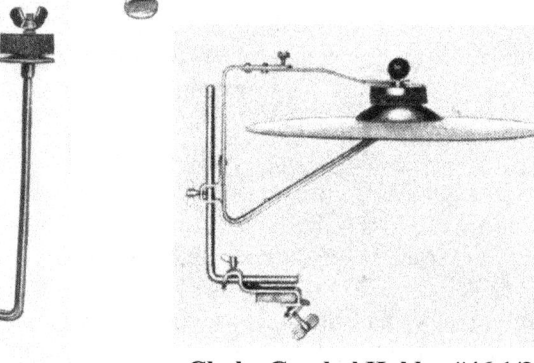

Choke Cymbal Holder #46 1/2
"swivels out of the way when not in use"
1936

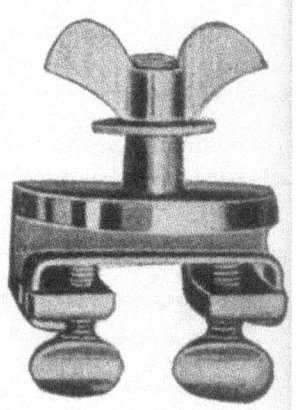

#26   1927-36

"Right Spot"
Cymbal Holder #45-1/2
1936
for choke cymbals

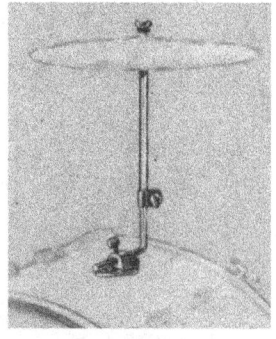

4804
Shell-mount adjustable-height
(hoop-clamp version 4806)
1948-1949

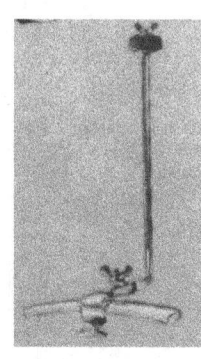

Fixed height hoop-clamp
series
14" to 22"
1950-66
Chrome:
#4811 14" height,
#4813 18", #4815 22"
Nickel:
#4810 14", #4812 18",
#4814 22"

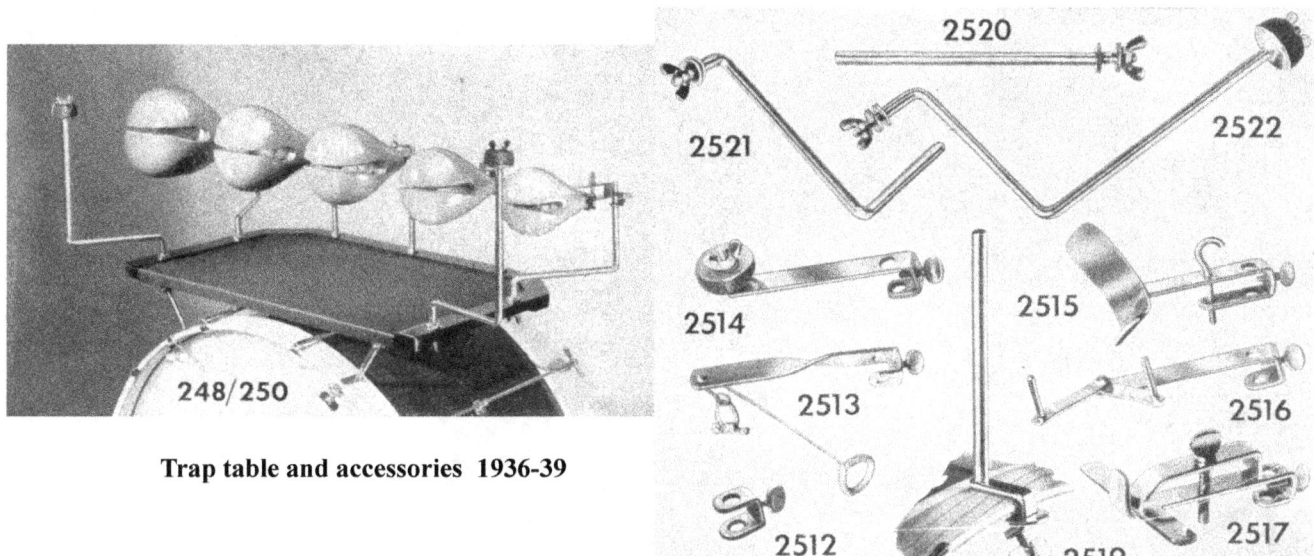

Trap table and accessories 1936-39

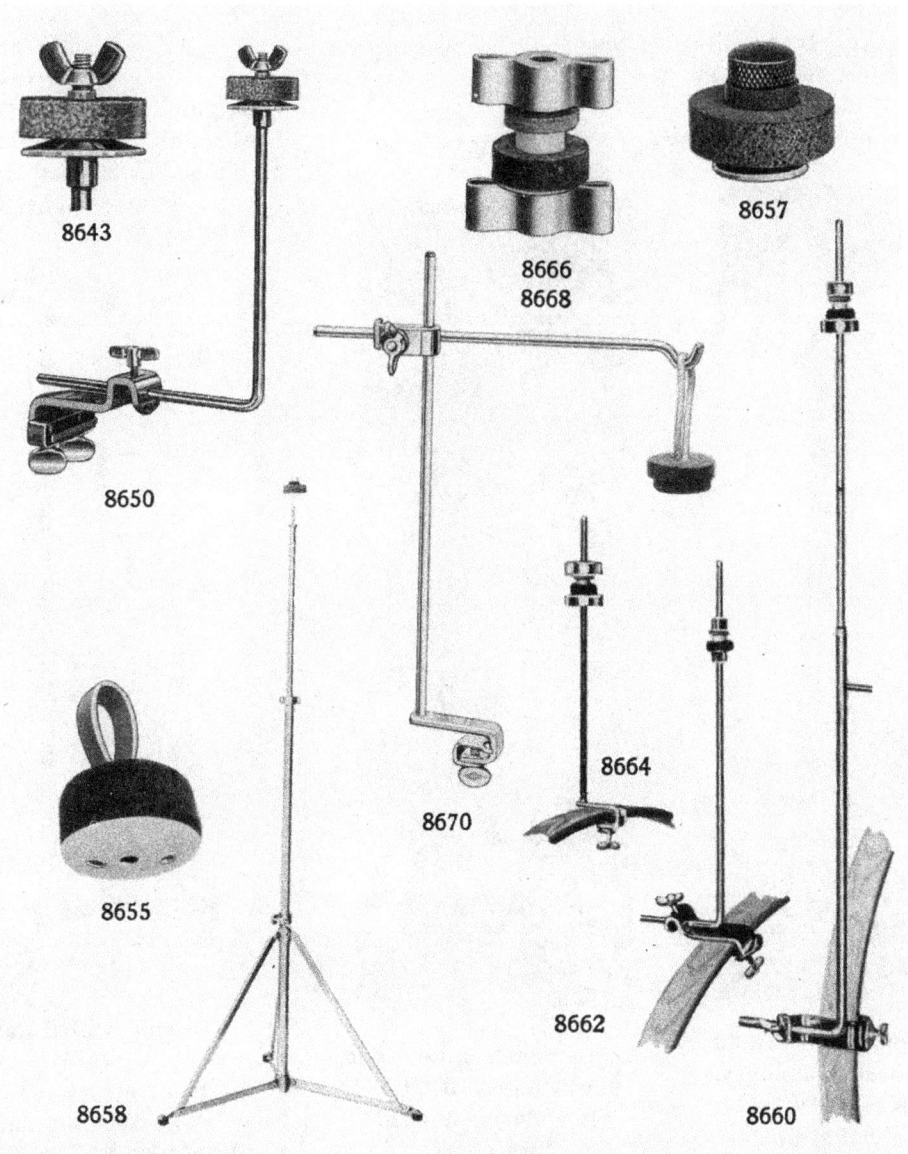

First folding floor stand (8658), first telescoping holder (8660), first "Rocking Cup" cymbal holders with convex washers (8643).

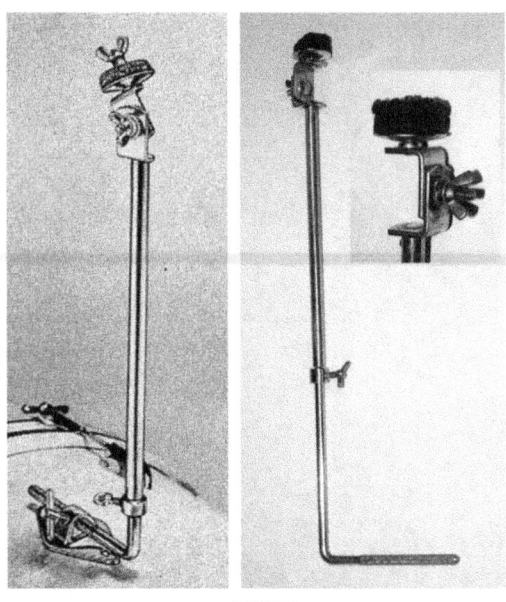
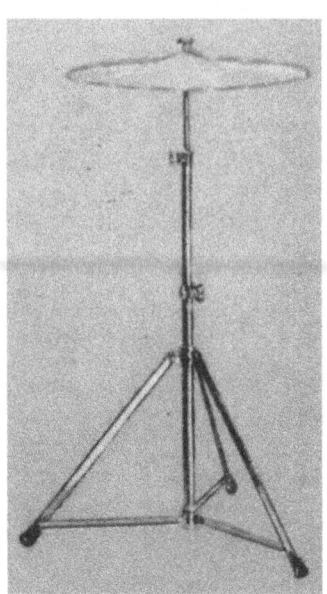
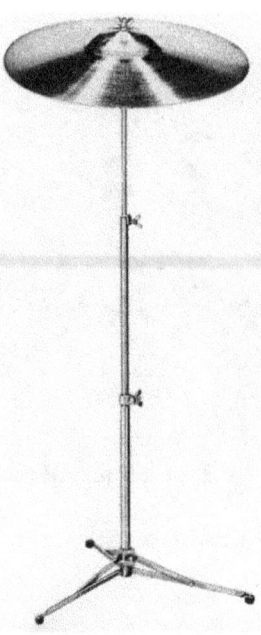

#4805
1948-1971; wing-bolt gave way to a threaded coupling (like a height-adjustment on a mic stand) from 1971-1978.
(hoop clamp version 4807 1954-1963)

#4825
1948-1958

#4826
1948-1978
Originally shown in the 1950 catalog with the "tripod" base design, but changed to flat-base style by 1961.
Extends to height of 48"

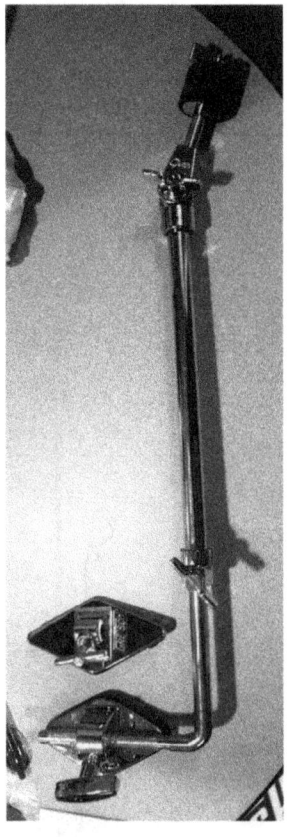
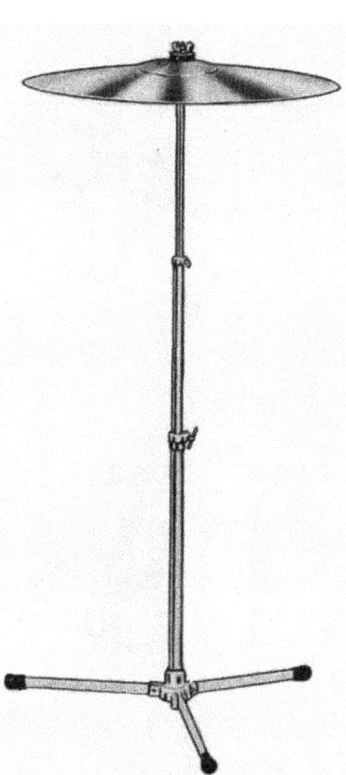

The shell-mount cymbal stand was brought back in January, 2010 as the #GS-VBDCH127 Vintage BD Cymbal Holder (12.7 mm) to fit 9020 or 9025 brackets.

Another came out early in 2011 as #GS-VBDCH103 (10.3 mm) to fit 4820 brackets.

Comet cymbal stand #4827
1961-1965
Probably made by Camco; identical to Camco #700.
Price lists of the mid-1970s also refer to a heavy version of the #4827 and a standard version #4828. This was about the time that longtime supplier Walberg & Auge went out of business. Gretsch bought cymbal stands from Camco before finding an overseas supplier.

An old model number with a new name, the Monster was a beefier tripod-based design that extended to 60" in height. This stand first appeared in the 1971 catalog and was last listed as "Temporarily Discontinued" in the 10-20-78 price list but never listed again.

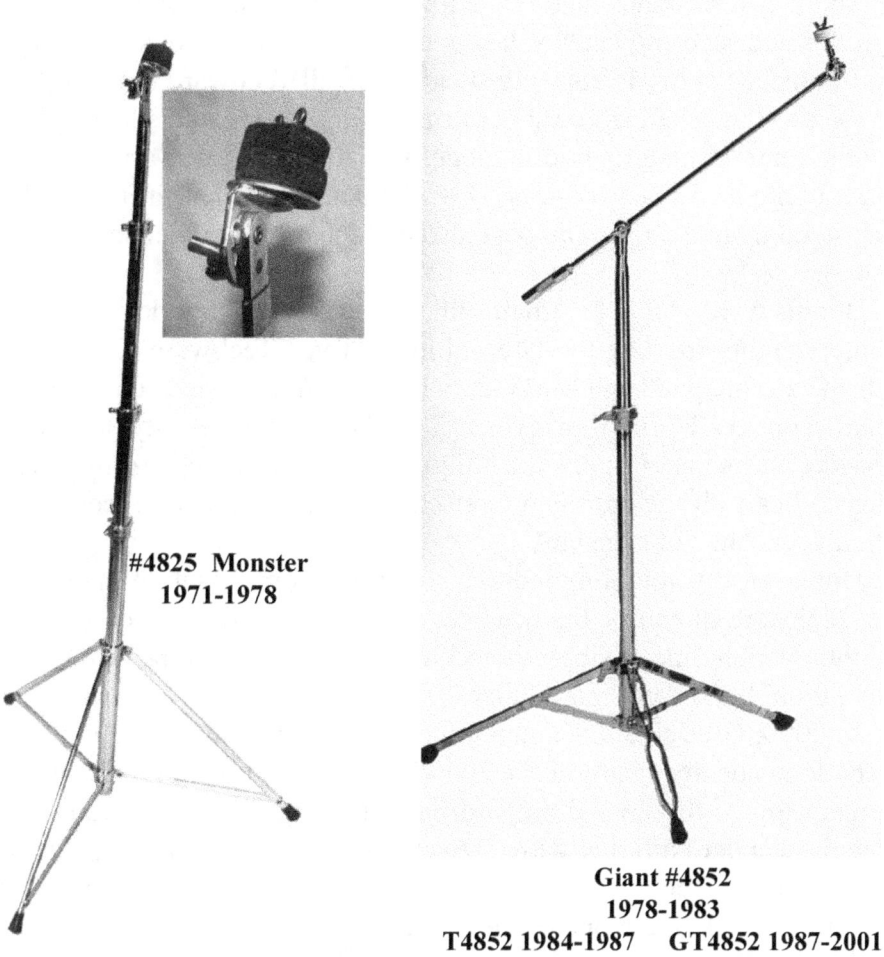

#4825 Monster
1971-1978

Giant #4852
1978-1983
T4852 1984-1987   GT4852 1987-2001

From John Sheridan's *Classic Drummer* article "Gretsch's Last Stand: The Techware Story"

Prior to 1975, practically all Gretsch hardware was manufactured by Walberg & Auge of Worcester, Massachusetts. W & A supplied other drum companies as well, but Gretsch likely remained their longest customer. This is evidenced by the fact that many of the stands Gretsch offered into the 1970s were precisely the same as the decade before, and in some cases, the decade before that!

The Monster series hardware was a clumsy transition that began in 1968 and lingered until Walberg & Auge's demise in 1975. Consequently, Baldwin (who purchased Gretsch in 1967) had to resort to new designs.

By 1978, Gretsch introduced a new and expanding line of seriously beefy (imported) stands called Giant. The Giant series continued to evolve while a new line of similarly beefy tom holders, brackets, legs & spurs was introduced as Creative Research in 1980.

In 1984, all Giant models became Deluxe models under the Techware banner. Though the former name was dropped, the "CR" abbreviation preceded all Techware model numbers until 1984, when it was mostly changed to "T." In 1987, the notation became "GT."

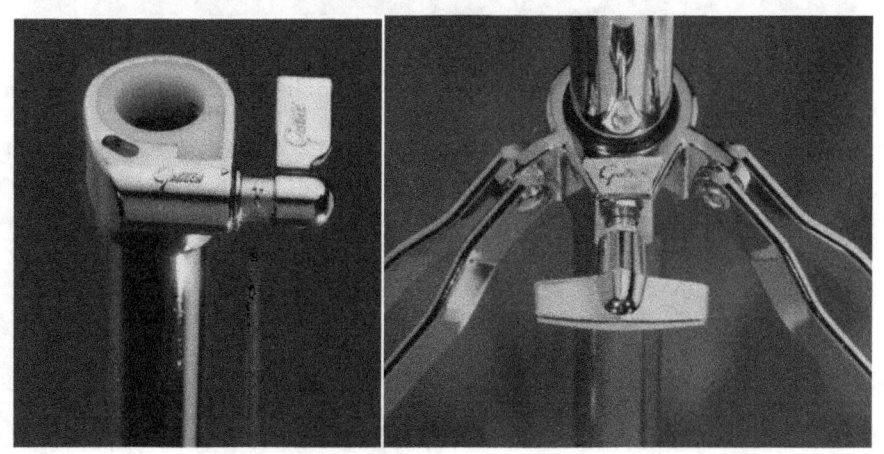

All Techware stands featured extra-long tubing (averaging 7/8" in diameter), with white nylon bushings and securing latches, heavy double-braced tri-pods with large rubber feet and heavy-duty wing-bolts. Memory locks were standard on all Techware models.

Snare stands had large rubber grips, sturdy tilting and securing latches. Thrones had thick, comfortable seats; even a hydraulic model was offered. An L-arm design tom-holder with large ratcheting slid onto an 18" or 20"-long, 7/8" diameter post that fit into a 1" receiving bass drum bracket or floor stand tri-pod base. The post also had the option of accommodating additional L-arm holders, if desired.

Booms were available as half, full, and telescoping models, with the latter two having heavy black counterweights sporting the Gretsch logo. Even Techware bass drum pedals were introduced along with an extremely tall and heavy-duty hi-hat stand. Large Techware brackets with notches for memory locks accepted 12.7mm L-arms as well as the new heavy-duty floor tom legs. Cymbal stands had hard, cork-like washers to insulate the unique doubled white felts from wing-nuts. Apparently, Baldwin had taken to heart all the criticism Gretsch hardware had been receiving for some time and struck back with a vengeance of a design!

However, this retooling led to a slight overcompensation in engineering designs that caused their new Techware line to be the heaviest, most over-built and expensive hardware in the drum industry! A lighter weight line of single-braced hardware was set to be introduced at the January, 1985, NAMM convention, but did not materialize.

In 2000, Gretsch and Kaman joined forces and suddenly a new G-Series hardware was being offered alongside Techware in the 2000/2001 Gretsch price lists. Of course, G-Series turned out to be Kaman's top-of-the-line Gibraltar drum hardware. By 2002, Techware disappeared, and Gibraltar became the standard offering with Gretsch drums. Not only is Gibraltar a more versatile and reasonably-priced line than Techware, it beautifully complements the current line of Gretsch drums while greatly reducing the risk of anyone busting a gut.

Techware assembly in the Rokkomann factory, Kobe, Japan

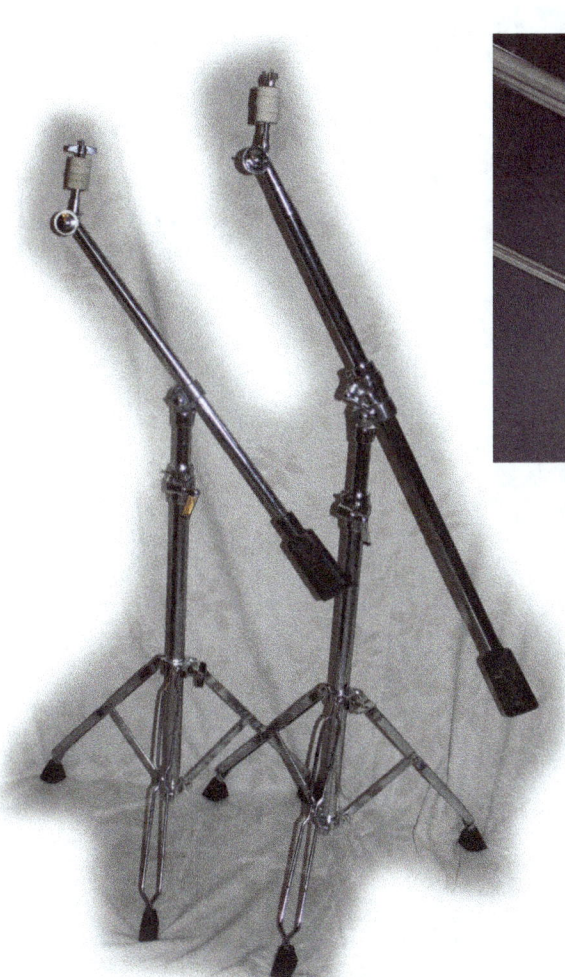

Top: telescoping boom counterweight
Bottom: "Full" boom counterweight

4853 Giant cymbal stand with half boom arm
1982-1983
T4853 1984-1987
GT4853 1987-2001

(L) 4852 Giant boom - 1978-1983
(R) 4854 telescoping boom
1982-1983
T4852, T4854 1984-1987
GT4852, GT4854 1987-2001

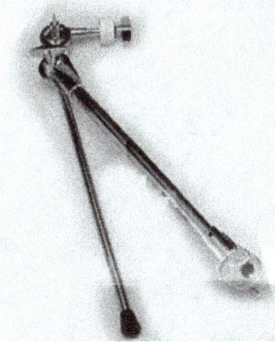

#4860 Giant cymbal holder. Short boom arm made to attach to another stand section
1982-2001
T4860 1984-1987
GT4860 1987-2001

4850 Giant Straight Cymbal Stand
1978-1983
T4850 1984-1987
GT4850 1987-2001
(note that the stand in the photo is a 2-piece. 3-piece versions of this stand were much more common.)

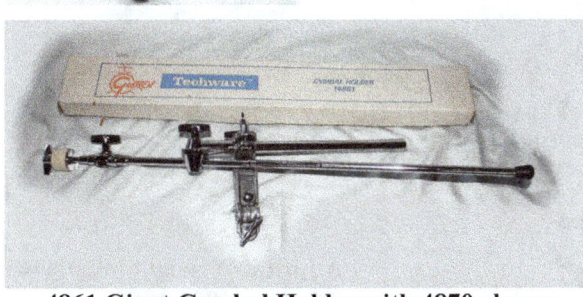

4861 Giant Cymbal Holder with 4870 clamp;
the combination was catalogued as #4871 1982-2001
T4861 & T4871 1984-1987, GT4861 & GT4871 1987-2001

HI-HAT STANDS

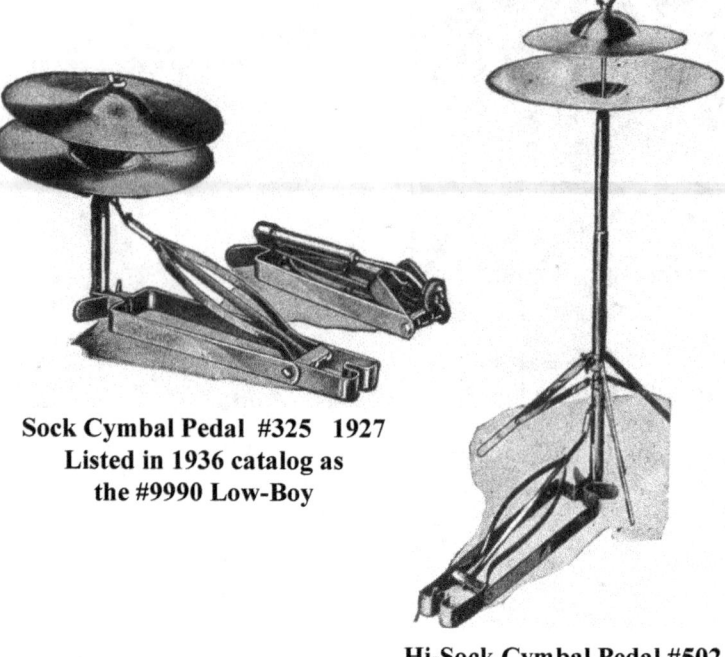

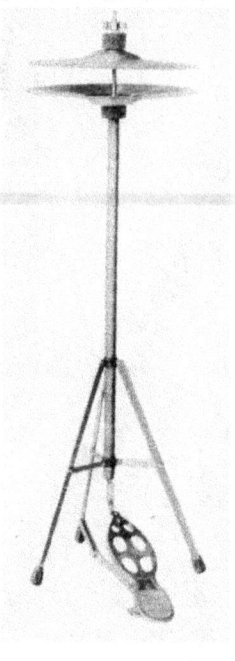

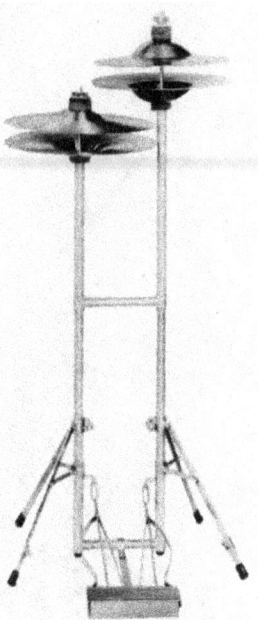

Sock Cymbal Pedal #325 1927
Listed in 1936 catalog as
the #9990 Low-Boy

Hi-Sock Cymbal Pedal #502
1927
Same photo in 1936 catalog refers
to this as the #9980 Hi-Hat

"Single Unit Hi Hat"
#8635 1939

"Twin Hat" #8638
1939
(limited to use with
cymbals 11" and
smaller)

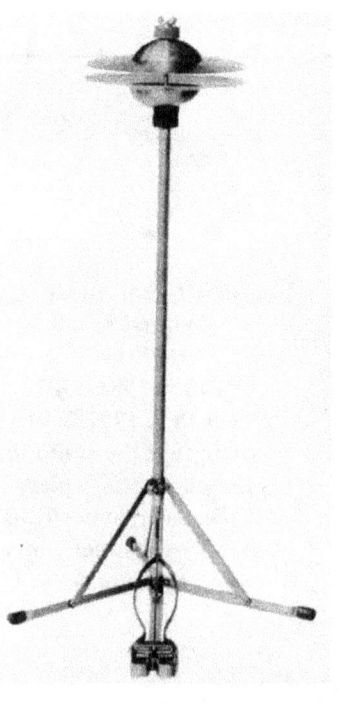

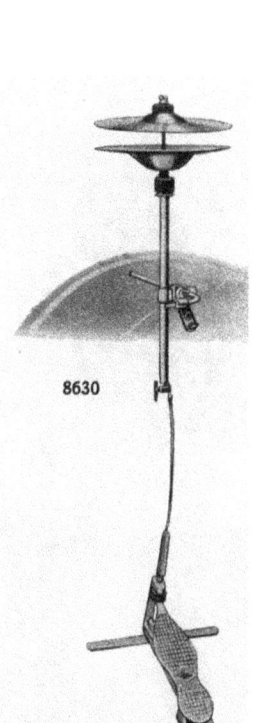

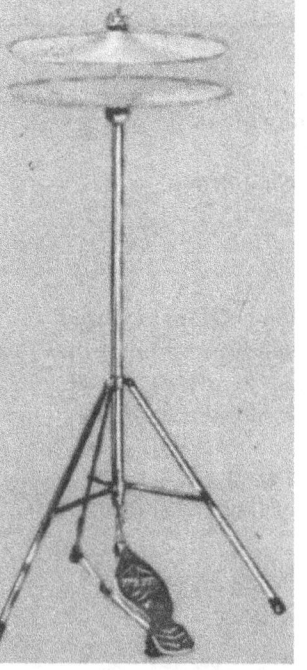

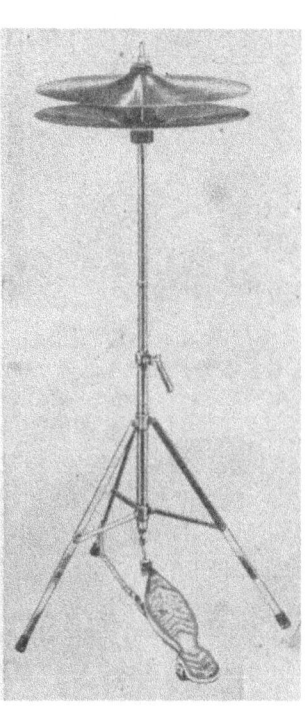

"Improved Hi-Hat" #3633
1939

New Gretsch-Gladstone
hihat pedal 1939

4840 (fixed height)
1948-1958

Adjustable Height hihat 4843
1954-1958

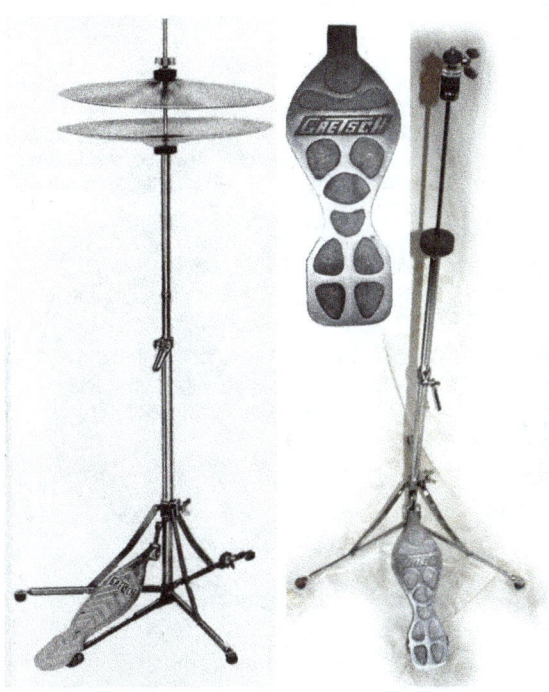
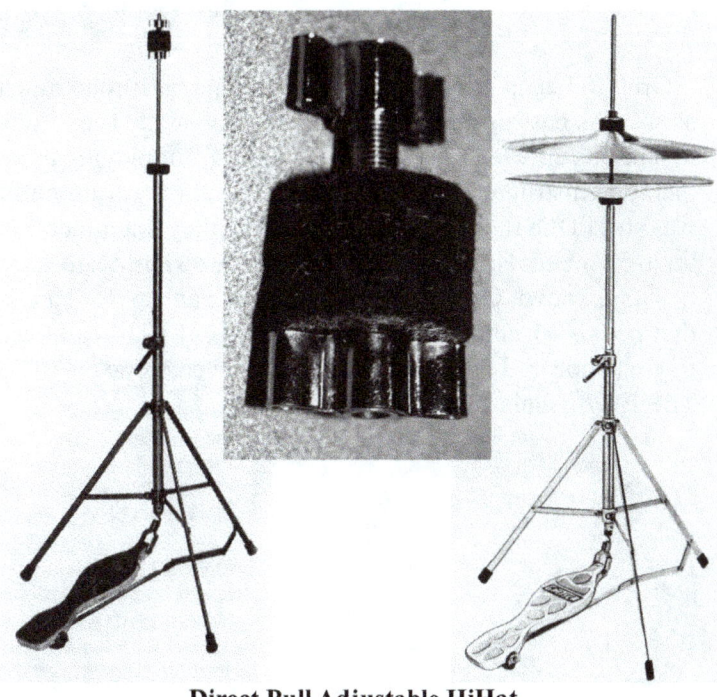

Flush Base Adjustable HiHat #4844 1954-1966

Flush Base Adjustable HiHat #4844 (Wider footboard) 1966-1978

Direct Pull Adjustable HiHat #4845
narrow footboard 1963-66

wider footboard 1966-1978

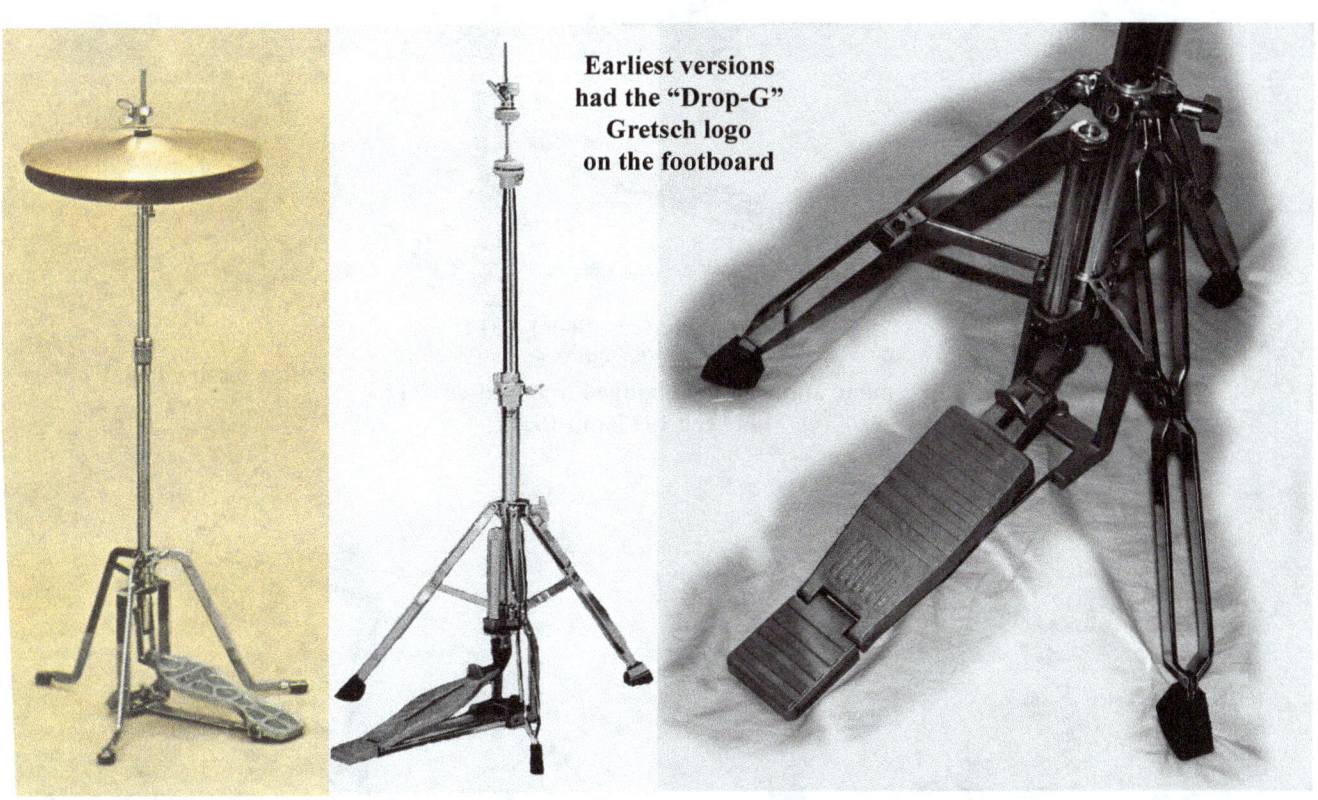

Earliest versions had the "Drop-G" Gretsch logo on the footboard

Hi-hat #4846
1968-1974, 1977-1978
Inroduced as "New Deluxe," name changed to "Monster" by 1971

Giant #4849
As pictured left: 1978-1983
T4849 1984-1987 footboard widened, above right
GT4849 1987-2001 First double-braced Gretsch hi-hat stand, above right
Last referred to as "Giant" in the June 1983 poster catalog, listed as Techware from 1984-1987, then became GT4849

PEDALS

Gretsch began offering bass drum foot pedals pretty much as soon as bass drum foot pedals were invented. These new inventions allowed for "double drumming," or playing more than one instrument at a time. The concept of a drum outfit was still in the future... It is unlikely that they manufactured their own pedals. At this writing there are significant gaps between known Gretsch catalogs; all we can say for sure is that pedals #1 and #2 were in the 1912 and 1914 catalogs, #3 first appeared in the 1914 catalog; all were gone by 1927. The 1927 pedals were gone by 1936.

(overhead) #2 1912-1915

#1 1912-1915

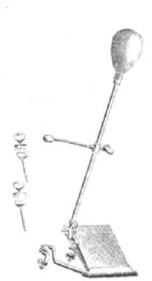

#3 1914

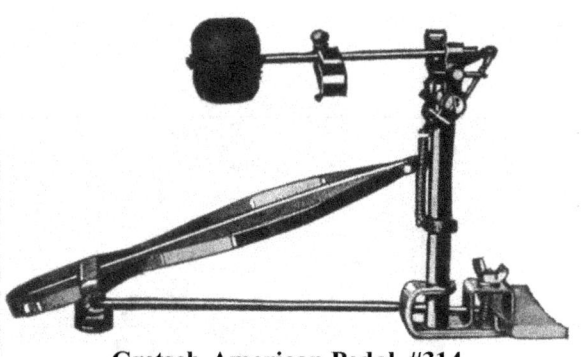

Gretsch-American Pedal #314
1927-1936
name and number changed to Speed-ee #312
between 1927 and 1936

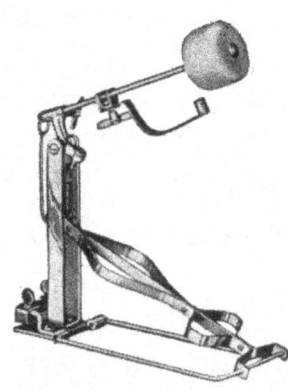

20th Century Pedal #350
1927

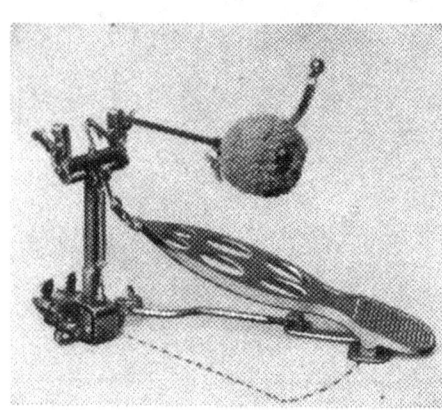

Gretsch "All-Position"
pedal #316
1936

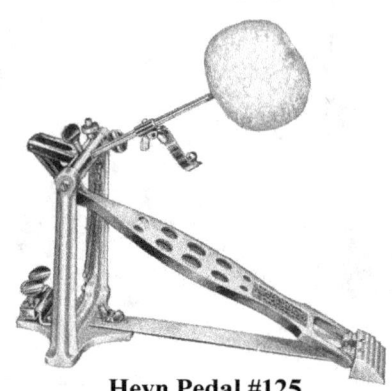

Heyn Pedal #125
1936
The Heyn pedal was definitely not one that they manufactured, but distributed. Several other major drum companies also catalogued the Heyn.

Heyn Pedal #8820
1939-41
catalogued 1949-1958 as:
Professional Drum Pedal #4956

SPEED-EE Gretsch identified at least one of its pedal models as the "Speed-ee," or "Speed-Dee" for over 30 years. Model numbers changed a bit and features such as the footboard design changed. Basically the Speed-ee was always an economy pedal and nearly all of them were produced by Walberg & Auge for Gretsch.

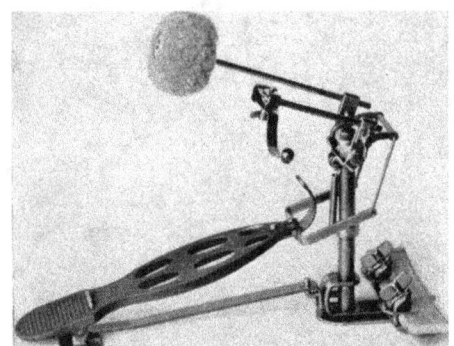

Professional pedal #314
1936
Appeared in 1939-41 catalogs as
#8800

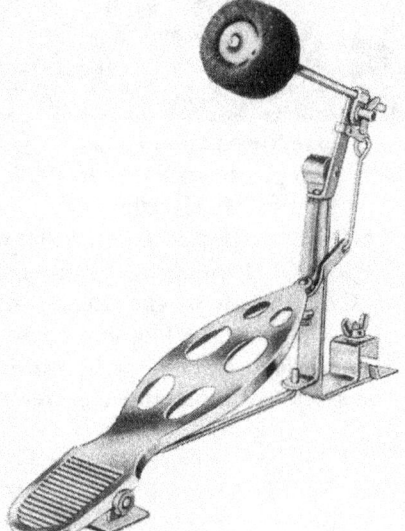

Speedee pedal #8804
1939–41
#8803
1948

Speed-ee
#4955 1949-54
#4950 1958

#4950 Speed-ee
1961-1966

Monster pedal #4956
1975-1979

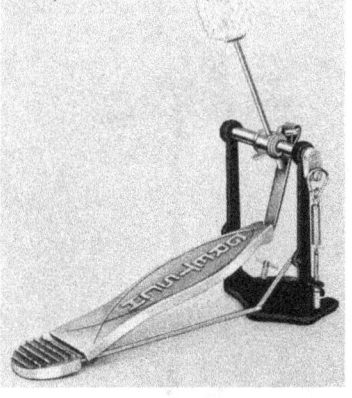

Professional Pedal #4956
1961-1969
Referred to by some collectors as the Gretsch "Christian" pedal because the footboard very much resembles the Jesus "fish" design. Has the same heel plate as the Floating Action, indicating the 4956 was probably also a Camco product.

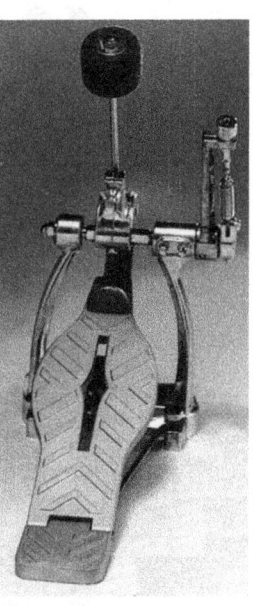

Giant #4958
1978
(imported)

**Deluxe Speed Cam Pedal #T4959
changed to #GT4959 in 1997
1983-2000**

This is an early 4959 Giant pedal with a generic footboard, distinguished as Gretsch only by the sticker on the side. By 1984, the footboard had the Gretsch logo cast into it, as shown in the assembly photo above center.

**Floating Action pedal #4955
1948-1996
Chain-Drive version #4960
1982-1996**

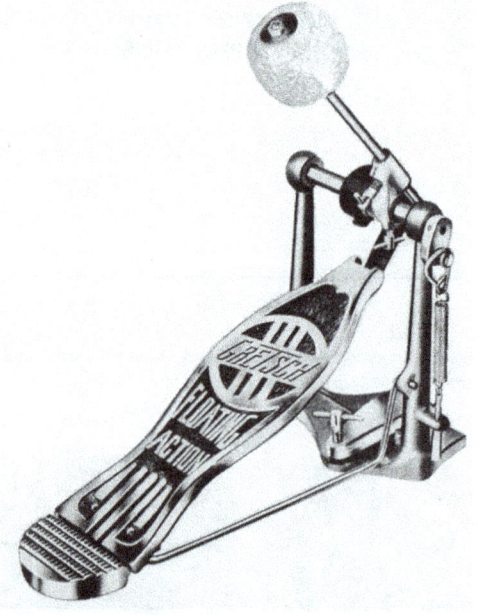

This pedal originally showed up in the marketplace as the Martin Fleetfoot pedal. Rights were purchased by Camco, who made it as the Floating Action pedal for Gretsch. This arrangement continued even after Camco was sold and broken up into pieces owned by Hoshino (Tama) and Drum Workshop. DW continued to supply pedals to Gretsch until about 2000 when Gretsch affiliated with Gibraltar and catalogued Gretsch pedals were made by Gibraltar.

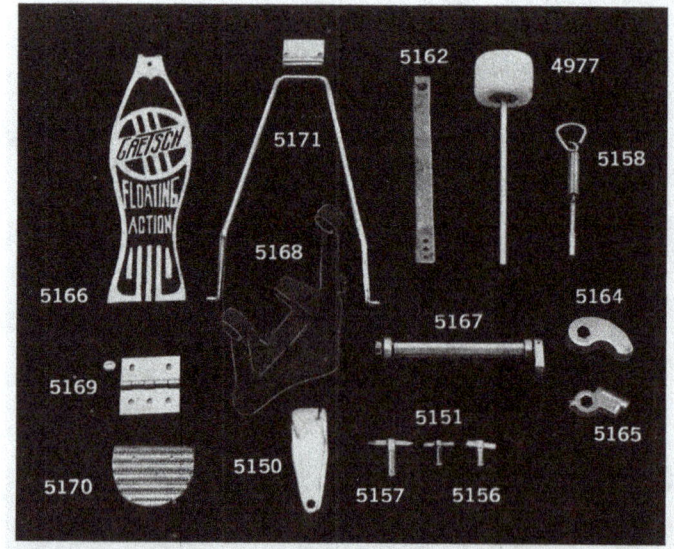

4977—Felt Beater Ball
5150—Hoop Clamp
5151—Hoop Clamp Screw
5156—Hub Lock Screw
5157—Beater Lock Screw
5158—Spring Assembly
5162—Cam Strap
5163—Strap Screw
5164—Cam Casting
5165—Beater Hub Casting
5166—Foot Board
5167—Hex Shaft Assembly
5168—Frame Assembly
5169—Metal Heel Plate Hinge
5170—Heel Plate
5171—Radius Rod Assembly w/clamp

TOM HOLDERS

Earliest Gretsch catalogs did not include snare drum stands or tom-tom holders, because at that time they had not become commonly used hardware. The drum "kit" did not exist; the marching or orchestra drums were worn and played by one drummer, the bass drums were played by another drummer. The invention of the bass drum pedal made "double drumming" possible, but the tom-tom as we know it today did not yet exist.

Adjustable tom-tom holder #2217 1936
(tom-toms were still Chinese-style and considered a special effect)

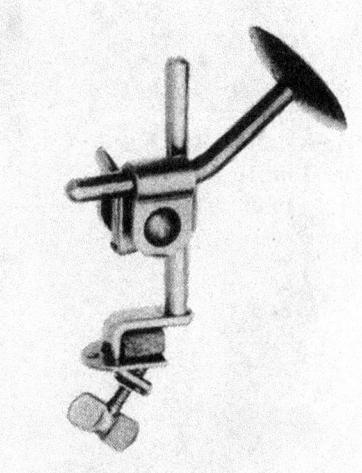

Tunable tom tom holder #8473 1939

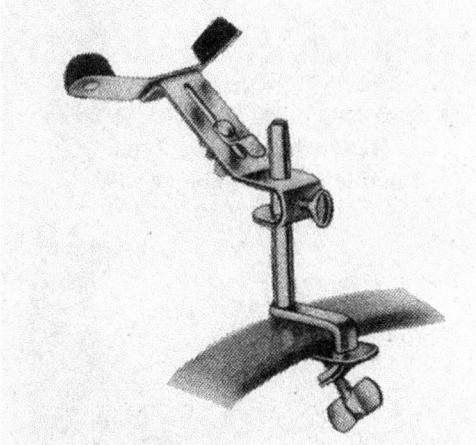

Chinese tom tom holder #8472 1939

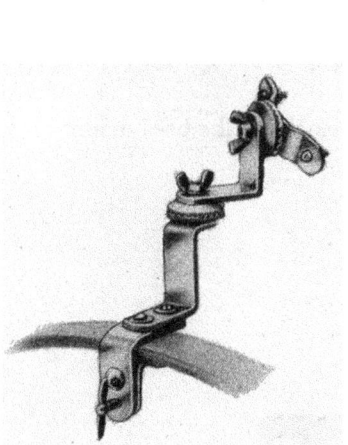

Tunable tom tom holder #8475 1939

Low-Boy tom tom holder #8486 1939

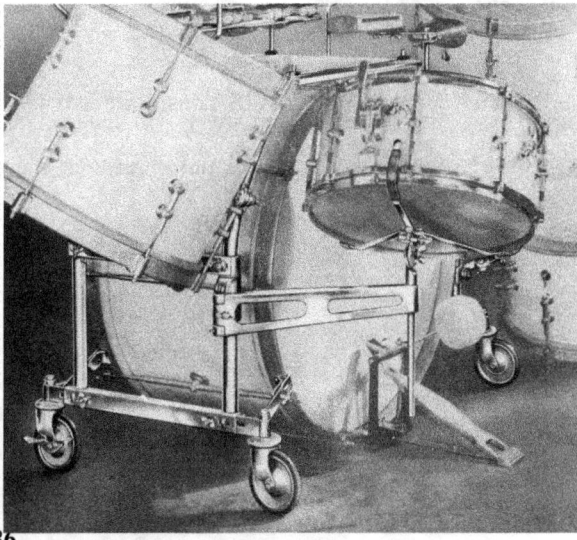

Drummer's Wheeled Console #8770 1939-1941

Porto Console #8788 26", #8789 28" 1939-1941

Roll-A-Ways bass drum wheels #8785 1939-1941

Heavy duty ratchet type tunable tom tom holder #4939
1948-1950

Heavy Duty Ratchet Tom Tom Holder #4940
1950-1971

Utility Model Ratchet-type tom tom holder #4939   1948-1971

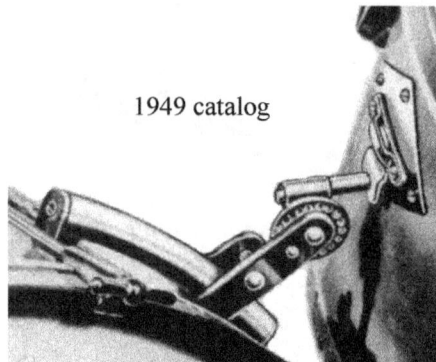
1949 catalog

1954 catalog

Rail Consolette #4942 (with diamond shape tom plate #4943)
1948-1971
Note that this is the "2-point" model; there are two bolts securing the rail assembly to the bass drum.

#4942 Rail Consolette with tom-tom height extension
(for use with small bass drums)
#4988 Long Lip Extension Rod,
#4997 Short Lip Extension Rod.

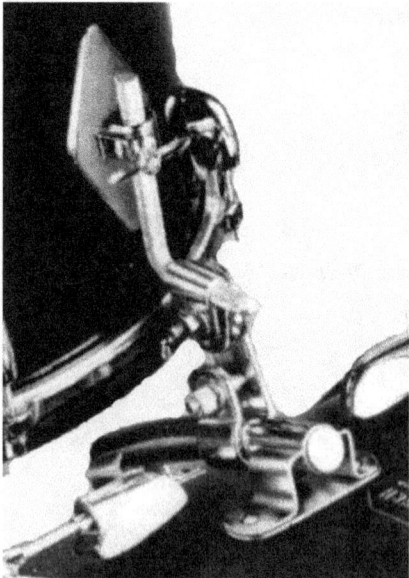

Rail Consolette #4942-1
1971-1976

Note that the tom diamond plate is now #4820 and there are 4 bolts attaching the rail assembly to the bass drum. See floor tom leg section for more on the 4820 bracket.

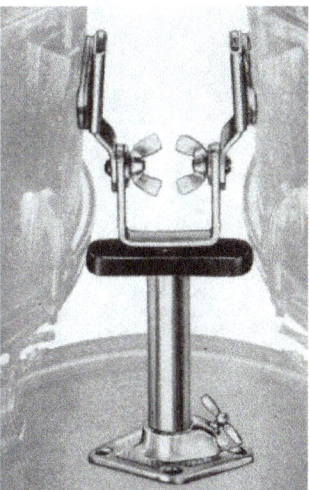

First version #4936 double tom holder, 1965-1966
Note black-painted wood spacer on post to keep bottom tom hoops stabilized and to keep toms angled toward each other. Nearly identical to Ludwig mount. Note the bass drum bracket is unplated aluminum,

Cut from Ludwig catalog

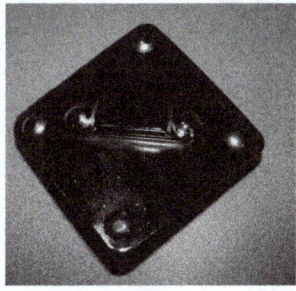

**#4943 Diamond plate
1949-1976**

Earliest felt gaskets were green, followed by brown, grey and black

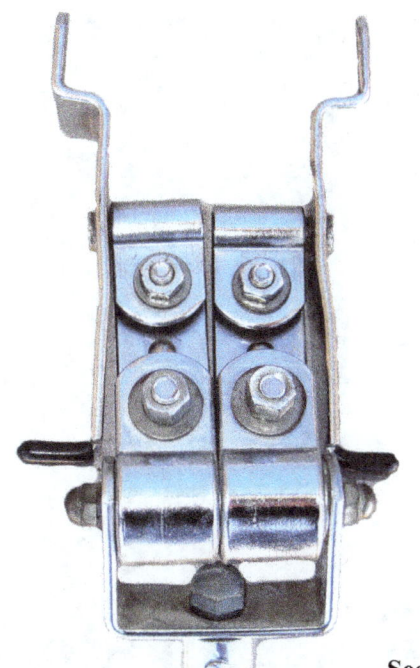
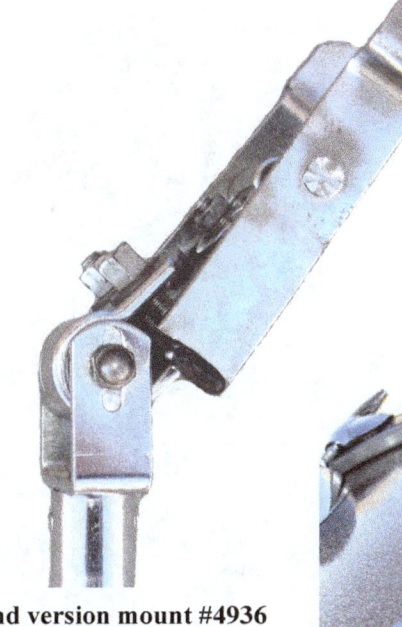

**Second version mount #4936
1967-1976**

not pictured:
Floor stand version
#4829 1968-1976

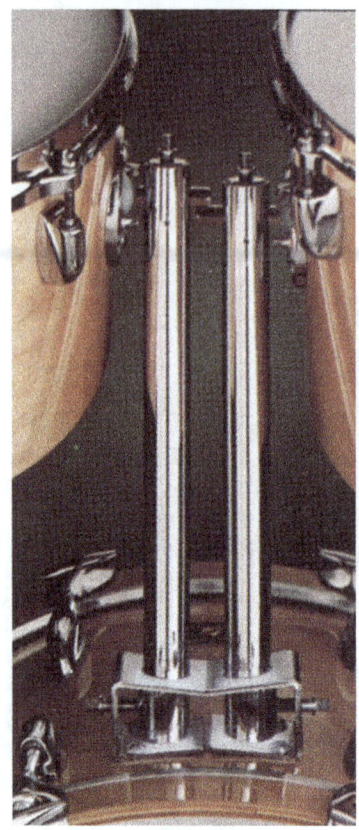

Monster Double Tom Tom Holder #4925
1975-1979 1993-1995

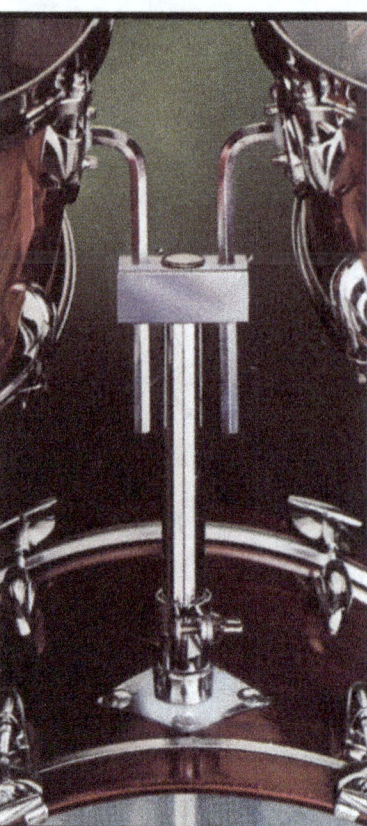

Dual Purpose Holder #4937
1976-1982 1993-2001
(floor stand version #4830)
1976-1978

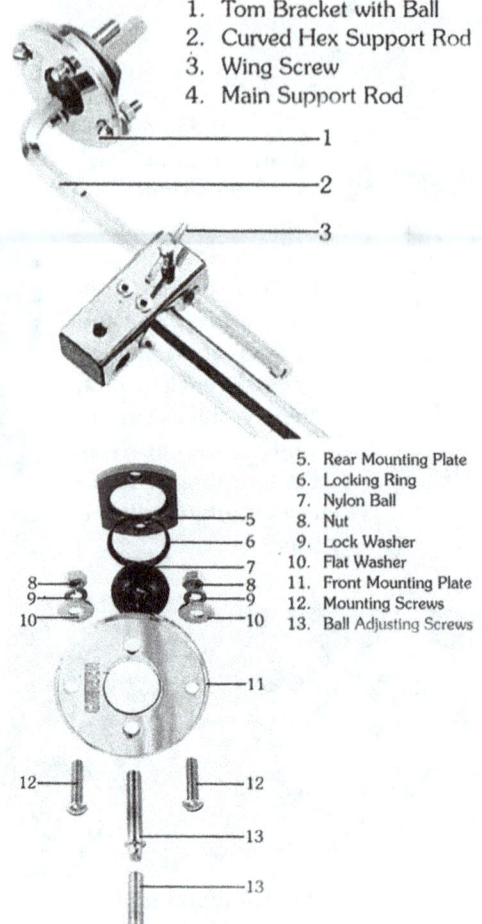

1. Tom Bracket with Ball
2. Curved Hex Support Rod
3. Wing Screw
4. Main Support Rod

5. Rear Mounting Plate
6. Locking Ring
7. Nylon Ball
8. Nut
9. Lock Washer
10. Flat Washer
11. Front Mounting Plate
12. Mounting Screws
13. Ball Adjusting Screws

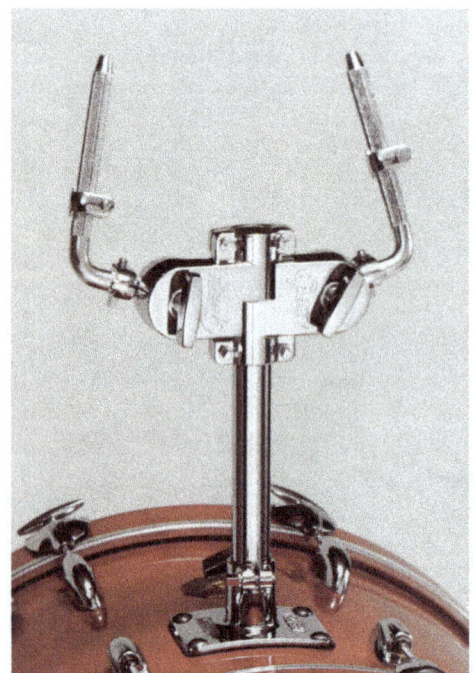

Creative Research series #9002 CR
1980-2009
floor stand version #9013 1980-2001

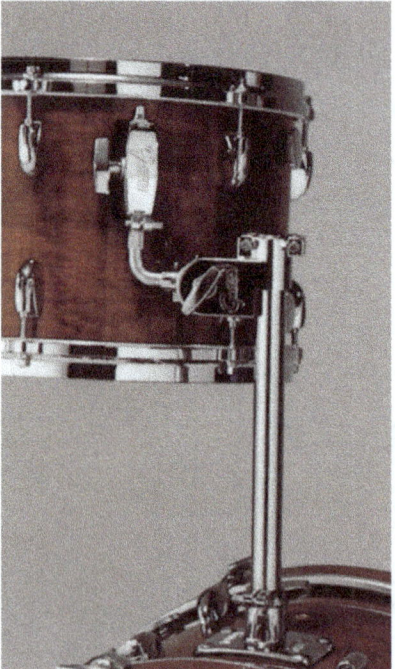

Creative Research series single tom holder #9001 CR
1980-2009
floor stand #9013 1980-2001

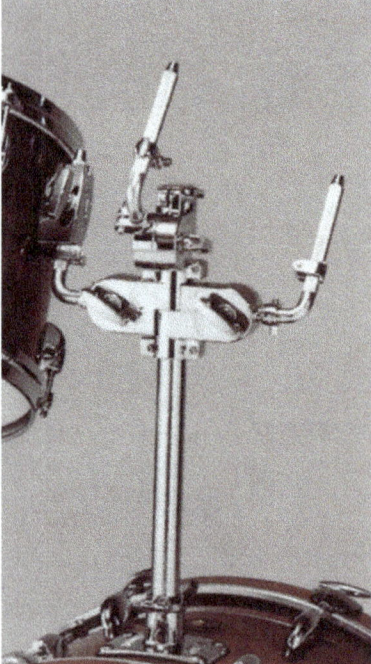

Creative Research series triple tom holder #9003 CR
1980-2001
floor stand #9014
1980-2001

The post-receiving bass drum bracket #4945 was introduced in the Creative Research era in 1979 and remains a current part as of this writing in 2013.

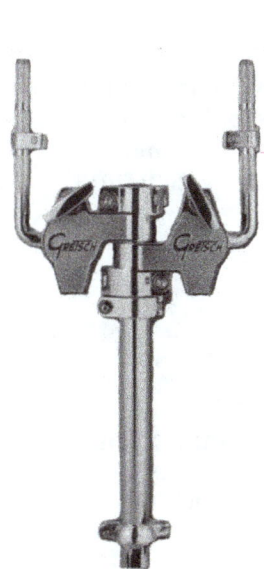

GTH-DL (12.7mm)
Professional/Deluxe
2001-2013

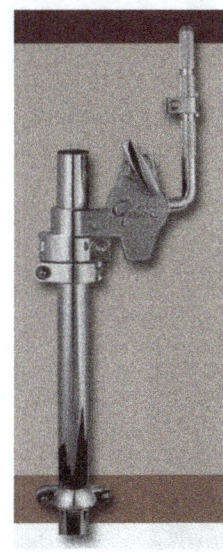

GTH-SL (12.7mm)
Professional/Deluxe
2001-20

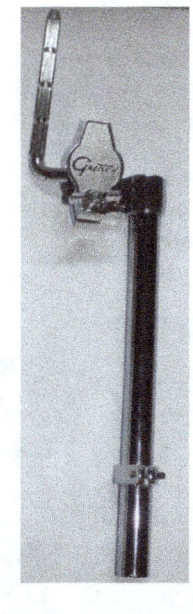

GBTH-SL (12.7mm)
Standard Single holder
2001-2013

GTH-DS Double Tom holder
(single version GTH-SS Single Tom holder)
Very similar to the 12.7 mm DTH-DL, but with smaller shafts of 10.5 mm and rather generic small tom brackets. This series was used on the Catalina series.
2001-2003

PC-DTHGB (10.5mm)
Catalina Series
2006-2010
(Has "Gretsch" name on it.)

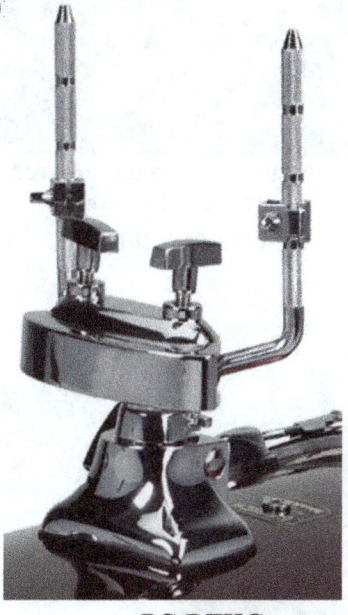

PC-DTHG
(10.5mm)
Blackhawk Series
2006-2010
(Does not have any name on it.)

GT-STCL Single Tom Arm
with multi-clamp
(high position)
2001-2013
Also GT-STCR
2001-2013
Same, only "low position"

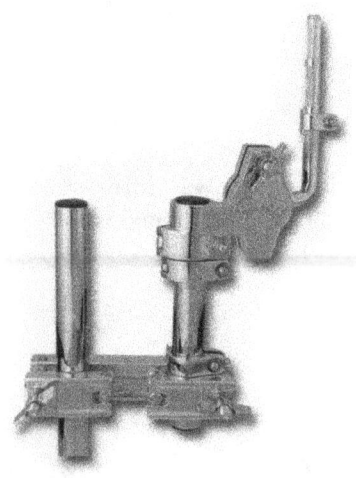
GT-STCR Single Tom Arm with Multi-Clamp (low position)
2004-2013

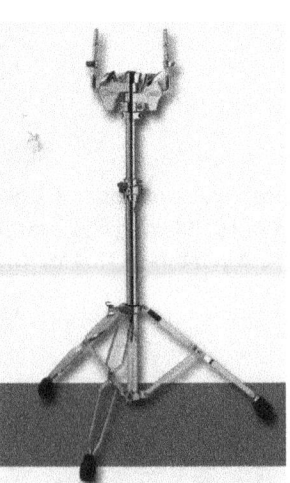
6613 GR
Double Tom Floor Stand (Professional)
2003

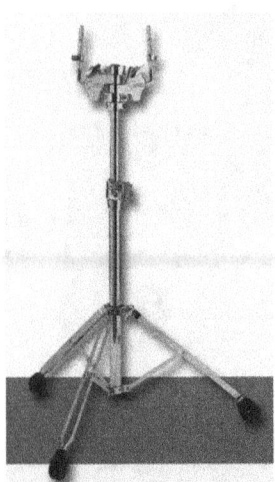
9613 GR
Double Tom Floor Stand (Standard)
2003

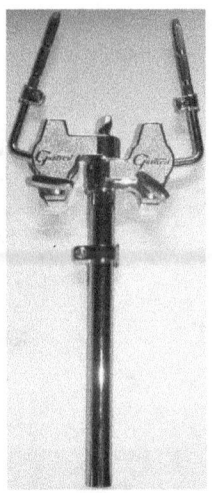
GBTH-DL
Standard double holder supplied on import kits only
2001-2013

SC-GVRM
2003-2013
The rail-mount mount was brought back in 2003 for the Anniversary kits; a total of 120 kits were made. The mount was added to the catalog in 2008.

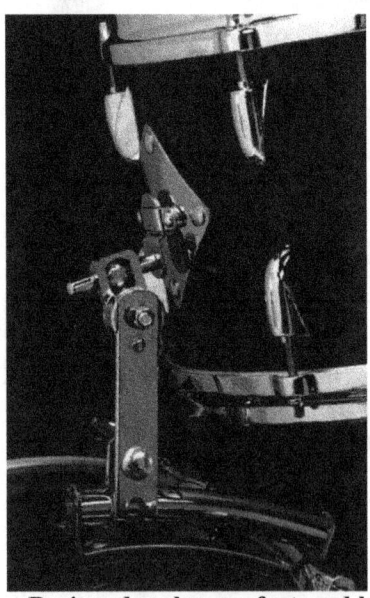
Designed and manufactured by Steve Maxwell
GVRM   2011-2013

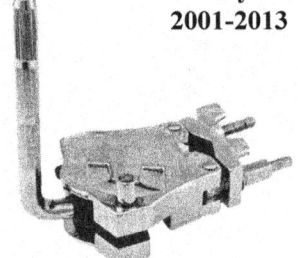
GS-SLLRM (12.7mm)
Gibraltar-type offered on Gretsch drums until 2011

PS-SLRM (12.7mm Gretsch)
2011-2013

PS-BDPM Bass Drum Riser
Simple chrome version offered on Catalina Jazz (CT-models)

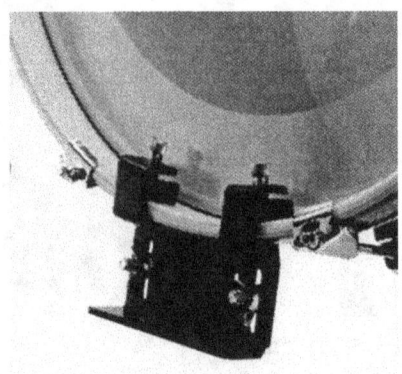
SC-BDPM Bass Drum Riser
Gibraltar part offered on Gretsch 16" & 18" Catalina (CC-model) bass drums from 2003-2013.

TOM LEGS

#4930 (nickel) #4931 (chrome)
"block" style bracket
1948-1950

#4930 "Gladstone" style bracket
two posts with holes, one threaded for the wing screw
1950-1958

Note: These earliest 4820 brackets (below) were rarely used as floor tom leg brackets, usually only as cymbal holder brackets. They are included in this section to demonstrate the difference between these and the newer 4820 brackets on the next page.

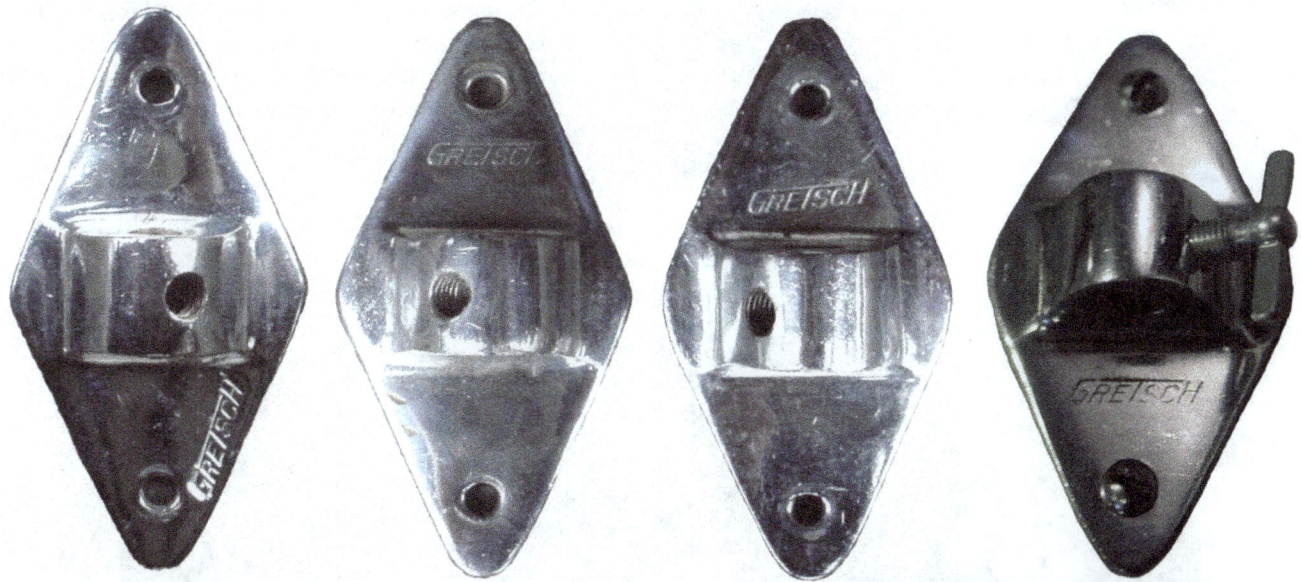

#4820 Diamond Plate for the #4805 Cymbal Holder or floor tom legs
1948-2013

Originally, the #4820 was a heavy chrome-over-brass die-cast bolt-through bracket. It was first introduced as a bass drum bracket for mounting cymbal arms. Earliest versions had the Gretsch name stamped heavily at an angle (far left). By the late 1950s the Gretsch name more lightly stamped and was applied inconsistently as demonstrated by the three examples pictured.

Earliest 4820 bolts were secured with washers and nuts (left). Speed nuts (right) came later.

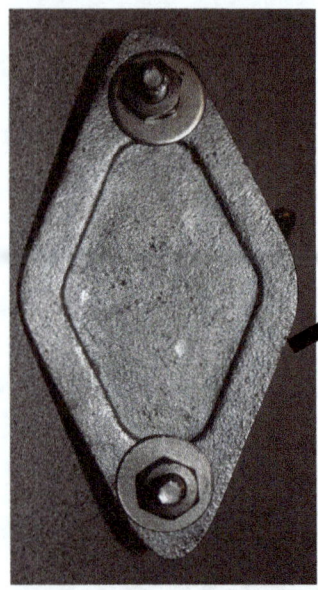

Back side of "older" 4820 Sand-cast

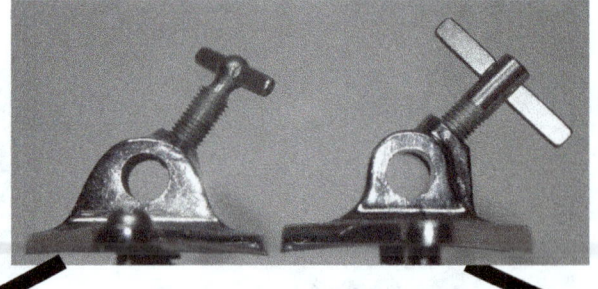

This photo shows the profile of both the "old" (left) and "new" (right) 4820 brackets. Note that the wing-bolts are different also.

Back side of "new" 4820 standard-cast

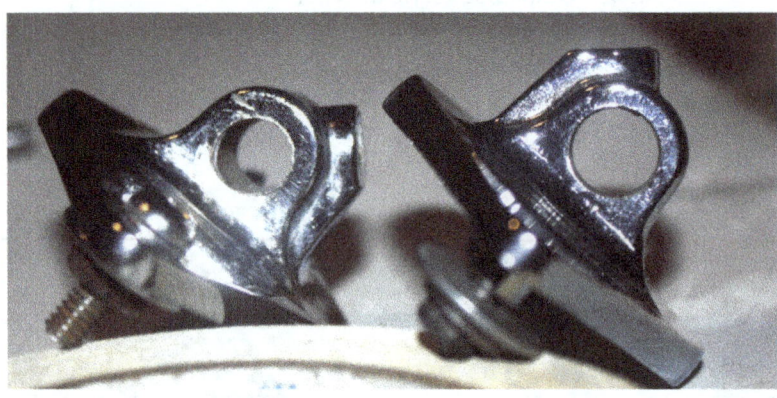

4820 variations
left: 3/8" for cymbal arms and some tom legs.
right: 7/16" for heavier floor tom legs and tom mount rods of the early 1970s. Never used for cymbal arms. This was the last variation of the 4820 until the Millenium versions of the KMC era. These two sizes ran concurrently for a time.

"New" 4820 with exposed screws 1959 to 1962.

By 1963, the bolts became concealed by mounting them underneath the bracket so the heads of the mounting screws were no longer visible

"New" 4820 with concealed screws about 1962 to 2013

1950s: 3/8" 18" "Knurled band" legs, 6 bands or 5 bands

1960s: 3/8" 18" and 20" "Knurled band" legs, 5 bands

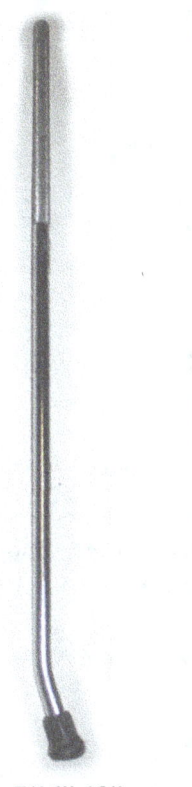

7/16" 18" entire top section knurled
1971-1976

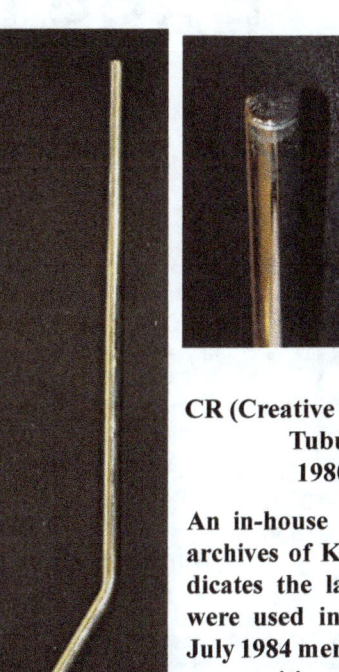

CR (Creative Research series) Tubular leg 1980-1984

An in-house memo from the archives of Karl Dustman indicates the last of these legs were used in late 1984. The July 1984 memo indicates they were waiting for a shipment of solid legs from the Far East and had a stock of about 50 legs to use in the meantime.

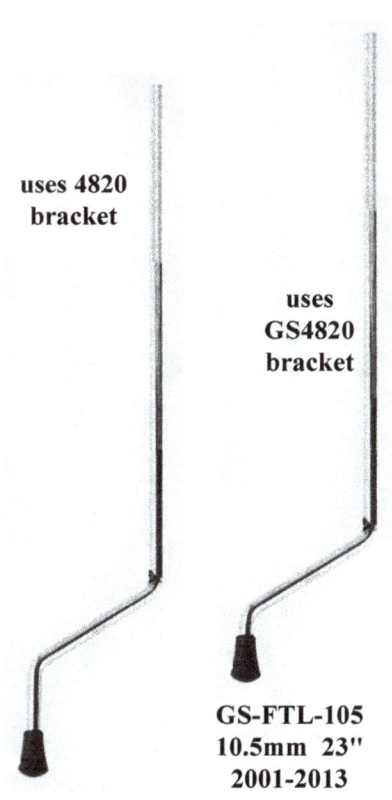

uses 4820 bracket

uses GS4820 bracket

uses 9020 bracket

#4939 Dual Purpose
9.5 mm (about 3/8") 23"
1977-2013

GS-FTL-105
10.5mm 23"
2001-2013

#9021 CR Series
12.7 mm 23"
1980-2013
tubular from 1980 to 1984 as seen above, then solid through 2013

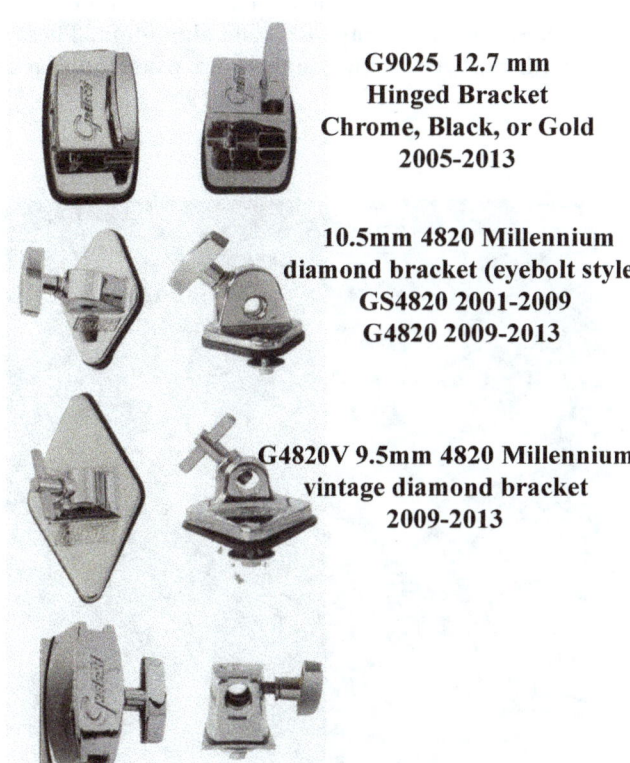

G9025 12.7 mm Hinged Bracket Chrome, Black, or Gold 2005-2013

10.5mm 4820 Millennium diamond bracket (eyebolt style) GS4820 2001-2009 G4820 2009-2013

G4820V 9.5mm 4820 Millennium vintage diamond bracket 2009-2013

G9020 Non-hinged bracket 12.7 mm Chrome or Black 1980-2013

BASS DRUM SPURS

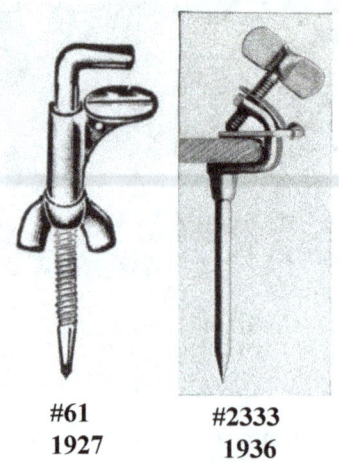

#61
1927

#2333
1936

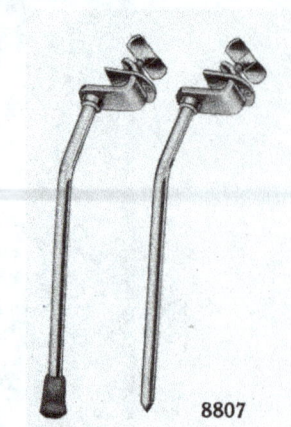

8807

#8807 1941–1949
Number changed to #4964 in 1949, remained in line until 1971.

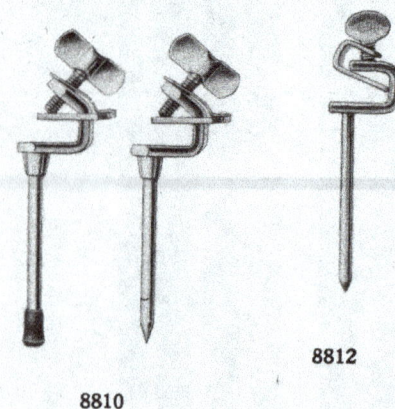

8810

8812

#8810 1941-1949
Number changed to #4968 in 1949, retained until 1971

#8812
1941

oldest   newest

Disappearing spurs #4960
These rods were unplated solid aluminum. These were shipped with rubber tips but the tips were usually discarded over time.
1949-1967

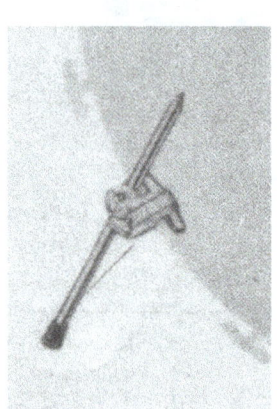

Double-End spurs
#4962
(point one end, rubber tip on other)
1948-1956

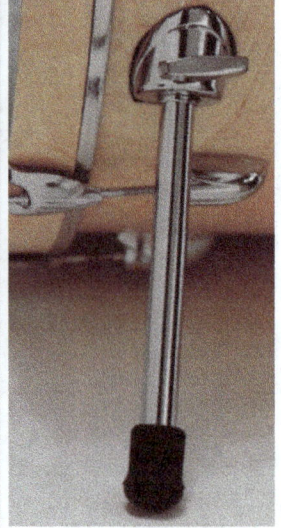

CR Series Internal Support Spur #9011

10. Upper Support Shaft
11. Spur Tube
12. Rubber Tip
13. Allen Head Mount Screws
14. Felt Pad — Inner
15. Wing Lock Screw
16. Front Plate
17. Felt Pad — Outer (Not Shown)
18. Nylon Disc (Not Shown)
19. Back Plate (Not Shown)

CR Series Internal Support Spurs #9011
1980-2001
The concept of these spurs was to maintain integrity of the bass drum shell while supporting up to three mounted toms. Became #G9011 in 1987.

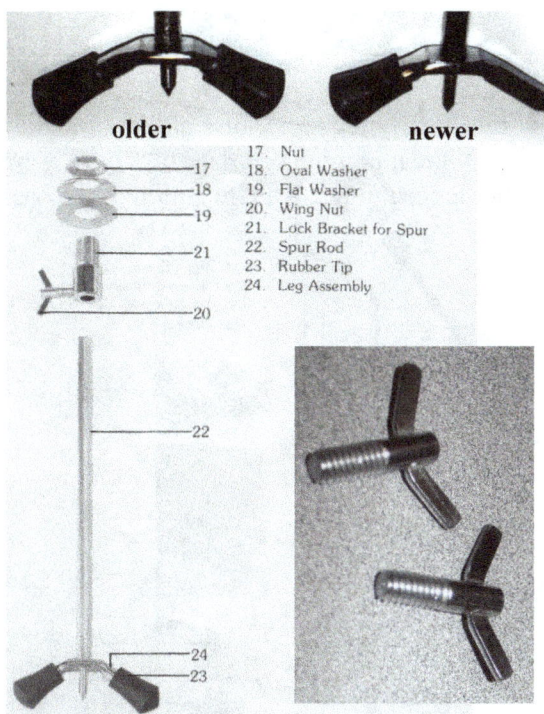

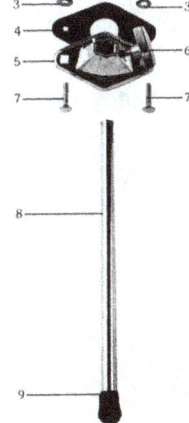
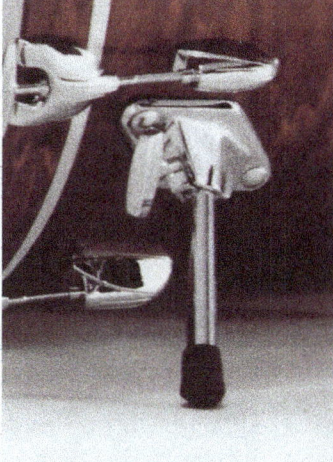

CR Series Retractable spurs #9012
1980-2000

#4966   1968–1982
Aluminum finish rods, self-adjusting double rubber-tip leg assembly
(this cut from Chanute parts catalog)

Brought back 1993-2001 under the heading of "Old Style Hardware"

Brought back again in 2005 (completely chrome plated) as "Vintage Spurs," still in the line in 2013

PC BS1
Blackhawk: 2001-2011
Catalina: 2003-2013

GS-BDS4
New Classic: 2006-2008
Renown: 2001-2008

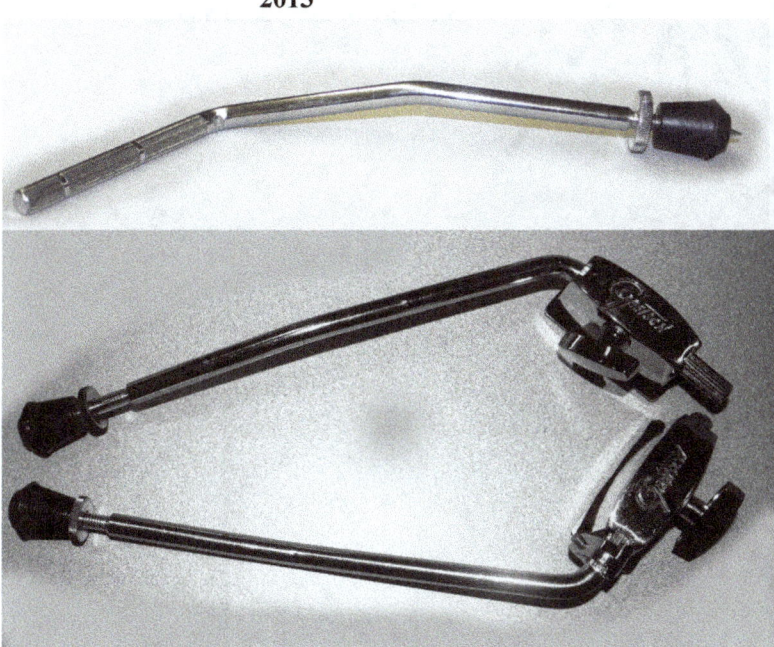

G5975 Gull Wing Spurs 1998-2013
The gull-wing spurs first appeared on Gretsch Broadkaster bass drums in 1998. Pictured brackets are # G9020. The Broadkaster line was discontinued in about 2003, but these spurs remained in the Gretsch line.

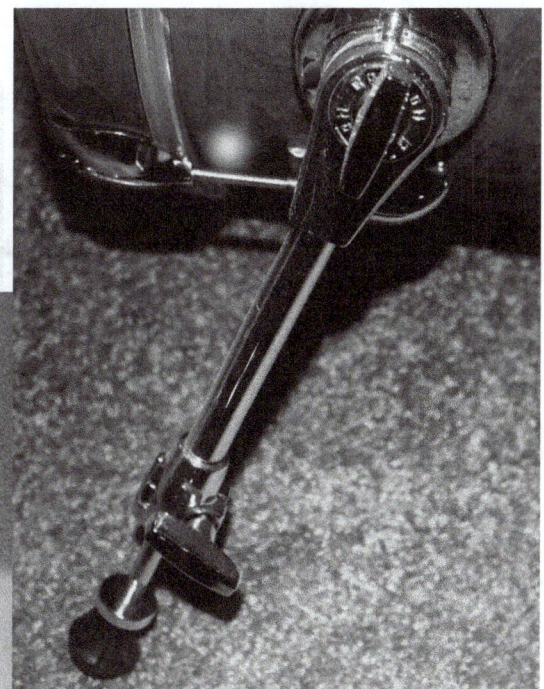

9013   2008-2013
Gibraltar GGSCBS4 spurs became standard on USA Gretsch bass drums in 2001. In 2008 when the number was changed to 9013, the Gretsch name was added to the round bracket as pictured.

SNARE DRUM STANDS

Earliest Gretsch catalogs did not include snare drum stands or tom-tom holders, because at that time they had not become commonly used hardware. The drum "kit" did not exist; the marching or orchestra drums were worn and played by one drummer, the bass drums were played by another drummer. The invention of the bass drum pedal made "double drumm
did not yet exist.

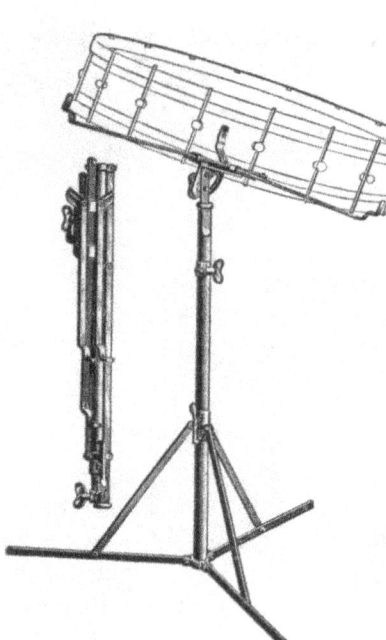

Hamilton Drum Stand #9
1928

Sturd-ee Drum Stand #G8
1936-1939
renumbered #8917 in 1939

Heavy Duty Drum Stand #G9
1936-1938
Renamed Safe-Tee 1939
#8920 14", #8921 15", #8922 16"

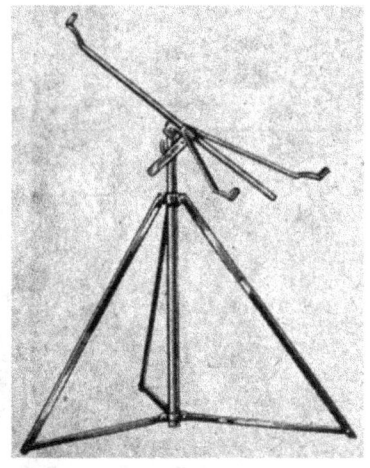

Student Drum Stand #4980
1948-1966

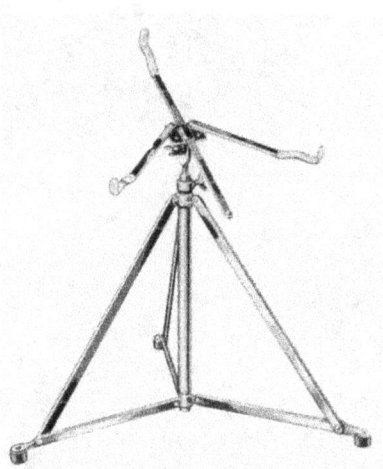

Super Safe-Tee Drum Stand
#8924 14", #8925 15", #8926 16"
1939-1941

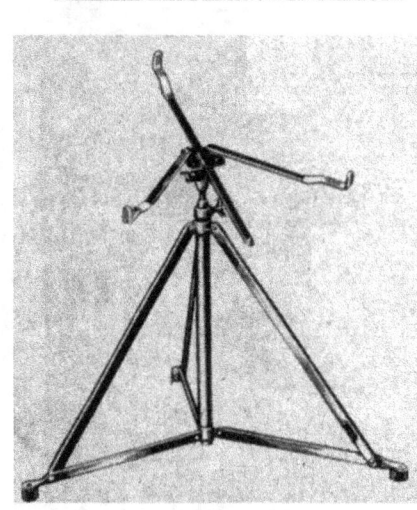

Heavy Duty Drum Stand #4982
1948-1958

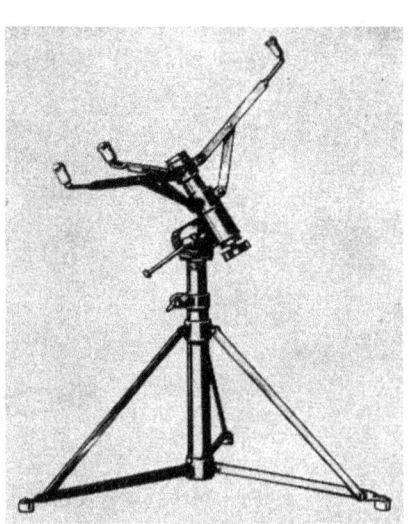

Artist Drum Stand #4985
(#4986 for 15" or 16" drum)
1954-1958

**Heavy Duty Drum Stand
#4983
1959-1978**
(Alternately appeared with round,
hard rubber disc feet.)

**Buck Rogers Drum Stand
#4986
1961-1978**
(Sometimes appeared as flush-base stand
with round, hard rubber disc feet by 1971.)

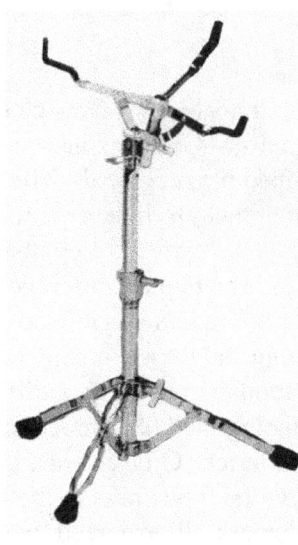

**Giant snare stand #4988
1978-1982**
**(A slightly heavier version of the #4988
remained in the line 1982-1984.)**

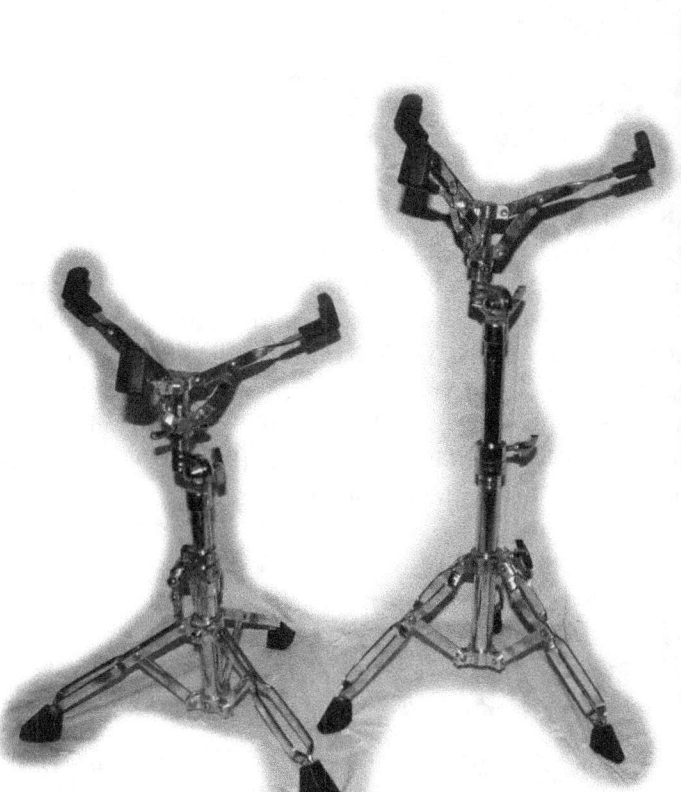

**Giant Short Deluxe Techware
#4987 (early lightweight version):
1975-1976
#4987: 1982-1983
#T4987: 1984-1987
#GT987: 1987-2001**

**Giant Orchestral Techware
#4839: 1983 only
#T4839: 1984-1987
#GT4939: 1987-1996**

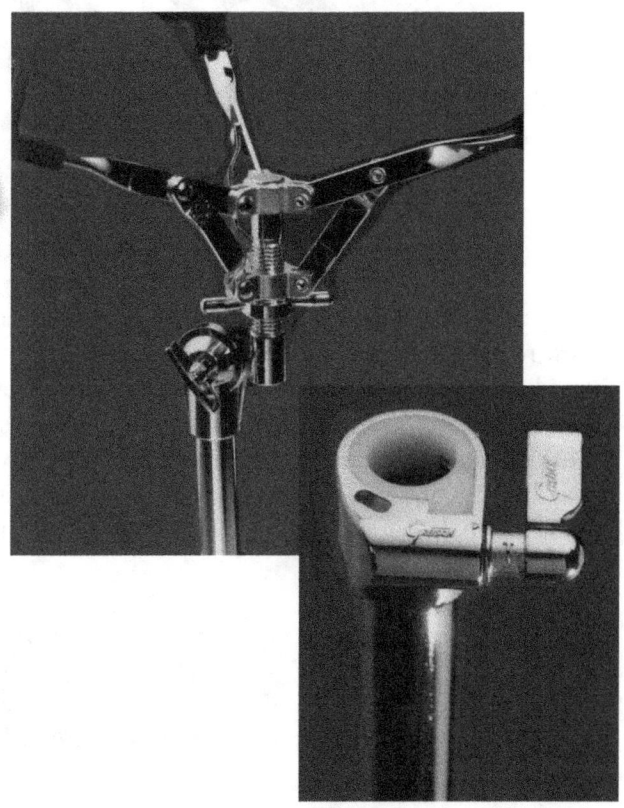

Giant Deluxe Techware (Same base and
basket as Short and Orchestral; the three
stands differ in height.)
**#4989: 1982-1983
#T4989: 1984-1987
#GT4989: 1987-1996**
(For more on Techware series hardware, see
the cymbal stand section.)

GRETSCH AND CYMBALS

Through it's history, Gretsch has distributed many brands of cymbals. There have been numerous specialty lines such as the "Genuine Chinese" cymbals and inexpensive stamped brass cymbals. This section will focus on the professional cymbals.

Although Gretsch never actually manufactured cymbals, the connection between Gretsch and the cymbals they distributed is unique compared to that of the other drum companies. The biggest difference is that fact that Gretsch successfully registered numerous U.S. Trademarks related to the cymbal lines they were importing and marketing. It is unusual for a company to be granted a U.S. Trademark for products manufactured in another country by a different company. Gretsch was able to accomplish this by convincing the U.S. Trademark Commissioner that Gretsch was much more than a mere importer. Gretsch was, they successfully argued, "commissioned to develop and expend [sic] business in the United States and Canada of the Turkish producer." The Trademark office agreed that the manufacturers meant to assign the good will of the business to Gretsch for the purpose of business development.

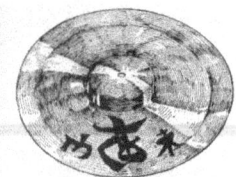

Listing for Chinese cymbals, 1927 Gretsch catalog

Trademark application image

Trademark 800,367 Ajaha

Serial number 193,357 filed May 13, 1964, registered December 14, 1965

The first U.S. Trademark granted to Gretsch for cymbals appears to be for Ajaha cymbals. The 1965 Trademark registration indicates that the first use was in 1922. The 1912 Gretsch catalog indicates that Ajaha was already a U.S. Government registered trademark at that time, but the Trademark office does not have accessible records for that era. Ajaha cymbals were presented as Turkish cymbals, later catalogs described them as "Turkish-style cymbals." They apparently were always manufactured in Italy. In a 1925 Music Trades article, Fred Gretsch Sr. is quoted as referring to them as Tuscany (a region in Italy) cymbals. By the 1950s Gretsch's Ajaha cymbals were being made in Italy by Ufip and in the 1970s by the Italian firm Tosco.

"ZILDJIAN"

Trademark application image

Trademark 245,846 "ZILDJIAN"

Serial number 263,082 filed March 13, 1928, registered August 21, 1928

Apparently the confusion created by multiple branches of the Zildjian family presenting "genuine" cymbals prompted Gretsch to also secure this trademark. This was in retrospect a wise choice, as by 1929 they found themselves defending their Trademarks in court in litigation brought by the newly formed Avedis Zildjian Company of Massachusetts.

Trademark application image

Trademark 228,592   A Zildjian & Cie
Serial number 237,857 filed September 28, 1926, registered June 7, 1927

According to the Trademark application and later paperwork related to defense of the Trademark, this trademark represents the company that Aram Zildjian formed in Bucharest, Romania in 1926. Since Aram had no experience making cymbals prior to this and was not the direct heir of the secret process, he formed the company with the assistance of Mikail Zilcan and his brother-in-law Vaha Injidjian. An order for 200 pairs of cymbals was secured from Gretsch on the basis of a prototype cymbal which later turned out to be a K Zildjian with the stamp obliterated. The A. Zildjian cymbals used to fill the order were of inferior quality, deemed unacceptable, and Gretsch stopped using this trademark. (The Avedis Zildjian Company of Massachusetts was later able to successfully register this as a U.S. Trademark after its abandonment by Gretsch.)

Trademark 247,623   K Zildjian & Cie
Serial number 263,083 filed March 13, 1928,

Registered October 2, 1928, second renewal 1968. Gretsch imported K. Zildjian cymbals as early as 1895. The earliest documented Gretsch catalog reference to K. Zildjian cymbals at this writing is 1912. Shortly after the introduction of the A. Zildjian & Cie. cymbals referenced above, the Constantinople-based K. Zildjian & Cie company went out of their way to make it clear (through magazine ads and the dispatch of a representative to the United States) that the Romanian A Zildjian & Cie were inferior imitations of the genuine article. Gretsch apparently agreed, as they pursued an agreement to become the exclusive distributors of K. Zildjian & Cie cymbals in the United States. The U.S. Trademark Commissioner agreed to grant Gretsch not only this trademark but also that of the word "Zildjian" (previous page.)

Trademark application image

GRETSCH CYMBAL DISTRIBUTION

1912   1926 1927   1958

AJAHA

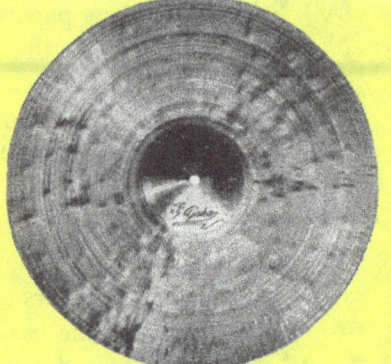

Gretsch was granted the U.S. Trademark for Ajaha cymbals some time prior to 1912. Gretsch distributed these Italian-made cymbals until well into the Baldwin era, 1979.

K. Zildjian & Cie (Co.)

1920s catalog trademark

Gretsch affiliation with the K. Zildjian company began in 1895. In the late 1920s Gretsch became the exclusive U.S. Trademark holder, importer, and distributor. Gretsch retained that position until 1972 when Baldwin gave the Trademark to the Avedis Zildjian company. Gretsch remained the exclusive U.S. distributor of K. Zildjian cymbals for ten more years, until 1982.

1960s catalog trademark

A. Zildjian & Cie (Co.)

Trademark and distribution rights to the Romanian-made A. Zildjian & Cie. cymbals were granted to Gretsch in 1926. The initial order of cymbals supplied to Gretsch were unsatisfactory, and the relationship was abandoned.

1920s catalog trademark

Founding Gretsch family era 1883-1967

GRETSCH CYMBAL DISTRIBUTION

1968　　1978　　1982　1984　　　1987　　　1995　　　2003　　　2012

AJAHA

Sabian was founded in 1981; Gretsch/Gallatin was one of their initial six U.S. distributors. The distribution agreement ceased with Baldwin's sale of Gretsch to Fred W. Gretsch. Sabian distribution again became linked to Gretsch when KMC (exclusive distributor of Gretsch drums) began to distribute Sabian in 2003.

K. Zildjian & Cie (Co.)

The first K Zildjian cymbals made by the Avedis Zildjian company were made in Canada from 1975-1979 and sported this block-K ink stamp on the underside.

K Zildjian production was moved to the USA by the Avedis Zildjian company in 1979 and were distinguished by this ink stamp on both the top and bottom through 1981.

UFIP

From 1978 to 1984, Gretsch/Gallatin distributed Ufip cymbals. The distribution agreement ceased with Baldwin's sale of Gretsch to Fred W. Gretsch.

ISTANBUL

From 1987 to 1995, Fred W. Gretsch distributed Istanbul cymbals.

Baldwin Era   1967-1984　　　Fred W. Gretsch 1985-2013   KMC 2000-2013

Bill Hartrick's K Zildjian Dating Guide

TYPE I OLD STAMP
1940-1945

Identifying features of this trademark are the thick crescent and large star touching the 'pincers' of the crescent. The height of the letters used in 'K. Zildjian' are the same as in the word 'Istanbul' and are taller than in any of the other old stamps. Also 'Cie.' is used instead of 'Co.' to abbreviate the word company. There is no 'Zildjian' stamped in below 'Istanbul' in this particular example, but it should be present as it is in most cases.

TYPE IIa OLD STAMP
1945-1949

Here there is the thick crescent and large star again, but this time the letters in 'K Zildjian' are smaller than in the type I. The letters in 'Istanbul' are larger. The word 'Zildjian' stamped in at the bottom is small as well, as is the case with the next two types. Finally, all the different components of the stamp are spread out quite a bit.

TYPE IIb OLD STAMP
1949-1950

This type also has the thick crescent and the large star as in the previous 2 types. As in the type IIa trademark, the components are spread apart. The presence of the large 'K' is the main difference between this and the type IIa. Both this type and the type IIa have what I call the thick crescent and the large star. As will be shown in the next examples, the type III's have the thin crescent and small star. Because both the type II and type III trademarks have the large 'K', then the best way to tell the II's from the III's is by looking for this characteristic. In some cases where the star and crescent may not have been stamped in well enough for this to be used as an identifying feature, then the location of the 'K' becomes the next best method to use. This example shows the usual location of the 'K' for this trademark. Typically it's located so that the top of the large 'K' is even with the tops of the letters in the word 'Zildjian'. In the type III stamps the bottom of the 'K' is usually even with the bottom of the letters in the word 'Zildjian', but it should be pointed out that this is true for the majority but not necessarily in all cases.

TYPE IIIa OLD STAMP
1950-1953

The difference between this and the type I, IIa, and IIb is that here the crescent is larger and thinner and the star is slightly smaller. The star doesn't appear to touch the 'pincers' of the crescent. The 'K' is the larger type that was present in the type IIb, and in general the bottom of the 'K' is even with the bottom of the letters in the word 'Zildjian'. In practically all cases, the word 'Zildjian' is stamped in at an angle and the letters are not all clear. These letters are also smaller on this trademark than on the other types to come.

TYPE IIIb OLD STAMP
1953-1956

In this type, the size of the letters in the 'Zildjian' are about 1mm larger than in the type IIIa, and are stamped in horizontally. In this example, each letter is readable, and although this is typical for most examples, it's not necessarily true in all cases. Strictly speaking, the larger letter height and the horizontal stamping of the word 'Zildjian' are the most reliable identifying features for this type.

Images and text this page copyright Bill Hartrick © 2013

Bill Hartrick's K Zildjian Dating Guide

TYPE IIIc OLD STAMP
1956-1957
Here, the star is above the crescent moon, and the semi-circle made by the letters 'Made in Turkey' are farther from the crescent (especially on the right and left sides). In all the other trademarks, the semi-circle is closer to being equi-distant around the crescent. Again, the 'Zildjian' is horizontal with the larger letter type as in the type IIIb.

TYPE IVa OLD STAMP
1957-1958
This one has an entirely different Arabic script than the other old stamps. As in the type IIIc the star is above the crescent. The quickest way to identify this type is to look at the first Arabic script letter. It looks like a hook or a cursive letter 'J'.

TYPE IVb OLD STAMP
1959
Here again we have the same Arabic script as in the type IVa only here, the words 'Made in Turkey' wrap closely around the moon, whereas in the type IVa they are more flattened out.

INTERMEDIATE STAMP
1959-1966
In this type, we see the third and final form of the Arabic script. This trademark is similar to what appears on the new stamps which come next. However, here, the star is small and is located above the crescent as it is in the type IVa and IVb old stamps. The 'Made in Turkey' hugs the moon as it did in the type IV old stamp. Also, this trademark is almost invariably, exactly midway between the bottom edge of the bell and the outer edge of the cymbal. There is also a slightly smaller version of this type of trademark that I've seen on a few cymbals.

OLDER NEW STAMP
1967-1972
The star is above the crescent and is larger than in the intermediate stamps. The 'Made in Turkey' hugs the moon as in the type IVb old stamp and the intermediate stamp. This trademark has slightly smaller lettering in both the English and the Arabic writing, and the font of the letters is slightly different than in the intermediate stamp. In the older new stamp, there is usually only a small space between the Arabic script and the 'K. Zildjian & Co'.

NEWER NEW STAMP
1972-1977
This type is just like the older new stamp, but more often with this type there is more space between the Arabic script and the 'K. Zildjian & Co.'

Images and text this page copyright Bill Hartrick © 2013

Cymbal Evolution

It is important to note that cymbals have evolved (and continue to) along with popular music. Gretsch was importing and distributing cymbals for nearly 3 decades before the drum set and the hi-hat pedal were invented, so it is no surprise that hi-hat cymbals are not listed in early catalogs.

AJAHA TURKISH CYMBALS.

The Genuine Bear this Trade Mark Signature.   Adopted by the U. S. Government.

No.	Size	Price	2012 Equiv.
1042.	12 inch	per pair $18.00	$416.00
1044.	13 inch	per pair 22.00	$509.00
1046.	14 inch	per pair 25.00	$579.00
1048.	15 inch	per pair 34.00	$787.00

GENUINE CONSTANTINOPLE—K. Zildjian & Cie.
(Not guaranteed against splitting.)

No.	Description	Price	2012 Equiv.
1060.	12 inch, Name Stamped on each Cymbal	per pair $35.00	$810.00
1062.	13 inch, Name Stamped on each Cymbal	per pair 40.00	$926.00
1064.	14 inch, Name Stamped on each Cymbal	per pair 45.00	$1042.00
1066.	15 inch, Name Stamped on each Cymbal	per pair 50.00	$1158.00

1912 Catalog listings for Ajaha and K. Zildjian cymbals — Figures in red are 2012 equivalents

No.	Size	Price	2012 Equiv.
8	Size, about 8 inches. Pair	$25.00	$332.00
12	Size, about 12 inches. Pair	35.00	$465.00
13	Size, about 13 inches. Pair	40.00	$531.00
14	Size, about 14 inches. Pair	45.00	$598.00
15	Size, about 15 inches. Pair	50.00	$664.00
16	Size, about 16 inches. Pair	60.00	$797.00

1927 Catalog listings for K. Zildjian cymbals — Figures in red are 2012 equivalents

K. ZILDJIAN PAPER THIN

No.	Size	Price	2012 Equiv.
X4700	Size 10"	$15.00 Ea.	$144.00
X4701	Size 11"	17.50 Ea.	$168.00
X4702	Size 12"	19.00 Ea.	$182.00
X4703	Size 13"	22.00 Ea.	$211.00
X4704	Size 14"	26.00 Ea.	$249.00

K. ZILDJIAN CRASH CYMBALS

No.	Size	Price	2012 Equiv.
X4708	Size 13"	$22.00 Ea.	$211.00
X4709	Size 14"	26.00 Ea.	$249.00
X4710	Size 15"	28.50 Ea.	$273.00
X4711	Size 16"	31.50 Ea.	$302.00

1948 Catalog listings for K. Zildjian cymbals — Figures in red are 2012 equivalents

Author's note: It is beyond the scope of this book to document the sequence of events within the Zildjian family that directly effected the succession of the "secret formula." This is, after all, a book about Gretsch. The author did find it neccessary to wade into those murky waters far enough to understand how the Gretsch cymbal business evolved. Should the reader be motivated to look into this situation further, he is encouraged to refer to the "resources" page near the end of this book. If you do so, be advised that part of the problem in understanding the situation is that many names have changed in many ways. Sometimes the reason is simply a difference in how the names were translated into the English language. Other times, individuals changed their names in order to more closely associate themselves with the Zildjian family legacy. Where you see the name "Zilcan" it is safe to read it as "Zildjian" because the Turkish government, when persecuting Armenians, prohibited the use of names ending in "ian," forcing Zildjians to become Zilcans or some other name of their own choice. Be advised that the references cited offer conflicting facts and certain individuals are referred to with different names and spellings in different sources.

APPENDIX I Promotional Items

Cookie Tin 2003

Pin 2008

Drumsticks 2008

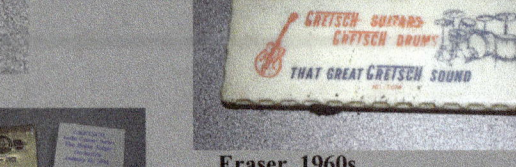
Eraser 1960s

Ashtray 1960s

Matchbooks 1993

2003

1940s

Drum-shaped hairpin box 1930s/1940s

2000s

Women's pendant watch
2000s

Desktop pen holder 1960s

2003

1960s

Ashtray with Gretsch sales rep name and number 1930s

All items on this page from the John Sheridan collection

APPENDIX II: Ridgeland, S.C. Production

Paul Cooper has been in charge of Gretsch drum production since Fred W. Gretsch hired him in 1998, prior to the involvment of KMC. In his early days with Gretsch, Paul consulted with Gene Haugh. Haugh had worked for Baldwin since 1966 and was involved with moving the Gretsch production equipment to South Carolina and getting it up and running.

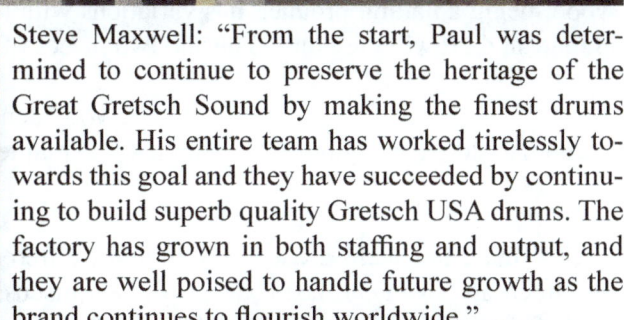

Steve Maxwell: "From the start, Paul was determined to continue to preserve the heritage of the Great Gretsch Sound by making the finest drums available. His entire team has worked tirelessly towards this goal and they have succeeded by continuing to build superb quality Gretsch USA drums. The factory has grown in both staffing and output, and they are well poised to handle future growth as the brand continues to flourish worldwide."

APPENDIX III : Drums and Wood

Making Drums Out of Wood
by Joe Partridge

The woods used in the manufacturing of musical instruments are typically known as tone woods due to their resonant qualities. The are chosen based on not just their tonal aspects, but also for their availability, workability, and appearance.

The two divisions of wood used for instruments are softwoods and hardwoods. These terms are deceptive in that it is more of an indication of how the seeds of the trees are borne, rather than the actual wood density. Softwoods such as pine cones have naked seeds, while hardwoods like walnut or pecan, for example, have covered seeds. There are softwoods that are denser than hardwoods and vice versa. That being said, most all drums are made from hardwoods. Among the more common species that have been used in drum manufacturing are maple, birch, mahogany, and poplar, as well as gum and walnut. The different and sometimes subtle differences in the densities of these woods are what help determine the tonal quality is a drum shell . Note the density chart on the more common wood varieties used. The larger the number, the denser the wood. It is helpful to note that wood, being a natural product, has variations within a species that are determined by many factors including climate and growing regions. Thus no two pieces of wood are exactly alike, so no two drums are exactly alike.

Wood densities   lb./cu. ft.

poplar 20-31   gum 35   birch 42   maple 35-47   mahogany 40   oak 41-60   walnut 40-43

Shells

Although drum shells are made from many different types of materials such as fiberglass, acrylic, metal, carbon fiber, and even cardboard, this will be a discussion about wooden shells. Modern drum shells were first made from a single sheet of steam-bent hardwood known as a one-piece, single-ply or solid-shell construction. They are manufactured by cutting a board to a predetermined length, cutting a scarf or angled cut to the ends and steaming the wood until it becomes pliable. After bending the wood in or around a cylinder form and allowing it to dry, it is then glued at the scarf and trued on a lathe. Some manufacturers cut the board to its desired thickness before the bending process to eliminate the need for lathing. Reinforcement rings are made by the same process and added to the inner edge of the shell to ensure trueness and rigidity.

Plywood shells

Although plywood has been used since ancient times, its use as a drum shell material was first introduced in the early 20th century by Gretsch. The advantages of plywood over solid wood include more uniform strength in all directions and the virtual elimination of both splitting and dimensional instability. It is also more cost-effective than bending single pieces of hardwood or segmenting pieces to form a shell.

Plywood is made up of veneers, or thin sheets of wood. These veneers can vary in thickness from less than 1/16th of an inch up to 1/8th of an inch. The methods and configurations for making plywood shells have changed as they developed over the years. The typical plywood shell has as few as three plies or as many as ten or more, depending on the desired pitch of the shell. As a rule, the thicker the shell, the higher the pitch relative to the types of wood used. The plies are usually, though not always, laid up perpendicular to one another, creating a cross-grained pattern.

Early methods of manufacturing plywood shells was similar to how solid, single-piece shells are made. Glued veneers were laid up flat and then bent around a heated form. The ends were scarfed and glued, then reinforcement rings were added just like the single steam-bent shells.

The modern plywood shell is most commonly made by placing thin veneers glued up inside a form and inserting an inflatable bladder inside the form to exert even pressure throughout. The glue is then cured using high frequency radio waves that create uniform heat within the form.

There are a number of factors to take into account when choosing species for building plywood shells. The appearance of the visible plies on the exterior and interior of the shell is always one of the main considerations. The more attractive veneers are more expensive, and therefore thinner than the plies that are sandwiched between them. A great many of the tonal properties of drum depend upon the thickness of the shell and the density of the wood used. The inner plies can be thicker, as they are chosen more for their tonal qualities. These thicker veneers allow the manufacturer to use less glue to achieve the overall thickness desired in the shell.

APPENDIX III : Drums and Wood

Maple is a popular outer veneer because it is closed-grained, and it is much easier to finish than an open-grained wood like mahogany. In the 1960s era drums, when acetate-based covering was used for finishing shells, the open grain of mahogany made it a good outer veneer for the application of the adhesives, preventing the delamination of the finish.

Stave and segmented shells

Yet another method for shell construction is the gluing together of small, solid pieces of wood in either a stave or segmented ring configuration, sometimes known as brick and barrel construction. The pieces are glued up into a rough cylinder shape and then trued up on a lathe or with a router. These methods are not very efficient in large-scale productions and are usually produced by individuals or small custom drum companies.

Bearing edges

Bearing edges are the contact point between the drum head and the shell. The way they interact depends on how and where that contact occurs. There are a lot of opinions as to what degree the effect different bearing edges have on the attack, sustain, decay, and projection of drums. No extensive studies have been done on the true physics of the differences between the various types of bearing edges, primarily due to the nearly limitless number of variables available in this kind of research, among them diameter, depth, head type, and mounting system. The experts in this field are the collectors, historians, and players who have concerned themselves with these differences and made observations accordingly. Not surprisingly, they don't always agree, but there is a broad general consensus within the drum community.

There are many types of edges and edge combinations that help give a drum its unique sound. The most popular are the 45- and 30-degree cuts, often in combination with various types of counter bevels or outer cuts. These bearing edge descriptions are quite broad, and an exception to any of these discussions can be readily found.

The 45-degree angle, the more common of the edge cuts, tends to yield an increased attack, sustain, and projection over most other cuts. The sharper the cut is made, the less contact occurs with the shell, thus allowing for more harmonics and resonation.

Adding a 45-degree counter bevel to this cut moves the contact surface closer to the center of the drum and changes where the shell makes contact with the head. Using a round-over counter bevel increases contact with the head and reduces the harmonics, promoting a rounder, more focused tone. A 30-degree angle appears to give a drum a fuller, rounder sound while lessening the attack and tonal range. It is said to give off a warmer, more focused sound.

The variations found in drum construction are nearly limitless, and it cannot be said that any one choice of wood, construction method, or type of edge, hardware, mounting system, etc. is best for every application. It is a matter of preference, based on everything from brand loyalty to experience in the field, to what you might have owned in the past.

Reinforcement hoops

Reinforcement hoops are as critical in stabilizing solid shell drums as they are in the vintage 3-ply shells of the 1950s to 1960s era. In solid steam-bent shells, the wood has a tendency to expand and contract based on the temperature and moisture content of the surrounding air. The fact that these shells are usually no more than a quarter-inch thick and bent into an unnatural shape, the absence of re-rings would cause the shell to twist, distort, and possibly split over time due to these seasonal movements. In the early 3-ply shells, the thick inner veneer of the shell ran perpendicular to the thin outer veneers. This arrangement allowed the thicker wood to be bent easily, but it did not add to the strength and stability found in modern plywood shells. These shells, like the solid shells, were scarf-joined at the seams, which requires reinforcement.

Modern plywood shells are very stable and require no reinforcement rings. They are added purely for sound enhancement. Re-rings add density and rigidity, raising the pitch and clarity of the shell. They also allow for more bearing edge options due to the increased thickness of the edges.

Ferit Odman
feritodman.com

Rob Cook: "A couple of years ago I boarded a plane in Detroit, the first leg of a journey to visit Fred Gretsch's offices in Pooler, Georgia. When I was seated I checked my phone one last time and found a message from my buddy Ferit wishing me luck on my trip and asking if I could inquire into a possible endorsement arrangement. I was surprised- I did not realize drummers around the world were following Fred's tweets and how many people knew about the trip.

I first met Ferit in the late 1990s. Just before one of my trips to Istanbul, my favorite city in the world. He wanted to buy a Gretsch kit and I wanted to buy some flight tickets for my son Will and myself; we were going to explore Turkey. The trade worked out great for both of us. Ferit was a student then but was already nationally known. In the years since Ferit's star has steadily risen. He got his B.A. on a full scholarship to a University in Istanbul, attended the School for Improvisation workshops in NYC (2004) and was granted a Fulbright Scholarship to study at William Patterson University in New York (2006). I didn't help with his endorsement deal; international artists are signed by regional Gretsch representatives. I was pleased to learn of Ferit's Gretsch affiliate status just in time to include him in the book– he richly deserves it!"

ANDY FLORIO

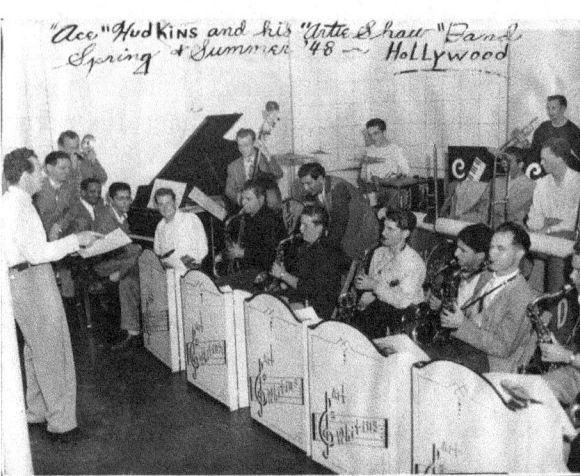

APPENDIX V Late Additions: Andy Florio

Andy Florio

MGM Musical *Looking For Love*, Connie Frances

APPENDIX VI Late Additions: Brooklyn Series Cocktail kits

2013 Brooklyn Series Cocktail Kits

GB-CKTL-RO: Red Oyster
GB-CKTL-BO: Blue Oyster
GB-CKTL-GO: Grey Oyster
GB-CKTL-CO: Cream Oyster

Gretsch Brooklyn Cocktail Kit Specs						
Sizes	Lugs	Leg Brackets/Legs	Batter Hoop	Resonant Hoop	Batter Head	Resonant Head
14"x24" Cocktail Bass	8/side	G9025 with G9013 legs	302	Wood	Permatone Coated with underside dot	Permatone Clear
6"x8" Tom	5/side	N/A	302	302	Permatone Coated	Permatone Clear
6"x10" Snare	6/side	N/A	302	302	Permatone Coated	Permatone Clear
Hardware						
SC-LGA	Ultra Adjust brackets for snare and tom holder					
SC-XHHR	X-Hat for Hi-Hat					
BD Pedal Bar	Support bar and clamp for BD Pedal					
BD Pedal	Not Included					

APPENDIX VII Late Additions: Hannah Ford

HANNAH FORD

"In 2006 I was approached by a teen drummer who wanted to perform at the Chicago Drum Show. I explained that the only performance opportunites are clinic presentations and I reserved those for artists who will boost show attendance. She came back to me a year later making a strong case for a clinic slot. She had a couple of endorsement deals and her playing had improved tremendously. Her comunication skills were highly developed. More important than all of that, I was impressed with how focused, persistent, and determined she was. That, I felt, had to be encouraged. I scheduled her for the opening slot of the 2007 show. When I introduced her, I kind of had the feeling that there were a lot of skeptics in the audience who wanted to know exactly why I was bringing them an unknown teenager. I tried to explain that they were about to meet someone on the way up. "In a few years," I told them, "Hannah will be nationally known with her picture on magazine covers and all that. I fully expect that some day I won't be able to afford to have her appear here."

Hannah came back to do another clinic in 2010 and was by then a known quantity. (She also responded to Danny Seraphine's invitation to trade 4s during his 2009 clinic to the delight of the clinic audience.)

It's been great fun to watch Hannah's star rise, and I'm certain she is still on the way up. At this writing she is preparing to tour with Prince as drummer for Prince's New Power Generation. (On the heels of a successful tour with Prince's 3rd Eye Girl.)" Rob Cook

Michael Hacala's action photo of Hannah at the 2010 Chicago Drum Show has been featured in a mail-order drum catalog and appears as a 2-page spread in the July 2013 issue of DRUM! magazine.

hannahforddrums.com

Hannah with her 3rd Eye Girl Gretsch kit

INDEX

120th Anniversary drums	151,180
125th Anniversary	44,52
125th Anniversary drums	150,183
130th Aniversary drums	155
Abadi, Yvo	54
Adams, Jack	54,68
Advanced Pressure Casting	21
Alexander, Pete	54
Anderson, Trent	54
Anniversary model snare drum	164
Apo, Earl	54
Atkins, Chet	21,26
Back cover photos	50
Badges	83-95
Baibai, Yves	54
Bailey, Colin	54
Bailey, Dave	54
Balbinot, Tony	54
Baldwin	23-38
Baron, Dutch	54
Barrett, Creighton	54
BayBay, Ives	54
Beaver	54
Beck, Paula Cole-	54
Beddoe, Rich	54,80
Bellerose, Jay	54,77
Belleville, Pierre	54,78
Belli, Remo	54,67
Bellson, Louis	22,54,62,63,66,68,128
Bennett, Alvino	54,76,80
Benson, Bernie	54,61
Bey, Sam	54
Best, Denzil	54,128
Bigay, Danny	54
Bigsby	48
Birdland outfits, Birdland jazz club	127-128
Biwandu, Roger	54
Black, James	54
Blackhawk drums	145
Blackman, Cindy	54,75,77,78
Blakey, Art	54,63,67,68,69,128
Blanchard, Amaury	54
Blane, Dewey	54,60
Bode, Frank	54
Bomba, Nicky	54
Bonner, Fred	54,67
Borden, Barbara	54
Bosarge, Harrell	54
Bourdon, Rob	54,76,79
Boutherre, David	54
Boyd, Raymond	54
Boydstun, Jack	54
Bram, Michael	54,80
Brande, Sherman	54
Braunagel, Tony	54
Brazil, Karl	54,78
Bridges, Reees	54
Brill, Rob	54
Brock, Tony	54,73
Brockstein, Herb	54,68
Brooks, Clyde	28,54,74
Brooks, Philip	54
Brown, Gerry	54
Brown, Jeff	54
Brown, Jerry	30,54
Brown, Les	54
Browne, Ian	54,77
Bruno, Jack	54
Bukowski, Nicolas	54
Burns guitar company	23
Burns, Roy	54,74
Byrne, Bobby	54
Byrne, Mike	54
C'Alberon, Alberto	54
Cafforio, Franco	54
Calderon, Alberto	54,59
Camco	224,231,232
Camera, Cesar	54
Cambre, Herman	54
Campbell, Harry	54
Capoloo, Carmine	15
Caputo, Greg	54
Carlock, Keith	54
Carlson, Peter	55
Carello, Tony	15
Carnegie Hall	61
Carrigan, Jerry	55,85
Carroll, Charlie	55
Carrorio, Franco	55
Carter, Lamar	55,79
Castka, Joseph	55
catalogs	96-104
Centenniel anniversary drums	27,30,141,176
Cester, Chris	55,78
champagne sparkle vs. peacock sparkle	106
Champion, Jared	55
Chapman, Steve	55
Christian, Bobby	55

Chanute, KS	26,30	Dolenz, Micky	55
Churilla, Scott	55	Donlinger, Tom	55
Clapp, Geoff	55	Drain, Ish	55
Clark, Brett	55,77	Droubay, Marc	55,72
Clark, Terry	55	Drummond, Billy	55
Clarke, Kenny	55,68	Duffy, Dan	15
Clegg, Joe	55	Duggins, Dan	55
Cobb, Jimmy	55	Dungannon Lumber Co.	42
Colaiuta, Vinnie	47,55,77,79,150	Dustman, Karl	26-38
Collins, Phil	28,30,55,72,77,85	D'Auria, Oscar	55,77
Colors	105-116	Dyrason, Orri Pall	55
Combs, J.C.	55	Eckberg, Paul	55
Connors, Norman	55	Edlin, Mike	55
Conway, AR	38	Edwards, Dennis	55
Cool, Tré	55	electronic drums	142
Cooper, Al	55	Ellison, Nathan	55
Coste, Yann	55	Ellner, Sam	55
Cottrill, Tony	55	Emphrey, Calep	55
Clarco, Dave	55	endorsers	53-81
counterfeit badges	86	Enyard, Ron	55,71,129
Crahan, M. Shawn "Clown"	55,79	Entressangle, Phillippe	55
Craney, Mark	55,72	Ernie, Francois	55
Crosby, Caleb	55,81	Esposito, Davide	55
Cruse, Will	55	Etkin, Norman	55
Cusatis, Joe	55	Eulinberg, Stefanie	55,79
cymbal stands	222	Evans, Darren	55
cymbals	246	Fa, Patrick	55
Gretsch cymbal distribution eras	248-249	Faberman, Leo	55
K Zildjian dating guide	250-251	Fadden, Jimmie	55,80
Dam, Kasper	55	Fagan, Aaron	55
Damin, Hugo	55	Farro, Zac	55
Danielson, Richard	55	Farrugia, Daniel	55
Danziger, Zach	55	Fatool, Nick	55,59
Dapper, Frank	55	Fiel, Max	55
date stamps	83	Fein, Paul	55
Davison, Daniel	55,78	Ferguson, Gary	55
Dawson, Alan	55	Ferrone, Steve	47,52,55,72,78
Day, Josh	55	Fineo, Mika	55
Didominico, Vincent	15	Fink, Herman	55,60
de Seta, Lucrezio	55	Fisher, Eddie	55,79,80
Deakin, Paul	55	Flores, Chuck	55,68
Dennis, Kenny	55	Flores, Martin	55
Dentz, John	55	Florio, Andy	55,65
Derge, David	55,76	Fogarino, Sam	55,78
dei Lazzaretti, Maurizio	55	Fontana, D.J.	55
Delong, Paul	55	Fonseca, Paulinho	55
Dentz, John	55	Ford, Hannah	55,80,260
DeRon, Cal	55	Forte, Nick	55
DeRosa, John	15	Frankel, Danny	55
Diaz, Carl	15	Frasure, Doug	55
Dickson, Richard	15-18	Frazier, Stan	55,77
Doksausky, Lukas	55	Freire, JJ	55,78

Friday, Johnny	55	Gretsch Gladstone	84,162,192,212
Fromm, Charlie	15	Gretsch House Telegram	104
Fryar, Chris	55	Gretsch News	103
Fryoux, Ray	55	Gretsch web sites	51
Fulterman, Harry	55	Grey, Trey	56
Gadzos, Ernie	45	Grossman, Steve	56
Gagon, Jeremy	55	Grupp, Dave	56
Gajo, Dragan Gajic	55	Guiliana, Mark	56,81
Galland, Stephane	56	Guitar Art	48
Gannon, Sean	56	Hagner, Bill	15,20-22,25,26,43
Garibaldi, Alonso	56	Hamilton, Chico	56,67,68,69
Garman, Greg	56	Hamilton, Jeff	56,72
Garofolo, Al	15	Hanna, Jake	56
Gary, Bruce	56,77	Harris, Eddie	56
Gates, Richard	56	Harrison, Richard	23,37
Gavin, Jack	47,56,76	Harte, Roy	56,63
Gier, Rick	83	Haugh, Gene	43
Gladstone, Billy	22,56,60	Hawkes & Son Drum Co.	16
gold-plated drums	169	Hawkins, Taylor	56
Goldberg, Paul	56,76	heads	211
Goldman, Dr Edwin Franco	56	Helmecke, Gus	56,61
Gonzalez, Paul Alexander	56,76	Herman, Sam	56
Goodman, Saul	56,61	Herndon, Mark	30,56,73
Goodwin, Garrett	56,79	Hervol, Sergio	56
Goossens, Mario	56	hi-hat stands	228
Grainger, Sebastien	56,77	Hiraoka, Yoichi	56
Graham, Kim	53	Hodgson, Nick	56,76
Grant, Phil	15,18,22,24, 26,40,41,56,61	Holland, Milt	56
Graves, Justin	56	Honnet, Davy	56
Gretsch & Brenner	97	hoops	198-200
GRETSCH FACILITIES	viii	Horowitz, Dick	56
Booneville, AR	23-25,27	Horton, Chaun	56
Brooklyn	42	Houck, Randy	28
De Queen, AR	22,27,32-36	Houdlett Banjo & Drum Factory	39
Gallatin, TN	26	Huff, David	56,77
Ridgeland, SC	43	Hyde, Dave	56
GRETSCH FAMILY MEMBERS		Hyndman, Clint	56

GRETSCH FAMILY MEMBERS

This index lists only the descendants of Fritz Gretsch and Rosa Behman Schnapauff who became directly involved with the Gretsch drum business as they are mentioned beginning with Chapter 1-III. Please refer to the family tree on page ix. Chapter One's first two sections include detail on numerous other Gretsch family members.

Gretsch, Dinah	47-51,100	Ichinose, Hisashi	56
Gretsch, Fred Junior	8,9,12,15,20,39	Imamura, Mai	56
Gretsch, Fred Senior	10,20,39	Imbrechts, David	56
Gretsch, Fred W.	22,39-45,47-51,100	Infusino, Chris	56,80
Gretsch, Richard	12-14	Izumitani, Makoto	56,77
Gretsch, William Walter "Bill"	8-12,15,20	Jablonski, Kuba	56
Thomas, Lena	49	Jaeger, Rick	56
Gretsch Foundation	48	Jansen, Ken	56
		Jasper Wood Products	30,202
		Jean, Norma	56
		Jenkins, John	56
		Jenkins, Phillip	56
		John Jr, Paul "Phinkky"	56,76,79
		Johnson, Ben	31-35
		Jones, Elvin	56,67,68,69,128

Jones, Harold	56,67	Masaki, Garo	56
Jones, Jo	18,56,62,63,68,128	Mason, Harvey	30,56,144
Jones, "Philly" Joe	56,68,70,128	Mason, Nick	56
Judd, Harry	56	Mason, Paul	56
Kajitani, Masahiro	56	Mason, Tony	56
Kalafus, Caitlin	56	Masui, Remio	57
Kamoosi, John	56	Mattinson, Bernie	57,59
Keeling, Bryan	56,78,79	McCarthy, Margaret	15
Kelly, Kitty	56,64	McClanahan, Mary	57,59,61,64
Kerrigan, Jerry	28,56	McClure, Rick	57
Kerswill, Derek	56,79,80	McDonald, Pat	57,76
Kidd, Chip	56	McGlinchey, Cameron	57
Kiri	56	McHugh, Chris	57,77
Kirkpatrick, Scott	56	Medeles, Jose	57
Koba, Dean	56	Meissner, Konrad	57
Kramer, Duke	15,19,24,37,39	Mela, Francisco	57
Krom, Ro	56	Mendelsohn, Jules	57
Kreutzman, Bill	56	Mendolia, Francesco	57,79
Krom, Ro	56,79	Messina, Louis Jr.	57
Kustom	26	Mette, Dave	57,78
Kutak, Frank	56, 69,61	Micali, Eric	57
Labarbera, Joe	56,76,81	Micro-Sensitive Strainer	
labels, shell	87-95	214-215	
Labovitz, Jesse	56,77	Milovac, Joe	57
Lackey, Jim	56	Mitchell, J.R.	57
Lakin, Sid	15	Miyauchi, Kosuke	57
Lamond, Don	56,63,68,69,70,128	Moffatt, Al Sr.	57,61
Lane, Johnny	56	Moffett, Jonathan	57
Larsen, Claus Andre	56	Montgomery, Mike	57
Lauro, Albert	56	Morgan, Doug	57
Layne, Larry	56	Morgan, Barry	57
Lazzaretti, Maurizio dei,	56	Morgenthaler, Bobby	57
Lear, Graham	30,56	Moore, Stanton	57,76,79
Leedy	46	Mossis, Cameron	57
Lebrosa, Joe	56	Morris, Lee	57
Lenailly, Eric	56	Moy, Russ	57
Lenga, Zeke	56,60	mufflers	219-221
Lewis, Mel	56,68,69,72	Musiate, Oscar	57,78
Lightning throw-off	216-217	Nakamura, Tatsuya	57
lugs	191-197	Nash, Phil	15
Bakelite	191	Neal, Bob	57,128
rocket	191	Neblett, Nate	57
Mackley, Linda	56	Negron, Didi	57
MacMillan, Ryan	56,79	Norman, Duane	57,76
Maher, Mark "KRAM"	56	Northrup, David	57,77,80
Malen, Phil	56,60	Norvo, Red	57
Mann, Howie	56	Oakes, Warren	57,79
Manne, Shelly	56,62,63,67,128	Odman, Ferit	57
Maronet, George	56	Owczarz, Radek	57
Marsh, Mike	56,76	Owens, Ulysses Jr.	57,81
Martin, Stu	56	Palermo, Matt	57
Marucci, Mat	56	Palmer, Carl	57,71,72

Parito, Jerry	15	rocket drums	97,161
Parolin, Robi	57	rocket lugs	191
Parrish, Ryan	57	Rodriguez, Alex	57,79
Pasillas, Tiki	57,81	Rogers drums	161
Payne, Sonny	57,68	Romaine, Van	57,76
pedals, bass drum	230	Ross, Kent	57
Pent, Mark	57	Roth, Bob	57,60
Perry, Charlie	57,67,68	Rottella, Bill	57
Petri, Sven	57	Roy, Charlie	26-30,37,100
Payne, Sonny	57	Russo, Rich	57,78,81
Pedersen, Nathan	57	Ruth, Milton	57
Pemberton, Brad	57,80	Saito, Syuuichiri, Saito	57
Perito, Jerry	24	Sakiyama, Tatsuo	57
Perkinson, Tommy	57	Sakurai, Masumi	57
Perry, Charlie	57	Salmins, Ralph	57
Persip, Charlie	57,67,68,69,128	Sanders, Mark	57
Peterson, Debbi	57	Sanford, Kevin	57
Petri, Sven	57	Savage, Scott	57
Phantom, Slim Jim	57,72,76,79	Saxton, Dusty	58
Pierce, Ray	57	Saxton, Mark	58
Pillado, Joe	57,60	Scaffidi, Anthony	58
Plummer, Kenny	57,60	Schild, Daniel	58,78
Pluta, Jan	57	Schulman, Mark	47,58,77,78,79,80
Pontius, Mark	57	Seiwell, Denny	58,77
Pope, Jarred	57	Seixo	58
Powell, Chris	57	Senda, Akiharu	58
Pratt, Jimmie	40,57,68	Serial number dating	83
Jimmie Pratt muffler	219	Seta, Lucrezio de	58
Price, Nick	57,80	Shanahan, Dick	58,62
Progressive Jazz outfit	132	Sharp, Lee	58
Progressive Jazz snare drum	168	shells	201-210
Pruitt, Brian	57	oversized shells	207
Pryor, Wesley	57,77	Super Structure shells	205
Ramos, Mauro	57	"Sheridan's Rule" for serial number dating	83
Rausch, Seth	57	Shiino, Kyoichi	58
Receli, George	57	Shlosser, Rick	58
Reed, Ted	57	Sho-Bud	48
Reid, Frank	57	Shrieve, Mike	58
Richmond, Bill	57,68	Silver Sealer	206
Rickard, Tommy	57	Silverlight, Terry	58,76
Riddle, Paul	57,72	Silvio, Andrew	58
Ridgeland, SC	22	Simmons, Paul	58
Rieflin, Bill	57,72	Simpson, Boomer	58
reinforcement rings	203	Sims, Ben	58
Rickard, Tommy	57	Simms, Zach	58,78
Rivera, Anthony	57	Sinai, Joe	58,60
Roach, Max	57,63,66,68,69,70,128	Skinner, Carl	58,60
Max Roach model snare drum	84,166,167	Slingerland	38,46
Max Roach model lugs	192	Sloan, James	58
Robinson, Forrest	57,77	Smith, Aaron	58
Robley, Bart	57,80	Smith, Charlie	58,128
Robson, Paul	57	Smith, Harold	23,37

Smith, Wayne	58,72	Walberg & Auge	21, 24, 225
Smith, Ty	58	Waltzer, Jack	58,60
Smith, Viola	58,61,64	War Effort (WWII)	21
snare drums	157-190	Watson, Sammy	58,79
snare drum stands	244	Watts, Charlie	58,71,72,76
Soule, Kenny	58	Webb, Chick	58,59
Soulier, Francois	58	Webster, Jimmy	15
Spencer, Joel	58	Weisbach, Ken	58
spurs, bass drum	242	Weiss, Sammy	58,60
Starosta, Maciek "Slimak"	58	Wells, Tommy	58,76,81
Spencer, O'Neil	58	Wettling, George	58,62,68
Stephens, Michael	58	White, Lenny	58
Stewart, Bill	58,76	White, Noel	58
Stocki, Gregg	58,77,78	White, Skip	58
Stoeck, Martin	58,78	Wilk, Brad	58,76
strainers	212-218	Williams, Tony	58,68,72,73,85
Strong, Emerson	15	Wilson, Chris	58
Stroud, Keio	58	Wilson, Damon	58
Stroud, Melvin	58	Wilson, Shadow	58
Studer, Fredy	58	Wolf, Teddy	58
Summers, Wayne	28	Wolfe, Jim	58
Super Structure shells	205	Wood, Nate	58,77
Synsonics	142	Woods, Harold	15
Tavares, Omar	58	Woodyard, Sam	58
Taylor, Art	58,68,69,128	Woolstenhulme Jr., Rick	58
Taylor, Daren	58,80	Wolfe, Jim	58
Techware	29, 225	Worf, Neil	58
Teixeira, Cuca	58	Wrennell, Jarred	58,76
Thompson, Morley	23	Woolstenhulme, Ricky	58,79
Thompson, Tony	58	Wynn, Donnie	58
Thomson, Paul	58,78	Yagami, Toll	58
Thornton, Billy Bob	58,80	Yerdon, Ryan	58
tom holders	223	Yoshizawa, Kyo	58
tom legs	239	Young, Brandon	58
Tough, Dave	58,62	Zhu, Dawn	58
Trafton, Casey	58	Zotta, Bill	15
Tribolet, Xavier	58	Zotta, Mike	15
Trucks, Butch	58		
Twentieth Century drums	96		
Ulano, Sam	58,68,99		
Underwood, Scott	58,76		
Vander, Christian	58,78		
Vanalli, Northon	58		
van den Broeck, Joost	58		
van Tornhout, Wouter	58		
van Wijk, Wouter	58		
Vargas, Paulo	58		
Vasquez, Roland	58		
Very, Mike	58		
Von Ohlen, John	58		
Waits, Freddy	58,72		
Walker, Matt	58,80		

RESOURCES

Contact the Gretsch Drum Company in the U.S.A.:
KMC Music Inc.,
55 Griffin Road South
Bloomfield, CT 06002-9005
email: info@gretschdrums.com
www.kmcmusic.com

Rob Cook can be contacted at:
rob@rebeats.com

Lee Ruff can be contacted at:
jazcym@gmail.com

John Sheridan can be contacted at:
P.O. Box 4
Old Bridge, NJ 08857
gretscher@earthlink.net
sheridan@gretschgear.com

Gretsch Gear
GretschGear.com
P.O. Box 126
Ringoes, NJ 08551
1-609-466-4485
email: info@gretschgear.com
www.GretschGear.com

drum covering material:
Precision Drum Company, Inc.
2012 Route 44
Pleasant Valley, NY 12569
1- 888- 512- DRUM (3786)
845- 635- 9820
Fax: 845 - 635 - 8442

Rick Gier's "Dating of Vintage Gretsch Drums Based Upon Serial Numbers: Challenging The Legend, Lore, and Lies" is available from Rebeats. Rick Gier continues his research and can be contacted at Rick@GretschDrumDatingGuide.com

The 1941 Gretsch drum catalog reproduction is available from Rebeats.

Chet Falzerano's books *Gretsch Drums- The Legacy Of That Great Gretsch Sound* and *Billy Gladstone* are both published by Centerstream Publications and distributed by the Hal Leonard Corporation.

DRUM SHOPS KNOWN FOR GRETSCH EXPERTISE

Memphis Drum Shop
878 S Cooper St
Memphis, TN 38104
901-276-2328
sales@memphisdrumshop.com

Professional Drum Shop
854 Vine Street,
Hollywood, CA USA 90038
(323) 469-6285
info@prodrumshop.com

Steve Maxwell Vintage
& Custom Drums
2000 Bloomingdale Rd #110,
Glendale Heights, IL 60139
630-778-8060
www.maxwelldrums.com

REBEATS PUBLICATIONS
visit the Rebeats website or contact us for details

THE GRETSCH DRUM BOOK
by Rob Cook
with John Sheridan
Business history,
dating guide

THE SLINGERLAND BOOK
by Rob Cook
Business history,
dating guide

THE ROGERS BOOK
by Rob Cook
Business history,
dating guide

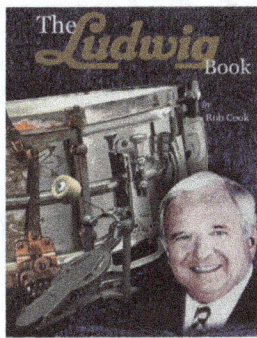

THE LUDWIG BOOK
by Rob Cook
Business history,
dating guide

THE MAKING OF A DRUM COMPANY
The autobiography of Wm. F. Ludwig II,
with Rob Cook

LEEDY DRUM TOPICS

THE LEEDY WAY
Biography of George Way,
History of Leedy, Camco, Conn, L&S

MY LIFE IN PERCUSSION
Five Decades In The Music Products Industry
Karl Dustman memoir

Franks For The Memories

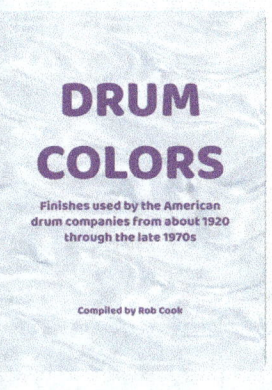

DRUM COLORS

George Way
mini-biography,
vendor directory

GENE KRUPA, HIS LIFE AND TIMES
biography of Gene Krupa,
by Bruce Crowther

THE BABY DODDS STORY

Gretsch 1941 Catalog Reprint

The Rebeats Calfskin Head Book

Best Seat In The House

HAL BLAINE & THE WRECKING CREW

P.O. Box 6, Alma, Michigan 48801
989 463 4757
www.Rebeats.com rob@rebeats.com

Gretsch from the Steve Maxwell Collection

Gladstones

BDP Gladstone

Gold Sparkle 18, 12, 14, 4x14

Anniversary 20, 12, 14, 5.5x14

new stock: center band of Capri, upper and lower bands of Fiesta

Gretsch from the Steve Maxwell Collection

Gold Satin Flame 18,12,14, COB

Andy Florio kit. 22,13,16,18,20

Elvin Jones kit 18,12,13,16,18

Cadillac Green 20,12,14

Champgne 18, 12,14, 4x14

We are the experts in vintage Gretsch drums

The world's largest showroom for new & used USA Gretsch drums

- Worldwide client base
- Always buying and selling vintage Gretsch drum sets
- Special unique product offerings for new USA Custom Gretsch including unique colors such as espresso burst, mardi gras, fiesta pearl, vintage copper, burgundy sparkle

- Visit our NY showroom in Manhattan, and our Chicagoland store in Naperville, Illinois
- Steve is always available!
  630-865-6849
  vintagedrums@aol.com

New for 2013: Espresso Burst.

A new exclusive wrap finish available only through us and only on Gretsch USA Custom drums.

Beautiful classic white marine pearl with an espresso fade at the edges. Standard build out or vintage build out (pictured).

Iroquois Center
1163 E. Ogden Avenue, #709
Naperville, Illinois 60563
Ph: 630-778-8060

Midtown Manhattan
723 Seventh Avenue, 3rd & 4th Floor
New York, NY 10019
Ph: 212-730-8138

maxwelldrums.com

www.ingramcontent.com/pod-product-compliance
Lightning Source LLC
Chambersburg PA
CBHW081105080526
44587CB00021B/3454